Advance Praise

Edward Panico is a meticulous thinker and a dedicated investigator, and his latest book showcases his extensive experience in both the public and private sectors. The Daily Investigator offers a thorough examination of what it takes to succeed and build solid cases, reflecting the high standards expected of Diplomatic Security Service Special Agents worldwide. Presented in a concise, accessible format, the book serves as both a daily read and a valuable reference. New and experienced investigators alike will find the information practical and immediately applicable.

—Kory M. Hammond,
Supervisory Special Agent (ret.), Diplomatic Security Service (DSS)
Former Member, Senior Foreign Service

The Daily Investigator reflects the investigative discipline required at the highest levels of federal law enforcement and the same rigor demanded in complex corporate environments. Ed distills practical lessons rooted in fundamentals—accuracy, judgment, and accountability—that align with FBI investigative standards and translate directly to enterprise risk and security operations. This book reinforces habits that protect cases, organizations, and people, making it a valuable resource for professionals responsible for uncovering the truth and leading investigative efforts across sectors.

—Richard W. Kollmar
Deputy Assistant Director (ret.), Federal Bureau of Investigation (FBI)
Vice President & Chief Security Officer, Wellstar Health System

The Daily Investigator reflects the lessons I've learned over decades of investigative work across law enforcement and the military. Ed always emphasizes the fundamentals that young investigators must master early if they want a long, credible career. This book serves as both a guide and a reminder that the craft is built over time, through training, reflection, and doing the job right when it matters most. It's the kind of resource I would recommend to anyone serious about growing in this profession.

—Paul F. Perriello
Police Officer (ret.), Prince George's County Police Department
Chief Warrant Officer 3 (ret.), U.S. Army
Deputy Sheriff, Prince George's County Sheriff's Office

The Daily Investigator reflects the core investigative principles I relied on throughout my service in the Jordan Public Security Directorate and continue to apply in my support of U.S. Embassy operations. These fundamentals are essential across public safety roles, whether in policing, emergency response, or security operations. The lessons in this book translate seamlessly to multinational and joint investigative environments, where trust, standards, and cooperation between partners are critical. It is a valuable guide for investigators working alongside international counterparts in complex operational settings.

—Basem Kharabsheh
Brigadier General (ret.), Jordan Public Security Directorate
Senior Foreign Service National Investigator, U.S. Embassy Amman

The Daily Investigator captures the investigative fundamentals that drive effective risk management, fraud prevention, and organizational integrity in the private sector. Edward Panico presents lessons that translate seamlessly from field investigations to executive decision-making, reflecting the realities of white-collar crime, brand protection, and enterprise risk. This book reinforces disciplined thinking, professional judgment, and systems-based approaches that are critical to protecting companies, investors, and reputations. It is a valuable resource for investigators and leaders operating in complex, global business environments.

—Vincent L. Volpi
Chairman & CEO, PICA Corporation

The Daily Investigator:

366 Lessons To Make You A Better Investigator

Edward Panico

This book is dedicated to the men and women of the investigative community—especially the giants whose shoulders we stand upon. Thank you for paving the way.

Other Books by Edward Panico

- *The Daily Investigator: 366 Lessons to Make You a Better Investigator (2026)*

- *How to Start a Private Investigation Business: A Proven Blueprint for Success (2021)*

Table of Contents

Preface

"If I have seen further, it is by standing on the shoulders of giants." —Sir Isaac Newton

This book started with a simple idea: every great investigator I have ever met had one thing in common—they mastered the fundamentals. Over the years, I have seen new technology, new tactics, and new threats change how we work. But the core of investigation has not changed at all. It still takes discipline, critical thinking, patience, and the willingness to do things the right way, even when nobody is looking.

When I started my career, I was lucky. I had good people around me—men and women from the military, law enforcement, and the Intelligence Community. Some are still with us. Others are not. But their lessons stuck. They did not hand me fancy tools. They handed me a foundation. They taught me that investigations are not won by luck or shortcuts. They are built day by day, decision by decision, detail by detail.

The Daily Investigator grew out of that foundation. This is not a book you read once and shelve. It is meant to be a daily companion, a way to sharpen your edge over time. Each month covers a core part of the job—from surveillance and OSINT to interviewing, analysis, and professional development. Each day gives you a single, focused lesson you can actually use. There are hundreds, if not thousands, of variations of investigation. This book is meant to be as universal as possible, imparting these lessons across the public and private sectors for someone in or entering the field.

This book is for anyone who takes the craft seriously—the new investigator learning the ropes, the working professional trying to stay sharp, or the seasoned vet who knows the basics matter most. Mastery does not come from a single training course or a big case. It comes from consistency. Reps. Repetition. Showing up every day.

I do not have all the answers. What I do have are lessons learned the hard way, shaped by real work and the people who came before me. Some days will be reminders. Others might challenge the way you do things. Either way, they will make you think like an investigator.

Whether you use this book in the morning, during shift briefings, or during a quiet moment at the end of the day, I hope it makes you better. The strength of this profession has always been its people. If this book sharpens even one investigator's skills, then it has done its job.

Edward Panico
Abuja, Nigeria
2026

How to Use This Book

The Daily Investigator was designed to be experienced one day at a time. Each page contains a focused idea—a practical tip, principle, or reminder—tied to a monthly theme. The structure encourages consistency, reflection, and real-world application rather than information overload.

You do not need to read this book from cover to cover in a single sitting. In fact, you should not. Investigative skill is built through repetition, habit, and attention to detail—the same way this book is meant to be used.

Daily Reading

Read one entry per day. Take a few minutes to reflect on how that idea connects to your work, your training, or your operational mindset. If possible, find one way to apply the principle in real time—whether in the field, during planning, or in how you approach a problem. Investigators sharpen their craft not by theory alone, but by daily application.

Monthly Themes

Each month focuses on a core investigative domain—from foundational skills to OSINT, surveillance, interviewing, analysis, and more. The content is structured to **progress logically**, building capability over time. You can follow the calendar year or start wherever you are; the lessons are timeless and not date-dependent.

Reflection and Reinforcement

Investigators know that **writing things down** reinforces learning. Keep a small notebook or digital journal with you. Use it to:

- Capture your thoughts on each daily tip.
- Record how you applied or observed the concept in practice.
- Identify areas you want to develop further.

This simple habit will multiply the impact of what you read.

Revisiting the Material

Good investigators revisit their notes and refine their approach over time. This book is meant to be:

- A **daily companion**, not a one-time read.
- A **reference guide** when you need clarity or inspiration.
- A **training supplement** for teams, mentors, or self-study.

There will be days when a single page will resonate deeply, and others when it simply sharpens your edge. Either way, the daily discipline builds over time.

A Final Thought

The best investigators are students of the craft for life. As I mentioned in another book I wrote, *How to Start a Private Investigation Business: A Proven Blueprint for Success*, try to embrace the **shokunin** mindset—a Japanese way of life centered on dedication to mastery, attention to detail, and honor in one's craft.

Skills fade without practice. Habits sharpen with use. However you choose to work through this book—as part of a morning ritual, during shift briefings, or personal downtime—the value lies in showing up every day. Small, consistent effort compounds into lasting capability.

January: Foundations of Investigation

"Practice isn't the thing you do once you're good. It's the thing you do that makes you good." —Malcolm Gladwell

Every solid investigation starts with the basics. Fancy gear, software, or tactics will not save a case built on a shaky foundation. I have seen it across every part of my career—military, the Intelligence Community, law enforcement, and the private sector. The best investigators are not the loudest or the flashiest. They are the ones who do the small things right, over and over again.

During U.S. Army Basic Combat Training, our unit's First Sergeant oversaw the drill sergeants as they taught weapons presentations—moving the rifle from the low ready to the firing position. We had just completed 10 reps. He walked up with his trademark bag of David sunflower seeds (I do not think I ever saw him without them) and said, "It takes about 3,000 reps for something to become muscle memory." He spit out a seed and added, *"That is 10 reps. It's going to be a long day for you all."*

That lesson stuck with me. After all, here I am telling you about something from more than 20 years ago. Mastery is not about knowing something once. It is about doing it so many times that it becomes part of who you are. Investigative work is no different. Repetition builds discipline. Discipline builds skill. And skill, under pressure, is what holds everything together.

This month is about getting back to what actually matters: your mindset, discipline, integrity, and attention to detail. If those four things are not rock solid, nothing else will hold up—not in the field, not in the courtroom, not anywhere. If you do not have these soft skills, how can you have hard skills?

Here are some of the things we are focusing on this month:

- **Mindset:** Thinking like an investigator. Seeing what others miss. Asking the questions others do not.
- **Ethics:** Your credibility is your most valuable asset. Lose that, and nothing else matters.
- **Situational Awareness:** Know what is happening around you before anyone else does.
- **Discipline:** The unglamorous part of this job. Do it right every time.

I made plenty of mistakes early on. I was motivated, but motivation alone isn't enough. What truly helped me wasn't fancy tech or luck—it was learning to slow down, think clearly, and do the job correctly. The men and women who trained me were strict about the fundamentals, and they were right.

Mastering the basics is not optional. It is the difference between a case that stands and a case that falls apart. This is where it starts. As Todd Beamer said shortly before his heroic demise on 11 September 2001, *"Let's roll."*

January 1: Build the Foundation

*"The most dangerous phrase in the language is, 'We've always done it this way." —
Grace Hopper*

When I was a young intelligence officer, the very first day of training was not spent learning some advanced tactic or technical skill. It was spent adjusting our mindset. Many of us had come from other specialties, and the instructors made it clear: before we could do the job, we all had to think like intelligence professionals. Soft skills like mindset and situational awareness were harped on more than any hard skills we would learn. At the time, I didn't fully get it—but years later, I understood exactly why they drilled it so hard. It's the same for investigators. Before you can build any technical skill, your mindset must be solid.

Everything starts with the foundation. If your fundamentals are weak, everything else eventually fails. Every solid investigation begins with mindset, not equipment, not software, not luck. Your foundation determines everything that follows. If your approach is sloppy, your work will be too. If your foundation is sharp, everything built on it will hold.

The investigators I respect most—military, law enforcement, or private—have one thing in common: they never get too experienced to practice the basics. They do not skip steps. They do not rush the process. They pay attention to detail.

Before you move into tactics, gear, or techniques this year, set your base. Be methodical. Be disciplined. Be humble enough to know the fundamentals matter, and sharp enough to keep them strong.

Takeaway: Every good investigation starts with a solid foundation. The most successful people are ready to learn, open to new suggestions, and always striving for improvement.

January 2: Think Like an Investigator

"The real voyage of discovery consists not in seeking new landscapes, but in having new eyes." —Marcel Proust

Investigators see what others overlook. That is the edge. Long before you interview a subject, write a report, or set up surveillance, your most valuable tool is your mindset. How you see, listen to, and process information separates an average investigation from a sharp one.

When I train new investigators, I tell them: take time to step back and see the big picture. Be alert to behavior, context, and the small, seemingly meaningless details that can break cases open. Often, the solution to the puzzle is what no one else noticed.

This applies everywhere. When I play chess with my daughter, I will sometimes have her stand up and view the board from the other side. It's a habit I picked up as a kid—one you will see grandmasters use: change the angle, see more. In tactical movements during room clearing, the team leader hangs back to see the whole picture—watching sectors, timing, and flow—while the front elements focus on their immediate slices. Same principle: Widen your perspective to make better decisions.

Mindset is simply disciplined awareness. It is learning to slow down just enough to catch what is really happening, not just what is on the surface. You can't fake that. You build it one observation at a time, day after day.

Takeaway: An investigator's greatest asset is not gear—it is how they think. Train your mind to see what others miss.

January 3: Trust, But Verify

"Trust but verify." —Russian Proverb

When I was attending the Criminal Investigator Training Program (CITP) at the Federal Law Enforcement Training Center (FLETC), we conducted search-warrant exercises in mock residences. Our team was supposed to systematically search for items listed in a warrant inside a mock apartment. Someone asked if the kitchen had been cleared. A couple of teammates had just come from there, so everyone assumed it was done.

It wasn't.

A handgun was tucked behind the oven. The trainee who asked the right question didn't follow up after sensing uncertainty, and the rest of us hesitated instead of confirming. One missed verification almost sank the exercise. Lesson learned.

Assumptions creep in fast—but you can't let them dictate how you operate. If you have ever been a patrol officer, you know the drill; after one officer searches for a suspect, the next officer searches again, and then they are searched again at the jail. It's not micromanaging or disrespecting a colleague's work. It's standard procedure. It's professional. It's trust but verify.

The same applies across every aspect of investigations—whether it is surveillance handoffs, chain of custody, or corroborating witness statements. Trust is earned. Verification is mandatory.

Practical Ways to Build a Verify-First Habit:

- **Clarify, don't assume.** A simple follow-up question can prevent big mistakes.
- **Doublecheck high-risk points.** Evidence, warrants, and critical timelines deserve extra scrutiny.
- **Redundancy is good.** Multiple eyes on the same detail isn't overkill—it's insurance.
- **Document verification steps.** If you checked it, log it. Don't rely on memory.
- **Create a culture of verification.** Encourage teammates to cross-check without ego.

Takeaway: Strip your case to facts, assumptions, and hypotheses—and actively look for what would break your theory. Verification beats confidence every time.

January 4: Credibility Is Your Currency

"If you tell the truth, you don't have to remember anything." —Mark Twain

In law enforcement, *Giglio v. United States* (1972) put it plainly: The government must disclose information that can impeach a witness's credibility. You don't want to be "Giglio-impaired." That is how law enforcement officers end up on the Rubber Gun Squad (desk duty). Private investigators don't fare any better. If you are impeached on the stand for credibility issues, clients and counsel stop calling.

Everything you do rides on trust—not just from a court or a client, but from your team and from yourself. If people can't trust your observations, your notes, or your word, nothing else matters. Gear can fail, and plans can change; credibility is what keeps a case standing under stress. It's as old as the gentleman's handshake.

I have had moments where the easy choice was to round a detail, smooth a timeline, or let a small inconsistency slide. That's a trap. Fix the inconsistency. Say you don't know. Own the mistake and correct it fast. The fastest way to build trust is to be brutally honest—especially when it costs you time or pride in the short term.

Credibility Is Built on Small Decisions:

- Don't overstate. Say what you saw, not what you *think* you saw.
- Don't guess—label it as an **assumption** or a **hypothesis** until it's proven.
- If new facts change your conclusion, say so and update the record.
- Keep your tone neutral. Facts don't need drama to be strong.

Remember: People won't judge you for not knowing everything. They will judge you for pretending you do. Your name is on your work. Protect it.

Takeaway: Guard your credibility like evidence—secure, untampered, defensible. When your word is trusted, your work holds.

January 5: Be the Lynx

"I can tell you the license plate numbers of all six cars outside." —Jason Bourne

In mythology, the lynx is known for heightened perception, even the ability to see through solid objects. A real lynx doesn't rush. It studies. It knows what belongs in its environment and what doesn't. That's your job: Establish a baseline—what "normal" looks like for this person, place, time, and pattern—so you can spot the anomalies when they show up. Situational awareness is one of the most powerful tools in an investigator's arsenal.

During long stretches of surveillance, I have watched team members or students miss the tell because they never took the time to define normal. Traffic flow, lights on/off, delivery windows, who parks where, who smokes where—baseline those first. Then the out-of-place van, the shifted trash day, or the back door that's never used suddenly opening aren't random anymore. They are leads. In the U.S. government, we call it area familiarization—another way of saying *"know the baseline."*

Use a Quick Mental Checklist When You Hit a Scene:

- Exits, cameras, mirrors, lines of sight
- Usual flow—people, vehicles, timing
- What changed? Haircut, gait, companion, bag, parking spot
- Does it have a simple explanation—or does it warrant a closer look?

U.S. military units in Iraq and Afghanistan got good at this. They would patrol a busy bazaar for days—then one day it was quiet as a mouse. Locals would be warned about an improvised explosive device placed in the bazaar. The service members were now in imminent danger. The anomaly wasn't the lack of activity; it was a signal.

Always ask: *What's normal here? What's different today? Why?* Build the habit. The right observation at the right time saves hours of dead-end work and keeps you safe.

Takeaway: Establish the baseline first. Anomalies aren't random—they're signals. Be the lynx: patient, quiet, observant.

January 6: Run Your Reps

"Chance favors the prepared mind." —Louis Pasteur

I had the absolute privilege of working alongside an active-duty Delta Force Sergeant Major during a training exercise overseas. We were waiting for a visitor neither of us had seen before. He clocked the visitor from a long way off in the parking lot. I asked how he did it. He said one word: reps. For those of us not currently at the tip of the spear, the tools below can provide structure to help your attention, memory, and decisions improve under pressure.

Kim's Game (Observation & Memory)

Used by scouts and snipers to sharpen recall. Place 12–20 small items on a table. Study for 60 seconds, cover them, then list everything you remember (items, order, colors, positions). Repeat with variations (fewer seconds, more items, moved positions). Do it anywhere—desk, glovebox, hotel nightstand.

COL John Boyd's OODA Loop (Decision Speed)

Observe (what's here), **Orient** (what it means), **Decide** (choose), **Act** (execute). The goal is to cycle faster and cleaner than the problem or adversary. Practice by narrating your loop during low-risk tasks (parking lot approach, lobby entry, checkout line). Speed comes from clarity, not hurry.

Jeff Cooper's Color Code (Readiness Level)

- **White:** Unaware. (Avoid except when truly safe.)
- **Yellow**: Relaxed alert—baseline scanning. (Live here.)
- **Orange**: Specific alert—something is off; define the if/then.
- **Red**: Action—execute the plan you set in Orange. Train yourself to name your state and deliberately return to **Yellow** after the event.

One-Minute Drill (Today)

- Name three **normals** for a place you're already going.
- Spot one **anomaly** and write a plausible reason.
- Set one **if/then**: "If X happens, I will do Y."

Takeaway: Make situational awareness a daily habit. Run Kim's Game, tighten your OODA, and live in Yellow. Reps build clarity; clarity drives good decisions.

January 7: Protect the Work

"Loose lips sink ships." —WWII Security Slogan

Whether you're in the private sector or public service, your job is to protect client and victim information—and keep your investigative steps under wraps. I have seen investigators try to impress people at bars and end up sharing case details. That isn't storytelling; it is a leak. Today, we will focus on operational security (OPSEC), and later in the year, we will focus on the legal privileges to back you up.

Good investigators don't just find information—they protect it. A case can die from leaks long before it dies from lack of evidence. Most leaks aren't malicious; they are casual. A hallway comment outside a cleared space. A social post that gives away time, place, or pattern. OPSEC isn't paranoia; it's professionalism—and every investigator needs it.

Use Simple Rules That Hold Under Pressure:

- **Need-to-know only.** Share specifics with people who have a role, not with those who have an opinion.
- **Delay details.** Talk about what happened **after** it's done, not before.
- **Watch your patterns.** Same coffee shop, same time, same route = a map you don't want to publish. Anyone can benefit from making themselves a hard target.
- **Assume you're being observed.** Hallways, rideshares, lobbies, elevators, and phones aren't secure. In the era of doxxing, remember you have no reasonable expectation of privacy.
- **Police your colleagues.** OPSEC fails when one person doesn't know the standard.

Remember: Trust inside the team doesn't mean total visibility. Curiosity is healthy; over-sharing is not. Protecting the work protects the people, the evidence, and the outcome.

Takeaway: Treat operational details like evidence—handle with care, share only when needed, and never telegraph your next move.

January 8: Checklists Win Under Stress

"Under conditions of complexity, not only are checklists a help; they are required for success." —Atul Gawande

People roll their eyes at checklists—especially very intelligent people—right up until the moment they need one. Stress strips working memory. Fatigue narrows attention. Under load, even pros miss obvious steps. I've seen it everywhere, from investigative interviews to protection operations. Checklists don't replace judgment; they protect it.

Former Navy SEAL and entrepreneur Jocko Willink is a big fan of checklists for operational planning, and investor Charlie Munger used investment checklists to avoid repeat errors. On a lighter note, a military commander of mine once told me that as a young private on immediate recall for Operation Just Cause (Panama, 1989), he started a packing checklist in his car—then got the go call and left it half-finished on the seat. He returned after the mission to find the unfinished list. It became a core memory of his when he told me the story in 2007!

Before a surveillance, interview, or warrant service, I run a short, boring list. It's saved me more times than I can count: a dead camera battery, a mismatched timestamp from daylight saving time, a missing lens, a gas tank under half. Skill matters. So does process.

Build a few micro-checklists you can run in sixty seconds, such as:

Surveillance Start

- Time sync across team devices
- Batteries/camcorders/cameras on
- Plates, covers, handoffs, rally point, spare equipment
- Primary/contingency comms (call signs, brevity)

Interview Setup

- Legal authority/notices, question sets, location control
- Recorder test + backup recorder
- Roles: lead, note-taker, observer
- Objectives, exit criteria, post-brief plan

Takeaway: Under stress, memory fails. Checklists don't. Build short, repeatable lists that protect your judgment when it matters most.

January 9: Lines You Don't Cross

"This Special Agent is commended as worthy of trust and confidence." —Diplomatic Security Service Special Agent credentials

Many law enforcement credentials explicitly speak to trust and integrity in the person who carries them. Every investigator eventually faces gray areas: a shortcut "no one will notice," a call you should not make, a detail you're tempted to round off to make the story better. That is where careers go sideways. Plenty of investigators have been fired—or imprisoned—for taking bribes, intimidating witnesses, planting evidence, or lying under oath.

Early on, a mentor told me: If you're debating whether it's ethical or not, you already know the answer. He was right. I have seen good investigators hurt cases and their reputations by trying to "help" the facts. Don't. If the evidence isn't there, say so. If the method is questionable, stop and re-route. If you make a mistake, own it fast and fix it.

Example of Quick Ethics Checks (Public or Private Sector):

- **Conflicts of interest:** Would a reasonable person question my neutrality? If yes, disclose or reassign.
- **Truthfulness:** Am I stating only what I saw/heard, or am I filling gaps?
- **Pretext:** Is my ruse lawful, necessary, and proportionate—or just lazy?
- **Promises:** Did I imply outcomes I can't control? Never guarantee a specific result.
- **Chain of custody:** Can I defend every handoff, time, and place—cleanly?
- **Need-to-know:** Am I sharing details with someone who needs them, not just wants them?

Takeaway: Choose the hard right over the easy wrong. When your ethics are non-negotiable, your work—and your name—stand up under scrutiny.

January 10: Control the Pace

"Slow is smooth, smooth is fast." —Marksmanship adage

Speed without control creates mistakes that take hours to unwind. The best investigators aren't the ones who move the fastest; they are the ones who set the tempo—and keep it. Under pressure, make space to think before you act.

In the field, pacing is a tactic:

- **Before you knock:** Breathe, visualize the first 30 seconds, confirm roles.
- **Before you surveil:** Set comms, mark landmarks, and decide break-off points.
- **Before you dial:** Define the objective, the boundary, and the exit line.

Navy SEALs use box breathing to lower stress and widen attention. I teach it to my private investigation students before their written exam—it works under pressure:

- **One breath box (4–4–4–4):** Inhale through the nose from the belly for four seconds, hold four, exhale through the mouth for four seconds, hold four. Repeat until your pulse and focus settle.

Tempo also means knowing when to slow the room. Ask for the question to be repeated. Don't let a defense attorney rush you. Re-state the objective or call a quick "time out" to sync roles. Fifteen seconds up front can save fifteen hours later.

Takeaway: Don't let the situation set your speed. Set your tempo—pause, define the next move, execute clean. Slow is smooth. Smooth becomes fast.

January 11: Own the Clock

"You may delay, but time will not." —Benjamin Franklin

Busy is not productive. Investigations stall not from lack of effort, but from scattered attention and orphaned tasks. Time and task management is an investigative skill: It protects focus, prevents rework, and purposefully moves cases forward.

An old platoon sergeant taught me to sort work into glass balls and rubber balls. Drop a rubber ball, and it bounces—you will get another turn. Drop a glass ball, and it shatters. Those are your must-do priorities. Pair that with former President and General of the Army Dwight D. Eisenhower's simple matrix:

- Urgent/Important—Do
- Urgent/Not Important—Delegate
- Not Urgent/Important—Decide (schedule)
- Not Urgent/Not Important—Delete

Run Your Day Like an Operation:

- Set three outcomes (not tasks). "By 1700, I will ___, ___, ___." Tie each to a case number.
- Single source of truth. One board/list for all cases (status, next action, owner, due date).
- Capture everything. Notes, voicemails, ideas → one inbox. Process twice daily.
- Triage with 4 Ds. Do (≤2 min), Defer (time-block), Delegate (name/date), Delete.
- Block golden hours. Reserve your best 90 minutes for deep work; guard it.
- Batch the noise. Email/DMs at set windows. Outside those windows, they wait.
- Sprint the hard stuff. 25/5 or 50/10 timers—when it runs, do only that task.
- Weekly case review. Objective, status, risks, next action, date. Kill zombie tasks.
- Deconflict with the team. Shared calendar for surveillance windows, interviews, and court.

If a task doesn't have a next action, owner, or a specific time, it isn't real—it's a wish. Make it real or take it off the board.

Takeaway: Time is an investigative tool. Protect the glass balls, delegate the rest, and run your day like ops—clear outcomes, owners, and dates.

January 12: Discipline Is a System

"We are what we repeatedly do. Excellence, then, is not an act but a habit." —Will Durant (summarizing Aristotle)

Discipline isn't motivation. It's the system that keeps your work clean on the days you're tired, busy, or under pressure. Great cases don't come from heroic bursts—they come from boring, repeatable habits that prevent small errors from becoming big problems. If you're looking to enter the field, you will learn fast that it is not all Hollywood shootouts and drug busts. If you're already in it, you know. Either way, without discipline, you won't go the distance. When I first received a black belt in Tang Soo Do, the instructor put the freshly minted black belt on me, and he said, *"Congratulations, you have mastered the basics. Now you can start learning Tang Soo Do."* If hundreds of hours weren't spent mastering those basics, how could I do hard stuff? If you can't do the little things, you will never be able to do the big things.

Build Small Non-Negotiables You Run Every Day:

- **Start-of-shift reset:** Sync time across devices; check batteries, storage, and date/time stamps.
- **Naming convention:** If your organization doesn't have one, standardize it. *Example:* Case#_YYYYMMDD_SurveillanceReport_Subject.
- **Note discipline:** Timestamp every entry; separate facts, observations, and assumptions. No doodles or personal notes.
- **Evidence ritual:** Immediate tag, bag, log. Update the chain of custody before moving on.
- **Admin blocks:** Two short windows (e.g., 1100/1600) for email, calls, scheduling—then back to work.
- **Post-brief cleanup:** File notes, upload media, set the case next action, stage gear for tomorrow.
- **Weekly standards check:** Sample a report, a photo set, and a log. Fix drift before it spreads.

As the Greek poet Archilochus put it, *"We don't rise to the level of our expectations; we fall to the level of our training."* Make your standards visible. Make them automatic. Make them yours.

Takeaway: Discipline isn't intensity—it's consistency. Set simple, repeatable standards and let the system carry you on hard days.

January 13: Communicate Like a Pro

"Wise men speak because they have something to say; fools because they have to say something." —Plato

Every investigator eventually learns this truth: Your ability to communicate determines how far your work goes. You can be the sharpest investigator on the team—but if you can't get your point across clearly, none of it matters. Whether you're briefing superiors to secure resources, testifying in court, debriefing a witness, or writing a report for a client, communication is part of the job.

I once had to brief a military officer who was notorious for wanting things short. If you couldn't give him the concept in less than a minute, he would already have moved on. I even had to brief him on a case for the length of an elevator ride. Talk about having to be clear and concise!

Practical Communication Skills for Investigators:

- **Be clear, not clever.** Speak in plain language, especially when briefing non-investigators. Jargon doesn't make you look smarter—clarity does.
- **Know your audience.** A judge, a jury, a supervisor, a client—each needs a different level of detail and tone. Adjust accordingly.
- **Structure your message.** Situation → Actions → Results → Recommendation. A clean structure makes people listen.
- **Control your delivery.** Steady pace, calm tone, confident posture. How you say something can matter as much as what you say.
- **Brief like time matters.** Assume attention spans are short. Lead with the bottom line up front (BLUF). Then fill in the details if needed.
- **Write like it will be read in court.** Because one day, it might be. Reports should be tight, factual, and free of fluff.

I have briefed senior officials influencing how they made a decision—and testified in court where every word mattered. In both places, how I said something shaped what happened next. Communication isn't just a soft skill; it's a fundamental one for getting what you want.

Takeaway: Clear communication builds trust, drives decisions, and protects your work. Speak clearly, write cleanly, and brief with purpose.

January 14: Calibrate Your Intuition

"It is a capital mistake to theorize before one has data." —Sir Arthur Conan Doyle

When I transitioned from active military service to the reserves, I attended several private investigation academies. One instructor ran a short module on intuition calibration. I had never heard of the term, but every investigator should. "Gut feel" isn't magic—it's pattern recognition built from reps. Useful when it's calibrated, dangerous when it isn't. The goal isn't to ignore intuition; it's to test and refine it so facts verify your quick judgment.

How to Calibrate Your Gut (Field-Ready):

- **Prediction + Confidence.** Before you act, write a one-line forecast and a confidence score (0–100%). Later, compare result vs. confidence. Over time, your confidence should match reality.
- **Base-rate check.** Ask: *What usually happens in cases like this?* Use historical rates, not vibes.
- **Two-hypothesis default.** State your primary theory and a credible alternative. List what would **disprove** each.
- **Disconfirming question.** "What evidence here would make me change my mind?" Look for that first.
- **Pre-mortem.** Imagine it's two weeks from now, and your conclusion was wrong. *What failed?* Add checks for those points.
- **90-second scan → 3-minute challenge.** Take 90 seconds to form your read, then spend 3 minutes trying to **break it**. If it survives, proceed.
- **After-action notes.** When you're right (or wrong), capture why. Was it a real cue or a coincidence? Turn lessons into named cues.

Cues worth logging (examples): sequence/timing changes; concealment behaviors (hands/eyes/objects); clothing mismatched to context; language hedges in interviews; inconsistent timelines across sources.

Takeaway: Treat intuition like a tool. Log it, test it, and tune it—so your fast read stays honest, and your decisions stay sharp.

January 15: Remember Your Why

"The only way to do great work is to love what you do." —Steve Jobs

In service circles (the military, law enforcement, Intelligence Community, etc.), you will often hear: "Remember your why." In investigations, that matters. Parts of the job are tedious. Passion isn't hype; it's the steady fuel that keeps you learning on your own time, finishing the last 5%, and showing up when the weather, schedule, or case turns ugly. Passion without direction burns hot and fizzles. Passion with purpose compounds—and it's infectious.

Your why should come from within, rarely from external sources. The money from closing a good private investigation or the award for closing a good government case is a byproduct and should never be the primary reason.

How to Keep the Fire Productive:

- **Define your "why."** One line: *Who do you serve and how does your work protect them?* Put it where you'll see it daily.
- **Invest in craft time.** 30–60 minutes a day (or 3×/week) on a skill block—interview drills, OSINT reps, camera work.
- **Chase curiosity.** One case-related question per week, you don't have to answer... then answer it anyway.
- **Find a standard-bearer.** A mentor, unit, or author whose work you emulate. Reverse-engineer their quality.
- **Guard against burnout.** Passion ≠ 24/7. Schedule recovery blocks to sustain the pace. (More on self-care later.)

Takeaway: Let passion drive consistency, not chaos. Point it at craft time, curiosity, and measurable standards.

January 16: Innovate in Inches

"Small deeds done are better than great deeds planned." —*Peter Marshall*

Innovation in investigations isn't a moonshot. It's minor, intentional tweaks that make your work faster, cleaner, and more dependable. Whenever I go somewhere, I ask two questions: How can I leave this better than I found it? And what is the next goal line? Most people absorb information and stop there. I don't. If I am in a training course, I observe how the instructor teaches, which training aids they use, why that practical exercise, why that venue, and why that audience. On cases, I try to think outside the box, step into the subject's shoes, or apply underused techniques—especially in missing-persons cases or when trying to locate a subject. Those small shifts often break the stalemate and lead to the individual's location.

Run the Innovation Loop (Field-Ready):

- **Observe:** Spot friction. "We have always done it this way." Why?
- **Hypothesize:** Name one tiny change that could help (camera location, interview order, call script, template tweak).
- **Try & Standardize:** Document the winning tweak so the team can repeat it, and your organization can scale it.

One Small Experiment per Week (Ideas):

- **Surveillance:** Try a new partner, camera technique, or vehicle out
- **Interviews:** Swap techniques. For example, an accusatory approach to a narrative approach.
- **OSINT:** Add one new aggregator or site-specific search operator; incorporate it into your workflow.

Borrow and Adapt from Other Trades:

- **Aviation:** checklists and sterile periods (no chatter during critical phases).
- **EMS:** clear handoffs with SBAR-style summaries (Situation, Background, Assessment, Recommendation).
- **Newsrooms:** style guides—create one for names, dates, times, and photo captions.

Guardrails so Innovation Doesn't Become Chaos:

- **Ethics & law first.** If a tweak touches authority, consent, or privacy—stop and clear it.
- **One change at a time.** Two changes = unclear results.
- **Write it down.** If it's not documented, it won't spread.

Takeaway: Innovate in inches. Test one small improvement, measure it, then decide whether to keep or kill it. Tiny wins compound into better cases.

January 17: Progress, Not Perfection

"It ain't about how hard you're hit, it's about how you can get hit and keep moving forward." – Rocky Balboa

There is no better Hollywood movie series than the Rocky series to showcase a man's unwavering persistence on a mission. Persistence is a vital trait for an investigator. You need to have the drive and relentless pursuit to see a case through to the end, never taking no for an answer. Always aim for yes. Your client, the victim, the victim's family, the taxpayer, or your agency relies on you. Your country depends on you. Cases rarely break cleanly, and more often than not, you don't have the smoking gun to make a case slam dunk. Leads stall. The difference between a cold trail and a closed case is usually persistence—small, consistent efforts that add up over time. Progress beats perfection.

Make Persistence a Habit:

- **Next action, always.** End every day and every entry with one concrete step, an owner, and a date. If it's not scheduled, it's not real.
- **Stall breakers.** Change one variable: time of day, day of week, door vs. phone, language, or pretext.
- **Return to the baseline.** Re-read the first report, photos, and call notes. Fresh eyes + fundamentals = missed cues found. Better yet, bring in a different set of eyes to help achieve a breakthrough.
- **Log what didn't work.** Your future self (or teammate) won't waste time repeating dead ends.
- **Don't confuse motion with progress.** Busy isn't forward. Ask: *What outcome did today's push move closer to?* If you can't answer in one line, you might be spinning.
- **A quick persistence drill (today).** Pick one stuck lead. Think of two different ways to approach it. Execute on them. Document what worked and what didn't.

Takeaway: Keep nudging the ball forward. One clear next action, every day. Persistence compounds—and closes cases.

January 18: Dress as a Tactic

"Elegance is not standing out, but being remembered." —Giorgio Armani

On my first intelligence assignment in Afghanistan, I worked with a Soldier who mastered the ebb and flow of dressing for success. In one day, he might rotate through MultiCam, a suit and tie, field-office casual, and local Afghan garb—all based on who he was meeting: village elders, line troops, or senior officers. He understood a simple truth: how you dress shapes rapport, authority, and outcomes.

Uniformed police academies teach **officer presence** for a reason. Appearance can escalate or defuse. Investigations are no different. Whether you're blending in on surveillance, meeting a client, interviewing a witness, or testifying in court, **clothing is a tool.** Use it on purpose. There are two modes to master:

- **Power of the suit (signal credibility).** Court, formal interviews, and client briefings. Prioritize tailored fit over brand: a dark, quiet suit; a crisp shirt; a conservative tie; polished shoes. Slim your pocket load—no bulges.
- **Blend with the environment (disappear).** Match the setting first by footwear, then outer layer, then accessories. Consider neutral colors, avoid flashy logos, choose a practical watch, and opt for a low-profile bag. Avoid tell-tale "tactical tourist" markers like Velcro and MOLLE.

Rapport by Attire

- **Respect local norms.** When appropriate and lawful, modesty or local dress signals respect and unlocks conversations.
- **Signal role clarity.** A suit says "decision-maker." Field office casual says "working." Each has a place.

Grooming = Credibility

- Hair/nails clean; scent light or none; lint and scuffs removed
- Keep jewelry minimal; cover distracting tattoos when it helps the mission
- Credentials carried discreetly; shown only when appropriate

Takeaway: Dress isn't vanity—it's strategy. Use the suit to project credibility, blend when surveilling or interviewing. Make deliberate choices to move the case forward.

January 19: Resourcefulness on Demand

"Do what you can, with what you have, where you are." —President Theodore Roosevelt

While serving in Amman, Jordan, with the Diplomatic Security Service (DSS), I sought armored-vehicle breaching training for a team I helped create that specialized in urban search and rescue. The problem was that we had no armored vehicles! I tracked down a contact who was decommissioning a few and persuaded management to allow our team to train on them. Afterward, the vehicles were damaged and undriveable, so I coordinated transportation to a demolition range where another team and I practiced explosive entry and post-blast investigation before the vehicles were ultimately destroyed. We turned unwanted equipment into a valuable cross-unit training resource for multiple U.S. Government elements.

Am I telling this to impress you? No. I am telling you so you see resourcefulness is a core investigator skill. When budgets, access, or equipment are missing, find alternatives, borrow, barter, or improvise—ethically and legally.

Practical Moves for Resourceful Investigators:

- **Identify available resources.** Know which agencies, contractors, universities, or NGOs have gear, ranges, or venues you can lawfully access or borrow. Keep names and contact information current.
- **Ask for cross-use.** Show the value: training A helps B. Frame requests as force multipliers for other units or offices.
- **Create low-cost reps.** Simulate scenarios with volunteers, mock props, or table-top exercises before you ask for the real thing.
- **Leverage grants & sponsors.** Some vendors, trade groups, or foundations underwrite training—ask and document the return on investment.
- **Barter skills, not secrets.** Offer instructor time, after-action reports, or venue support in exchange for access.
- **Use regional centers.** Intelligence fusion centers, regional task forces, and state teams often loan equipment out for short periods of time.
- **Ethical guardrails:** Always clear legal authority, safety, and OPSEC. Never shortcut lawful process for convenience.

Takeaway: Constraints are opportunities. When you can't buy a solution, build one, borrow one, or swap value. Resourcefulness closes gaps and delivers training and operational wins.

January 20: Self-Care Is Operational Readiness

"Fatigue makes cowards of us all." —Vince Lombardi

Investigative work isn't a sprint. It's long hours, high stakes, and the kind of stress that slowly grinds down performance if left unchecked. Early in my career, I treated self-care like a luxury. A wise platoon sergeant once told me, *"If you can't take care of yourself, how are you going to take care of your squad?"* Self-care isn't a luxury—it's a tactical advantage. An investigator who's burned out, dehydrated, or sleep-deprived makes bad calls, misses details, and puts the mission and team at risk. Think of self-care like gear maintenance: you don't let your vehicle run without gas, and you shouldn't let your body or mind run on empty either.

The Operational Cost of Neglecting Yourself:

- Slower reaction time
- Foggy judgment under pressure
- Irritability with witnesses, partners, or clients
- Lower baseline situational awareness
- Increased risk of burnout and career-ending mistakes

Practical Self-Care for Investigators:

- **Sleep like it matters.** Fatigue doesn't make you tough; it makes you sloppy. Prioritize a real sleep block when operations allow.
- **Fuel strategically.** A pocket full of caffeine and sugar isn't a plan. Think protein, hydration, and sustained energy for long ops. Consider eliminating alcohol and tobacco.
- **Train for endurance, not vanity.** Mobility, strength, and cardio directly affect how you move in the field—and recover after.
- **Schedule decompression.** Whether it's the gym, hobbies, family, or prayer, build a ritual that resets your baseline.
- **Control the inputs.** Be deliberate about what you consume—news, social media, vices. Garbage in = garbage out.
- **Know your redline.** Learn to recognize when fatigue or stress is changing your decision-making. Then act to correct it.

Team self-care matters too. A burned-out partner isn't just tired—they're a liability. Build a culture where taking care of yourself isn't a weakness; it is standard operating procedure.

Takeaway: Self-care isn't a spa day; it is operational readiness. A sharp investigator takes care of their mind and body so they can take care of the mission.

January 21: Initiative Wins Quietly

"The best way to predict the future is to create it." —Peter Drucker

Good investigators don't wait for something to happen; they make something happen. You have to be a self-starter in this business. This is especially true if you are—or plan to be—a private investigator. Cases aren't going to fall into your lap. Seizing the initiative works equally well in the private and public sectors and can make the difference between closing a case quickly or never closing it at all.

In investigations, no one's going to hand you a roadmap. The best investigators are the ones who see a gap, step up, and move the ball forward without being asked. Initiative doesn't mean freelancing—it means anticipating needs, taking ownership of your role, and creating momentum when things stall.

I have seen investigations stagnate not for lack of leads, but because everyone waited for someone else to act. The case never needed a genius. It needed someone to move it forward.

I once inherited a criminal case that kept getting passed around the office as people came and went. It was the "ugly baby" no one wanted to hold. I worked every lead and resurrected it from the grave. When it came time for case presentation, the AUSA told me, *"I can tell you did a lot of work on this case—let's move on it,"* even though it was four years old. That is initiative in action.

Practical Ways to Show Initiative:

- **Own the "orphan" tasks.** Those small, unglamorous jobs no one wants—background checks, schedule coordination, site sketches—often produce the lead that cracks the case.
- **Think two steps ahead.** If surveillance is planned, pre-check comms, vehicles, and cover stories without being told.
- **Solve problems, don't just spot them.** If you have ever heard me conduct an after-action review, you will often hear me say: *"Don't just bring problems, bring solutions."*
- **Respect the chain, but don't wait for permission to think.** Clear actions that need clearance while keeping the planning ball rolling.
- **Document and communicate.** Quiet initiative fails if the team doesn't know what's happening. Keep others in the loop.

Initiative isn't about ego. It's about being the person others can count on when things go sideways. It's what turns routine investigators into trusted operators.

Takeaway: Initiative isn't loud—it's steady, reliable action that moves cases forward. Don't wait. Anticipate. Act.

January 22: Adaptability Keeps You Alive

"Everyone has a plan until they get punched in the mouth." —Mike Tyson

No matter how solid your plan is, reality will find a way to undermine it. A surveillance target changes their route after using the same one for three straight months, slipping past the surveillance box despite any intelligence training. A key witness ghosts you after swearing they would be there for you. A warrant service goes wrong because an officer claims to be on the perimeter—but isn't. (All based on actual events.) Investigations don't reward rigidity—they favor those who adapt quickly without losing discipline.

I have had to learn and relearn this lesson, often during surveillance. Just start observing people, and you will realize they do things like sit in cars for long stretches. It's not some counterintelligence tactic—it's just human nature. Now you look awkward, either loitering in a store waiting for them to leave or dealing with a busybody knocking on your car window to ask why you're parked there. That's where adaptability separates the pros from everyone else.

Building Adaptability Into Your Craft:

- **Plan A is great. Plan B is mandatory.** Always ask, "What's the move if this goes wrong?" before stepping off.
- **Know your thresholds.** Identify what breaks the plan (vehicle swap, subject split, bad weather) and pre-decide the pivot.
- **Keep your ego out of it.** A broken plan doesn't mean failure. It means reality showed up.
- **Train for chaos.** Build uncertainty into scenarios. Role-play lost targets, late intel drops, and real-world curveballs.
- **Anchor to fundamentals.** When the script is useless, fall back on principles, legal authorities, and sound judgment.

Adaptability isn't about winging it—it's about being structured enough to bend without breaking.

Takeaway: Plans break. Good investigators don't. Build adaptability into your mindset, so when reality hits, you're the calmest person in the room.

January 23: Time and Task Discipline

"If you're on time, you're late. If you're late, you're dead." —Drill Sergeant Baker

Drill Sergeant Baker—*first name Drill Sergeant, last name Baker*—was one of my drill sergeants during U.S. Army basic training. Anyone who's been through that experience can probably hear the gravel in his voice already. He didn't whisper it over a cup of coffee either; it was delivered at a volume that could be heard two zip codes away.

Sure, his statement might be a little extreme for the investigative world, but the point still lands: **time is everything in operations**. In investigations, showing up on time—and managing your time—isn't optional. It's a marker of discipline, reliability, and respect for the mission.

Time management for investigators boils down to two things: being where you say you will be and managing your load.

If you tell a witness to meet at 10:00 AM, don't roll in at 10:32 AM because "your time is more valuable." If the hood brief is at 3:00 AM to serve a warrant or set up surveillance, don't wander in at 4:00 AM like the main character who just decided to show up for the big finale. These habits erode credibility fast.

The second piece is load management. Don't be the person who stacks their calendar so tight that the smallest ripple sinks the whole ship. Leave white space. You will need it.

Field-Ready Principles for Time and Task Discipline:

- **Early is on time.** Build in buffer time for every meet, movement, or operational step. Your team shouldn't wait on you.
- **Respect others' time.** Witnesses, subjects, and partners all notice lateness—even if they don't say it. It signals how much you respect the mission.
- **Guard calendar space.** White space isn't wasted time; it's operational insurance. It lets you adapt when leads change or emergencies hit.
- **Know your capacity.** Taking on too much isn't ambitious—it's sloppy. If everything's a priority, nothing is.
- **Set alarms and rituals.** Time discipline is a system, not memory. Use alarms, buffers, and prep rituals to make it automatic. *(I'm a fan of redundant alarms—phone or plug-in, and battery-operated.)*
- **Hold yourself accountable.** If you blow a time mark, own it. Don't make excuses—fix the habit.

Takeaway: Time is a tactical asset. Be early. Manage your load. Respect the clock like your investigation depends on it—because it does.

January 24: Details Win Cases

"A man's accomplishments in life are the cumulative effect of his attention to detail."
—John Foster Dulles

It doesn't matter if you're a private investigator working an infidelity case or a federal agent on a transnational criminal ring—details matter (as Jack Reacher would say). Consider the cognitive bias *WYSIATI*—"what you see is all there is" — described by Daniel Kahneman in *Thinking, Fast and Slow*. We judge based on whatever information we have on hand, no matter how incomplete. Confirmation bias then piles on: we look for data that supports our existing belief and ignore the rest.

Big cases rarely collapse from big mistakes. They fall apart from one small, missed detail that snowballs: a wrong timestamp, a bad transcription, a misspelled name on a warrant. One loose thread can unravel months of work.

Attention to detail isn't glamorous. No one hands out medals for clean time stamps or consistent formatting. But those little things are the backbone of defensible investigations.

A quick parallel example from a protective detail that could have caused international issues: I was working the Iraqi Foreign Minister during one of the U.N. General Assembly sessions. His schedule listed a meeting with the Belgians at their mission; the Belgian Foreign Minister's schedule listed the same meeting at their hotel. I flagged both staffs, they reconciled the conflict, and we avoided embarrassment to our protectee—one of protection's two cardinal rules: prevent harm, and prevent embarrassment.

How to Sharpen Your Detail Discipline:

- **Slow is smooth.** Double-check names, dates, times, and locations—every time.
- **Use checklists.** (Yes, again.) Make accuracy repeatable, not heroic.
- **Cross-verify.** Two sources, two sets of eyes. For Lynx cases: field investigator drafts → self-review after a short time block → case manager review → my review → client/attorney.
- **Standardize formats.** Keep dates, times, filenames, and evidence labels uniform across your work.
- **Annotate everything.** If it isn't written down, it didn't happen. If it's sloppy, it won't hold up.

Takeaway: The small stuff isn't small. Attention to detail is what separates good investigators from great ones. Check it twice—your case depends on it.

January 25: Humility Keeps You Sharp

"It is impossible for a man to learn what he thinks he already knows." —Epictetus

In investigations, confidence is a tool. Ego is a liability. The moment you start believing you've "seen it all," the job will find a way to humble you—usually at the worst possible time.

Humility isn't weakness. It's strength. It keeps your mind open, your ego in check, and your learning curve alive. It's what lets you admit, "I don't know," and then go find the answer. It's also what earns you trust—because no one wants to work with the know-it-all who talks more than they listen. I have worked with a handful of braggarts who forgot what humility looks like—and more importantly, why they serve in the first place. I have also seen doors close on them that remained open for me simply because of how I approached the situation. If you enter an interview, a confidential informant meeting, or any operational encounter with an open mind and a positive attitude, you dramatically increase your chances of building rapport and advancing your case.

I once deployed to support a specialized unit. My element had to be spread across the country to support their operations as an intelligence-enabling element. One of my colleagues' very first words to a seasoned operator were, "I'm just as trained as you." (He was not.) The unit sent him home the same day and asked for another agent to replace him. That single lapse in humility cost him the chance to work alongside some of the best in the business. The unit didn't need another ego in the room—they needed a teammate.

How to Practice Professional Humility:

- **Ask, don't assume.** Even if you think you know the answer, ask the extra question. You might catch the blind spot.
- **Respect every role.** Analysts, surveillance teams, translators, techs—they all see things you don't.
- **Invite critique.** A tough after-action review makes you sharper, not smaller.
- **Own your misses.** Admitting an error early protects the case and your credibility.
- **Keep learning.** Training isn't for rookies. The best investigators know they never really "arrive." Stay curious, keep training, and keep sharpening.

Humility doesn't mean doubting yourself. It means respecting the craft enough to know you can always get better. The best investigators I've ever known were confident in their skills—but humble enough to keep growing.

Takeaway: Humility isn't soft. It's steel wrapped in quiet. It protects you from your own blind spots and earns you trust in the room. Stay teachable. Stay sharp.

January 26: Curiosity as a Force Multiplier

"The important thing is not to stop questioning. Curiosity has its own reason for existing." —Dr. Albert Einstein

Every great investigator I have ever met had one trait in common: curiosity. The kind that drives you to ask one more question, open one more report, or rewind one more minute of surveillance footage, even when everyone else says, "We're good." Curiosity isn't about nosiness—it's about the relentless drive to understand.

Curiosity turns routine work into discovery. It's what helps you spot the anomaly in a stack of reports, notice the one vehicle that doesn't belong, or ask the witness the question no one else thought to ask. It's the quiet, steady force that powers every major breakthrough.

I use it constantly when interviewing or dealing with people. I'm not just looking at what they say—I'm paying attention to their environment. I'll ask about the family photo on their desk, the diploma on their wall, the painting behind them, or the tattoo peeking out from under a sleeve. I'm not redecorating their office or starting a lifestyle blog—it's a subtle way to build rapport, make people drop their guard, and learn what matters to them. Nine times out of ten, those small, curious questions reveal something useful that a scripted interview would have missed.

How to Apply Curiosity in Your Daily Work:

- **Ask one more question.** Don't stop at the first answer—ask what it means, what it connects to, and what's missing.
- **Follow the thread.** When something feels off, don't shrug it away. Track it until you can prove or disprove it.
- **Study laterally.** Learn how other disciplines solve problems—aviation, medicine, journalism, and intelligence. Borrow their methods.
- **Keep a curiosity log.** Write down one question a day that your case raises. Circle back later.
- **Turn boredom into fuel.** When things get routine, challenge yourself to find one new pattern or insight.

Curiosity isn't just a personality trait. It keeps your work alive, your edge sharp, and your understanding deep. When others stop digging, curiosity is what pushes you past the obvious.

Takeaway: Curiosity isn't chaos—it's focused exploration. Ask, notice, and dig. The case may hinge on the question no one else bothered to ask.

January 27: The Power of Listening

"Most people do not listen with the intent to understand; they listen with the intent to reply." —Stephen R. Covey

It doesn't matter if you're doing a client intake interview for a private investigation, listening to a confidential informant tell you their woes, negotiating with a hostage taker during a crisis negotiation, or talking with a witness—listening is a fundamental skill. Conversations aren't won by the person who talks the most—they are won by the person who listens best.

One of the most valuable lessons I ever learned was to let the silence work for you. You can see it in interviews: people hate dead air. Give them space, and they will often fill it with something unplanned—sometimes the one detail you actually need. You can't fake good listening; it shows in your body language, your timing, and your follow-up. The same principle applies when you're running an intelligence operation and trying to elicit information from a potential spy. Sometimes the best thing you can do is... nothing at all. Bonus points if you wait to speak on the witness stand so the prosecutor has time to object to the defense attorney.

Practical Listening Skills:

- **Listen for what's not said.** Gaps, hesitations, and evasions often speak louder than words.
- **Embrace the silence.** Count to five in your head before filling dead air. Let them talk themselves into the next detail.
- **Mirror and echo.** Repeating their last phrase or word prompts elaboration—without confrontation.
- **Take light notes.** Staring at your notepad isn't listening. Capture keywords and return to eye contact.
- **Respond with precision.** One good, thoughtful question after listening beats ten rushed ones.
- **Control your tells.** Nodding too much or reacting too quickly gives away your angle.

Good listening isn't passive. It's active, disciplined, and tactical. It builds rapport, reveals inconsistencies, and earns trust. More than once, I have solved a problem not because I was the smartest person in the room, but because I shut up long enough to hear the answer.

Takeaway: Listening is a superpower. It breaks cases, builds trust, and exposes what questions alone can't. Say less. Hear more.

January 28: Check Your Bias

"What we see depends mainly on what we look for." —John Lubbock

Bias is one of the quietest poisons in investigation. It seeps in through first impressions, preconceptions, or social norms. Investigators must watch for it every time they look at a victim, a client, or a suspect.

One of the most insidious forms of bias is the halo effect—when one positive trait (appearance, education, demeanor) causes you to overvalue everything else about that person. You see the well-dressed suspect and assume credibility. You speak with the respectful client and assume honesty. You interview the polished victim and dismiss their possible contradictions. None of those assumptions is evidence. A powerful historical example is Kim Philby, one of the infamous Cambridge Five. Because Philby looked the part—educated at Cambridge, impeccably mannered, well-connected—many in the British establishment simply could not believe he could be a traitor. That halo protected him for years, allowing one of the most damaging acts of espionage in modern history to unfold right under their noses.

I saw a version of this dynamic in an internal investigation I once supported. An American employee accused a host-nation citizen of theft. Many were quick to lean toward the American's story simply because of who was making the complaint. But the investigation revealed the opposite: the American was the one stealing. I had to remind the lead investigator—just because the complaint came from an American didn't make it more (or less) credible. Facts make cases. Nationality, appearance, or demeanor don't. How to keep bias in check:

- **Name your snap judgment.** Acknowledge it internally ("He seems trustworthy")—then deliberately set it aside.
- **Separate style from substance.** Good manners don't prove truth. Poor behavior doesn't prove guilt. Always demand evidence.
- **Use counter-narrative drills.** Ask yourself, "What if the opposite is true?"
- **Double-down on verification.** Test everyone's claims with equal rigor—even those who seem "above suspicion."
- **Invite a filter.** A second set of eyes can catch what your brain has already decided to overlook.

Bias isn't disqualifying, but it is dangerous if unchecked. Great investigators don't pretend they don't have bias—they build systems to catch it before it contaminates the work.

Takeaway: The halo casts a long shadow. Watch for it. Test through it. It's not how someone looks—it's their behavior and the evidence that tells the story.

January 29: Sense of Urgency

"A good plan violently executed now is better than a perfect plan executed next week." —*General George S. Patton*

Investigations don't wait for perfect conditions. Neither should you. A sense of urgency isn't panic—it's disciplined movement. It's the difference between investigators who react and those who drive cases and the profession forward.

Urgency is about acting quickly when tasks land on your desk. As Benjamin Franklin said: *"Don't put off to tomorrow what can be done today."* Too many cases stall not because of a lack of skill, but because of delay. Reports sit half-written. Leads go uncalled. E-mails wait for "the right time." Meanwhile, opportunities disappear. Every day you let a task linger, it grows heavier—and your case gets colder. Great investigators don't wait for the perfect moment. They *make* the moment.

How to Build Urgency Into Your Habits:

- **Act same-day.** If it takes less than five minutes, do it immediately. Don't "put it on the list."
- **Set hard edges.** Time-block key tasks so they don't drift into "someday."
- **Kill analysis paralysis.** Progress beats polish. You can clean a draft later.
- **Create daily momentum.** One completed action snowballs into the next.
- **Make urgency a culture.** If everyone treats time like a tactical resource, fewer balls get dropped.

Sometimes, public-sector investigators grow complacent because cases just land in their laps. In the private sector, a lack of urgency can sink your business. I try to apply this principle in every facet of life: **Get it done. Just get the task done.**

Takeaway: A sense of urgency isn't about rushing. It's about intentional speed— pushing your case forward before opportunity slips away. Act before the window closes.

January 30: Relentless Pursuit

"Genius is 1% inspiration and 99% perspiration." —Thomas Edison

The difference between a cold case and a closed case often isn't brilliance. It's follow-up. Most people don't do it. They get the initial statement, write the report, make a few calls, and then move on. Good investigators circle back. Great investigators don't stop circling until the job's done.

I have seen it time and again: an unanswered email to a records clerk that just needed one follow-up, a case that could have been solved with a quick camera review, a potential client who only needed one more call to sign on. And if someone won't respond to impersonal communication, go to their office in person. It's a lot harder to ignore someone standing in the doorway.

On my second deployment to Afghanistan, I worked in more of an intelligence management role. I spent at least two-thirds of my time following up with staff, partners, and interlocutors—making sure cases were closed, administrative actions were completed, and people were actually working. It would have been easy to just make the initial request and let it fade. One supervisor told me, *"Ed, you always get to yes."* That is what relentless pursuit looks like.

Follow-up isn't about pestering. It's about intentional persistence—steady pressure, polite professionalism, and never letting the thread die.

Practical Ways to Build a Follow-Up Habit:

- **Calendar every lead.** If it's not scheduled, it's forgotten. Numerous calendar apps make this easy—I just use Microsoft Outlook.
- **Vary the approach.** If a call doesn't work, try email. If email doesn't work, knock on the door. Change the angle, not just the date.
- **Be politely relentless.** Professionalism plus persistence earns more results than aggressiveness ever will.
- **Log every attempt.** A clean paper trail shows diligence—and sometimes the record itself nudges people to respond.
- **Re-read your case notes.** Hidden opportunities live in old pages. I once picked up a case where the original investigator had written a note to review surveillance footage—but never did. No one else followed up. By the time I got it, the footage had been sent to archives, which only retained records for 90 days. I tracked it down just before the deadline and got the evidence we needed. That wasn't luck. That was follow-up.

Takeaway: Be the one who follows up—again and again—until the door finally opens.

January 31: Execution Wins

"An idea is nothing. Execution is everything." —Edward Panico

Execute. It's one of my favorite words in the English language. In investigations, ideas are cheap. Execution is what closes cases. You can have the best plan in the world—the most brilliant theory, the cleverest investigative angle—but if it never leaves the notebook, it's worthless. I have watched cases die not because someone didn't know what to do, but because they didn't do it.

Let me tell you a story. In 2005, a young Soldier in a U.S. Army barracks had a pizza delivered to his room. He thought, *Why can't I get a cheeseburger from McDonalds or a steak from a steakhouse delivered the same way?* He had the idea. He didn't execute. Nearly a decade later, a company launched a platform to do exactly that. How do I know this story? Well, that Soldier was me. The company was Uber Eats—and now dozens of competitors around the world. A billion-dollar idea that stayed just that: an idea. If you have an idea on how to move a case forward, execute. Don't wait for someone else to pick it up. Don't let it die in a planning session. Action separates wishful thinking from results.

A friend of mine once was favorably assessed into a specialized intelligence unit. Before starting, he imagined the grass would be greener. When he got there, he was stunned: no sources on the books. Everyone was too busy talking about how great they were to have been in the unit instead of actually working! Within a month, he had spotted and developed two solid sources. When his supervisor asked how he did it, his answer was simple: *"I thought about what to do, and then I executed."* This applies everywhere, from a lead you think might be worth a phone call to a question you think might open a witness up.

How to Make Execution Your Default:

- **Start immediately.** If your idea is solid, act before the spark fades.
- **Make it real.** Put it on the calendar, assign a time, give it a name.
- **Keep it simple.** Execution isn't about perfection—it's about movement.
- **Don't overthink it.** The first step doesn't need to solve the case; it just needs to move it forward.
- **Close the loop.** Once it's done, document it, communicate it, and set the next action.

I have seen too many people talk themselves out of great moves because they waited for the "right time." Here is the truth: **it never is.** The investigators who act—who execute—are the ones who build momentum, catch breaks, and close cases.

Takeaway: Most good investigative work isn't flashy. It's just executed ideas.

February: Case Management and Report Writing

"Plans are nothing; planning is everything." —*President Dwight D. Eisenhower*

Investigations aren't won with a cool story—they're won with structure. A sharp investigator isn't just someone who can find the facts; it's someone who can manage those facts, document them clearly, and make sure nothing slips through the cracks. Poor case management burns time and resources. Bad reporting kills otherwise strong cases.

I've seen it too many times. A brilliant piece of investigative work goes nowhere because no one can follow the paper trail. Leads get lost because there is no system. Reports end up vague, incomplete, or written like diary entries instead of professional case files. It doesn't matter how good your fieldwork is if you can't document it, communicate it, and defend it.

Case management is how you steer the investigation. Report writing is how you prove it happened. This chapter will walk through both—how to keep your cases tight, organized, and moving forward, and how to write reports that stand up in court, in a boardroom, or in front of a client.

Here is what we will focus on this month:

- **Case structure:** Building repeatable systems that keep you on track.
- **Documentation:** If it's not written down, it didn't happen. Period.
- **Timelines and tracking:** Managing leads, deadlines, and evidence flow.
- **Professional reporting:** Writing with clarity, precision, and legal defensibility.
- **Communication through reports:** Making your findings understandable to non-investigators.
- **Efficiency:** Turning chaos into clean workflows that save time and money.

In my line of work—whether in the public or private sector—the strongest investigators I've seen are not just good at collecting information. They are exceptional at turning that information into a structured, defensible story. That's what moves cases forward. That's what wins trust. And that's what keeps you from being buried under your own paperwork. Onward!

February 1: Document Everything

"If it's not written down, it didn't happen." —Investigative proverb

Every investigator has heard that line at some point in their career—and the good ones live by it. Documentation isn't just a box to check. It's the backbone of your case. It's how you prove what you did, when you did it, and why it mattered. Memory fades. Witnesses recant. People retire or move on. The only thing that holds up is what's on paper (or in a secure digital system). As a CIA case officer once told me, *"I might forget, but Agency records do not."*

In both the public and private sectors, your reports, logs, and notes become part of the record. If the case ends up in court, they will be scrutinized by opposing counsel. If it's a private investigation, your documentation may be the only thing your client ever sees. That's why every action should leave a clear, factual trail. In the private sector, documentation isn't just good practice—in some states, it's legally required. Certain jurisdictions require investigators to provide a written work product to clients. In states that don't, some firms try to avoid producing reports altogether. Often, that's not strategy—it's fear. Many simply lack confidence in their writing or worry about what might surface during discovery.

There are times when it's appropriate to limit what goes into a written product— but that should be the exception, not the rule. Clear, factual documentation protects you, your client (or victim), and the integrity of the investigation. A concise written report paired with relevant evidence isn't just professional; it builds trust, adds value, and creates a defensible record of what was done.

Practical Documentation Habits:

- **Write it now, not later.** Details decay fast. Log your actions and observations while they are fresh.
- **Be precise.** Times, dates, locations, and identities should be accurate down to the minute. Vague language kills clarity.
- **Assume it will be read in court.** If it can't stand up to cross-examination, rewrite it until it can.

When I was learning to be an intelligence officer, an instructor often reminded us: *the reports you're writing aren't for you—they are for the next officer, a policymaker, an attorney, or a judge.* When I train young investigators today, I tell them the same thing.

Takeaway: Documentation is the skeleton of your case. Without it, the whole thing collapses. Write everything down. Make it clear, accurate, and defensible.

February 2: Reports That Work

"Writing is easy. All you have to do is cross out the wrong words." —Mark Twain

If documentation is the backbone of an investigation, the report is its voice. It's what speaks for you when you're not in the room. A clear, factual, well-structured report can make or break how a case is understood—by supervisors, clients, attorneys, or juries. I have seen sloppy reports create more work than the actual investigation itself. I have also seen clean, tight reporting drive quick decisions, secure funding, and stand up in court without breaking a sweat.

Whether you're in the public or private sector, good reports share one trait: they tell the story of the investigation without unnecessary drama. They are clear, complete, and credible. The very first thing I tell aspiring investigators when it comes to hard skills is that if you can't write, you won't last long in this field.

I was once coaching an investigator who was frustrated that a client would not pay him for his report. I offered to take a look at it—and after reading it, I told him bluntly, "I wouldn't pay for this either." He was flabbergasted at first, but after we walked through the issues together, he realized the client wasn't wrong. He agreed to tighten up his report writing moving forward to keep his clients happy.

Field-Tested Report Writing Tips:

- **Start with the bottom line.** Lead with the key finding or outcome. Don't bury the headline three pages deep.
- **Stick to the facts.** Separate what you observed, what others said, and what can be verified. Keep opinions out.
- **Be chronological and logical.** If your reader can't follow the flow, they won't trust the content.
- **Use standardized formats.** Headers, timestamps, and labeling should match across all reports in your organization. It builds consistency and speeds review.
- **Attach the right exhibits.** Photos, videos, diagrams, and supporting documents give weight to your words. Reference them clearly in the body of the report.
- **Proof it like your name's on it—because it is.** Spelling errors, bad grammar, or sloppy formatting make people doubt your professionalism.

Good reports don't just document what happened—they make people care enough to act on it. They reflect your credibility, your competence, and your respect for the case.

Takeaway: Write reports that earn respect. If you wouldn't pay for it, no one else should have too either.

February 3: Write in the Active Voice

"Clarity is the courtesy of professionals." —George Bernard Shaw

The way you write can make or break how your report is understood. One of the fastest ways to strengthen your reports is to use **active voice** rather than **passive voice**. Active voice is direct, clear, and shows responsibility. Passive voice is vague, clunky, and leaves your reader wondering who did what. For the rest of this lesson, we will shorten *'investigator' to 'INV'* and focus on that distinction.

- **Active:** "INV Doe observed Subject exit the vehicle at approximately 0930 hours."
- **Passive:** "Subject was observed exiting the vehicle at approximately 0930 hours by INV Doe."

The second version might sound "official," but it hides the actor until the end of the sentence. Who observed the subject? Was it you? A camera? A neighbor? Passive voice creates distance between the writer and the action—and that distance can be exploited in court, questioned by supervisors, or misunderstood by clients.

A note on **"the Subject" versus "Subject."** While I do not control government-wide writing standards, I do control Lynx writing standards. Although it may not be grammatically traditional, dropping "the" is logical to me. "Subject" functions as a stand-in for a person's name. You would not write, "INV Doe observed *the* Dominic exit the vehicle." You would write, "INV Doe observed Dominic exit the vehicle." For the same reason, "INV Doe observed Subject exit the vehicle at 0930 hours" makes more sense to me.

Quick Tips to Stay Active:

If you can add "by zombies" to a sentence and it still makes sense, it is passive.

- "The evidence was collected *(by* zombies*)*." → Passive
- "INV Doe collected the evidence." → Active

Identify who performed the action and put them at the front of the sentence.

Avoid unnecessary "was" or "were" constructions.

Finally, read your report out loud. Passive voice sounds distant; active voice sounds decisive.

Takeaway: Own your sentences. Active voice makes your writing stronger, sharper, and harder to pick apart.

February 4: Use Templates

"You cannot increase the quality or quantity of your achievement or performance except to the degree in which you increase your ability to use your time effectively."
—Brian Tracy

Templates are one of the simplest force multipliers you can use as an investigator. They save time, keep your documentation consistent, and ensure key information isn't missed. But—and this is important—a template is a starting point, not an excuse to turn off your brain.

I've seen people treat templates like autopilot, and it shows. Here is a funny but cringeworthy example: in the military, when someone gets assigned to a new unit, they often receive a digital welcome letter from their unit sponsor. You can always tell who actually read the letter before sending it. More than once, I have received one that proudly began with: "Dear [Insert Name Here], welcome to the [XXX] battalion!"

Templates can make you look organized—or careless. In investigative work, that can be the difference between your report being taken seriously or looking sloppy. Whether in the public or private sector, using templates effectively means reviewing every line, ensuring the details match the case, and removing placeholder language.

Why Templates Matter:

- They save time and reduce the mental load of repetitive tasks.
- They standardize language, structure, and formatting across teams.
- They help ensure the required information isn't forgotten or skipped.
- They allow new investigators to learn best practices through structure.

How to Use Templates Without Embarrassing Yourself:

- **Review every word.** Never assume the placeholders were cleared.
- **Customize the language.** Adjust phrasing to fit the tone, sector, or case.
- **Verify details.** Case numbers, names, dates, and times are the first errors people miss.
- **Match the template to the situation.** A surveillance report isn't a witness interview summary—use the right tool.
- **Stay within policy.** Many agencies or companies have approved formats you must follow.
- **Protect the master.** Keep a clean, read-only master; save edits as a new file.

P.S. If you need private investigation report templates, reach out.

Takeaway: Templates don't replace thinking—they free your brain to focus on the case. Review them carefully and own every word.

February 5: Write for the Reader

"Good writing is clear thinking made visible." —Bill Wheeler

When investigators write, they often focus on what *they* want to say rather than what the reader needs to understand. But your report isn't for you—it's for the next person in the chain: your supervisor, prosecutor, client, or judge. If they can't quickly grasp what happened and why it matters, your hard work gets lost in translation.

I've reviewed countless reports that technically included all the right details—but were structured like a stream of consciousness. It might make sense to the writer, but if the reader must hunt for key facts, they won't trust or use your work. In many cases, it's not the investigation that fails—it's the communication.

The best reports guide the reader through the story logically, step by step. They don't make the reader work to understand the facts. If you've ever seen me prepare a training exercise, draft an action memo, or (yes) write a book, you know I always aim for logical, step-by-step lucidity.

Write Like the Reader:

- **Lead with what matters.** Give them the bottom line up front. Don't bury key findings on page four.
- **Anticipate their questions.** Who, what, when, where, why, how? Answer these early and clearly.
- **Make it skimmable.** Clear headers, logical flow, and clean formatting help the reader find what they need fast.
- **Be specific.** Vague language forces the reader to guess—and guessing kills confidence.
- **Explain acronyms once.** Then stick to plain language wherever possible.
- **Trim the fat.** Every word should earn its place. If it doesn't move the case forward, cut it.

I once had an attorney tell me she loved reading my reports because she didn't have to guess what happened. That wasn't because I'm a literary genius—it was because I wrote them like she was standing in my shoes, seeing what I saw. That's the standard.

Takeaway: Write reports for the person who will use them, not the person who wrote them. When the reader can understand your work on the first pass, you've done your job.

February 6: Write as You Go

"The faintest ink is better than the best memory." —Chinese Proverb

One of the biggest mistakes investigators make with report writing is waiting until the end of the day—or worse, the end of the case—to start documenting. By then, details blur, timelines shift, and your "mental notes" are gone. Writing as you go isn't just efficient—it's an insurance policy for your case.

I occasionally must relearn this lesson. I recently went to a meeting with Nigerian police officials and took some decent notes. Then other duties pulled me in different directions, and before I knew it, two days had passed. By the time I sat down to write the report cable, the crisp details of the meeting were gone. My memory filled in the gaps, but the product was degraded. It wasn't a disaster, but it was far from my best work—and it never should have happened.

I have seen it happen to others, too: strong operations supported by weak reports because the writing came too late. Times and sequences get fuzzy, quotes get paraphrased, and key context is lost. A half-remembered observation isn't evidence—it's a liability.

Why Writing as You Go Matters:

- **Accuracy is highest in the moment.** Every minute you wait, you lose precision.
- **Your future self will thank you.** It's easier to polish a draft than reconstruct one from memory.
- **Your report becomes a living document.** It grows with the case instead of being a last-minute scramble.
- **It locks in timelines.** Clean, contemporaneous notes beat after-the-fact guesswork every time.

I've never regretted writing something down right away. I have regretted trying to remember it later.

Takeaway: Report writing isn't a single event—it's a running process. Document in real time, and your reports will always be sharper, more accurate, and harder to tear apart.

February 7: Describe What You See

"Accuracy is the twin brother of honesty; inaccuracy, of dishonesty." —Nathaniel Hawthorne

A good physical description can make or break surveillance, suspect identification, and witness interviews. Reports aren't just about what happened—they are about *who* was involved. A crisp, detailed description helps your team locate, track, and identify individuals in the real world. A vague description, on the other hand, can send people chasing shadows. When writing a description, think like the field personnel who will rely on it. This isn't about poetic language—it's about usable data. You want the kind of description that lets someone step into the scene hours or days later and still recognize the individual immediately.

Key Elements of a Solid Physical Description:

- **Height:** Useful for surveillance teams in crowded environments. Narrow it down to a two-inch range if possible. Don't be surprised if sources or clients only give estimates—just note it clearly.
- **Weight:** Aim for a 10-pound range. Treat it as an approximation, not a hard fact.
- **Race:** An important piece of information for differentiation during initial identification or online research.
- **Hair:** Record length, color, and style. Hairstyles change frequently, so always verify the current status.
- **Eye color:** Straightforward but helpful. You might even encounter heterochromia iridium (different colors in each eye)—rare but useful.
- **Complexion:** Use simple terms like "light," "medium," or "dark." The medical Fitzpatrick Scale exists, but your report doesn't need to sound like a dermatology text.
- **Facial hair:** Length, color, and style matter—and they change often. Don't rely on old photos.
- **Build:** Think in terms of "small," "medium," or "large." If a witness says "athletic build" or "heavyset," translate that into something your team can use.
- **Distinguishing features:** Tattoos, scars, birthmarks, piercings, prosthetics, or anything else unique. People often *advertise* their individuality.

I have seen plenty of cases where a single tattoo, a hairstyle update, or a missing detail like eye color made the difference between a team picking up a subject or losing them entirely. A solid description is a tactical asset.

Takeaway: Don't write vague descriptions. Write usable ones. Height, build, hair, features—these aren't filler details. Describe what you see clearly, consistently, and with purpose.

February 8: Write for the Worst Day in Court

"By failing to prepare, you are preparing to fail." —Benjamin Franklin

Every investigator has a "worst day in court." It's the day opposing counsel dissects your report word by word, line by line, looking for holes to exploit. It's the day your credibility isn't assumed—it's tested. And when that day comes, sloppy writing, vague language, or fuzzy timelines will hurt you more than any aggressive cross-examination ever could. It's not personal—it's a defense attorney's strategy. And they're good at it.

A report isn't just a record of what you did. It's your sworn testimony on paper. It can protect you—or it can expose you. The time to prepare for that courtroom grilling isn't the night before testimony. It's the day you write the report. Write like the defense is already reading.

Why This Mindset Matters:

- Court is unforgiving—what's unclear will be challenged.
- A clean report reduces your stress when testifying. You won't be scrambling to remember or explain unclear writing.
- Even if your case never goes to trial, solid writing stands up to internal review, client scrutiny, or administrative hearings.

For the Lynx private investigation academy, I bring in one of my instructors—a prosecutor in his day job—for a courtroom testimony practical exercise. He usually only spends five minutes reviewing the students' reports before going on the offensive. In those five minutes, he gives them a run for their money. Imagine what he could do with several weeks or months to prepare. Make no mistake; that is what you are up against.

Takeaway: Don't write reports for your best day. Write for your worst day in court.

February 9: Timelines Are Your Friend

"Order and simplification are the first steps toward mastery." —Thomas Mann

A messy timeline can tank a strong case. It doesn't matter how good your evidence is—if the sequence of events isn't clear, you'll lose credibility fast. A clean, structured timeline is one of the most powerful tools in an investigator's reporting toolkit. It helps you tell the story logically, makes it easier for others to follow, and cuts off a defense attorney's ability to create confusion.

Timelines don't just help in court—they help *you*. When you come back to a case weeks later, you will be able to pick up right where you left off without re-reading an entire narrative. They are also gold for supervisors, attorneys, or clients who need to understand the sequence quickly. That's why most agencies require a Report of Investigation or a Summary of Investigation that lays out every step you took in the case. If you're not doing this, start.

A good timeline should read like a GPS track of your case: clear, chronological, and easy to follow—even months or years later.

Practical Timeline Tips:

- **Go chronological.** Start with the first event and build forward. Resist the urge to jump around.
- **Timestamp everything.** Dates and times (even approximate) give your reader a map, not a maze.
- **Log actions as they happen.** Don't reconstruct after the fact—memory is unreliable.
- **Use consistent formatting.** Example: 2025-02-09 0930—Subject observed exiting vehicle at gas station. Follow your company or agency policy—or set the standard if one doesn't exist.
- **Separate facts from analysis.** The timeline is for what happened, not your theory about why it happened.
- **Align evidence with events.** Link photos, surveillance video, or documents directly to their corresponding time stamps (when policy allows).

I once worked on a complex passport fraud case where we were trying to identify gaps in movement and establish a pattern of life. Once we mapped it on the timeline, we knew exactly when to serve the arrest and search warrants. As a bonus, we pulled a bunch of drugs and guns off the street.

Takeaway: Timelines are the skeleton key of good reporting. A clear sequence of events brings your case to life, keeps your narrative defensible, and saves you (and everyone else) hours of confusion down the line.

February 10: Reports Aren't Play Time

"Don't say anything in writing that you wouldn't want read in court." —Unknown

This isn't a long lesson, but it's an important one: **watch what you put in writing.** If you're documenting something, keep it professional. If your notes, e-mails, or texts become evidence, every word will be scrutinized.

You don't want to be the investigator who described a suspect as "a clown" or sprinkled little jokes through their notes. You definitely don't want your handwriting with an "i" dotted by a heart or smiley faces projected on a courtroom screen. And yes—if you write "I wish I could eat an egg salad sandwich" in the middle of a surveillance note, it might just come back to haunt you.

This goes beyond case notes. E-mails, text messages, chat threads—anything written can be discovered, subpoenaed, or shared. Write like a jury, a judge, your mother, or opposing counsel may one day read it out loud. One day, they just might.

Takeaway: Your report isn't your creative outlet. It's a legal, operational, and professional document. Keep it clean. Keep it clear. Let the facts speak for themselves.

February 11: Proof It Early and Often

"Details matter. It's worth waiting to get it right." —Steve Jobs

The fastest way to make a solid investigation look sloppy is to submit a report full of spelling errors, poor grammar, and inconsistent formatting. It doesn't matter how good your case is—if your writing looks careless, people will assume the investigation was too. I have seen outstanding work lose credibility in seconds because the report looked unprofessional.

Proofreading isn't glamorous, but it's part of the job. Judges, juries, prosecutors, clients, opposing counsel—they all notice the details. A well-written report says you care about your work. A sloppy one says the opposite.

Practical Proofreading Habits:

- **Read it out loud.** You will catch awkward phrasing and missing words that your eyes skipped over.
- **Double-check names, dates, and times.** The big errors are usually the simplest ones.
- Run spell check—but don't rely on it. Technology won't catch everything.
- **Look at formatting.** Headers, spacing, numbering, and labels should be clean and consistent.
- **Take a short break before reviewing.** Fresh eyes find errors the tired ones miss.
- Have someone else review it when possible. A second set of eyes is the minimum. In the public sector, a typical path is: **you → you (fresh eyes) → peer → supervisor → government attorney.**

I have read and processed thousands of Intelligence Information Reports (IIRs), diplomatic cables, investigative reports, and other products over the last 20+ years. Once you start doing that, little errors—an extra space or a misspelling—jump out. And still, I have my own work proofread.

Takeaway: Proofreading isn't busy work. It's professional insurance. A clean, polished report makes your work stronger—and harder to pick apart.

February 12: Places and Things (Part One)

"Details make perfection, and perfection is not a detail." —Leonardo da Vinci

Reports aren't only about people; they are about where things happened and what was involved. Your standard is a description so clear that someone who wasn't there can recognize the vehicle or locate the place without you. Think usable data, not poetry.

Vehicles (Work and Personal): Capture the Identifiers Your Surveillance Team and Partners Need:

- **Year/Make/Model/Trim/Body style:** Sedan, coupe, SUV, pickup, van, motorcycle, boat
- **Color:** Plain language; note two-tone or vinyl wrap
- **Plate:** Number, state, type if relevant; temp tag; trailer plate if any
- **Distinguishers:** Visible damage, bumper stickers, dealer frames, tint, roof rack, sunroof, aftermarket wheels, running boards, hitch, unusual lights/exhaust; interior items in plain view (car seat, sun shade, beads)
- **Where allowed/authorized:** VIN/HIN, registration state
- **Status:** Primary daily driver vs. secondary/recreational; employer-owned vs. personal
- **Photos:** Wide/medium/tight; 360° if possible; time-stamped; note direction (e.g., "front quarter, facing N")

If a private-sector client can't supply plate info, obtain it lawfully through approved databases. Stock photos are fine for reference only—never as evidence.

Places (Exterior): Give the reader a Map They Can Actually Use:

- **Address:** Include unit, nearest cross street(s), optional GPS
- **Type & construction:** Single-family, duplex, apartment, office, warehouse; brick/stucco/metal; number of stories
- **Entrances/exits & access control:** Front, rear, garage, gated, keycard, buzzer
- **Cameras & lighting:** Count, placement, apparent coverage, obvious blind spots
- **Parking & approaches:** Street/lot, typical occupancy, choke points, sight lines
- **Adjacencies/landmarks:** Corner lot; next to pharmacy; behind school
- **Signage/business hours:** If relevant (useful for surveillance planning)

Takeaway: Don't write vague descriptions. Write actionable ones.

February 13: Places and Things (Part Two)

"You might be a redneck if... you've been on TV more than once describing the sound of a tornado." —Jeff Foxworthy (paraphrased)

Continuing from yesterday, get even more specific so your write-ups work in the field and hold up later.

Places (Interior): Document Layout to Speed Follow-On Work and Withstand Scrutiny

- **Sketch:** Not to scale, rooms, doors, windows; mark **N** arrow; label key areas ("office," "safe," "server rack")
- **Security:** Alarms, interior cameras, safes, locks
- **Lines of sight/choke points:** Mirrors, long hallways, stairwells
- **Environmental notes:** Noise, lighting, strong odors—gas/solvent
- **Things/Equipment:** If an object matters, identify it as if it were exhibit 1
- **Make/model/serial:** Phones: IMEI/MEID; computers: serial/MAC; firearms: make/model/serial/caliber)
- **Color/condition:** Case, decals, damage
- **Photo log:** Linking images to the narrative; preserve metadata where policy allows
- **Chain of custody:** Entries if seized/handled
- **Specific beats vague:** "2017 Toyota Camry SE, gray, MD 9AB-1234" > "gray Toyota"
- **Use a standard order:** Year–Make–Model–Color–Plate–Distinguishers
- **Wide → medium → tight:** Photos; number and caption each image (e.g., "Img 07—rear plate, MD 9AB-1234, 02/12/2025 0914L")
- **Keep opinions out:** "Well-kept" → "no visible body damage; new tires"

Takeaway: The more precise your descriptions, the more operational value you give the reader.

February 14: Quote Precisely

"The difference between the almost right word and the right word is really a large matter—'tis the difference between the lightning bug and the lightning." —Mark Twain

In investigations, words matter. A single phrase, quoted exactly, can withstand cross-examination. A fuzzy paraphrase can fall apart. Your job is to capture speech accurately, fairly, and usefully. That means knowing when to quote verbatim and when to paraphrase—and labeling each clearly.

When to Quote Verbatim:

- **Admissions/intent:** "Fine, I took it." "I'll deal with him tomorrow."
- **Key facts/figures:** Times, dates, amounts, addresses.
- **Unique phrasing/slang:** The exact words carry meaning (threats, coded terms).
- Statements likely to be challenged: Preserve the exact language.
- **Digital messages:** Quote texts, emails, DMs as written (typos/emojis included).

When to Paraphrase:

- **Rambling or repetitive:** Answers that obscure the point.
- **Non-critical details:** Where precision adds noise, not clarity.
- **Sensitive/redacted:** Portions where policy requires summarizing.

Common Pitfalls to Avoid:

- Mixing quotes and paraphrasing without labeling the change.
- "Polishing" quotes to sound better.
- Ellipses that change meaning; if you elide, ensure the sense is intact.
- Passive attribution ("It was stated…")—own it: "Witness stated…"

Takeaway: Quote exactly when precision matters; paraphrase clearly when it improves readability—then label which one you used.

February 15: Murder Boards Make You Sharper

"Criticism may not be agreeable, but it is necessary. It fulfills the same function as pain in the human body." —Winston Churchill

A good report or presentation isn't just written—it's tested. One of the best ways to tighten your work before it ever reaches a courtroom, a client, or a command briefing is to run it through a murder board. This concept, borrowed from military and government planning circles, brings a team of sharp, skeptical peers together to tear your work apart so it can't be torn apart later.

I was once studying abroad at the University of Oxford, and one of my tutors was a retired British General Officer. He had been detailed to the Pentagon at the start of the Iraq War in 2003. He fondly remembered presenting invasion plans to a murder board of U.S. military captains who dubbed themselves "the Jedi Knights" because they loved cutting through senior officers' battle plans and leaving red marks all over them. Brutal? Yes. Effective? Absolutely.

That story stuck with me because I have seen the same principle play out in investigations. If your reporting, timeline, or exhibits can survive a tough internal review, they can survive anything. But if your first real test is in front of a prosecutor, defense attorney, client, or the media, you're already behind.

How to Run a Murder Board for Investigations:

- **Assemble the skeptics.** Pick peers who aren't afraid to ask hard questions.
- **Present like it's real.** Walk through your report, exhibits, and findings as if you were on the stand or briefing leadership.
- **Invite attack.** Tell the board to find weak points, missing links, and sloppy language.
- **Fix what breaks.** Patch gaps in logic, tighten wording, clean exhibits, and clarify timelines.
- **Repeat if needed.** Big cases benefit from multiple rounds.

I have sat on plenty of murder boards, and they have saved more cases than I can count. Weak points exposed in a room full of colleagues are exactly what a defense attorney, senior official, or client will pick up on. Murder boards create controlled stress—the kind that builds resilience, clarity, and confidence.

Takeaway: If your agency, department, or company doesn't have murder boards, start them. It's one of the most effective tools for bulletproofing your work before anyone else gets a chance.

February 16: Scope Before You Sprint

"A goal without a plan is just a wish." —Antoine de Saint-Exupéry

Scope is the shared map for the investigation. It is the objective, constraints (legal, ethical, budget, etc.), stakeholders and roles, deliverables, and exit criteria. When the scope is clear, teams move fast in the same direction. When it isn't, hours burn, risks rise, and "just one more thing..." turns into scope creep that buries progress. Most cases don't fail in the field—they fail at intake.

The 10-Point Scope Checklist (Public & Private)

1. **Objective & success criteria:** One line: "Prove/disprove __ by __." Define the deliverable (e.g., affidavit-ready report with exhibits; client memo + recommendations).
2. **Authority & constraints**: Predicate, consent/warrant posture, licensing/jurisdiction limits, privacy policy, use-of-force/safety rules, discovery/FOIA posture.
3. **Stakeholders & roles:** Investigator-in-charge, case manager, client/prosecutor POC, approvals, escalation path. (Private: SOW signatory. Public: supervisor/ASA/AUSA.)
4. **Milestones & timeline:** Backward-plan from court dates or client deadlines. List week-1/week-2 actions and decision points.
5. **Resources & budget/time:** People, gear, travel, databases. Set a ceiling (hours/dollars) and a trigger for re-scoping.
6. **Risk register (top five):** Legal, safety, OPSEC, reputational, and schedule. List one mitigation for each risk.
7. **File architecture & naming:** Standard folders (Admin, Logs, Evidence, Photos/Video, Legal, Reports), a locked naming convention, and a live case timeline doc.
8. **Comms cadence:** Who gets updates, how often, and in what format. Adopt a no-surprises rule.
9. **Deconfliction:** Parallel cases, task forces, fusion centers, prosecutors— notify/coordinate appropriately; protect sources/methods.
10. **Exit criteria:** What must be true to close, pause, or escalate. Write it down.

The beauty of private investigation is that you can always turn down or refer out. Use it to your advantage.

Takeaway: If you open sloppy, you manage sloppy. Define the objective, constraints, owners, deliverables, and exit criteria before you sprint.

February 17: Triage & Prioritization

"The main thing is to keep the main thing the main thing." —Stephen R. Covey

Investigations rarely stall because no one is working; they stall because people are working on the wrong thing first. Triage is the discipline of deciding *what must happen now*, *what happens next*, and *what hasn't happened yet*. Done well, it protects perishables, prevents rework, and keeps the whole team pointed at the outcome.

Field Triage: What Comes First

1. **Safety & legality:** Life safety, scene integrity, and lawful authority (predicate, consent/warrant) beat everything.
2. **Perishables clock:** Grab what will disappear: CCTV that overwrites (often 24–72 hours, sometimes 7–30 days, archival up to 90 days?), ephemeral messages, ride-share logs, hotel folios, tow lots, flight manifests. Send holds/preservation letters *today*.
3. **High-signal interviews:** Uncontaminated witnesses fade fast; schedule while memory is fresh.
4. **Dependencies:** Do the task that unlocks five others (e.g., authority approval, preservation letters, device imaging window, master timeline start).
5. **Long lead items:** Forensics lab queues, travel approvals, subpoenas—start the clock early.
6. **Stakeholder beats:** Prosecutor/client update cadence and statutory deadlines (discovery, statute of limitations).
7. **Batch the low-signal work:** Vouchers, filing, noncritical admin → batch windows.

Public vs. Private Notes

- **Public sector:** Anchor triage to legal deadlines, discovery obligations, and coordination with prosecutors/partner agencies.
- **Private sector:** Guard budget/time caps, stop scope creep, and prioritize items that drive client decisions.

Takeaway: If everything is a priority, nothing is. Triage sets the order of operations.

February 18: Backward Planning

"What gets measured gets managed." —*Peter F. Drucker*

Great case management starts at the end and works backward. Court dates, statute of limitation (SOL) deadlines, client deliverables, lab queues, and travel windows. All of those are the anchors. When you backward-plan from fixed dates and set milestones, you create a critical path that keeps the whole team honest about time, dependencies, and risk.

You can backward plan with anything. For example, you have a domestic flight leaving Atlanta Airport at 6:30 AM. You know you have to allow 30 minutes for boarding, one hour to get through security, and 30 minutes to check in, so you should plan on arriving at the airport by 4:30 AM. You also know it takes 15. minutes for the shuttle to get from the short-term parking lot to the airport, and 15 minutes from your house to the airport. You also know it takes you one hour to get ready in the morning, so you should leave your house at 4:00 AM and get up at 3:00 AM. You should also account for Murphy's Law.

Start with the End in Mind:

- **Final deliverable:** What exactly will exist on the finish line? (Affidavit-ready report + exhibits? Client memo + recommendations?)
- **Hard dates:** Court/discovery/SOL on the public side; client board meeting/contract dates on the private side.
- **Success criteria:** "Prove/disprove ___ by ___" so everyone knows what "done" looks like.

Build the Milestones:

1. **Report submissions:** Discovery packets, subpoenas, report draft to counsel/client.
2. **Evidence complete:** All returns imaged, logged, and indexed; photos/video labeled to timeline.
3. **Interviews locked:** Priority witnesses scheduled; alternates identified.
4. **Preservations sent & confirmed-** CCTV/records with overwrite clocks.
5. **Authority secured:** Predicate/consent/warrant approvals; licensing checks cleared.
6. **Kickoff & scope lock:** Owners, budget/time ceiling, risks, comms cadence.

Takeaway: Deadlines drive decisions. Backward-plan from the finish line, set milestones with owners, and account for Murphy.

February 19: Deconfliction & Coordination

"The single biggest problem in communication is the illusion that it has taken place."
—George Bernard Shaw

Nothing derails cases faster or more dangerously than blue-on-blue conflicts, duplicate efforts, and crossed wires. Deconfliction is how you prevent that: you identify who else is touching the same target, venue, or witnesses, and coordinate so everyone stays safe, legal, and effective.

Why It Matters:

- **Safety:** Avoid operational collisions and compromised surveillance/ warrant service.
- **Integrity:** Prevent witness contamination, evidence duplication, or loss.
- **Credibility:** Partners, prosecutors, and clients expect you to control the left/right limits.

Core Deconfliction Moves:

- **Check first:** Task force channels, prosecutor's office, fusion centers, internal case index. (Private: client security/legal, corporate investigations, outside counsel.)
- **Name a coordinator:** One case lead owns external communications and logs every touchpoint.
- **Notify appropriately:** Share what's necessary (no more), document who/when/why.
- **Protect sources & methods:** Share outcomes and timings; mask sensitive collection where possible.
- **Sequence interviews:** Agree on the order to avoid taint and keep statements clean.
- **Calendar the ops window:** Lock times/locations so surveillance, interviews, and service don't collide.
- **Write it down:** Maintain a simple deconfliction log (agency/POC, date, topic, decisions, next step).

Red Flags That Demand Immediate Coordination:

- Another team shows interest in your target/location/witness.
- Defense counsel or media appears unexpectedly.
- You hear "we've got something similar" or "we're serving something there today."

Takeaway: Don't assume coordination happened—make it happen. Deconflict early, share smartly, and keep a log.

February 20: Build Your Case File Architecture

"For every minute spent in organizing, an hour is earned." —attributed to Benjamin Franklin

A messy case file wastes time, confuses partners, and falls apart under scrutiny. A clean file architecture turns your work into a system anyone can enter, understand, and defend. Think single source of truth, consistent naming, and a structure that mirrors how the case actually runs.

Standard folders (top level):

1. **Admin:** SOW/authority letters, approvals, COI/ethics checks
2. **Notes & Timeline:** daily logs, contact sheets, master chronological timeline
3. **Evidence (Physical/Digital):** intake forms, chain of custody, hashes, storage references
4. **Photos & Video:** labeled by date/location/event; captions + link to timeline entries
5. **Legal:** subpoenas/warrants/returns, correspondence. preservation letters,
6. **Reports & Briefs:** drafts/finals, BLUF updates, AARs
7. **Comms:** client/prosecutor updates, deconfliction log, stakeholder decisions

Naming Conventions (Lock Them In):

Case#_YYYYMMDD_Context_Detail_v1.0.ext

Examples:

- 23-0417_2025-02-20_Timeline_Master_v3.1.docx
- 23-0417_2025-02-09_Photo_Img07_RearPlate_MD9AB1234.jpg
- 23-0417_2025-02-14_Subpoena_Return_TelcoA.pdf

Timeline + Index = Navigation:

- Maintain a master case timeline (date/time → action/observation → source/exhibit link → owner).
- Add a simple case index on page 1: folder map, contact list, milestones, SOL/critical dates.

Also, don't forget to use version numbers and archive finals as read-only.

Takeaway: File chaos is case chaos. Build a predictable structure, name things consistently, and keep a living timeline.

February 21: Take Notes That Hold Up

"Amateurs rely on memory. Professionals rely on notes." —Field Training Officer Maxim

Notes are the connective tissue of any good investigation. They bridge the moment something happens to the day it is briefed, reported, or challenged in court. They will be read—or at least relied upon—by fellow investigators, attorneys, judges, juries, clients, and sometimes even the press. Your notes are not personal; they are evidence. More importantly, they aid memory. My friend once worked a five-year undercover narcotics assignment for a major metropolitan police department. Can you imagine trying to recall what happened in detail five years later? Notes made that possible. The primary functions of notes are simple:

1. Aid your memory when preparing formal reports.
2. Serve as a contemporaneous record of contacts and activities before they are fully documented.
3. Stand up as part of the case file in court or administrative review.

And remember, original notes must be maintained. They are not scratch paper—they are part of the official record.

Practical Note-Taking Principles

- **Redundancy matters.** Always carry two pens and a clean, bound legal pad or notebook. Never rely on memory—or a single pen.
- **Listen first, write second.** Be present during interviews and surveillance. Observe, process, then record. Accuracy beats speed.
- **Think proactively.** Don't just write what's said—capture what matters. Ask the right questions.
- **Develop shorthand.** Create a personal but consistent system for abbreviations (e.g., W-1, Veh-A, Subj).
- **Review your notes.** Go over them soon after the activity while your memory is fresh. Fill gaps, clarify handwriting, and log follow-ups.
- **Time-stamp and label.** Every entry needs date/time, location, and identifiers. Use local time and note the time zone.
- **Transcribe promptly.** Convert rough notes to your official case log within 24 hours. Mark clearly: "Transcribed from field notes on [date/time] by [name]."
- **Protect originals.** Store securely in the case file. Never rewrite, tear out, or destroy pages

Takeaway: Notes outlive memory and defend your integrity. Your notebook is a witness—treat it like one.

February 22: Use Every Tool in the Toolbox

"I have not failed. I've just found 10,000 ways that won't work." —Thomas Edison

When you manage a case, you're not just tracking leads—you're orchestrating an entire system of investigative tools and people. Each method you deploy, whether surveillance, financial tracing, or digital forensics, is a different instrument in the same orchestra. Knowing which one to use and when separates a good investigator from a great one.

Sometimes, when I'm coaching private investigators, they come to me saying they have hit a wall: *"Ed, I have done everything I can think of."* We sit down, walk through the case, and I start throwing ideas on the table—interviews, a certain record, a trash pull, a quick site survey, a targeted social-media lookup. Within minutes, they realize there is always another rock to overturn. The client is paying you to look under *every* one of them. In the public sector, the taxpayer is paying you to do the same. Experience helps, but the real driver is mindset—refusing to stop thinking creatively just because the easy leads are gone.

Just a Small Sample of Investigative Techniques at Your Disposal:

- **Informants:** Properly managed human sources reveal what paper can't.
- **Trash pulls:** Lawful, low-tech, surprisingly revealing.
- **Mail covers:** Administrative tools that expose communication patterns.
- **Financial review:** Follow the money; it rarely lies.
- **Wiretaps:** powerful, high-oversight, and precise.
- **Psychological profiles:** Behavioral insights shape interviews and priorities.
- **Undercover operations:** High-risk, high-reward; oversight is everything.
- **Asset forfeiture:** A tactical way to dismantle criminal infrastructure.
- **Computer forensics** – digital evidence is now the rule, not the exception.
- **Grand-jury subpoenas:** Compel what cooperation can't.
- **Polygraphs:** Assessment tools, never an absolute truth.
- **Storefront operations:** Controlled settings for controlled collection.

A seasoned case manager doesn't use every tool on every case—they know which lever to pull, when, and why. The value lies in seeing the full toolbox and choosing wisely.

Takeaway: Whether you work for a client or the country, someone is trusting you to turn over every stone. Use every lawful tool available—and when one fails, find the next that won't.

February 23: Track the Task

"The essence of strategy is choosing what not to do." —Michael E. Porter

A good investigation moves like a machine—deliberate, coordinated, and constantly monitored. A bad one drifts. The difference almost always comes down to task tracking and case progress. Whether you're a solo private investigator managing multiple clients or a public-sector agent handling a complex case file, disciplined case management keeps momentum alive and prevents important details from falling through the cracks. Every case, no matter the scale, follows a general rhythm:

1. **Case Initiation:** Every investigation starts with intake—a complaint, a lead, a tip, or a directive. Log it immediately, note who originated it, and confirm authority and jurisdiction. This is your case foundation.
2. **Assessment of the Allegation/Information:** Vet the claim before you sprint. What's credible? What's actionable? What's outside your authority? This prevents wasted effort and early missteps.
3. **Development of the Investigative Plan:** Build your road map: objectives, tasks, timelines, and responsible parties. Define your resources and scope.
4. **Conduct the Investigation with your Techniques:** Execute with precision and discipline. Use every lawful tool—from interviews to digital forensics—and document as you go. Always operate within policy and safety parameters.
5. **Prepare Your Report of Investigation and Supporting Reports:** Write it as if it's going to court. Clear, chronological, and factual. Reports tell your story when you're not in the room.
6. **Process Additional Evidence:** As new material surfaces, preserve the chain of custody, verify authenticity, and update your case. Each piece of evidence either confirms, refutes, or redirects your hypothesis.
7. **Testify in Court if Needed:** Courtroom preparation starts the day the case opens. Every note and report should withstand cross-examination.
8. **Close the Case:** Don't just mark it complete. Conduct a postmortem. Were objectives met? Lessons learned? Follow-up referrals needed?

Effective task tracking keeps investigators honest with themselves and their teams. It maintains momentum, clarifies responsibilities, and offers transparency when supervisors, clients, or prosecutors ask, "Where are we with this?"

Takeaway: Case management isn't paperwork—it's operational control. Know your process, track your progress, and keep every case moving forward until it's done.

February 24: Own the File

"Responsibility equals accountability equals ownership. And a sense of ownership is the most powerful weapon a team or organization can have." —Pat Summitt

In every investigation, someone must own the file. Not share it. Not assume someone else is tracking it. Own it.

Cases rarely fall apart because of one catastrophic mistake. They unravel because of small gaps: a follow-up not made, an exhibit not uploaded, a deadline not tracked, a clarification not requested. When responsibility is diffused, those gaps multiply. When ownership is clear, they close.

Whether you are a solo private investigator juggling multiple clients or part of a federal task force with layers of supervision, one principle remains constant: one investigator must have operational control of the case. Supervisors oversee. Prosecutors advise. Analysts assist. But someone drives.

Many people shirk ownership and responsibility to the best of their ability. It doesn't have to be that way. Ownership allows you to have pride in your work and for everyone to benefit. Ownership changes posture. When you own a file:

- You know the status of every lead.
- You track every deadline without being reminded.
- You anticipate questions before supervisors or clients ask them.
- You ensure documentation is current, not "almost done."
- You close loops instead of assuming someone else will.

In the private sector, ownership protects your reputation and your client's investment. In the public sector, it protects taxpayer resources and prosecutorial confidence. Either way, it protects you.

Owning the file does not mean doing everything yourself. It means knowing what has been done, what remains, and who is responsible for each task. It means reviewing the case with fresh eyes periodically and asking: *If this went to court tomorrow, am I ready?*

Takeaway: Shared work still requires singular ownership. If your name is on the case, treat it like it's yours alone, even if it is not.

February 25: Eliminate Ambiguity

"There is no greater impediment to the advancement of knowledge than the ambiguity of words" —Thomas Reid

In investigations, clarity isn't optional—it's survival. An ambiguous report entry can derail an entire case, confuse a supervisor or prosecutor, or worse, create reasonable doubt in court. Every sentence you write should communicate one thing only: what actually happened.

When editing or reviewing reports, remember this rule: **any change that goes beyond basic spelling, grammar, or clarity corrections must be approved by the authoring investigator.** The person who wrote the report owns the facts. Anything unclear or open to interpretation should always be sent back to the author for clarification—never assumed, "fixed," or guessed at. Here is an example of how ambiguity can quietly wreck your report:

When asked if Daniel REED discussed the break-in with his neighbor, SMITH stated that it was unusual how REED mentioned the missing tools the day before.

That one sentence could mean several things: Did REED talk about the break-in the day before it happened? Did he talk about the tools missing the day before the interview? Or did SMITH simply find it odd that REED knew about the missing items early? The ambiguity makes it impossible to know what really happened— and invites misinterpretation by defense, management, or the media. When writing or reviewing, use this mental checklist to stay precise:

- **Confirm meaning with the author:** Never assume you "get it." Ask.
- **Avoid vague pronouns:** Replace "he," "she," or "they" with names when multiple people are involved.
- **Untangle timelines:** If events are connected, state the sequence explicitly ("REED mentioned the missing tools on June 4, one day before the burglary was discovered").
- **Keep sentences short:** Long, compound sentences breed confusion.
- **Read it out loud:** If you have to stop and think about what it means, so will the reader.

Cases can be slowed down—often between supervisors and field investigators— leading to reports being sent back, witnesses re-interviewed, and attorneys frustrated. It's an easy problem to prevent if you slow down and write with precision.

Takeaway: Write so there's only one possible interpretation—the truth. Clarity protects your credibility, your team, and your case.

February 26: The Language of Reports (Part 1)

"Details create the big picture." —Sanford I. Weill

In investigations, precision in language isn't about grammar snobbery—it's about credibility. A misplaced initial, a wrong date, or an inconsistent title can create confusion that ripples all the way into court. Your report is often read by people who don't know the context, so we are going to discuss some cheat codes over the next couple of lessons on terminology you most likely will encounter in your investigative report writing. If your agency has its own go-by, please use it; this is a way, not *the* way. If you have ever reviewed an old case file and wondered, "Wait, is this the same Johnson or another one?" you already know how small inconsistencies can cause big problems.

Names and Identifiers

- Use full legal names the first time, then last names only.
- When a name is unknown, use FNU (First Name Unknown), MNU (Middle Name Unknown), or LNU (Last Name Unknown).
- Record aliases clearly: "John DOE, aka 'Slim.'"
- Keep job titles and ranks consistent: don't bounce between "Det. Johnson" and "Lt. Johnson." Pick the correct title and stick with it.
- Titles and honorifics (Mr., Ms., Dr.) are rarely needed—use them only for clarity or respect in private-sector reporting.

Abbreviations and Acronyms

- Spell out the full phrase on first mention, followed by the abbreviation in parentheses—"Bureau of Alcohol, Tobacco, Firearms and Explosives (ATF)" —then use the acronym consistently.
- Avoid creating new acronyms that others won't understand.

Numbers, Currency, and Time

- Spell out numbers one through nine; use numerals for 10 and above (unless policy differs).
- Use a consistent currency format—"$5,000.00," not "5K."
- Always record times in the 24-hour clock with "hours" noted: "0930 hours."
- Indicate time zone when relevant: "0930 hours (EST)."
- All times are approximate; say so: "approximately 0930 hours."

Takeaway: Write names and numbers as if someone who's never met you will rely on them—because they will.

February 27: The Language of Reports (Part 2)

"Accuracy is the foundation of everything else." —*Niels Bohr*

Yesterday, we covered names and numbers; today, we turn to how you describe places and measures. These details may seem small, but they're what let others—from supervisors to prosecutors, to your own future self—visualize what happened and where. A missing unit number, a vague direction, or a wrong measurement can make your reader question your accuracy or credibility.

Addresses and Geography

- Record the full address, including apartment, suite, or unit number.
- Use standard abbreviations for street types (St., Rd., Ave., Blvd.) and compass directions (N, S, E, W).
- If the address is approximate, say so—"vicinity of 1200 Block, Main St."
- Include cross streets, landmarks, or GPS coordinates when helpful.

Measurements and Quantities

- Use U.S. customary units unless your agency or client specifies metric.
- Be consistent—don't switch between systems in the same report.
- Approximate when necessary, but label it clearly ("approximately 15 feet").
- Avoid imprecise terms like "a few," "several," or "some." Use specific estimates or counts whenever possible.
- For weights and dimensions, be uniform: "approximately 6 feet tall," "3 inches in diameter," "weighing 15 pounds."

Directions and Orientation

- Use cardinal directions (north, south, east, west) or relational descriptions ("the vehicle was parked facing north," "the suspect entered from the rear door on the west side").
- Avoid relative phrases like "to the left" or "in front of" unless they're anchored to a fixed point.
- Identify rooms, floors, and features clearly: "second-floor office, northeast corner," "garage attached to the south side."
- Note environmental context: lighting, terrain, or visibility. These details are critical for surveillance and for preparing search warrants.

Have you ever hit the wrong house on a search warrant? My buddy has. He was serving on a local SWAT team before going federal. The FBI insisted that the target location was at a specific house, but it was actually the one next door. Try explaining that on the big boss's luxury carpet.

Takeaway: Describe places and measurements like you're writing for someone who's never been there—because one day, you will be gone, but your report won't be.

February 28: The Language of Reports (Part 3)

"Clarity is the most important style element; it's the writer's equivalent of courage."
—William Zinsser

The last piece of the three-part mini-report writing series isn't just *what* you say—it's *how* you say it. Structure and style determine whether your reader understands your work or gets lost in it. Good reports sound calm, factual, and deliberate. They avoid emotion, opinion, and filler words. Remember: when your report is read in court, your tone will speak louder than your voice.

Tone and Professionalism

- Write like a neutral observer, not a participant. Avoid slang, sarcasm, or emotional phrasing.
- Never speculate. If something is unclear, state it plainly: "It could not be determined…" or "The witness was uncertain…"
- Avoid intensifiers like "very," "extremely," or "clearly." Let the facts prove the point.
- Keep sentences simple and declarative. Long, meandering sentences create confusion.

Punctuation and Mechanics

- Commas clarify meaning—use them to separate thoughts, not decorate the sentence.
- Avoid overusing colons and semicolons; periods are your friend.
- No contractions ("don't," "isn't") in formal reports—write the words out.
- Maintain single spacing after periods for consistency and readability.

Clarity and Flow

- Use paragraph breaks to signal new actions, locations, or subjects.
- Start each paragraph with a time, date, or action cue.
- Keep transitions clean: "Following the interview…" or "Later that same day…"
- Maintain consistent tense—past tense for completed actions, present tense only for ongoing conditions.

The U.S. military is the master of short, concise writing geared towards people of all educational levels. The U.S. State Department prides itself on flowery writing, which still drives the point home (enveloped in a 10-person+ clearance process for cables). No matter your organization, know that report writing is a fundamental skill in any investigation that must be mastered.

Takeaway: Style reflects your organization's writing standards. Regardless of who employs you, write with structure, precision, and restraint.

February 29: Audit Your Reports

"Quality means doing it right when no one is looking." —Henry Ford

Every few years, you should take time to audit your own work—and leap years make a perfect reminder. In finance, medicine, and law, audits are built-in processes to verify accuracy, compliance, and accountability. Investigations deserve the same rigor. An audit, whether conducted by you or a supervisor, is a structured review of your case documentation, evidence handling, and process flow. The goal is to confirm that every action is supported, every piece of evidence is accounted for, and every report could stand alone years later without you to explain it.

Why Auditing Matters:

- **Defensibility:** If a case resurfaces years later, your audit trail should prove integrity from start to finish.
- **Consistency:** Ensures every investigator follows the same standards for documentation, naming, and structure.
- **Continuity:** A well-audited case lets another investigator pick it up seamlessly if you transfer or retire.
- **Accountability:** Protects you and your agency or firm from legal exposure and professional embarrassment.

How to Audit Your Own Work:

1. **Check Completeness:** Is every document, photo, and exhibit where it should be? Are all investigative steps recorded?
2. **Verify Cross-References:** Do your reports align with logs, timelines, and evidence records?
3. **Review for Clarity:** Could a third party read your report and understand the case without additional context?
4. **Evaluate File Structure:** Are folders logically organized (Admin, Logs, Evidence, Legal, Reports, etc.) and consistently labeled?
5. **Spot Ambiguity or Gaps:** Any unclear wording, missing dates, or unanswered leads? Address them now, not later.

I have participated in my share of internal audits—government and private—and one truth remains: the strongest investigators welcome them. They don't fear scrutiny because they have built their work to withstand it. The weak ones dread the process because they know what it will reveal.

Takeaway: Take advantage of the extra day this leap year. Open a few old case files, audit them line by line, and make sure your work is as strong as your reputation.

March: People Tools: The Interview and The Interrogation

"The most important thing in communication is hearing what isn't said." —Peter Drucker

Technology evolves. Laws change. Techniques come and go. But one skill remains timeless—the ability to talk to people and uncover the truth. Interviewing is where information turns into intelligence and facts become evidence. It's the investigator's most powerful tool, and it's as much an art as it is a science.

Interviewing is not interrogation, though both share structure and discipline. An interview is a conversation with purpose—a chance to gather information, test credibility, and build rapport. Whether you're a private investigator speaking with a client's employee, a federal agent interviewing a suspect, or a corporate investigator conducting an internal review, success depends on how you communicate.

The best investigators don't just ask questions—they *listen between the words.* They know when to stay silent, when to challenge gently, and when to let the subject fill the space. They read posture, tone, and hesitation as carefully as they read statements. And they understand that every interview is two-way intelligence collection—you're learning about the person, but they are also learning about you.

I have conducted interviews in embassies, safe houses, corporate boardrooms, on roadsides, in cars, fast-food restaurants, and hotel lobbies—just to name a few. The details change, but the fundamentals don't. Preparation, rapport, observation, and precision are what win the moment. A well-run interview can break open a case; a sloppy one can close doors forever.

This month's entries focus on the skills that define effective interviewing and interrogation—from setting the room to documenting the results. We will explore:

- How to create the right environment for honesty and control.
- Building rapport without crossing professional lines.
- Interview structures—narrative, cognitive, and accusatory.
- Working with interpreters and conducting interviews across cultures.
- Techniques for detecting deception and truth indicators.
- Recording, documenting, and preserving statements ethically.
- Interrogation strategies when the conversation turns confrontational.

No matter where you operate—public, private, or military—mastering interviewing makes everything else in investigations stronger. Let's execute.

March 1: Traits Needed

"Communication is the most important skill any leader can possess." —John C. Maxwell

The success of any interview or interrogation depends less on the questions asked and more on who's asking them. Tools and techniques matter, but the investigator's traits determine how effective those tools become. The best interviewers aren't born with special instincts—they develop habits of discipline, empathy, and emotional control that make people open up and speak truthfully.

Across government, corporate, and private investigations, I've seen a consistent pattern: the investigators who get results are the ones who listen more than they speak, project calm under pressure, and adapt their approach to the personality across the table. The core traits of an effective interviewer include:

- **Self-Concept:** Know who you are and what role you're playing. Interviews collapse when the investigator confuses their mission—you're there to gather facts, not win arguments.
- **Active Listening:** Hearing isn't listening. The best investigators absorb tone, pacing, and word choice—the gaps between the lines.
- **Confidence:** Not arrogance—composure. Confidence reassures the interviewee that they are in capable hands and encourages cooperation.
- **Empathy:** Understand and, to a degree, share the other person's feelings. It's not about sympathy; it's about reading emotional context and adjusting your tone accordingly.
- **Emotional Control:** Interviews can test patience and push boundaries. Keep your own emotions in check; your calm sets the temperature of the room.
- **Wide Knowledge:** The more you know about the topic, culture, or context, the more rapport you can build and the less you'll rely on guesswork.

All of the above apply to interrogators, but you should add precision and control. They manage the tempo, read micro-behaviors, and exploit inconsistencies without crossing ethical lines. They are patient tacticians, allowing silence and discomfort to do the work rather than intimidation. I have trained agents, analysts, and private-sector investigators alike, and I tell them the same thing: your first interview will probably feel awkward. Your hundredth will feel natural. But the best interviewers never stop improving—they debrief themselves after every session, asking what worked, what didn't, and what they will do differently next time.

Takeaway: The most effective interviewers and interrogators master themselves before managing anyone else.

March 2: Safety First

"The essence of good discipline is respect." —*President Dwight D. Eisenhower*

Before you ever sit down with a witness or a subject, consider the most important factor of all—safety. Interviews and interrogations can change tone quickly. A conversation that begins calmly can turn defensive or volatile in seconds. Whether you're in a secure facility, a corporate office, or a parking lot, anything can happen. That second investigator can help you physically in case things take a turn for the worse.

Safety also extends beyond the physical. It's about protecting your career. People will lie. They will claim you asked for sexual favors or accuse you of taking a bribe. That is why it's always prudent to have a second investigator present. It's much harder for false accusations to stick when there is another professional in the room saying otherwise.

In private investigation, if I know a service of process or a field interview is required, I tell the client we will use two investigators. If they refuse to authorize the additional cost, I tell them we can't do it. The safety of my investigators comes before profit—always. In law enforcement work, we often notify the local police department in person before conducting an interview, just in case things go sideways. Knowledge is power. Ask clients or witnesses about any history of violence. If you're law enforcement or intelligence, check the subject's wants and warrants before you go. Safety in interviews is about prevention, not reaction. Some key principles include:

- **Assess Risk Beforehand:** Know your subject's history, temperament, and stressors. Review prior reports, HR complaints, or intelligence notes.
- **Choose the Right Location:** Neutral, controlled spaces reduce tension. Avoid a subject's home or personal space unless policy or necessity dictates.
- **Set the Room:** Position yourself between the subject and the exit. Keep your path clear. Avoid cluttered desks and sharp corners.
- **Bring Backup When Needed:** Two-person teams allow one to lead and one to observe. They offer both a second set of eyes and career protection. Always deconflict who speaks.
- **Trust Your Gut:** If something feels off, it usually is. Stop, pause, or relocate. No interview is worth injury or compromise.
- **Stay Professional:** Never match emotion with emotion. Your calm sets the tone—and can de-escalate nearly any situation.

Takeaway: Preparation protects. The safest interviewer is the one who controls the space, reads the person, and knows when to walk away.

March 3: Timing Is Everything

"The right time is any time that one is still so lucky as to have." —Henry James

When it comes to interviews, timing shapes truth. Choose the wrong time, and even the most willing witness will shut down. Choose the right one, and the truth flows naturally.

I could tell you something sophisticated—like trying to match the person's circadian rhythm—but the reality is simpler: plan around the person you're interviewing and when it's best for them.

I once worked on an identity theft case where the victim didn't even realize he *was* a victim. He was a security guard on the midnight-to-8 a.m. shift. When I contacted him, he said the only time he could talk was during his break at 3:30 a.m.—and he couldn't leave the premises. So, when he returned to work that night, there I was, standing beside him at 3:30 a.m. during his break, clipboard in hand, under the flicker of fluorescent lights. Not ideal, but it worked. Timing matters more than comfort.

Strategic Timing:

- **Set the Stage Early:** Conduct interviews when attention is highest—typically mornings. Fatigue and distractions grow as the day wears on.
- **Mind Emotional Context:** After major incidents, allow brief decompression, but don't wait so long that memories fade or stories shift.
- **Avoid Stacking Interviews:** Give yourself time to process notes, reflect, and adjust your next line of questioning.
- **Respect Their Schedule:** People who feel rushed or trapped give short, unreliable answers. Flexibility earns cooperation.
- **Don't Force the Clock:** Some situations require urgency (e.g., safety concerns), but when possible, patience produces better results.

Timing isn't just about when—it's about readiness. Both you and your subject need the mental space to think, speak, and process clearly.

Takeaway: Interviews run on rhythm, not just questions. Pick the right moment, and the truth will have time to breathe.

March 4: Order of Battle

"Strategy without tactics is the slowest route to victory. Tactics without strategy is the noise before defeat." —Sun Tzu

Who you interview first determines what you know later. Interview order is your investigative battle plan. A smart sequence clarifies contradictions, builds leverage, and exposes deception faster than any trick.

Some agencies mandate sequence (e.g., subject last). If yours does not, a common cadence is victim → witnesses → subject. There *are* times to lead with the subject—you might secure a quick confession or, in the public sector, lock them into a false-statement violation (e.g., 18 U.S.C. § 1001) if your prosecutor is engaged. But you also risk tipping your hand and inviting evidence to be destroyed. Choose deliberately.

Years ago, on a passport-fraud case, a woman admitted she had hired a man to pose as her husband. Asked where they had met, she described a nearby shop. Shortly after, a colleague and I walked into the shop, and the man—standing right there—blurted, "I did it, please don't send me back to Ghana," before we had even identified ourselves. Right order, right moment—facts came fast.

Establishing Interview Sequence:

- **Victim:** The victim will provide the initial information needed. Depending on your agency, you might not interface with them.
- **Onward to cooperative witnesses:** They give context, names, and leads you didn't know existed.
- **Move to peripheral subjects:** Fill gaps and lock timelines before confronting the primary subject.
- **Finish with the primary subject:** Arrive with facts, documents, and contradictions—your leverage.
- **Revisit as needed:** Follow-up interviews after new information surfaces often reveal cracks.
- **Coordinate up and across:** Loop in counsel/supervisors early and often.

Takeaway: Plan your sequence. Each interview should set up the next one—not undo the previous one.

March 5: The Right Approach

"Tact is the art of making a point without making an enemy." —Sir Isaac Newton

Every interview has a personality. Some subjects need calm conversation; others require structured control. The key is choosing the right approach before you ever sit down. There are dozens of interview and interrogation styles—from narrative-based, rapport-driven approaches to firm, accusatory ones—but the wrong choice can end the conversation before it starts.

I once saw an investigator begin an employee interview ready for battle: hard tone, rigid posture, zero rapport. Within seconds, the administrative assistant across from him froze. The interview was over before it began. A follow-up session, handled gently by another investigator, revealed everything the first one had missed.

Gender can sometimes play a role, too. People may open up more easily to someone of the opposite sex, depending on personal history or trauma. During a deployment to Afghanistan, one of my intelligence reports led to us doing a subsequent raid and capturing a high-value Taliban target. When it came time for interrogation, a young female interrogator was chosen. She used what the military calls the *'emotional love approach'*—reminding the man of his daughter. Without a single threat or raised voice, she broke through every barrier. He cried and confessed to everything.

Choosing Your Approach:

- **Conversational:** For cooperative or neutral witnesses. Use open-ended questions, a relaxed tone, and genuine curiosity.
- **Structured:** For cautious or professional subjects. Keep a clear sequence, deliberate pacing, and consistent documentation.
- **Direct/Confrontational:** For deceptive or resistant individuals—but only when supported by solid evidence.
- **Adaptive:** The best interviewers adjust midstream. As behavior shifts, so should your style.

Takeaway: Match your approach to the person, not your ego. Adaptability is a strength, not a compromise.

March 6: Know the Violation

"If you can't explain it simply, you don't understand it well enough." —Dr. Albert Einstein

Never walk into an interview without fully understanding the violation. You can't ask the right questions about what you don't grasp. Every law, policy, or regulation has defined elements—and those elements form the structure of your questioning. Build your interview around them to confirm or deny whether someone committed a violation, witnessed one, or knows who did.

I have seen investigators stumble through interviews because they didn't understand the underlying rule or statute. They asked vague questions, missed contradictions, and failed to follow up when the subject slipped. Preparation isn't just about logistics—it's about comprehension.

If you're conducting a debriefing or intelligence interview, it might be best to have a subject-matter expert or analyst present—someone who understands the technical or contextual details beyond your lane if the collection requirement calls for it. It's hubris to think you can probe a PhD-level particle physics professor on physics when the last time you studied basic physics was in college 20 years ago. The same goes for investigations. Know your limits and bring in help when needed.

Understanding the Violation:

- **Define It Clearly:** What rule, policy, or law is at issue? Be able to summarize it in one sentence.
- **Know the Evidence:** Review files, reports, and exhibits. Walk into the room knowing the facts better than the person across from you.
- **Anticipate Explanations:** People justify their actions differently—ignorance, necessity, mistake, or denial. Prepare for each.
- **Understand the Consequences:** Know potential penalties and administrative outcomes. It builds authority and accuracy.
- **Clarify Jurisdiction:** Don't chase violations outside your organization's authority or geographic reach.

Takeaway: If you can't explain the alleged violation clearly to yourself, you can't test anyone else's explanation of it.

March 7: Setting the Scene

"Luck is what happens when preparation meets opportunity." —Seneca

Control is built, not demanded. Whether you're conducting an interview in a corporate conference room, a police station, or a hotel lobby, the physical environment communicates authority, comfort, and intent. The scene you choose tells your subject what kind of conversation this will be long before the first question.

Lighting, temperature, seating position, and distractions all influence cooperation. You can't always choose the location—but you can always shape it.

I once worked in a counterintelligence field office where the interview room could barely seat three people. It had three chairs, a small table, and barren walls except for a framed copy of the U.S. Constitution—meant to remind subjects of their oath. In some cultures, such as in Afghanistan, sitting closer to someone conveys respect and familiarity rather than intrusion. In that small room, the proximity helped build rapport while limiting distractions. With no electronics allowed in the building, the environment forced both sides to stay focused and present.

Key Points:

- **Command of Space:** Position yourself where you can observe exits and maintain a clear line of sight to the subject. Avoid barriers like desks or tables that imply confrontation unless they are used purposefully.
- **Control of Lighting:** Natural light fosters openness; dim or harsh lighting increases anxiety. Adjust the tone to your desired effect.
- **Distraction Management:** Silence phones, remove clutter, and minimize interruptions. The fewer sensory disruptions, the greater your control.
- **Neutral Territory:** Whenever possible, choose a neutral setting. Subjects are more candid in spaces that don't feel adversarial.
- **Documentation Setup:** Keep your notepad or recorder visible but non-intrusive. Transparency builds confidence and trust.

Takeaway: Before you begin questioning, ask yourself—*what story does this space tell?* If it communicates comfort and control, you have already won half the battle.

March 8: Psychological Readiness

"He who conquers himself is the mightiest warrior." —Confucius

Before you can read others, you must first read yourself. Psychological readiness is the quiet foundation of every successful interview, surveillance, or operational encounter. Investigators who enter the room flustered, distracted, or emotionally unregulated surrender control before the first question. Composure is not an act—it's a discipline.

There are days when readiness feels impossible: too many cases, too little sleep, or personal issues gnawing at your attention. This is where professionalism separates the good from the great. Before every interview or operation, take a moment to clear your mind. Review the facts, visualize the flow, and regulate your breathing. Something as simple as a brief pause before entering the room can reset your baseline and sharpen focus.

I once had to conduct debriefings shortly after learning a teammate had been killed overseas. We had been talking about stock tips earlier that same day. My thoughts were elsewhere, and had I carried that emotion into the room, it would have torpedoed the team's efforts to locate the insurgents responsible. Instead, I excused myself, took one minute alone in a hallway, and forced a mental reset. That moment of control preserved both composure and mission focus.

Key Points:

- **Check Your Baseline:** Recognize your emotional state before engaging. If you're off balance, recalibrate before proceeding.
- **Control Your Physiology:** Breathing, posture, and tone anchor composure. The body leads the mind as much as the mind leads the body.
- **Mental Visualization:** Picture the sequence of the interview or operation—anticipate, adapt, and adjust before first contact.
- **Emotional Detachment:** Empathize without absorbing emotion. You can understand a person's pain without carrying it.
- **Resilience as Routine:** Build habits—sleep, exercise, reflection—that sustain clarity under pressure. Readiness isn't a mood; it's maintenance.

Takeaway: You can't manage an interview if you can't manage yourself. Psychological readiness isn't about perfection—it's about discipline.

March 9: Breaking Barriers

"The most important space in any interview is the one between two people." —My academy instructor

Barriers are both physical and psychological. Tables, chairs, crossed arms, or even the wrong tone can divide you from the truth. The investigator's task is to identify and remove the invisible walls that keep people guarded—without losing command of the room. Every movement, word, and gesture either builds trust or fortifies resistance.

Start with positioning. Avoid sitting directly across from the subject unless confrontation is your goal. Angled seating—about 45 degrees—creates collaboration rather than conflict. Keep the table clear; it's not a barricade, it's a workspace. When possible, match your subject's posture and pace. Mirroring is subtle, but it tells their subconscious: *we're on the same side of the table, even if the tables between us.*

The same principle applies to tone. A neutral, conversational cadence invites dialogue; an interrogative rhythm shuts it down. People respond better to curiosity than accusation. If you can make someone forget, even momentarily, that they are in an interview, you have already opened the door to honesty.

A colleague and I once had to interview an inmate in prison, and it was great seeing my colleague work. As you might expect, inmates can be notoriously difficult to interview when they want to be. My colleague started the interview by sitting rigidly behind the desk, arms folded, voice clipped. The subject mirrored his defensiveness word for word. My colleague then lowered his tone and changed his posture. The subject's posture changed within seconds. The conversation turned from denial to detail, and we eventually got the lead information we needed. The information didn't come because of a better question—it came because the barrier came down.

Takeaway: Barriers aren't just in rooms—they are in minds. Remove them with intent and presence to get to the information needed.

March 10: Managing Third Parties

"I have always thought the actions of men the best interpreters of their thoughts." — John Locke

Every extra person in the room changes the interview dynamic. Whether it's an interpreter, an attorney, an analyst, a union representative, or an HR manager, their presence alters what's said—and how it's heard. The investigator's challenge is to maintain control of the process without undermining others' rights or roles.

Third parties can either stabilize the room or fracture it. In fact, during an advanced Survival, Evasion, Resistance, and Escape (SERE) debriefing course, the instructors always insisted that the room be kept to two or fewer investigators, including the returnee, to avoid overstimulation. An attorney might interrupt to protect a client, an HR observer might unintentionally signal disapproval, or an interpreter might subtly adjust phrasing, thereby shifting meaning. Your job is to set boundaries early and manage the flow with quiet authority.

Start with a pre-brief. Clarify roles, expectations, and procedures before anyone sits down. If using an interpreter, discuss the format: simultaneous translation versus alternating. Debrief afterward to confirm fidelity. With attorneys or reps, set the tone professionally but firmly—respect their presence while making it clear you're conducting the interview, not negotiating control.

Key Points:

- **Establish Roles Early:** Clarify each participant's function before questioning begins. Boundaries prevent confusion and conflict.
- **Control Eye Contact:** Focus on the subject, not the interpreter or observer. Direct engagement reinforces authority.
- **Brief and Debrief Interpreters:** Discuss format, tone, and terminology beforehand; review accuracy immediately after.
- **Document Participants:** Record names, roles, and any notable interjections for transparency and future reference.
- **Maintain Neutrality:** Stay professional with third parties—even when they test your patience. Control is quiet, not combative.

Takeaway: Third parties and interpreters can either amplify clarity or distort it. The difference lies in your preparation and presence.

March 11: Other Considerations

"Amateurs talk strategy. Professionals talk logistics." —General of the Army Omar N. Bradley

The most successful interviews rarely fail because of questioning—they fail because of everything else. A chair that creaks. A recorder that dies. A subject who can't focus because the room feels like a freezer. Details that seem small in the moment can derail months of work. The seasoned investigator knows that logistics and comfort are not luxuries—they are part of the interview strategy.

Every environment demands foresight. A field interview in a remote area may require backup power for recording devices, cold bottled water, and printed forms. A corporate interview may call for arranging building access, sending security notifications, or securing a non-disclosure agreement in advance.

If you have ever worked in Nigeria, you know the local power grid is unreliable. A colleague and I were interviewing someone when the lights failed. What could have been a disaster turned into a productive interview only because we had flashlights and paper notes ready until the power resumed. Preparation doesn't just protect the process—it protects credibility. You can explain an evasive subject. You can't explain poor planning.

The same level of attention applies to comfort and safety. The goal isn't to pamper the subject; it's to remove distractions. If someone is cold, thirsty, or interrupted every five minutes, their focus—and their willingness to cooperate—evaporates. I once had an Iraqi detainee thank me for offering him a soda—his first in five years. Unfortunately, it was a little warm. He brought it up multiple times during the interview, and I could tell it lingered in his mind. Not my best work—and a reminder that small oversights can cost you big.

Key Points:

- **Plan for Failure:** Test every piece of equipment before the subject arrives. Assume that what can fail, will.
- **Prioritize Comfort:** Temperature, seating, and privacy affect focus more than you think. Remove avoidable distractions.
- **Account for Technology:** Bring backups—recorders, chargers, batteries, and pens. Digital convenience is no substitute for redundancy.
- **Think Safety and Security:** Know your exits, maintain situational awareness, and secure sensitive materials before and after.

Takeaway: Interviews succeed because of what happens before they start. Logistics, comfort, and foresight don't just support professionalism—they define it.

March 12: Introduction: Owning the Room

"Own the room. Confidence has nothing to do with what you look like." —*Marian Seldes*

Before the first question, before the first note, before a single word is spoken—you have already told the subject who's in charge. The way you enter the room, the pace of your movements, your tone, posture, and eye contact—all communicate authority and intent. In those opening moments, you don't just occupy space—you set the atmosphere that will define everything that follows.

Owning the room doesn't mean dominating it. It means projecting calm confidence that steadies everyone present. The person being interviewed, whether a CEO or a homeless person, is reading your cues as closely as you're reading theirs. If you walk in rushed, distracted, or uncertain, they will sense it. If you appear focused, prepared, and in control, they will mirror that stability.

First impressions happen fast—usually within thirty seconds. That window determines whether the person views you as credible, competent, and trustworthy. The introduction phase is not a formality; it's an opportunity to establish control through professionalism. When you begin an interview, make sure to:

- **Identify with whom you are speaking:** Confirm the subject's name and identity before proceeding.
- **Introduce yourself clearly:** "My name is John Doe. I am an investigator with Lynx Security Group." or "My name is Detective John Doe with the NYPD."
- **Present credentials when appropriate:** Show your badge or ID if requested or when policy or context makes it necessary.
- **State the purpose of the interview:** Explain why the conversation is taking place in a calm, professional manner.
- **Control first impressions:** From your handshake to your posture, everything about your presence communicates intent and authority.

Takeaway: You never get a second chance to start an interview. The room is yours the moment you walk in—if you choose to own it.

March 13: Building Rapport (Part One)

"When people talk, listen completely. Most people never listen." —*Ernest Hemingway*

Every successful interview starts with connection, not confrontation. Before you can uncover the truth, you must first earn enough trust for someone to share it. Rapport isn't a trick or a tactic—it's the authentic bridge between two people who need something from each other. For you, it's information. For them, it might be understanding, dignity, or relief.

True rapport begins before the first question. It starts with the tone of your introduction, your body language, and how you acknowledge the subject as a person—not just a source. The small gestures—offering a seat, using their name, making eye contact without staring—signal respect and stability. These moments lower defenses faster than any polished question set.

Working in South Korea, you quickly realize that many interactions are built on shared experience before business begins. Social rituals—like communal meals or a drink—establish familiarity and trust. The same principle applies in interviews: connection before content. When people feel comfortable, they communicate more freely.

The secret to connection is genuine curiosity. People can tell when they are being managed, and when someone is sincerely interested. The human need to be heard often outweighs the instinct to hide. Interviewing someone in their home or office provides valuable insight into who they are. Diplomas reveal education, photos show priorities, and souvenirs hint at experiences. These details build context— and context builds connection. When you observe with respect rather than judgment, people feel seen rather than scrutinized.

Takeaway: Connection always comes before confession. When people feel seen and heard, they reveal more than they intended—because, for the first time, they feel safe doing so.

March 14: Building Rapport (Part Two)

"The greatest compliment that was ever paid me was when one asked me what I thought, and attended to my answer." —Henry David Thoreau

Rapport doesn't stop once the conversation starts; it evolves. Building a connection is only the first step; maintaining it requires awareness. Reading the room is about recognizing what isn't said as much as what is. Every shift in tone, posture, or eye contact provides real-time feedback on how your subject feels. The skilled investigator notices these cues and adjusts accordingly.

You can sense when energy shifts. Maybe the source leans back, crosses their arms, or avoids eye contact when a sensitive topic surfaces. That's your cue to pause, reframe, or soften your approach. Likewise, a relaxed posture, steady gaze, or small smile signals comfort—permission to go deeper. Reading the room isn't intuition; it's disciplined observation trained over time.

Cultural awareness also plays a major role. In some cultures, silence signals respect; in others, it reflects discomfort. Averted eyes may mean guilt in one country and politeness in another. Understanding these nuances prevents misinterpretation—and missteps. The room you are reading isn't just physical; it's emotional and cultural, too.

Key Points:

- **Observe, Don't Assume:** Let behavior guide your approach; resist the urge to project meaning onto every reaction.
- **Adjust in Real Time:** Use pacing, tone, and posture to respond to changing dynamics.
- **Cultural Awareness Matters:** Interpret cues within context. Respect doesn't look the same everywhere.
- **Stay Present:** Don't chase your next question—watch the person in front of you.
- **Protect the Connection:** Rapport isn't something you earn once; it's something you maintain every minute.

Takeaway: Rapport is a living exchange, not a static state. It must be monitored, adjusted, and maintained.

March 15: Questioning Techniques (Part One)

"Silence is one of the great arts of conversation." —Marcus Tullius Cicero

The best interviews start with one thing: silence. You ask the question, then get out of the way. The more the person talks, the clearer the truth becomes. The less you interrupt, the more authentic the story that unfolds. Every investigator is tempted to jump in—to clarify, correct, or guide. Resist that urge. Let the person narrate. Their story, told in their own words, will reveal far more than anything you could extract by force. The key is to open the funnel wide, then narrow it as you go.

The **TED method**—*Tell, Explain, Describe*—is a simple, proven framework for starting broad:

- *Tell me what hap*pened.
- Explain how you got involved.
- Describe what you *saw.*

These prompts are open enough to invite a full narrative but structured enough to keep the person focused. They foster psychological safety by giving people permission to speak freely without feeling cornered. Once they have laid out the story, you can begin to clarify details with the traditional **5Ws and 1H**—*Who, What, When, Where, Why,* and *How.* But not yet. Let the funnel stay wide until they've emptied their version first. When the story begins to slow, you can gently guide it:

- Tell me more about that.
- Explain what you mean by...
- Describe what happened next.

These questions extend the narrative without confrontation. The person being interviewed feels heard, and you gain unfiltered data before steering toward precision later.

Takeaway: The best investigators talk less and learn more. Open the funnel, ask broad TED questions, and let silence do the heavy lifting.

March 16: Questioning Techniques (Part Two)

"The art and science of asking questions is the source of all knowledge." —*Thomas Berger*

Yesterday, you learned—or relearned—the **TED method** (*Tell, Explain, Describe*) for opening the funnel and allowing a person to talk themselves empty. Once their narrative naturally slows, that's your moment to begin narrowing the funnel with focused, factual questions: the **5Ws and 1H**.

- **Who:** "Who else was there?" / "Who made that decision?"
- **What:** "What happened next?" / "What was said in that meeting?"
- **When:** "When did you first notice the problem?" / "When did you leave the building?"
- **Where:** "Where were you sitting?" / "Where did the conversation take place?"
- **Why:** "Why did you think that was necessary?" / "Why did you report it to Jonathan first and not Amy?"
- **How:** "How did you know about it?" / "How did that make you feel at the time?"

These precision questions transform vague stories into verifiable facts. The key is to use them sparingly—and to use silence deliberately between them. Each pause invites elaboration, reflection, and sometimes self-correction. Most people feel compelled to fill that quiet space, often revealing details they had not planned to share.

"Why" questions, in particular, can be revealing but must be handled with care. They expose motivation, justification, and emotion—but they can also sound accusatory if poorly timed or poorly worded. Use them when rapport is strong, and your tone communicates curiosity, not challenge.

I once interviewed a woman reporting a series of alleged intelligence crimes her ex-husband had committed over several years. After she detailed the events, I asked, "Why didn't you report these sooner?" Her answer was telling; she explained that her ex had been paying her $1,000 a week in an unofficial custody arrangement, and that his new wife had put an end to it. She concluded, "He needs to pay one way or another." That single *why* revealed everything we needed to understand her motivation—and the credibility gap behind her claims.

Takeaway: Precision questions, built around the 5Ws and 1H, help you move from story to substance.

March 17: Questioning Techniques (Part Three)

"Memory is the diary we all carry about with us." —Oscar Wilde

An interview isn't just about gathering statements—it's about helping someone retrieve and reconstruct memory. The most accurate information often lies beneath the surface, buried under time, stress, or emotion. Cognitive and narrative approaches help uncover those details by using the brain's natural storytelling patterns rather than forcing recollection through direct questioning.

The cognitive interview relies on psychological principles of memory retrieval. Instead of asking, *"What did you see?"* you guide the person through mental reconstruction:

- *Close your eyes and picture the scene.*
- *What were you hearing just before that?*
- *If you were standing somewhere else, what would you have seen?*
- *What stands out most when you think back on that moment?*

This method works because memory isn't a photograph—it's a network. Triggering one sensory detail often activates others. Shifting perspective or prompting recall in reverse order forces the brain to reconstruct, not recite—revealing hidden details and inconsistencies that linear storytelling can mask.

Narrative-based approaches complement this by allowing people to tell their story in their own way. Humans naturally organize experiences into stories with beginnings, middles, and ends. When you let them narrate uninterrupted, you gain insight not just into what happened, but how they perceive it. Their structure, language, and emphasis expose what matters most to them—and sometimes, what they want to conceal.

I once interviewed a potential human intelligence source who claimed to have witnessed a critical event. When asked for a simple summary, his story was disjointed and vague. When I had him close his eyes and describe the event as if replaying a movie, details poured out—background noises, time of day, even the smell of the room. Later, when asked to tell it backward—from the end to the beginning—his timeline fell apart. That inconsistency confirmed we were dealing with fabrication, not faulty memory.

Cognitive and narrative techniques require patience and subtlety, but they yield powerful results. You're not interrogating—you're reconstructing. The more vividly someone recalls, the more accurately you can separate truth from fiction.

Takeaway: By guiding recall instead of forcing it, you transform vague recollections into vivid, verifiable accounts.

March 18: Questioning Techniques (Part Four)

"When you have to kill a man, it costs nothing to be polite." —*Sir Winston Churchill*

There comes a point in some interviews where the tone shifts—where patience meets pressure. You have listened, clarified, and tested, and now the person's story doesn't match the facts. That is when the accusatory or confrontational approach comes into play. These techniques aren't about aggression; they are about controlled pressure—using evidence, demeanor, and timing to break through resistance while preserving integrity.

Confrontation starts with evidence, not emotion. Before challenging inconsistencies, make sure your information is accurate, documented, and defensible. The goal is to confront the contradiction, not the person. Instead of saying, *"You're lying,"* say, *"That doesn't match the records I have."* You're testing facts, not attacking character.

Accusatory questioning requires a balance of logic and empathy. People rarely confess because you corner them; they confess because you give them a reason to. That's where the **RPM method—Rationalization, Projection, and Minimization**—comes in. It's a way to allow the person to save face while guiding them toward admission.

- **Rationalization:** Offer an explanation that justifies their behavior in their own mind. (e.g., *"I understand why you did it—you were under pressure, and money was tight."*)
- **Projection:** Shift some blame outward to reduce shame or defensiveness. (e.g., *"You didn't really want to sell the drugs—your friend pushed you into it."*)
- **Minimization:** Downplay the act's severity to make acknowledgment easier. (.e.g., *"It's just some document fraud; anyone could have made that mistake."*)

These techniques don't excuse the behavior—they simply lower emotional resistance, opening the path to truth. Used ethically, RPM can turn denial into dialogue and confrontation into cooperation.

Some people are what we call "deny until they die," and that's okay. You might not get the confession, but the rest of the evidence will put them away. The confession is usually just the cherry on top. Confrontation done right is not about breaking people—it's about breaking barriers. Done wrong, it damages trust, credibility, and the case itself.

Takeaway: Accusatory and confrontational questioning isn't about dominance—it's about precision, empathy, and control.

March 19: Questioning Techniques (Part Five)

"If you do not know how to ask the right question, you discover nothing." —W. Edwards Deming

Asking questions is easy. Asking the *right* questions is an art. But knowing which ones to avoid—that's mastery. The wrong question doesn't just derail the interview—it contaminates the information you're trying to collect. Poor phrasing can plant ideas, distort memory, or lead the person being interviewed exactly where you didn't intend. Recognizing and avoiding these traps is essential to keeping your interview clean, credible, and defensible. Some common questioning pitfalls are:

- **Complex Questions:** These sound sophisticated but confuse recall. *"What factors contributed to your decision to engage in the observed behavior?"* You might as well be asking for a thesis. Keep it plain: *"Why did you do it?"* Complex language leads to *"I don't know"* because the brain stops processing the question.

- **Compound Questions:** Two or more questions in one sentence create mental overload. *"Where were you standing and who were you talking to when it happened?"* You will get an answer to one, not both. Break it apart: ask each separately. Simplicity ensures accuracy.

- **Leading Questions:** These subtly suggest the answer you're fishing for. *"Could it have been a blue car?"* is not neutral—it plants an image. Instead, ask, *"What color was the car?"* Let the subject tell you. Leading questions feed confirmation bias and turn witnesses into echo chambers.

- **Negative Questions:** These invite agreement or confusion instead of clarity. *"You didn't see which way she went, did you?"* The subject often hears only the last part—*"did you?"* —and nods without thinking. Always ask in the affirmative: *"Did you see which way she went?"*

- **Polite Speak:** Courtesy has its place, but excessive softening weakens authority. *"Could you tell me..."* or *"Would you mind sharing..."* can signal hesitation or insecurity. Instead, state the question directly and respectfully: *"Tell me what happened next."* Authority and politeness aren't opposites— clarity is the ultimate form of respect.

Takeaway: The wrong question leads people away from the truth. The right one leads them straight to it.

March 20: Summarizing the Interview

"When you're interviewing someone, you're in control. When you're being interviewed, you think you're in control, but you're not." —Barbara Walters

Every good interview ends the same way it began—with control. Summarizing the interview isn't just a courtesy; it's a tactical step that ensures accuracy, clarity, and credibility. By the time you close your notebook, both you and the person you have interviewed should share the same understanding of what was said, what matters, and what comes next. You should repeat back everything the interviewee told you, which should enable them to add or clarify any information. Some agencies have the secondary take notes and do the summary portion so the primary can focus on questioning. This is their time to shine. You can use the 3C system to summarize: **confirm, clarify, and close.**

1. **Confirm the Facts:** Reiterate key statements and details in neutral language. This gives the person a chance to correct, add, or clarify. For example: "So, to make sure I understand—you arrived around 8:30, spoke briefly with the supervisor, and left at 9:00, correct?" This step serves two functions: it strengthens accuracy and signals professionalism. When your notes and the subject's recollection match, your documentation becomes far more defensible.
2. **Clarify the Ambiguities:** Before wrapping up, address anything vague or inconsistent. People often speak more clearly the second time around, especially when they realize you're paying attention to detail. Ask: "Earlier, you mentioned hearing voices before the alarm went off—can you describe that again for me?" "You said you met twice that week; was that Monday and Wednesday or different days?" These gentle follow-ups aren't confrontational—they are housekeeping for the record.
3. **Close with Professionalism:** End the interview with the same control and composure you began with. Thank the person for their time, explain what happens next, and give them an opportunity to add anything else. A simple prompt like: "Is there anything you'd like to clarify or add before we finish?" demonstrates fairness and transparency—two things that can later make or break your credibility.

A strong summary anchors your interview in professionalism. It closes the loop, reduces disputes, and shows your work was deliberate and disciplined.

Takeaway: The summary is your insurance policy. It validates the accuracy of your record and reinforces your control of the process.

March 21: Closing the Interview

"Well done is better than well said." —Benjamin Franklin

The close of an interview is just as important as the start. How you finish influences what happens afterward—whether the person stays cooperative, if follow-up is possible, and how your professionalism is remembered. The conclusion isn't a sign that you're done; it's the moment you shift from conversation to documentation, from interaction to evidence.

Closing well requires composure, structure, and respect. Even when the interview was difficult—or emotional—you must leave the room with control, not conflict. The best investigators know how to exit gracefully while maintaining authority.

Key Points:

- **Reinforce Professionalism:** Thank them for their time and continue building rapport.
- **Set Expectations:** Provide re-contact information (usually a business card) in case they think of something. See if they are willing to be contacted again. If they must sign a statement, you might need to bring them in after it is typed up, unless your agency allows handwritten.
- **Secure Materials and the Record:** Secure notes and any equipment you brought.
- **Read the Room Before You Leave It:** Don't race out. Leave the room as professionally as you entered it.

Takeaway: Closing an interview isn't about walking out—it's about sealing the process. End with precision, calm, and professionalism.

March 22: Interviewing Across Cultures

"To understand another culture, you must first be humble enough to admit you don't know it." —My orientation specialist at the U.S. Department of State

Investigations don't stop at borders—and neither should your understanding. Whether you're conducting an interview in a major U.S. city or a remote village halfway across the world, every interview carries cultural context. How people communicate, what they value, and how they respond to authority vary widely. Cultural awareness doesn't just make you polite—it makes you effective.

Throughout my career, I have had the privilege of working in dozens of countries across five continents (so far), and it has given me a deep appreciation for how alike—and how different—people truly are. No matter where you go, people want the same things: respect, safety, and to be heard. But the ways they express those needs can vary greatly. A small act of respect in one country might be meaningless—or even offensive—in another.

Doing just a little homework before an interview can pay huge dividends. Learn what is considered respectful, how people address authority, and which behaviors build rapport rather than suspicion. Something as simple as knowing when to shake hands, whether to remove your shoes, or how to greet elders can change everything.

When I worked alongside female agents in the Middle East, many chose to cover their hair out of respect for local customs. It wasn't about conforming—it was about credibility. The gesture often softened tension before the first question was even asked. In other regions, I found that learning about the local food or picking up a few words of the local language opened doors faster than any credential I carried. Even mentioning a piece of local history or geography can show that you value more than just the facts—you value the person.

Cultural sensitivity isn't political correctness; it's operational awareness. A culturally tone-deaf interview can just as quickly derail cooperation as a procedural mistake. Likewise, showing genuine curiosity about someone's background can transform a cold interview into a candid conversation.

Takeaway: Every culture has its rhythm. Learn to move with it, and you'll find people open up faster and share more freely.

March 23: Telephonic and Remote Interviews

"Technology is a useful servant but a dangerous master." —Christian Lous Lange

Not every interview takes place across a table anymore. Today, investigators have just as many conversations through screens and phones as they do in person. Whether it's Zoom, Microsoft Teams, or whatever platform is popular at the moment, remote interviewing has become a permanent part of an investigator's toolkit. But while technology saves time and resources, it also brings new challenges to control, credibility, and connection.

Advantages: Remote interviews offer flexibility and reach. They allow you to talk to people who might otherwise be unavailable—subjects across the country or witnesses who can't travel. They save money, reduce scheduling headaches, and, in most jurisdictions, are considered non-custodial, which reduces legal and procedural complications. For witnesses, the familiar environment can make them more relaxed and forthcoming. They also give investigators immediate access to digital resources—such as case files, timelines, and maps—without the constraints of a physical setup.

Disadvantages: What you gain in convenience, you lose in control. Remote interviews limit your ability to read the room—the posture, subtle shifts, or energy you rely on in person. You also can't control distractions: background noise, poor connections, or even unseen third parties listening off-camera. The screen creates distance that can flatten rapport and make deception harder to detect. Technical issues can also erode momentum. A delayed response or frozen screen can kill rhythm and credibility. Worse, security risks are real—unsecured networks, unauthorized recordings, or data leaks can compromise confidentiality.

Practical Considerations:

- **Verify Identity:** Confirm who you're speaking with. If remote, have them show ID and confirm whether anyone else is present.
- **Control the Environment:** Ask participants to silence notifications, use headphones, and ensure privacy.
- **Document Consent:** Clearly state whether the session is being recorded and obtain agreement.
- **Maintain Professional Presence:** Dress and act as if you were in the room— your tone and body language still project through the screen.
- **Adjust for Delay:** Leave pauses before responding to avoid cutting people off.

Takeaway: Remote interviewing is here to stay. Technology may bridge the miles, but professionalism bridges the gap.

March 24: The Secondary Interviewer

"If you want to go fast, go alone. If you want to go far, go together." —African Proverb (often attributed to the Akan people of Ghana)

Not every interview is a one-person operation. In many agencies and organizations, interviews are conducted by a two-person team: a primary and a secondary interviewer. When this dynamic works well, it provides balance, safety, and structure. When it doesn't, it creates confusion, overlap, and distraction.

The primary interviewer carries the conversation—building rapport, controlling flow, and guiding the questioning strategy. The secondary plays a supporting but equally vital role: documenting, observing, and maintaining situational awareness. Every agency has its preferences—some assign the secondary to take notes and handle the summary, while others use them as a silent overwatch to ensure officer safety or control the environment. The key is clarity of roles before the interview begins.

I've worked in places where the secondary's main job was to make sure the primary didn't get attacked—literally. In others, they were responsible for note accuracy and could step in if the primary began losing rapport or direction. The secondary must read both the room and the primary interviewer, sensing when to step in and when to stay silent.

A strong secondary anticipates, but doesn't react. They monitor tone shifts, watch for physical tells, and flag inconsistencies for follow-up without disrupting flow. When rapport begins to falter, or the primary gets tunnel vision, the secondary can tactfully take over the questioning, providing a reset for both sides. The best interview teams function like a good patrol pair—each member knows the other's rhythm. It's about coordination, not competition. Some tips:

- **Define Roles Early:** Establish who leads, who records, and who manages logistics before the interviewee enters.
- **Stay in Sync:** Communicate through subtle cues—eye contact, gestures, or written notes.
- **Support, Don't Overshadow:** The secondary enhances the interview, never competes for control.
- **Step In Strategically:** If rapport breaks down or fatigue sets in, take over smoothly to maintain momentum.

Takeaway: Two investigators working in sync can accomplish what one alone might miss. The secondary interviewer isn't a backup—they are a force multiplier.

March 25: Detecting Deception (Part One)

"Most lies fail because of words, not gestures." —Dr. Aldert Vrij

Detecting deception isn't about catching someone in a twitch or glance—it's about recognizing change. While nonverbal behavior reveals emotion, verbal behavior exposes contradiction. Research by Dr. Paul Ekman and Dr. Aldert Vrij, two of the leading experts in deception science, shows that no single cue—verbal or nonverbal—by itself proves deceit. Instead, truth and lies reveal themselves through shifts in how people communicate when the pressure rises.

The popular idea that "90% of communication is nonverbal" is based on a misinterpretation of older psychology studies. In fact, that number applies to emotional tone, not factual content. In investigations, words matter first because they carry logic, sequence, and intent—things liars struggle to maintain consistently. The key is to establish a **baseline**—how someone speaks when relaxed—and watch how that changes when discomfort appears. Sudden adjustments in tone, pace, or structure are often the first ripples of deception. Some common verbal indicators of deception:

- **Qualifiers and Distancing Phrases:** "To the best of my knowledge..." "As far as I can recall...", "That's what I was told." These statements soften ownership and create psychological distance.
- **Unnecessary Detail:** Liars often overload their stories with irrelevant specifics to sound convincing. "I parked on the left side, by the big oak tree, next to a red car—might've been a Honda..." Real memories flow; false ones are overdesigned.
- **Evasive Language:** "Did you take the money?" → "I would never do something like that." A moral declaration replaces a factual denial. The subject argues from ethics rather than facts.
- **Shifts in Pronouns or Tense:** "We were there when it happened" (when no "we" existed). "He *is* walking toward me" (when describing the past). Subtle shifts reflect stress or fabrication.
- **Repeating the Question:** When inventing a response, deceptive speakers often echo your question before answering—an unconscious stalling tactic.
- **Inconsistencies Across Retellings:** Truth holds steady; lies evolve. Changes in sequencing, emphasis, or word choice across versions are red flags.

Takeaway: Verbal deception lives in the details. The liar's challenge isn't the story—it's keeping the story straight. Listen closely.

March 26: Detecting Deception (Part Two)

"No single sign of lying is proof. Clusters of behavior, linked in context, are what reveal the truth." —Dr. Paul Ekman

Deception is never about one word, one pause, or one glance—it's about the pattern. Experienced investigators don't react to individual anomalies; they identify **clusters** of verbal and behavioral indicators that appear together under stress. A single hesitation means nothing. But hesitation, over-detail, and distancing language—all around a sensitive topic—form a pattern that deserves attention.

Clusters reveal deception because lying is hard work. It taxes memory, attention, and emotion simultaneously. That strain leaks into multiple channels—words, tone, posture, timing—creating alignment between what is said and what is avoided.

Recognizing Clusters:

- **Timing Clusters:** A pause before sensitive topics, followed by speed afterward.
- **Content Clusters:** Over-detailing unimportant facts while skipping key ones.
- **Tone Clusters:** Sudden defensiveness, moralizing, or overexplaining.
- **Behavioral Clusters:** Shifts in language coupled with posture or gaze changes.

The key is **correlation, not accusation.** Clusters point you toward the truth—they don't prove it. Once you identify them, probe gently. Change the sequence of questions, revisit topics, or ask for retelling. True memories replay naturally; fabricated ones crumble under reorganization.

I once had a Soldier who, when he was lying about what he did, would restate your question in a long, deliberate format: "Where...was...I...at...2300...hours...last...night..."

He was buying time to come up with a cover story. It always made me chuckle—but it also told me exactly when to pay attention.

Takeaway: Deception is a mosaic, not a moment. The investigator's job isn't to jump at single clues—it's to assemble patterns until the picture makes sense.

March 27: Detecting Deception (Part Three)

"The body never lies." —Martha Graham

Words can be crafted; behavior cannot. The face, posture, and small physical gestures often reveal what the voice conceals. Yet, contrary to popular belief, deception isn't exposed by a single "tell." There is no magic eye twitch or fidget that proves someone is lying. Nonverbal detection is about change—not movement. Much of human communication is nonverbal, but that doesn't mean 90% of deception is. The investigator's task is to interpret how comfort, stress, and control show themselves when the topic shifts.

1. **Establish a Baseline:** Every subject has a natural rhythm. Some gesture wildly when relaxed; others barely move. Spend a few minutes discussing neutral topics—sports, weather, travel—to see how they look and sound under no pressure. That baseline becomes your control sample.
2. **Watch for Change, Not Movement:** When the topic turns sensitive, note what changes. Breathing slows or quickens. Arms cross. Posture shifts. The body's comfort leaks through small adaptations. These are not proof of lies—but signals of stress worth exploring.
3. **Observe Congruence:** Truthful communication aligns across channels. When words and gestures don't match, trust the gestures. "I didn't take it," he says—while nodding yes. That disconnect between verbal and nonverbal expression is where the story begins to crack.
4. **Comfort vs. Discomfort Behaviors:** Truthful subjects tend to relax as they speak. Deceptive ones tighten up. Watch for self-soothing gestures like rubbing the neck, crossing the arms, twisting a ring, or shielding the body when questions strike close to home.

Takeaway: Nonverbal observation is the study of contrast. Truth and deception often look alike until the topic turns difficult.

March 28: Detecting Deception (Part Four)

"What you do speaks so loudly that I cannot hear what you say." —Ralph Waldo Emerson

Nonverbal deception detection becomes powerful when patterns form. Just as with language, the body reveals truth through **clusters**—groups of behaviors that appear together under stress or conflict. A single gesture may mean nothing, but several occurring in sequence can tell a story words refuse to.

1. **Microexpressions and Timing:** Dr. Paul Ekman's research showed that emotions leak through the face in brief, involuntary flashes called microexpressions, which last less than a second. These are windows into suppressed feelings like fear, anger, or guilt. Spotting them requires patience, timing, and practice.
2. **Timing and Synchronization:** Truthful subjects' gestures usually match their words—appearing simultaneously or slightly before the statement. When deception creeps in, gestures often lag, appearing a half-second after the words. The mind is editing faster than the body can follow.
3. **The Cluster Effect:** Cluster analysis means combining multiple signals: tone, gaze, posture, hand movements, and timing. When several stress-related cues appear at once—especially around sensitive questions—pay attention. Stress clusters, not isolated gestures, point to potential deception.
4. **Behavioral Leakage and Control:** Liars tend to overcontrol their upper bodies—especially hands and face—while their feet, legs, and posture reveal tension. Watch below the table. Restless legs, tapping feet, or angling toward the exit betray internal conflict long before the face does.
5. **Integrating Channels:** The best investigators synchronize what they hear and see. A subject who says, "I'm calm," while fidgeting or clutching the armrest isn't lying about facts—they're revealing emotion. That emotional contradiction is where the truth begins to surface.

Takeaway: Nonverbal deception isn't about spotting guilt—it's about reading human stress. Clusters, timing, and control all tell you when emotion and logic are at odds.

March 29: Ethical Boundaries in Interrogation

"Power corrupts, but absolute power corrupts absolutely." —Lord Acton

Pressure can produce answers. Coercion produces problems. The line between tactical pressure and abuse is the single most important rule in any interrogation: cross it once and credibility, evidence, and careers can be destroyed.

I trained at Fort Huachuca, Arizona, and I remember the annual protests aimed at alleged "torture" instruction—a reaction rooted in the well-documented, unacceptable treatment of detainees at Abu Ghraib, Iraq. My high school civics teacher once said to me regarding this, *"Americans don't do this."* He was right in principle: our procedures, laws, and training exist to prevent it. The moral and legal costs of crossing that line are simply too high.

There are legendary figures in the history of interrogation who demonstrate the contrast. Hanns Scharff, the Luftwaffe interrogator, extracted information by disarming rapport rather than force—so much so that he once allowed a captured pilot to fly a German plane under controlled conditions. That method shows the power of skill over brutality: respect, cleverness, and psychology can outperform coercion every time.

Core Limits and Practical Points:

- **Pressure ≠ Coercion:** Use evidence, timing, and calm confrontation. Avoid threats, promises, deprivation, or humiliation.
- **Law and Policy Matter:** Miranda, due process, corporate policy, and local statutes are not optional—violating them ruins cases. In private investigation, physically preventing someone from leaving can amount to kidnapping; know the law before you act.
- **Emotional Control:** Anger and impatience are liabilities. A steady tone maintains authority and protects the integrity of the process.
- **Ethical Deception vs. Corruption:** Tactical omissions within legal bounds are acceptable; fabricating evidence or making false promises is not. One falsehood can nullify an otherwise solid investigation.

Takeaway: Ethics are not obstacles—they are your operational backbone. The best interrogators get results without breaking rules or people.

March 30: The Debrief

"The unexamined experience is wasted experience." —Adapted from Socrates

Every investigator improves—or declines—after every interview. What happens after the subject leaves the room determines which direction you go. The debrief is not an afterthought; it's where skill turns into mastery.

A professional debrief looks beyond the facts of the case. It examines **how** the interview unfolded: what worked, what didn't, and what could be sharpened next time. Even a "perfect" interview contains lessons. Reviewing performance builds awareness, consistency, and confidence for the next one.

1. **Review the Process, Not Just the Product:** Don't just ask, *"Did I get the confession?"* Ask, *"Did I control the room?" "Was my questioning sequence effective?" "Did I miss cues?"* Treat the interview like a training film—replay it in your mind and critique your own tactics.
2. **Conduct Team Debriefs When Possible:** If you worked with a secondary interviewer, compare notes. What did they notice that you didn't? How did the subject respond when you paused, pressed, or softened? A second perspective often reveals the blind spots of the first.
3. **Document Emotional Dynamics:** Was the subject defensive, cooperative, evasive, or emotional? Note their behavioral rhythm. These patterns become invaluable for future contact or cross-interviews.
4. **Capture Lessons While They're Fresh:** The longer you wait, the more detail fades. Immediately after the interview, jot down improvements for next time: phrasing that worked, timing that didn't, or cues you missed. This becomes your personal playbook for continuous growth.

Takeaway: The interview isn't over when the subject leaves—it ends when you have learned from it. The best investigators are lifelong students of their own performance.

March 31: Statement Analysis

"If thought corrupts language, language can also corrupt thought." —George Orwell

Statement analysis is the examination of a person's written words for indicators of truthfulness, deception, and emotional state. It's an emerging discipline—part psychology, part linguistics, and entirely practical for investigators. The goal isn't to play word games; it's to recognize how people betray their intentions through syntax and omission.

1. **Word Choice and Ownership:** Liars often distance themselves from responsibility. "The gun went off" shifts blame to the object. "I fired the gun" accepts it. Words like "somebody," "they," or "we" can blur ownership when the writer wants emotional distance.
2. **Sequence and Gaps:** Truthful statements usually follow a natural timeline. Deceptive ones jump or stall. Phrases like "Next thing I remember…" or "After that…" can indicate missing events or selective memory. Gaps in the sequence point to places worth probing.
3. **Pronouns and Consistency:** Pronouns are the anchors of honesty. When someone shifts from "I" to "we" or "they" midway through a story, it can signal detachment from responsibility. Likewise, inconsistent use of proper names or titles—such as switching between "my wife" and "Sarah" —can reflect emotional distance.
4. **Tense and Detail:** Truthful memories are described in the past tense: "I walked in," "I saw," "He said." When a writer slips into the present—"He's standing there," "I see him" —they may be reconstructing events rather than recalling them. Overly specific minor details ("It was exactly 8:03 p.m.") can also suggest rehearsed fabrication.
5. **Omission and Brevity:** What's missing often matters most. Writers tend to gloss over the most incriminating or emotional parts. A statement that describes the beginning and end of an event but skips the middle is rarely accidental.

Takeaway: Written statement analysis is still a relatively new tool in modern investigations, but it's gaining momentum. When properly applied, it can corroborate other evidence or reveal inconsistencies long before a re-interview.

April: Tools of the Trade

"The tools don't make the craftsman, but the craftsman knows every tool." —*My father*

Every investigator relies on tools—from cameras and drones to vehicles, data platforms, and the humble pen. But tools alone don't solve cases; the people who understand, maintain, and adapt them do. Having equipment doesn't make you capable. Knowing how and when to use it—and how to keep it ready—is what separates a professional from an amateur.

In the military, we used to joke about *"Gear-dos."* These were the folks who always had the latest tactical gadget strapped to them—every pouch, clip, and attachment money could buy—but half the time, they couldn't find what they actually needed when it mattered. I remember one Soldier who looked like he had just walked off a Surefire catalog cover: brand-new everything, from gloves to optics. But when it came time to operate, he fumbled with his equipment and couldn't perform basic tasks efficiently. The lesson was clear—gear doesn't make you better. Mastery of your tools does.

Investigators fall into the same trap. It's easy to chase the latest camera system, drone, or software instead of focusing on the fundamentals—situational awareness, timing, and judgment. Fancy tech is worthless if you don't know how to use it, maintain it, or if it fails and you can't adapt. True professionals balance practicality with preparedness. They choose the right tool, not the newest one.

In the military, we also lived by another truth: *"Take care of your gear, and it will take care of you."* That lesson applies directly to investigations. A dead battery, an uncalibrated lens, or a corrupted memory card can wreck an operation just as surely as a bad lead. Preventive maintenance isn't exciting, but it's what separates amateurs from professionals.

Whether you're managing a drone program for a public agency or operating a small private-sector surveillance firm, your gear is an extension of your capability—and your credibility. How you acquire, care for, and apply it reflects how you treat your craft.

This month focuses on the full life cycle of investigative tools—selecting the right ones, maintaining them, and thinking creatively about how to use them. We'll also touch on the logistics behind the scenes: funding, supply, interagency borrowing, and accountability.

The goal isn't to turn you into a gearhead. It's to make you efficient, adaptive, and professional—the kind of investigator who doesn't just *have* the tools, but knows how to make them count.

April 1: The Right Tool for the Right Job

"A good tool improves the way you work. A great tool improves the way you think."
—Jeff Duntemann

The right equipment in the wrong hands—or used for the wrong task—is just expensive clutter. Every investigator needs tools, but the best investigators know that tools don't replace skill, judgment, or experience. They amplify them.

I have seen both sides of the spectrum. On one end, the "Gear-do" —someone buried in gadgets who can't operate without them. On the other hand, the minimalist who refuses to adapt or try new technology. The sweet spot is in between: practical efficiency. You don't need every new toy, but you do need the right tool for the right job—and you need to know how to use it when it counts.

Principles for Smart Tool Use:

- **Mission drives equipment-** Don't buy or deploy anything without a clear use case. The operation should dictate the gear—not the other way around.
- **Know your gear's limits-** Understand the operational envelope—range, power, weather, battery life, legal restrictions—before you depend on it.
- **Train with it before you trust it-** Your tools should feel second nature. If you fumble with buttons or manuals under pressure, you're not ready to use it in the field.
- **Have a backup plan-** Batteries die. Signals drop. Cameras fail. A notepad and pen never run out of power.
- **Stay legal and ethical-** Some "tactical" tools—trackers, covert cameras, intercept devices—have strict laws governing their use. Ignorance isn't an excuse.
- **Don't get sentimental-** If something doesn't work, replace it or adapt. Equipment isn't sacred—it's a means to an end.

A Practical Tip: Before any operation, run a "gear sanity check." Line up your tools, ask:

1. Do I know how to use this?
2. Do I need it for *this* job?
3. Do I have a simpler backup?

If you can't answer "yes" to all three, rethink it. The best investigators I've ever known had simple setups, but they could make those tools sing. They weren't dependent on gear—they were empowered by it.

Takeaway: Technology evolves, but fundamentals endure. Don't chase every gadget. Master your tools, pick them with intent, and make each one earn its place in your kit.

April 2: Building Your Investigator's Kit

"The more you know, the less you carry." —*Mors Kochanski*

Every investigator—whether a government agent, corporate compliance officer, or solo private detective eventually faces the question: *What should I carry?* The answer isn't found in a catalog or online forum; it's earned through time in the field. Your kit is more than a collection of tools—it's a reflection of your investigative mindset.

An effective investigator's kit isn't about volume; it's about intent. The inexperienced investigator packs for every imaginable scenario, convinced that preparedness is measured in pounds. Ask any light infantryman how that goes after ten miles under a rucksack, and you'll understand why efficiency matters. The professional packs deliberately, balancing capability with mobility. Whether you're conducting surveillance, interviewing witnesses, or managing evidence, every item you carry should serve a specific function—and justify its weight.

There's a difference between having tools and having a system. A system anticipates contingencies: batteries fail, light fades, weather turns, or subjects change direction. Each piece of equipment should integrate into how you observe, communicate, document, and adapt. The kit becomes an extension of your discipline—not just what you carry, but how you operate.

Key Points:

- **Purpose Before Purchase:** Never carry a tool you can't justify. If it doesn't directly support observation, documentation, or safety, leave it behind.
- **Tailor to Mission:** No two investigations are the same. Build your kit to suit the environment—urban, rural, corporate, or maritime.
- **Balance Weight and Worth:** Every ounce slows you down. Identify what you will use 80% of the time and streamline the rest.
- **Modularity Matters:** Use adaptable bags and pouches that can move from car to foot pursuit seamlessly.
- **Redundancy Smartly:** Carry backups for essentials only—batteries, pens, and memory cards.
- **Field-Test Everything:** Don't discover in the middle of an operation that your flashlight flickers or your mount doesn't fit. Check your gear before the mission, not during it.

Takeaway: The more you refine your kit, the less you will need to think about it—and that's when you're free to focus on what matters most: the investigation itself.

April 3: Preventive Maintenance

"Take care of your gear, and it will take care of you." —Old Soldier's Proverb

Preventive maintenance isn't glamorous. No one brags about charging batteries, cleaning lenses, or checking tire pressure before a surveillance run. But when your equipment fails at the wrong time, you learn fast why the U.S. military built an entire culture around PMCS—*Preventive Maintenance Checks and Services.* In the investigative world, the same principle applies: check it now or pay for it later.

The term PMCS comes from the U.S. Army and Marine Corps, where it refers to the structured inspection and servicing of vehicles, weapons, and field equipment. Soldiers and Marines conduct PMCS before, during, and after every mission—not because it's fun, but because lives depend on it. Their maintenance consistency is one of the defining traits that set them apart from other organizations and militaries worldwide.

Investigative work often involves long days, unpredictable weather, and technology pushed to its limits. Cameras, recorders, vehicles, and drones don't care how critical your mission is—they will fail if neglected. A good investigator develops a ritual of readiness: inspecting, testing, cleaning, charging, and logging before the operation begins. It's not just about equipment; it's about mindset.

Key Points:

- **Inspect Before Use:** Conduct pre-mission checks on all critical gear—cameras, batteries, lenses, radios, GPS units, and vehicles. Small issues become big ones under stress.
- **Create a Routine:** Establish a personal PMCS cycle. Daily for field gear, weekly for vehicles and power sources, monthly for backups and storage.
- **Keep Maintenance Logs:** Track what was checked, repaired, or replaced. A written record prevents missed steps and builds accountability.
- **Label and Rotate Gear:** Number batteries, SD cards, and cables. Rotate them to extend lifespan and identify failures quickly.
- **Clean as You Go:** Dust and moisture are silent killers. Keep microfiber cloths, compressed air, and silica packs handy.
- **Test Before Rolling Out:** Every morning, confirm operational readiness—not in theory, but in practice. Power on, test record, check playback.

Takeaway: PMCS is a habit that separates professionals from hobbyists.

April 4: Batteries, Backups, and Redundancy

"Two is one, one is none, three is better." —U.S. Military Saying

Today's investigative work is digital. Cameras, camcorders, drones, GPS trackers, laptops, and phones all draw from the same invisible reservoir: battery life. You might have the best optics and software in the world, but they are useless if they can't turn on. Power planning, then, is as essential as your gear itself. You would not leave home without fuel in your vehicle—don't leave for an operation without a full charge in your equipment.

Power management starts with diversity. Don't depend on a single energy source or charging method. A field-ready investigator uses multiple layers: charged batteries, power banks, solar panels, vehicle inverters, and even AC adapters for stationary ops. Each option provides an insurance policy against the realities of the job—long hours, harsh conditions, and the unpredictable rhythm of surveillance.

I once assisted on a multi-day rural surveillance mission in which the target's location had no nearby outlets or charging stations. One investigator brought a small solar panel charger and a power bank the size of a paperback. While everyone else rationed battery life, he kept his optics, phone, and recorder running indefinitely. That small investment kept him operational when others were dead in the water. It's not about being flashy; it's about being functional.

The same principle applies in vehicles. A DC-to-AC inverter turns a cigarette lighter into a charging hub for laptops, radios, or external battery packs. Keep an inverter rated for your most power-hungry device—and test it beforehand. Portable power banks are your lifeline for phones and cameras, while solar panels and foldable chargers offer sustainable power when outlets are out of reach. Compact jump-start batteries with USB ports can even start your car and recharge your phone. These are not gimmicks—they are survival tools for modern investigators.

Takeaway: Technology is powerful only when powered. Battery management isn't just technical—it's tactical. Redundancy is a mark of professionalism, not paranoia.

April 5: Cameras and Optics (Overview)

"The camera is an instrument that teaches people how to see without a camera." — *Dorothea Lange*

In investigations, the camera is more than a recording device—it's your witness. Whether documenting a crime scene or conducting surveillance, your camera becomes the lens through which truth is preserved. The right one doesn't just take pictures; it captures credibility.

New investigators often chase the highest megapixel count or the newest model. Professionals match equipment to mission. A mid-range camera you know inside and out will outperform a top-shelf model you barely understand. Capability and control matter more than cost.

For surveillance, choose a camera with a long optical zoom, image stabilization, a quiet shutter, and a viewfinder to avoid screen glare or reflection. Compact mirrorless models are ideal—light, fast, and discreet. Pair that with simple concealment techniques and steady hands; you don't need a giant lens to get quality footage, just smart positioning and patience.

For crime-scene or evidentiary work, precision outweighs concealment. DSLR or mirrorless systems with interchangeable lenses let you shoot wide for context and close for detail. Always enable date and timestamp functions and shoot in RAW when possible, to preserve metadata and detail integrity. Every image should be defensible in court.

Don't overlook action or waterproof cameras like GoPro. They are small, durable, and invaluable in rain, marine, or rugged environments. They can mount in vehicles, on vests, or in confined spaces to capture critical footage when your main camera can't.

Takeaway: A camera is only as capable as the investigator behind it. Learn its settings, practice in low light, and treat every shot like evidence.

April 6: Camcorders vs. Still Cameras

"Make sure that you always have the right tools for the job. It's no use trying to eat a steak with a teaspoon and a straw." —Anthony T. Hincks

Still cameras and camcorders may seem interchangeable, but they serve different investigative roles. Understanding what each piece of gear offers helps you choose the right tool for the right job—and that decision often determines whether you bring back usable evidence or just excuses.

Camcorders are designed for motion, endurance, and ease of use under pressure. They excel at documenting activity over time—surveillance, interviews, and operational walk-throughs. Look for models with an **electronic viewfinder (EVF)** so you can monitor discreetly without drawing attention with a glowing screen. **Filter threads** on the lens allow you to attach UV, polarizing, or neutral density filters—useful for reducing glare or for bright outdoor conditions.

Professional-grade camcorders often include **external focus controls**, giving you smooth, precise manual adjustments without fumbling through menus. Just as important, they come equipped with an **external microphone jack** and a **headphone port**. These features let you capture clear audio and monitor it in real time—something still cameras rarely do well. Built-in microphones are fine for reference, but external mics make the difference between intelligible dialogue and useless noise. The above features represent the minimum you should have on your camcorder and are typically found in prosumer-grade camcorders (one grade above consumer-grade and one grade below professional-grade).

By contrast, still cameras are optimized for clarity and detail. They produce high-resolution images for identification, documentation, and evidentiary reports. Most modern DSLRs and mirrorless cameras can record video, but that's not their primary function. They lack the long battery life, ergonomic grip, and dedicated audio ports of a camcorder.

Takeaway: For static scenes—crime-scene photography, property damage, environmental context—a still camera is your best bet. For dynamic, unfolding events, the camcorder wins every time.

April 7: Camera Accessories

"Quality is never an accident; it is always the result of intelligent effort." —John Ruskin

The best investigators know that cameras don't capture evidence—stability does. Blurry photos and shaky footage can turn strong documentation into weak proof. The right accessories transform your camera from a handheld device into a reliable evidence-gathering instrument.

Stabilization tools are the foundation of image quality. A **monopod** offers quick, lightweight support ideal for mobile surveillance or use in confined spaces. When you need complete steadiness—interviews, fixed-point documentation, or long-lens work—a **tripod** is the answer. In vehicles, a simple handheld **beanbag** provides quiet stability and absorbs dashboard vibration without drawing attention.

Lens filters should not be overlooked. A **clear (UV) filter** adds a protective layer over your camera or camcorder lens—it's far cheaper to replace a scratched filter than an entire lens. A **neutral density (ND) filter** reduces exposure to sunlight, allowing you to capture properly balanced footage in bright conditions. A **circular polarizing filter** minimizes glare and reflections—perfect for photographing through glass, whether during a drug buy or an infidelity surveillance.

Equally important is data integrity. Use high-quality SD or CFexpress cards from reputable manufacturers. Pay attention to read/write speeds, capacity, and compatibility. Inferior cards corrupt files—and you won't know until it's too late. Carry multiple smaller-capacity cards instead of a single large one; this limits data loss if a card fails or must be surrendered as evidence. Keep cards labeled, organized, and stored in a weatherproof case to prevent loss or damage.

Key Points:

- **Monopods:** Portable stability for mobile surveillance.
- **Tripods:** Maximum steadiness for static shots or interviews.
- **Beanbags:** Perfect for in-vehicle or low-profile setups.
- **Lens Filters:** UV for protection, ND for sunlight, polarizer for glare.

Takeaway: Accessories may be a small addition to your kit, but they define professionalism.

April 8: Covert Cameras and Concealment

"Cars and cameras are the two things I let myself be materialistic about. I don't care about the other stuff." —Louis C.K.

Aside from camcorders and traditional cameras, an investigator should also maintain a selection of covert cameras. These tools document behavior, corroborate testimony, and collect evidence when overt observation would compromise safety or effectiveness. There are generally three types of covert cameras:

- **Body Worn:** Hats, eyeglasses, shirt buttons, or other clothing-based devices. Keep in mind the camera's orientation—if it's tilted or off-center, you'll record nothing but the ground.
- **Handheld:** Key fobs, coffee cup lids, or phone cases. These are perfect for up-close operations such as drug buys or contact meetings.
- **Stationary:** Smoke detectors, computer mice, alarm clocks, or other functional disguises. Best for controlled environments where movement isn't possible or advisable.

Tradeoffs: All consumer off-the-shelf (COTS) devices share one weakness: familiarity. Because these designs are mass-produced and widely sold, even a moderately observant person could recognize them, which may pose a safety issue for investigators. What you gain in portability, you lose in image quality and range. Covert cameras lack optical zoom and often have a restricted field of view. If something goes offline, an undercover investigator can't easily fix it without compromising the operation.

COTS vs. Custom Builds: COTS covert cameras are sufficient for many private investigations—affordable, fast to deploy, and available in dozens of designs. But quality varies drastically. Cheap, no-name models often feature poor optics, unreliable firmware, and security flaws such as hardcoded cloud accounts. Avoid devices that transmit data to unknown servers or lack firmware updates. If your agency or organization maintains a technical services shop, use it. A skilled tech can build covert systems tailored to your environment—disguised for the mission, secure storage, and powered for long operations.

During intelligence work overseas, I had the benefit of using custom-made covert devices from a tech shop. The limits of what we built were only constrained by available materials—not imagination. A good technician can hide a camera anywhere, including drywall, and only a professional-grade Technical Surveillance Countermeasures (TSCM) sweep would ever find it.

Takeaway: Covert cameras can make or break a case—but only when used with discipline, legality, and technical precision.

April 9: Drones: Eye in the Sky

"I fly because it releases my mind from the tyranny of petty things." —Antoine de Saint-Exupéry

Drones have redefined modern surveillance and scene documentation. What once required aircraft, ladders, or risky proximity can now be done safely from the sky, at a cheaper cost than ever. If your department or organization isn't using drones, they should start. Drones fall into three general categories for investigative use:

- **Micro/Compact Drones:** Small, portable, and easy to deploy from almost anywhere. Ideal for confined urban areas, such as before warrant service. Their limited battery life and wind sensitivity require careful planning, but they are less conspicuous.
- **Standard Quadcopters:** The workhorses of field operations—stable, GPS-assisted, and capable of carrying quality optical or thermal sensors. These are best for crime scene mapping, accident reconstruction, search operations, or rural surveillance.
- **Fixed-Wing or Hybrid Drones:** Designed for long-distance and endurance flights. They are less common in the private sector, but invaluable for large-area mapping or disaster assessment.

Tactics and Application: A drone should never replace field presence—it should extend it. Use them for perimeter reconnaissance before serving a warrant, subject surveillance, or crime scene overviews. For law enforcement, they provide command visibility and safety during tactical operations. Private investigators can safely monitor large properties or follow subjects in open terrain. Always coordinate airspace use, respect privacy, and document your flights for legal transparency. Plan each flight as an operation: location, weather, battery rotation, recovery route, and data handling. Securely store your footage, label it, and note flight logs for potential discovery requests.

Legal and Operational Considerations: Regulations differ by country. In the U.S., FAA Part 107 governs commercial drone operations. In some countries, like Jordan, drones are illegal (including for Jordanian police) unless granted permission by the Jordanian Air Force. Always check local no-fly zones, altitude restrictions, and licensing requirements. Many states also have specific privacy laws addressing aerial surveillance and recording. For international operations, coordinate with host-nation authorities before deploying any unmanned system—violating local airspace laws can have severe consequences.

Takeaway: Drones extend your reach but also your responsibility. They can turn good investigators into great ones—or careless ones into liabilities.

April 10: Drone Operations and Safety

"There is simply no substitute for experience in terms of aviation safety" —Chesley *"Sully" Sullenberger*

Drones are everywhere now—from hobbyists flying over beaches to investigators mapping scenes and tracking subjects. Their accessibility is both a strength and a weakness: anyone can fly one, but few operate them correctly. Given how common drones have become, every investigator should understand the basics of drone care, maintenance, and operational discipline. Just because the tool is modern doesn't mean the principles have changed.

Pre-Flight Checks: Every flight starts before takeoff. Inspect propellers for cracks, motors for debris, and mounts for looseness. Confirm that the firmware and controller software are up to date and that your memory cards are formatted and secure. Verify GPS lock and compass calibration before launch. A five-minute inspection prevents a five-hundred-dollar crash. Always review your area for no-fly zones, obstacles, and electronic interference before arming the motors.

Battery Management: Battery health is the heartbeat of your platform. Label each battery and record charge cycles. Store them at roughly 50% charge when not in use to extend lifespan. Avoid flying in extreme heat or cold, which can cause voltage drops mid-flight. Bring more power than you think you will need—redundancy applies here as much as anywhere else. A drone that dies mid-flight is a liability.

Emergency Procedures: Every operator should know what to do when—not if—something fails. Program your drone's Return-to-Home (RTH) altitude above nearby obstacles, and rehearse manual flight recovery. If GPS or video feed is lost, maintain a visual line of sight and rely on the compass and attitude indicators. Always have a safe landing zone identified before takeoff.

Weather Considerations: Weather grounds more drones than bad piloting. Wind gusts, rain, and temperature extremes degrade sensors and drain batteries faster than expected. Check wind speeds at altitude, not just on the ground. Dust and humidity can foul gimbals or lenses, so carry microfiber cloths and protective cases. Sometimes the smartest move is to cancel the flight.

Data Capture and Workflow: After every mission, immediately secure and back up your footage. Maintain a standardized naming and storage system that links the data to the date, time, and flight log.

Takeaway: Drones may look like disposable tech, but they are operational aircraft—and they demand the same respect as any other platform.

April 11: Audio Monitoring and Recording

"The quieter you become, the more you can hear." —Ram Dass

Audio is different. Good video can show what happened; good audio tells you what was said. But distance is the enemy. A camera's onboard microphone is for ambient sound and close-range reference—not surveillance from a parking lot. If you count on a camera to capture distant conversation, you'll capture wind, your partner's conversation, radio traffic, and a lot of useless noise.

Audio laws vary. Some states and countries require **all-party consent** for recording private conversations; others allow **one-party consent**. Recording in areas where individuals have a reasonable expectation of privacy is usually illegal. I learned this from an old PI and later confirmed it in a formal video-surveillance course: proximity matters, and so does choosing the right equipment.

Knockout (Dead-Short) Plug: If you don't want ambient capture from your camcorder—or if local law requires no audio on overt recordings—install a knockout or dead-short plug to disable the onboard microphone. It's a simple hardware change that prevents accidental audio capture and avoids creating legal exposure when you only meant to collect video.

Shotgun Microphones: For directional, long-range pickup, shotgun mics are the workhorse. They attenuate sound from the sides and rear and focus on what's in front of the barrel. Mounted on a camcorder, boom, or temporary pole, they can extend useful pickup range substantially—but they are not magic. Wind, distance, and obstructions still reduce clarity. Use windshields and position the mic as close to the subject as possible, while remaining as unobtrusive as possible.

Handheld & Lavalier Microphones: For interviews and controlled contacts, handheld microphones and lavaliers are your go-to. Handhelds give you presence and control during live interviews; lavalier (lapel) mics are ideal for discreet, high-quality audio capture during consensual interviews or recorded statements. Wired lavs are more reliable than cheap wireless units; if you must use wireless, buy reputable systems that support encrypted channels and stable frequencies.

Takeaway: Choose microphones that match the mission, test them in real conditions, and silence any onboard audio when it creates risk.

April 12: Tracking Devices

"Everything that can be automated will be automated." —Robert Cannon

Tracking technology has changed the investigative landscape. GPS, Bluetooth, and cellular-based devices can provide real-time location data, once limited to law enforcement with warrants and expensive equipment. But as these tools have become cheaper and more common, so have the legal pitfalls that come with them. Consider using trackers to supplement your investigation. There are generally three types of tracking devices:

- **GPS Trackers:** The most widely used. These transmit positional data via satellite or cellular networks and can log or live-stream a target's movements. Used correctly, they are powerful tools for surveillance continuity, stolen-property recovery, or fleet management.
- **Bluetooth & RF Tags:** Compact and affordable. Products like AirTags or Tiles use proximity pings through nearby phones to approximate location. They are useful for tracking equipment, luggage, or marked assets—*not people*. Their short range and reliance on public networks make them unreliable and often unethical for covert use.
- **Cellular Beacons:** Advanced trackers that combine GPS and GSM triangulation. Some transmitters support two-way communication or long-range data bursts, but they require robust battery management and often require subscription services.

A tracker doesn't replace observation; it supplements it. Devices can fail, lose signal, or get discovered. Magnets weaken, batteries die, and subjects notice tampering. A well-placed GPS can save hours of tail work, but an unplanned signal loss at a critical moment can compromise the entire operation. Always confirm data accuracy with direct observation when possible.

In the United States, law enforcement must generally obtain a warrant to install a GPS device on a private vehicle (see *United States v. Jones*, 2012). Private investigators can face civil and criminal exposure under federal and state privacy and stalking statutes if they deploy trackers without the owner's consent or legitimate interest. Tracking a vehicle you don't own, lease, or have written consent to monitor is a fast way to lose your license—and possibly your freedom. Internationally, laws vary even more. Some countries classify GPS tracking as electronic surveillance requiring judicial approval. Always check your local statutes and document *who owns the property* and *who authorized the placement.*

Takeaway: Before you place a tracker, know the ownership, the jurisdiction, and your authority. Tracking devices can make an investigation more efficient, but they also carry greater legal risks.

April 13: Vehicle Selection

"Everything in life is somewhere else, and you get there in a car." —E.B. White

Your agency's vehicle options may be limited to what is available in the motor pool. If you have a say, especially for surveillance, remember that your vehicle is just as important as your kit. For surveillance, it needs to do three things: disappear, support your operation, and get into the follow quickly. Choose a car that blends into the neighborhood, not one that reflects your personal preferences. Flashy will attract attention; a common one will help you blend in.

- **Color & Type:** Neutral colors—gray, black, white, dark blue—are the safest bets. In suburban zones, a mid-size sedan or crossover blends; downtown, compact sedans and hatchbacks are common. In rural areas, a truck or SUV reads as normal. Avoid modified suspensions, oversized wheels, or aftermarket lights that shout "look at me." A minivan is an all-around excellent option. For bonus points, put in a car seat and sprinkle some crushed Goldfish on the floor. Add some baby toys scattered about, and you will be good to go.
- **Tinted Windows:** About 30–35% tint gives privacy and hides gear in the back. Know the local laws—tint violations lead to stops and exposure. Use tint legally and wisely.
- **Interior & Exterior:** Internally, your car should be organized and nondescript. Remove brand logos or decals that attract attention. Externally, no rooftop racks, business signage, or personalized plates. Subtle license frames are fine; vanity plates are not.
- **Fit Your Environment:** Don't use a sports convertible for winter stakeouts or a beater in an upscale neighborhood. The vehicle must match local patterns—what looks ordinary there should look ordinary when you park it for hours.
- **Vans & Utility Vehicles:** Vans are great for static surveillance and equipment transport, but their size is conspicuous, and people often associate them with surveillance.
- **Short-Term Rentals (Car Apps, Traditional Rental):** Rentals are useful for deniability and are used by criminals and investigators alike for operations. Some platforms flag unusual use; insurers can deny claims for covert operations. Keep rental paperwork and document the legitimate business purpose. Use rentals legally and with documented justification. Car apps like Turo let you cycle through a large pool of vehicles on a budget without owning a fleet.

Takeaway: A good surveillance car disappears. Choose a vehicle that fits the mission and location, not your ego.

April 14: Vehicle PMCS

"The more you sweat in peace, the less you bleed in war." —*General Norman Schwarzkopf*

A broken-down car ends an operation faster than poor tradecraft ever will. Vehicle PMCS is a simple discipline: inspections, basic servicing, and documentation.

Pre-Shift / Daily Checks

- **Tires:** Pressure and visible damage. Low PSI kills fuel economy and handling.
- **Lights:** Head, tail, brake, turn, and interior—replace bulbs before duty.
- **Fluids:** Oil, coolant, brake fluid, and windshield washer levels. No warning lights.
- **Battery:** Clean terminals, secure mount, and firm charge.
- **Fuel:** No less than 1/2 tank, ideally no less than 3/4 tank.

Weekly / Periodic Checks

- **Belts & Hoses:** Look for cracks, bulges, or hardening. Small failures become big ones.
- **Charging & Inverters:** Test your vehicle's power system under load (inverter, USB ports).
- **Mounts & Fasteners:** Inspect camera mounts, suction bases, and dash fixtures for looseness.
- **Spare & Tools:** Verify spare tire pressure, jack, and emergency tools.

Secure the Gear: Loose equipment is a hazard. A sudden stop turns loose batteries, lenses, and other items into projectiles that damage gear and injure occupants. I remember doing convoy operations in Baghdad and cringing about unsecured .50 caliber ammunition cans in Soldiers' vehicles. That could be a death sentence in a vehicle rollover.

Recordkeeping: Keep a maintenance log in the glove box and a mirrored digital file. Documentation protects you administratively and creates a timeline if something goes wrong.

Cleanliness & Visibility: A tidy vehicle is a happy vehicle. Clean windows for better photos; stash visible branding or case paperwork.

Takeaway: PMCS isn't paperwork—it's mission assurance. Sweat in peace, and you will minimize the bleeding when it matters.

April 15: Vehicle Everyday Carry

"Hope is not a strategy. Luck is not a factor. Fear is not an option." —James Cameron

Your vehicle is more than transportation—it's your mobile base of operations. The right everyday carry (EDC) setup in the car keeps you more functional, safer, and more self-reliant. A well-equipped vehicle lets you operate for hours without support, adapt to changing weather and environmental conditions, and allows you to handle minor emergencies without calling for help.

Purposeful Packing: Think of your vehicle EDC as an extension of your investigative kit—not a dumping ground for random tools. Everything you keep should support observation, communication, evidence collection, or safety. Weight and space matter; clutter slows you down and draws attention.

Tools & Recovery Gear: A compact jump starter, air compressor, tire plug kit, multi-tool, adjustable wrench, and duct tape can keep you in the field. Include a tire pressure gauge and a folding shovel for rural operations. These small items turn delays into minor inconveniences instead of mission failure.

Evidence & Documentation: Store a small lockbox or Pelican-style case for evidence and other sensitive items. Keep tamper-evident bags, tags, and nitrile gloves. A notebook, clipboard, and pens—simple but essential—let you document times, locations, and statements even when tech fails.

Navigation & Communications: GPS and phone apps are useful, but they are no substitute for printed maps. Keep a paper road atlas, a compass, and a spare penlight. Radios or alternate comms can bridge dead zones when cell coverage drops. Never rely on a single device for situational awareness.

Comfort & Sustainment: Water bottles, non-perishable snacks, sunscreen, and weather-appropriate clothing live in the trunk. A basic trauma or first-aid kit with tourniquet, gloves, and gauze should be easy to reach. Keep a headlamp and flashlight with fresh batteries. Cold-weather gear or a rain poncho can keep you operational when others pack it in.

Administrative Essentials: Carry some cash, change for meters, spare documents, and business cards. Store copies of registration, insurance, and rental agreements in a labeled envelope.

Takeaway: Build your vehicle EDC loadout deliberately, maintain it regularly, and remember: hope is not a strategy.

April 16: Waterborne Operations (Part 1)

"Calm seas never made a skilled sailor." —President Franklin D. Roosevelt

Most investigators forget that boats and other watercraft are a legitimate investigative option—especially if you work in a region with abundant waterways. I have used them multiple times in private investigations to think outside the box. Your agency may not have a budget for a dedicated boat, but boat rentals exist, much like car rentals. Used properly, a vessel lets you conduct surveillance the same way you would from a car—and it opens new angles that are impossible from shore.

Operating on or around the water changes everything. Boats introduce motion, reflection, noise, and weather, complicating even simple investigative tasks. Platform selection comes down to choosing the vessel to match the mission, not speed or pride. They include:

- **Small boats (RIBs, jon boats):** Quick, maneuverable, and useful for short-range ops; limited payload and range.
- **Mid-size craft (center console, cabin cruiser):** Better stability, more gear capacity, and comfortable for multi-hour details.
- **Large vessels:** Good for extended operations and equipment transport, but require trained crews and coordination.

Safety & PMCS: Water does not forgive neglect. Life jackets for everyone, a pre-launch PMCS (bilge pumps, fuel, batteries, navigation lights, radios, flares), and a visible float plan are mandatory. Keep a throw bag, first-aid kit, and signaling devices within reach. Weather and tides change quickly—plan alternate exit routes and recovery points.

Comms & Navigation: VHF marine radios are standard for ship-to-ship and ship-to-shore communications. Test them before leaving the dock. Use GPS, handheld compasses, and paper charts as redundancy—cellular coverage on open water is unreliable. Log launch and recovery points, waypoint tracks, operator names, and any anomalies.

Operational Considerations: Use weatherproof housings or dry bags for cameras and electronics. Motion compensation (gimbals) and polarizing filters reduce blur and glare. Remember that sound carries over water—keep conversation volumes low during surveillance. Having a pilot operate the boat while the investigator does investigative work (i.e., surveillance videography) is a sound operating method.

Takeaway: Remember that boats and other maritime vehicles remain an investigative option. Identify operational needs and get to work.

April 17: Waterborne Operations (Part 2)

"Smooth seas do not make skillful sailors." —African Proverb

Continuing from yesterday's theme, you should also endeavor to understand legal requirements, logistics, and environmental responsibility.

Jurisdiction & Permissions: Water blurs legal boundaries. Jurisdiction can shift between municipal police, state agencies, port authorities, and national services. Before you launch, confirm who controls the body of water you intend to use and secure permission when required. Document every point of coordination—who you spoke with, when, and what authority was granted. That documentation protects the operation administratively and prevents diplomatic or legal complications later.

Logistics & Rentals: If your agency lacks its own craft, boat rentals, or dockside operators can be a viable option. Treat a rented boat like a rented car: document contracts, insurance, and purpose. Rentals offer flexibility and deniability, but read the terms carefully—some operators and insurers prohibit surveillance or law-enforcement use. Use rentals legally, with clear justification, and keep all paperwork organized and accessible.

Environmental Responsibility: We all have a responsibility to the planet we live on. Look no further than the Great Pacific Garbage Patch to see a live example of what not to do to our waterways. Prevent fuel spills, secure trash, and avoid contaminating the water. Environmental violations can end an operation and lead to fines or criminal exposure. Plan for waste control, fuel management, and secure storage of anything that could leak or pollute. Responsible operations preserve both reputation and future access to those environments.

Key Points:

- **Confirm authority:** Identify which agency controls the water and obtain permission.
- **Document coordination:** Record names, times, and written approvals.
- **Treat rentals like assets:** Contracts and insurance must be accurate and current.
- **Review terms:** Some providers restrict surveillance activities.
- **Protect the environment:** Fuel, trash, and contamination risks are operational hazards.

Takeaway: Boats extend your reach—but they also extend your responsibility. Know the laws, logistics, and your environmental responsibilities.

April 18: Bags and Cases

"With only one bag, you can change your outfit completely." —Sonia Rykiel

I love bags. I probably have too many bags. They all exist to serve an operational purpose—whether it's a military operation, protective detail, carrying items for EDC, going to a waterpark, or an investigation. Always consider weight and the human tendency to fill the bag to the brim. When choosing bags for undercover or surveillance work, avoid MOLLE webbing, Velcro, morale patches, tactical company labels/logos, or camouflage. Urban camouflage means being as nondescript as possible. You may have heard of Gray Man Theory; practice it with bags.

Your bag strategy should start with mission definition. Is this a day-long static surveillance? A mobility-heavy tail? A court-appearance evidence run? Each mission calls for a different carry solution. If it's a two-hour job, don't carry a two-day ruck. Some basic bag types:

- **Sling/Shoulder Bags:** Quick access, low profile, good for short durations and urban surveillance.
- **Messenger Bags:** Useful for paperwork, tablets, and files—but they scream "courier" if over-branded. Use plain colors and minimal straps.
- **Backpacks-** Best for longer ops and equipment loads. Choose low-profile packs without external webbing; internal organizers are ideal.
- **Hard Cases (Pelican-style):** For evidence, electronics, or items that must survive water, drops, and rough handling. Lockable, crushproof, and easy to inventory.
- **Go-Bags / Range Bags:** Pre-packed mission kits ready to deploy. Defined purpose, sealed, and rechecked before use.

Organization & Modular Thinking: Organize by *function*, not by device. Create pouches for Power, Audio, Optics, Tools, and Evidence. Color-code or label internally so you can find items by feel. Use cable wraps, zip pouches for SD cards, and transparent sleeves for quick ID. Keep a "last checked" tag or date label on each pouch to track battery and firmware status.

Materials, Durability & Weatherproofing: Choose water-resistant fabrics and reinforced stitching. For harsh conditions, use dry bags or waterproof inserts. Hard cases are best for fragile or evidentiary gear requiring lockable protection.

Takeaway: A good bag isn't just storage—it's strategy. The right bag fades into the background, allowing the investigator to focus on accomplishing the mission.

April 19: Light as a Force Multiplier

"Light is less something you see directly and more something by which you see all other things." —Richard Rohr

Across the pond, they call it a *torch*. Call it what you like—just don't make your phone the torch. A standalone flashlight is a must for every investigator. Phones are useful, but when you make a single device responsible for illumination, navigation, note-taking, recording, and communication, you have built a fragile system. The more you task your phone, the more single-point failures you create.

I once attended a low-light/no-light course where the instructor demonstrated this perfectly. He told us to walk in a circle—easy enough. Then weave in and out of each other. Then recite the alphabet, flap our arms, and look left and right. By the time we were doing all of it, people were colliding. The point: multitasking under stress destroys awareness. Relying on a phone to be your light, map, and recorder is the same mistake.

A flashlight is more than illumination—it's control. It can disorient a threat, locate a missing person, signal across distance, break glass (in models with porcelain tips), or serve as a last-resort defensive tool. It's a simple piece of gear that multiplies your capability when used correctly. Some basics:

- **Lumens ≠ usefulness:** High lumen counts look impressive, but beam type matters more. Spot beams reach far; flood beams give area awareness. However, strive for at least 1,000 lumens—3,000+ is optimal.
- **Modes & control:** Low/medium/high, with adjustable ramping output. A strobe has a place for signaling or disorientation. Tail switches give quick activation; side switches allow mode cycling—choose what fits your workflow.
- **Power system:** Rechargeable 18650 or 21700 cells are the workhorses— high capacity, replaceable, and rechargeable. AA models are fine for redundancy. Label batteries, rotate them, and keep spares charged and in a labeled pouch.
- **Durability & waterproofing:** Look for IPX7/IPX8 ratings and hardened glass or polycarbonate lenses. Metal bodies resist drops; knurling improves grip when wet.
- **Hands-free options:** Headlamps for close work (evidence collection, repairs), or small mounts when needed. Keep a belt-mounted holster for quick access.

Takeaway: Light is a force multiplier. It reveals, protects, and controls space. Carry a reliable flashlight, train with it, and make it an extension of your hands.

April 20: Lasers and IR (Part One)

"The eye sees only what the mind is prepared to comprehend." —Henri Bergson

Lasers and infrared (IR) illumination tools expand what the human eye—and standard optics—can do. They are the invisible edge in modern surveillance and tactical work. Yet many investigators don't realize these tools are available to them, or how vital they can be in the field. When used responsibly, lasers and IR systems help you observe, mark, and document without giving away your position.

Lasers: Visible and Invisible: Visible lasers have practical uses—marking targets, directing attention during an operation, or orienting team members in the field. Green lasers offer maximum visibility under daylight; red lasers are more discreet in low-light environments. Never point a laser at a person's eyes, aircraft, or vehicles—even brief exposure can cause permanent injury or legal issues. IR lasers operate in wavelengths invisible to the naked eye but visible through night-vision or infrared-capable cameras. They allow investigators to "paint" a target, mark a location, or coordinate silently with others using compatible equipment. However, anyone else with night-vision capability—including hostile surveillance—can also see your beam. Use IR responsibly and only in environments where it is safe to do so.

Infrared Illumination: IR illuminators act like flashlights for night-vision systems, creating invisible light that enhances imagery through NV or IR-sensitive lenses. They are critical for nighttime surveillance or low-signature operations when overt lighting would compromise your position. Pairing an IR illuminator with a capable camera or drone sensor turns darkness into usable detail, but remember: IR light reflects off glass and water differently. Test your setup before relying on it operationally. Fog, dust, and rain also scatter IR beams, reducing range and clarity—always plan for weather.

Laser and IR tips:

- **Covert Surveillance:** IR illuminators paired with hidden cameras enable nighttime documentation without visible light.
- **Search and Recovery:** Visible lasers can mark zones or signal to responders during wide-area searches.
- **Evidence Marking:** Low-power lasers assist in defining reference points for photos or mapping.
- **Navigation and Safety:** Small IR strobes or beacons can mark paths, vehicles, or personnel with minimal signature.

Takeaway: Lasers and IR are powerful tools that should be added to an investigator's toolkit. You should explore different employment options.

April 21: Lasers and IR (Part 2)

Any sufficiently advanced technology is equivalent to magic.—Arthur C. Clarke

Carrying on from yesterday, let us explore the legal, safety, and training aspects of laser and infrared (IR) use.

Legal and Safety Considerations: Laser misuse carries serious penalties. In the United States, pointing any laser at an aircraft is a federal crime. Even small handheld pointers can fall under import or safety restrictions in certain jurisdictions. Always document the purpose, environment, and operational use of any laser or IR device—good recordkeeping is part of professional risk management.

For private investigators, confirm that your use of IR or night-vision gear complies with local privacy and surveillance statutes. Some states and countries classify these systems as electronic surveillance tools. Using them without proper authority or consent can expose you and your client to civil or criminal liability. When in doubt, research first or consult counsel before deployment.

Training and Familiarity: Operate lasers and IR gear with the same seriousness you would apply to a weapon system. Understand range limits, beam divergence, safety classifications, and backscatter effects. Practice the operation in daylight before deploying at night—if you can't run it confidently under ideal conditions, you should not trust it under stress. Rehearse your workflow until it's automatic.

Key Points:

- **Visible lasers:** Use for marking and orientation—never at people or aircraft.
- **IR lasers and illuminators:** Enhance night-vision capability, but can also reveal your position.
- **Environmental effects:** Fog, glass, and rain distort IR performance.
- **Train before use:** Master the gear before relying on it operationally.

Takeaway: Lasers and IR illumination tools extend what you can see, record, and control—but only if you know they exist and how to use them safely.

April 22: Navigation

"If you do not change direction, you may end up where you are heading." —*Lao Tzu*

Some of you might not remember or even know life before GPS. Before satellites guided us turn-by-turn, we had these things called *maps*. They were made of paper, folded in impossible ways, and didn't yell in a British accent at you when you missed a turn. I learned physical surveillance using map books with colored indicator stickers to mark key intersections, meeting sites, and choke points. No voice prompts—just judgment and coordination.

Maps are part of your redundancy strategy. Electronics fail, batteries die, and signals drop at the worst possible time. A printed map doesn't lose reception or overheat on the dashboard. Every investigator should keep a map book or regional atlas in their vehicle, especially if they work in rural areas or frequently cross jurisdictions.

I remember early in the Iraq War when our commander's vehicle had a tech meltdown mid-convoy. GPS down. We pulled into a secure position, and he calmly broke out his map and compass, plotted bearings, and got us back to the Forward Operating Base like it was 1944. That moment reminded me: no matter how advanced your gear, the fundamentals still matter. Never hate on the trusty map and compass.

GPS, smartphone maps, and dedicated trackers are phenomenal—when they work. Use them, but don't worship them. Mark waypoints, save coordinates, and cache offline maps for areas without service. Apps like Google Maps, OnX, and Gaia GPS can store terrain data locally. Just remember: phones are power-hungry and fragile. Keep a charger, inverter, and printed backup.

Learn how to orient a map, identify terrain features, and shoot a bearing with a compass. Even in urban areas, analog navigation keeps you situationally aware in a way that screens can't. It forces you to think spatially—where your target could go, not just where the arrow points.

Takeaway: Technology may guide you, but it shouldn't own you. The best investigators can navigate with satellites or sunlight.

April 23: Medical Gear

"When seconds count, help is minutes away." —EMS Proverb

When you think of an investigator, medical supplies probably are not the first thing that comes to mind. But they should be. Since the Columbine High School massacre in 1999, law enforcement, security, and even corporate protection professionals have learned one truth: medical self-reliance saves lives. Every investigator—public or private—should understand basic emergency medicine and carry gear that can make the difference.

Time is everything in medicine. Ambulances get caught in traffic in places like NYC, with patients dying while waiting for them. Overseas, I have worked in regions where "ambulance" was a theoretical term—response time measured in hours, if at all. When you are injured in a developing country, a rural U.S. town, or an urban metropolis, you are the first responder, whether you're ready or not. In those moments, time isn't money; it's life. At a minimum, you need two categories of medical supplies: **trauma gear** for life-threatening injuries and **first-aid gear** for everything else. Trauma gear includes:

- **Tourniquet (CAT or SOF-T):** Life-saving for arterial bleeding; one per limb if possible.
- **Pressure Bandage:** Israeli or ACE-style for wound compression.
- **Hemostatic Agent:** Celox or QuikClot gauze for deep wound packing.
- **Chest Seals:** Vented seals for penetrating chest injuries; prevent lung collapse.
- **Decompression Needle:** (Advanced) relieves pressure from a tension pneumothorax.
- **Abdominal Bandage:** Large, absorbent pad for abdominal or junctional wounds.
- **Nasopharyngeal Airway (with lube):** Keeps the airway open in unconscious casualties.
- **Casualty Card:** Document injuries and treatments for handoff to EMS.
- **Hypothermia Survival Wrap:** Prevents shock and maintains body heat.
- **Medical Tape:** Secures dressings and equipment under stress.
- **Nitrile Gloves:** Protect you and your patient.
- **Trauma Shears:** Cut clothing and gear quickly.
- **Marker:** Record the time a tourniquet was applied—it matters in the ER.

First-aid supplies for minor incidents include, but are not limited to: adhesive bandages, gauze, antiseptic wipes, splints, elastic wraps, burn gel, over-the-counter meds (pain relievers, allergy tablets, electrolytes, personal prescriptions), eye wash, tweezers, and a CPR mask.

Takeaway: You can't investigate if you're bleeding out. Medical gear isn't optional. Learn it, carry it, and be ready to use it.

April 24: Firearms

"With great power comes great responsibility." —Widely attributed to Uncle Ben of Spider-Man

A firearm is a tool with a single, irreversible function: it can take a life. For investigators, especially in the private sector, a gun is not required to do the job. Many great investigations are conducted without one. If you are required to or choose to carry, you accept enormous moral, legal, and operational responsibility. That choice demands training beyond the minimum, serious maintenance, and constant self-assessment.

Do not kid yourself: skipping practice and paperwork is not saving money—it's creating liability. My first Regional Security Officer once told me about an agent who bragged she had not qualified in 12 years. That is not a flex. It's a hazard. Today, we will focus on the handgun as the tool most readily available to you (even if you can carry a rifle or shotgun). Your agency may require you to carry a specific model or give you wide latitude on selection, but here are some selection basics:

- **Fit and ergonomics:** A pistol must seat naturally in your hand. If your thumb, grip, and trigger finger don't align without fighting the gun, it's the wrong choice.
- **Size & concealability:** Balance between comfort, concealment, and controllability. Larger frames are easier to shoot; smaller frames conceal better.
- **Caliber & terminal performance:** Choose ammunition that balances stopping power, recoil management, and over-penetration risk given your environment (urban vs. rural).
- **Capacity & reloads:** Higher magazine capacity reduces reloads, but weight and concealment tradeoffs exist. Practice reloads until fast and safe.
- **Reliability & simplicity:** Mechanical simplicity and proven reliability beat novelty. Service history and a strong aftermarket (holsters, parts, mags) matter.
- **Holsters & retention:** Don't skimp on buying a quality holster. A good holster positions the gun for a smooth, consistent draw and, depending on its retention, can help prevent it from being taken.

Know local, state, and federal laws on use of force, defensive display, retention of evidence, and required notifications. Private and public investigators can face civil suits and criminal charges for bad decisions; ignorance is not a defense. Maintain insurance, licensing, and clear written policies about when and how force may be used. If you work internationally, understand host-nation restrictions—some countries forbid private carriage of firearms entirely.

Takeaway: If you carry a firearm, you must be better than average: better trained, better maintained, and better documented.

April 25: Evidence Collection and Storage

"Facts are stubborn things." —*John Adams*

Evidence is the language of a case. Collect it carelessly, and the story unravels; collect it correctly, and you build an argument that survives scrutiny. To collect it properly, ensure you have the necessary items available. You may benefit from a full-time evidence response team where you only handle ancillary collection matters, or you may work solo, relying on an independent lab. Evidence items needed for an investigator are broken down into physical and digital evidence:

Physical Evidence:

- **Evidence bags:** Various sizes with tamper-evident seals.
- **Breathable paper bags:** For biological materials; plastic promotes mold and degrades DNA.
- **Rigid, lockable hard cases:** For fragile items and electronics.
- **Evidence tags:** Pre-printed chain-of-custody forms and permanent markers.
- **Swabs and sterile containers:** For biological and trace collection; secure with evidence tape.
- **Small tools:** Tweezers, disposable scalpels, nitrile gloves, and clean-room wipes.
- **Paper binders or folders:** For photographed logs, scene notes, and witness forms.
- **Caution tape:** For marking or securing a scene.

Digital Evidence:

- **Faraday bags:** Prevent remote access, tracking, or data wipes on mobile or wireless devices.
- **Tamper-evident USB drives or SSDs:** For transporting digital evidence securely.
- **Anti-static bags:** For storing hard drives, circuit boards, or small electronics.
- **Digital evidence tags and logs:** Record serial numbers, device states, and collection details.
- **Cable kit:** USB-C, micro-USB, Lightning, and proprietary connectors for multiple devices.
- **Power banks:** Keep devices powered during imaging or documentation.
- **Digital evidence lockbox:** Padded, lockable transport case for items.

Like most items in the investigative space, ready-made kits are available to consolidate these essentials. As the old saying goes, *it's better to have and not need than to need and not have*—especially if you're the first on scene.

Takeaway: Evidence is only as strong as the care you give it. Prepare now.

April 26: Technology Integration

"The danger of technology is that it seduces you into thinking you're smarter than you are." —Brian Eno

Technology has revolutionized investigation—but it's also created new points of failure. Every new app, sensor, or system you adopt should serve your process, not complicate it. Investigators often confuse *having* technology with *using* it effectively. A poorly integrated system is just a digital paperweight.

Your goal isn't to chase every gadget; it's to build a networked, reliable, and redundant workflow that supports your investigative objectives. Always follow your agency's rules on what you are allowed to use during the course of an investigation.

Core Technology Categories:

- **Case Management Software:** Tools like CaseGuard, i-Sight, or proprietary platforms manage leads, reports, and digital evidence. Use what your organization supports—and encrypt data at rest and in transit.
- **Digital Note-Taking:** Tablets or digital pens (e.g., ReMarkable, iPad with stylus) reduce paperwork and sync securely with your cloud systems. Keep hard-copy backups for critical documents.
- **Cloud Integration:** Platforms like Google Workspace or Microsoft 365 can centralize reports, imagery, and communications—but always control access permissions and version tracking.
- **Mobile Device Management (MDM):** Protect agency or corporate devices from data leaks. Implement PIN locks, remote-wipe capability, and encryption.
- **AI & Automation Tools:** Transcription, facial recognition, and geolocation AI can accelerate analysis—but they are only as good as the operator's judgment. Always validate automated results.

Always assume every electronic device will fail. Download maps, store backup case files locally, and maintain printed contact rosters. Power outages and network failures don't stop investigations—but they stop unprepared investigators.

Untrained users are the biggest vulnerability. Every new tool requires familiarization, certification, and a written policy. Update firmware and software routinely to patch security gaps—and document who did it, when, and why.

Takeaway: Integrate systems intentionally, train thoroughly, and always plan for the day your battery dies. The best investigators use technology as a tool—not a crutch.

April 27: Everyday Carry Essentials

"Always Be Prepared." —Boy Scouts Motto

Everyday Carry—or EDC—means different things to different people. For some, it's a lifestyle; for professionals, it's a principle. I consider it a fundamental part of preparation. The EDC mindset grew out of self-reliance—the belief that you should be able to function independently and effectively, even when separated from your gear, your team, or your vehicle. You don't have to go overboard, but you do need the essentials on you.

At a minimum, I usually carry a sling bag that includes my badge and credentials (when not in my pocket), cash (in both local and U.S. currency), a lighter, compact medical kit, spare magazine, shoelace restraints, multitool, knife, police sash, tactical pen, flashlight, and notepad. Each item has a specific role: survival, communication, self-defense, or documentation.

Principles of EDC:

- **Preparedness:** You're responsible for your own readiness. Your gear should reflect your ability to handle the unexpected—injury, power outages, confrontations, or delays.
- **Practicality:** Carry what you will actually use. Tools that stay in a drawer are useless in a crisis.
- **Adaptability:** Environments change. Change with them.
- **Consistency:** Don't constantly rotate gear. Familiarity builds efficiency—know exactly where everything is by touch alone.
- **Compliance:** Always follow local and organizational laws and regulations on what you can carry, especially when traveling internationally.

Lessons Learned (Common EDC Mistakes)

- **Overloading:** If it's too heavy to carry all day, it will end up left behind.
- **Noncompliance:** Carrying restricted gear across borders or into courthouses can get you detained—or worse.
- **No Familiarization:** Gear you don't train with is dead weight. Know how to deploy, use, and re-stow every item.

Your EDC will evolve based on your mission and environment. A domestic case in downtown Washington, D.C., isn't the same as a field assignment in Damascus. Culture, law, and threat level all dictate what is reasonable to carry—and how you carry it.

Takeaway: EDC isn't about being tactical—it's about being ready. Be adaptable, be discreet, and above all, *always* be *prepared.*

April 28: Gear You Don't Need

"Perfection is achieved not when there is nothing more to add, but when there is nothing left to take away." —Antoine de Saint-Exupéry

Every investigator loves toys. I am a self-professed gear nerd and thoroughly enjoy testing new equipment. But gear can make you heavier, slower, and more legally exposed. The professional's kit gets lighter with experience. The amateur's kit gets heavier with compensatory gadgets. Know the difference.

Start with a principle: every item you carry must earn its place. If you can't state exactly when and how you will use it on a case, it doesn't belong in your EDC or vehicle kit.

Carrying an exotic piece of equipment you don't train with is worse than carrying nothing at all—it creates false confidence and maintenance problems. At my first field office, an investigator attended a breaching course and convinced leadership to buy a one-off breaching tool. It subsequently sat in the storage room for years, never used. Some common items you don't need:

- **Badges for private investigators:** A badge invites confusion with law enforcement. You only need your credential card. The legal and ethical risk of even accidental impersonation isn't worth the image.
- **Oversized optics for urban surveillance:** Massive telephotos and huge tripods scream "observer." In many neighborhoods, they draw unwanted attention. I once watched a local cop in a surveillance course get tripped up by a security guard while setting up an oversized tripod—every second spent explaining himself was a second not observing the subject.
- **Every "tactical" gadget on the shelf:** My favorites are the ones labeled *"operator approved"* because one operator used it once or was sent a free sample. Function beats style. Choose low-profile gear that works when you need it to.
- **High-end exotic tech you can't service:** Thermal, LIDAR, or military-grade gear is expensive and often service-dependent. If you can't maintain, calibrate, or legally justify it, don't buy it.
- **One-trick devices:** Tools that solve a rare problem—like a specialty lock pick you never practice—add liability and clutter. Train for common contingencies; outsource rare techniques to specialists.
- **Too many spares:** You need redundancy, not duplication. Five extra batteries make sense; five identical cameras do not. Rotate supplies, not devices.
- **Unvetted "cheap" tech:** Low-cost, no-name devices often have poor optics, insecure firmware, and short lifespans. Buy reputable, serviceable brands for anything mission-critical.

Takeaway: Every piece of gear should have a purpose. The professional investigator knows that effectiveness comes from preparation and proficiency.

April 29: Procurement

"I not only use all the brains that I have, but all that I can borrow" —*President Woodrow Wilson*

Despite what some in the U.S. Government may tell you, every time is *not* the first time. Systems exist for procurement, funding, and interagency resource sharing—you just have to learn how to navigate them. The tools and equipment you need for an investigation have likely been sourced, bought, or borrowed by someone before you. The key is knowing how to ask.

1. **Understand the System:** Every organization has a procurement mechanism—some faster, some slower. In government, it might be a contracting or logistics office; in the private sector, it's often an administrative or purchasing manager. Learn who handles requisitions and what formats they require.

2. **The Funding Chain:** Budget cycles control everything. Most agencies and companies operate on fiscal years, and funds may already be earmarked before you even identify your need. Get ahead by planning early—ideally during pre-budget or end-of-year cycles when funds need to be spent. Build a list of justifiable "must-haves" and "critical upgrades" to present when funding windows open. If you work in the U.S. federal government, you have an uphill battle—because saving money isn't rewarded. You're encouraged to spend it by the end of the fiscal year or lose it. That is how you end up with a 65-inch TV in the breakroom and 5,000 extra rolls of single-ply toilet paper. Ask me how I know...

3. **Borrowing and Shared Resources:** You don't always need to own the gear. Interagency or intra-departmental borrowing can be the most efficient route. In government, many offices maintain shared equipment pools—cameras, drones, GPS trackers, even vehicles. Build relationships with neighboring units or partner agencies. In the private sector, consider partnerships with other firms or vendors that can loan or lease specialized tools for short-term use. Borrowing also lets you test equipment before committing budget dollars.

4. **Writing a Proposal or Justification:** A well-written proposal turns "no budget" into "find the money." Keep it short but factual:

   - Define the mission gap and explain how the requested gear fills it.
   - Quantify the impact—time saved, efficiency gained, risk reduced.
   - Estimate cost and life cycle (purchase, maintenance, training).
   - Reference past or peer use—"this system is fielded by XYZ office" adds legitimacy.

Takeaway: The best investigators don't just collect evidence; they collect resources.

April 30: Inventory and Equipment Life Cycle

"The more inventory a company has, the less likely they will have what they need."
—Taiichi Ohno

Inventory management isn't glamorous, but it's the quiet backbone of professionalism. Whether you're in a government agency or a one-person investigative firm, knowing what you have, where it is, and what condition it's in separates the organized professional from the chaotic amateur.

Know What You Have: Start with a master list—cameras, lenses, radios, laptops, batteries, cases, cables, even the small stuff like flash drives and SD cards. Whether digital or written, this list should track:

- **Item description and serial number**
- **Location or custodian**
- **Date of purchase**
- **Condition and service history**

Maintenance and Rotation: Every piece of gear has a lifespan. Batteries degrade, lenses fog up, seals dry out, and firmware becomes outdated. Rotate perishable items, update software regularly, and conduct quarterly or semiannual inspections. Label expiration dates with visible markers. Treat your equipment like an aircraft crew chief treats a plane—the mission doesn't start until the gear passes inspection. If your agency or company uses pooled gear, sign it in and out like evidence. Accountability prevents loss, ensures fair access, and protects your reputation when something goes missing.

Replacement Planning and Budgeting: Don't wait for catastrophic failure to justify a replacement. Plan for it. Create a lifecycle schedule—typically three to five years for electronics, two for batteries, and annual replacement for consumables like gloves, tapes, or first-aid items. Build replacement costs into your yearly budget proposal so you're not scrambling at fiscal year-end. Borrowing gear is fine for surge operations, but owning reliable, well-maintained equipment for your core tasks is an investment—not a luxury.

Disposal and Security: When equipment reaches the end of its life, dispose of it responsibly. Destroy or sanitize drives, memory cards, and devices before discarding or donating them. Wipe serials from public records if policy allows. Old tech often still holds case data, sensitive information, and PII (personally identifiable information). I have dug through many trash cans as part of red-team operations, and I can confirm that this step is often overlooked.

Takeaway: Inventory isn't paperwork—it's preparedness. A well-managed equipment life cycle ensures you always have what you need, when you need it.

May: The Art of Surveillance

"Our society is not one of spectacle but of surveillance." —Michel Foucault

Surveillance is one of the backbones of investigative tradecraft. It's the quiet, patient discipline that separates real investigators from everyone else. Technology, training, and timing all help—but the foundation is observation: noticing what others miss and translating it into actionable intelligence. Whether you're watching a person, a facility, or a digital footprint, surveillance is how you confirm what's real and uncover what's hidden.

Movies sell the highlight reel—long lenses, car chases, and rooftop stakeouts. The truth is quieter and far more deliberate: hours of boredom punctuated by seconds of movement. Good surveillance is built on patience, documentation, and judgment. You're not collecting movie clips; you're collecting patterns. Over time, you learn that surveillance is less about *seeing* and more about *understanding what you see.*

I first learned surveillance inside the U.S. Intelligence Community—long days, longer nights, and relentless repetition of the fundamentals. Later, I adapted those same principles to private investigation, where budgets are smaller, and operations are often solo. Federal law enforcement added structure and accountability, reinforcing the same truth across every setting: every form of surveillance—physical, technical, aerial, or digital—lives or dies by preparation and attention to detail. If you don't prepare, you fail before you start.

This month, we will explore both the fundamentals and advanced applications across the full spectrum:

- **Physical Surveillance:** The cornerstone—vehicle tails, foot movement, coordination, and clean handoffs.
- **Technical Surveillance:** Cameras, trackers, covert tools. Technology should extend your awareness, not replace it.
- **Fixed and Static Operations:** How to establish observation posts, blend into environments, and endure long hours without compromise.
- **Aerial Surveillance:** Drones and other airborne assets—integrating overhead feeds safely and lawfully.
- **Multi-Modal Surveillance:** Using movement—cars, trains, boats, and planes—as cover and opportunity.
- **Documentation and Reporting:** Time stamps, logs, metadata—creating defensible, court-ready evidence.
- **Disguise and Deception:** Subtle, natural adjustments to posture, attire, and behavior to avoid detection.
- **Team Tactics:** Communication, control, and deconfliction—the hallmarks of a professional team.

- **Singleton Tactics:** If you can do it with a team, you can do it alone—planning, self-cover, and autonomy.
- **Counter-Surveillance:** Recognizing when you have been made, disengaging safely, and preserving operational integrity.

Surveillance is like room-clearing—there are a thousand ways to do it, and no single one is perfect. What matters is sound tradecraft and disciplined execution. The best camera on earth can't fix poor positioning, sloppy timing, or bad judgment. Whether you're tailing a subject through downtown traffic, watching a facility from a parked van, or managing a drone feed over open terrain, the principles remain the same: prepare, observe, adapt, and record.

This month, we will use the same foundational, team-based system I was taught—refined through years of operations, courses, and mistakes to bring you lessons learned. Some of this may be new to you. Some may be a refresher. Some you might not be authorized to use, but can still learn from. Either way, every lesson has value.

Let's get down to business.

May 1: Surveillance Tradecraft & Mindset

"You must do the thing you think you cannot do" —Eleanor Roosevelt

Surveillance isn't glamorous. It's a long game of patience, precision, and professionalism. Every investigator wants the Hollywood version—the fast car, the hidden camera, the dramatic reveal. The reality? Surveillance is 90% preparation, 9% boredom, and 1% chaos. If you can master the first two, you will survive the last.

When I teach surveillance for Lynx, I always start with mindset—not movement, not gear. As you can see, a proper mindset is at the cornerstone of professional investigation. In every form of surveillance—vehicular, foot, or technical—the same core principles apply:

1. **Patience over adrenaline:** Most investigators get burned because they rush. They swing wide on turns, stare too long, or close the distance too early. Patience buys you invisibility. The best operators are unremarkable—steady, predictable, and invisible to pattern analysis.
2. **Repetition over novelty:** The reason elite teams drill call-signs, four-part calls, and comms so often is that under pressure, your brain defaults to muscle memory. If you only practice once a month, you're gambling. If you rehearse daily, you're building instinct.
3. **Preparation over gear:** Fancy optics and covert cams mean nothing if your batteries die, your timestamps are off, or your team hasn't rehearsed a pickup plan. Preparation is your real force multiplier.
4. **Discipline over excitement:** Surveillance can feel painfully slow. You will spend hours watching a door that never opens. But the one time it does, you had better be ready. Professionals don't need stimulation—they need results.

Mindset in Action: Before any operation, visualize your posture and presence. Whether you're in a car, on foot, or sitting in a café, the goal is to blend. Ask yourself:

- What's my cover story if someone challenges me?
- What's my line of sight, and what gives me away?
- Can I stay here for three hours without drawing attention?

Then, don't forget to think through the "boring" details—vehicle fuel, comms check, restroom access, food, and water. You don't want to be the one to compromise the operation by being unprepared.

Takeaway: Surveillance begins in the mind, not the vehicle. Patience, repetition, and preparation are the true tradecraft.

May 2: Roles & Responsibilities

"The first rule of management is delegation. Don't try and do everything yourself because you can't." —Anthea Turner

Every successful surveillance operation is built on structure. Chaos starts where roles blur. If everyone is "just following," no one is leading. The best surveillance teams—whether law enforcement task forces or private-sector operators—run like clockwork because everyone knows their lane, communicates clearly, and respects the chain of command. Surveillance is a team sport, or like team chess. Each piece has a purpose: one moves, one covers, one coordinates. If everyone plays their position, the picture stays intact.

- **Case Manager (C/M): The Architect.** Referred to by different names in different organizations, but we at Lynx call it the Case Manager. The Case Manager owns the mission—planning, execution, and accountability. They develop the operational concept, assign roles, coordinate logistics, and oversee communication discipline. When the radio goes quiet, and decisions need to be made, the Case Manager's word is law.
- **Navigator: The Brain in Motion.** The Navigator sits in the passenger seat and runs the operation on the move. They keep the team oriented, track subject position, and ensure comms flow cleanly between call-signs. Think of them as air-traffic control on wheels. A strong Navigator balances calm narration with rapid analysis. They are the connective tissue of the follow.
- **Driver: The Steady Hand.** The Driver's first job isn't to chase—it's to drive safely and discreetly. The best drivers aren't the fastest; they are the smoothest. They maintain spacing, obey traffic laws, and make subtle adjustments to avoid pattern recognition. A careless driver draws attention faster than any taillight out. Professionalism behind the wheel keeps the whole team alive.
- **Trigger / Pick-Up: The Bridge.** The Trigger monitors transitions—the moments when a subject stops, exits, or changes modes of transportation. They act as the eyes when the lead can't move. The Trigger's discipline during "extended stays" prevents most losses.

Take a moment to review the positions above and see how they match your team. You potentially have identical or closely matching roles and responsibilities, or need a framework to establish your own team. Ensure everyone on your team knows the scope of their responsibilities.

Takeaway: A surveillance team succeeds through clarity of role and discipline of execution. Know your lane, trust your teammates, and communicate like lives—or cases—depend on it.

May 3: Call-Signs & Team Structure

"Precision and clarity in communication are not luxuries—they're leadership." —
Secretary James Mattis

Clear communication saves operations. Confused communication kills them. In surveillance, your voice on the radio is both your fingerprint and your lifeline. When a team operates with disciplined call-signs and structure, they sound like a single mind with many eyes. When they don't, they sound like panic. Every professional surveillance outfit—whether law enforcement or the private sector—uses **call signs** to maintain security, brevity, and accountability. Call-signs exist for three reasons:

1. **Security:** They protect real identities and reduce the risk of exposure if comms are intercepted or overheard.
2. **Clarity:** They prevent multiple voices from overlapping.
3. **Structure:** They remind everyone of their lane and role.

Vehicular Callsigns: Most surveillance teams assign phonetic identifiers—**Alpha, Bravo, Charlie, Delta, Echo**—to each vehicle in the convoy. The *Lead* holds primary control of the subject; *Back-Up* follows and stands ready to take over; *Additional* vehicles form the outer ring or "surveillance box."

Example: "That's Alpha, Subject straight at Fleming Street heading north on Columbus Drive."

Foot Callsigns: Foot operators use **first names or nicknames**—never "Jack." Distinct names make comms intuitive while still maintaining cover.

Example: "That's Chris, Subject straight at Panda Express heading toward the Apple Store."

Supplemental Callsigns: To enhance the picture, teams can add supplemental data, such as lane number, side of the street, or walking speed.

Example: "That's Alpha, Subject heading north on Cooper Street, lane two, speed 50–55."

I can tell you what happens if you don't have clear call signs. Chaos. When my colleague first arrived at his overseas embassy assignment, personnel were allowed to choose any radio call sign they wanted. This resulted in wild fluctuations and no one immediately knowing who was who on the radio. He quickly changed the call signs to a uniform system so personnel could easily be identified.

Takeaway: Call-signs and structure are the backbone of clean surveillance communication. The smoother your comms, the sharper your team.

May 4: The Four-Part Call

"If you just communicate, you can get by. But if you communicate skillfully, you can work miracles." —Jim Rohn

Radio discipline is the bloodstream of any surveillance operation. Without it, information clogs, confusion spreads, and control collapses. Plain talk on the radio only gets you so far. The **Four-Part Call** exists to keep everyone in sync—especially when the subject moves quickly or unpredictably. When done correctly, the Four-Part Call is short, factual, and calm. It's not a conversation. At Lynx, we drill this format into every operator until it becomes muscle memory.

The Four Parts:

1. **Who you are:** Identify your call-sign first. It immediately orients the team. "That's Alpha…"
2. **Subject:** Always specify the subject next. It eliminates ambiguity if multiple elements are in motion. "…Subject…"
3. **What the Subject is doing:** Movement, direction, or behavior—this is the action piece. "…gone right at Fleming Street…"
4. **Where the Subject is going:** Direction or landmark—end the call with clarity. "…heading west on Franklin Avenue."

Put it together: "That's Alpha, Subject gone right at Fleming Street heading west on Franklin Avenue."

The best way to build muscle memory is repetition. Set up a drill with your team where one person acts as the subject vehicle, and others practice live Four-Part Calls as you follow through traffic. Rotate roles until everyone can deliver clear, timed transmissions under stress. This is what we used to do in the Intelligence Community, and it worked like a charm. If you're solo, record yourself making calls during routine drives. You can practice with any vehicle you are following. Play recordings back and critique your calls. It's tedious—but it will save you in real operations. Develop your calling system or use ours for seamless radio communications.

Takeaway: The Four-Part Call is the heartbeat of surveillance communication. Identify yourself, describe the subject, report the action, and pinpoint the location.

May 5: Supplemental Calls

"Accuracy builds credibility." —Jim Rohn

Once you have mastered the Four-Part Call, the next level is refinement. The basics keep the team aligned. Supplemental Calls keep them precise. Supplemental Calls provide the small, sharp details that fill in the gaps—the extra seconds of clarity that keep a team invisible. When the operation moves quickly, or the subject behaves unpredictably, those few extra words can make the difference between a seamless handoff and total confusion.

When to Use a Supplemental Call: A Supplemental Call should *enhance* clarity, not overload the net. It's about precision, not chatter. You use them when additional information makes the follow easier for the team. Examples:

- **Lane Usage (Vehicular):** "That's Alpha, Subject straight at Cooper Street heading north, lane two."
- **Speed (Vehicular or Foot):** "Speed 45–50." / "Walking briskly."
- **Side of the Street (Foot):** "Subject on the left side, eastbound."
- **Landmarks (Both):** "Passing Walgreens on the right." / "Subject entering Starbucks."

Used together, these paint a live picture of what's happening without requiring anyone to ask, "Where are they now?" Full example: "That's Alpha, Subject straight at Cooper Street heading north, lane two, speed 40–45."

Now take a look at that. A lot of great information in a clear, concise package (once your team learns the language or the language of your radio call). You know who is making the call, where the subject is located, where they are going, which lane they are in, and how fast they are going. A navigator can now plan ahead for their next movement. Combine that with the known pattern of life information, and you can head to a location, already be at it before the subject arrives, and the subject will never know.

Takeaway: Supplemental Calls are the fine-tuning of professional surveillance communication. Keep them short, accurate, and actionable.

May 6: Route Planning

"The more you know yourself and your enemy, the less you will fear the result of a hundred battles." —Sun Tzu

Every successful surveillance follow starts days before the first ignition key turns. Mission planning and reconnaissance build the foundation for control—because when the subject starts moving, it's too late to start thinking. You must train your surveillance operators to treat surveillance prep like a pre-mission checklist.

Route Planning: Route planning is where intelligence meets instinct. It's not just about mapping—it's about thinking like the subject. Identify primary, secondary, and bailout (emergency) routes for both the subject and your team. Know choke points, construction zones, and alternate exits. A solid plan includes:

- **Start and end points:** Where surveillance begins and where it should end.
- **Known patterns:** Commute routes, frequent stops, timing habits.
- **Decision points:** Intersections or areas where the subject could diverge.
- **Safe zones:** Predefined areas to stage, rotate, or regroup unseen.

Mark your "bumper" points—predetermined locations where a new lead vehicle can position ahead of the subject. This is how professional teams stay one move ahead.

Route Reconnaissance (Recon) and Area Familiarization (Fam): Recon and Area Fam are your insurance policy. They give you the lay of the land before you need to operate in it. Walk it. Drive it. Time it. Study it. The goal is to turn unknowns into knowns. During recon and area fam, note:

- **Camera coverage:** Traffic cams, business CCTV, and parking lot systems.
- **Lighting conditions:** Day vs. night visibility.
- **Public access points:** Entrances, exits, and open lots.
- **Local rhythms:** When deliveries, rush hour, and pedestrian flow occur.

Recon and area fam also prevent exposure. If your team knows the layout of the operating area, they won't make awkward U-turns or unnecessary stops that draw attention.

Takeaway: The more you plan, the less you react—and the less you react, the less you're seen.

May 7: Safety Briefs & Legal Checkpoints

"Take calculated risks. That is quite different from being rash." —*General George S. Patton*

No matter how skilled your team is, a surveillance operation can unravel in seconds if safety and legality are not built into the plan. Professional surveillance isn't just about following the subject—it's about protecting your team, your client, and your integrity. If you are not incorporating safety briefs before your surveillance operation, start.

The Pre-Operation Safety Brief: Before every surveillance assignment—whether solo or as part of a team—conduct a safety brief. It doesn't have to be long, but it must be consistent. Cover the following essentials:

1. **Objective:** What are we doing today?
2. **Area Hazards:** Traffic, school zones, restricted property, or known criminal areas.
3. **Equipment Check:** Radios charged, vehicles fueled, optics tested, GPS devices functioning.
4. **Emergency Protocols:** What's the plan if there's an accident, confrontation, or loss of visual?
5. **Legal Boundaries:** What can and cannot be recorded, entered, or tracked?

In law enforcement, this is usually standard procedure. In private work, it's often neglected—until something goes wrong. A five-minute safety brief can prevent a lawsuit, a police report, or worse. Additionally:

- **Expectation of Privacy:** You can observe anything visible from a public space, but you cannot trespass or record audio where privacy is expected.
- **Recording Laws:** Understand one-party vs. all-party consent states. Know the law in your state and the surrounding states if a follow takes you out of state or out of the country.
- **Tracking Devices:** GPS tracking requires either owner consent or lawful authority. Never attach a tracker without explicit written permission.
- **Use of Force:** What do you do if a subject confronts you and says, "why are you following me?" Then gets hostile about it?
- **Firearms or Defensive Tools:** Only if licensed, authorized, and justified by a credible threat assessment.

Takeaway: Safety and legality are non-negotiable. Every operation must begin with a safety brief and a clear understanding of the law.

May 8: Additional Considerations (Part One)

"An ounce of prevention is worth a pound of cure." —Benjamin Franklin

Surveillance is essentially won or lost in the small choices you make between roll-out and return. You can run a flawless route, have perfect call-sign discipline, and still be compromised by predictable behavior, a single careless gesture, or a missed environmental cue. These "additional considerations" are the small but critical trades that separate seasoned teams from amateurs.

Disguise (Blend, Don't Become a Caricature): Disguise is not about costume theater. It's about fitting the environment. If you stand out, you're being watched. Change elements like your hat, jacket, glasses, or hair—and make it look natural. Avoid over-the-top props; they attract attention. For foot ops, rotate clothing layers to match the weather and local norms. Keep clothing change kits in other surveillance vehicles for quick swaps when needed.

Never Point (and Don't Touch Your Ear!): Pointing is an unconscious human signal—and in surveillance, it screams "look here." Never point at the subject, their vehicle, or their door. Use peripheral cues instead: a subtle nod, an eye shift, or a pre-arranged hand signal. Touching your ear is another giveaway, immortalized in every spy movie. It's unnecessary and draws attention to you instantly. It's the same as when someone subconsciously touches a concealed weapon or equipment—people notice.

51% Rule (Blend In): There is a principle known as the 51% Rule. It simply means to fit in with your environment. If 51% of cars are parked nose-in, don't park nose-out. If 51% of people in a bar are wearing shorts and flip-flops, don't walk in wearing a three-piece suit. Subjects running countersurveillance deliberately create contrast points to expose tails. If you blend even slightly better than the average person around you, you disappear into statistical noise.

3-Turn Rule (Follow, But Not Too Long): The 3-Turn Rule applies to following a subject. You should avoid making more than three operational turns with them—on foot or in a vehicle—without rotating positions or changing tactics. Sometimes this is unavoidable during solo work, but understand: every additional turn increases your exposure. Most people today are distracted by their phones, but complacency remains the enemy. The longer you stay in the subject's shadow, the greater the odds of being burned.

Takeaway: Blend into your surroundings, avoid broadcast signals (like pointing or ear-touching), and follow smart—never long. The operator who disappears into the environment wins every time.

May 9: Additional Considerations (Part Two)

"If you put good people in bad systems, you get bad results." —Stephen Covey

In keeping with yesterday's theme, there are a few more critical habits that set professionals apart from amateurs. These considerations focus on awareness, time management, and communication discipline—the systems that keep good people from making bad mistakes.

Manage Time on Subject (Don't Burn Resources or People): Every subject has a "clock" you must respect. Long tails increase exposure and fatigue—both of which erode judgment. Set clear thresholds before you start: maximum continuous visual (usually three to four hours), required breaks, and rotation schedules. Use relays and pre-planned pickup points to swap operators seamlessly. If a subject's routine is static (for example, working in a restaurant for eight hours), adapt your strategy—conduct area familiarization, use observation posts, or schedule timed intercepts instead of constant tailing.

Pay Attention to Your Surroundings (Baseline Everything First): Always establish the baseline normal for your environment—people, vehicles, lighting, and noise. A new delivery truck, a different traffic pattern, or a shifted bus route is not random—it's data. When you arrive, take ten seconds to baseline the area: who parks where, how fast traffic moves, and what the noise levels are. When something breaks that pattern, note it. That anomaly may indicate a lead—or your exposure. Either way, document it.

Be Aware of Call-Sign Locations (Mental Map of Your Team): Know not just who Alpha is, but *where* Alpha is relative to you—right now. Maintain a mental or physical map of call-sign spacing and roles. This prevents overlap, maintains control, and allows quick takeovers without radio chaos. A good Case Manager should constantly track and adjust positions using a whiteboard, map, or tablet interface. Modern surveillance software can assist, but a grease pencil on laminated maps still works when batteries die.

All Calls Are Made on the Subject's Location, Not Yours: One of the most common rookie mistakes is reporting your own position instead of the subject's. Radio calls paint a picture for the rest of the team—describe what *the subject* is doing and *where they are.* If you need to communicate a personal issue—flat tire, lost visual, law enforcement contact—state your call-sign, then clearly note your situation: "That's Bravo—vehicle issue, pausing at 1200 block Main Street, pulling to curb."

May 10: Control Calls (Part One)

"In the absence of clear orders, communicate." —*U.S. Marine Corps Adage*

Radio calls don't just report what's happening—they control the operation. The most efficient surveillance teams sound quiet, not because they're silent, but because every transmission has a purpose. When used properly, short control calls instantly identify who owns the subject, who's supporting, and who's locking down the area. You may have heard of various terms like the "eye, "eyeball", numerical terms, etc., but at Lynx, we use **Lead**, **Back-Up**, and **Trigger**. Today, let's discuss Lead and Back-up.

Lead (Positive Control of the Subject): The **Lead** vehicle or operator is the one with direct, positive visual on the subject and the authority to guide team actions. When you make this call, you're telling everyone else that you are in control and that further movement will flow from you. Example: "That's Alpha, Lead."

This call is made **once** when control is established—never "moving to Lead," "taking Lead," or any variation. The moment you're Lead, you already have control. Clear and simple.

If you lose sight or must break off, announce the transition: "That's Alpha, loss of visual, Bravo—take Lead." "Copy, Bravo, Lead."

Back-Up (Next in the Follow): The **Back-Up** vehicle or operator is immediately behind or near the Lead, ready to assume control if the subject changes direction, stops suddenly, or the Lead must break off. Back-Up acts as a safety net for continuity. Example: "That's Delta, Back-Up."

Like the Lead call, this is made **once** when positions are established. The Lead acknowledges the call to confirm structure: "Copy, Back-Up." This acknowledgment closes the loop and prevents overlap. Everyone on the net now knows who's covering the subject and who's ready to take over.

Takeaway: Control calls like Lead and Back-Up aren't just words; they are structure in clean radio communications. Whether you use them or something similar, mark these positions as essential for controlling a subject.

May 11: Control Calls (Part Two)

"The great enemy of communication, we find, is the illusion of it." —*William H. Whyte*

In keeping with our theme on control calls, let's look at the Trigger position and put the whole package together.

Trigger (Stationary Control / Extended Stay): A **Trigger** call means the operator has the subject in view but cannot move—usually during an extended stay such as a stop at a residence, office, or café. When Trigger is declared, the team immediately adjusts around it. Example: "That's Bravo, Trigger."

This tells other call signs to **control the area**, not the subject. The Lead and Back-Up reposition, extending coverage or "setting the box." If the subject leaves, the Trigger announces movement: "That's Bravo, Subject on the move, eastbound on Cooper Street."

The Trigger is the anchor point during static periods. Everyone else orbits around it. The Trigger does not initially move with the Subject when they resume moving. This is because if someone is looking for surveillance, they are expecting a vehicle or person to move with them.

Putting It Together (Example Sequence):

1. **Initial Movement:**

    - "That's Alpha, Lead."
    - "That's Bravo, Back-Up."
    - "Copy, Back-Up."

2. **Subject Stops:**

    - "That's Bravo, Trigger."
    - (Lead and Back-Up set area containment.)

3. **Subject Moves Again:**

    - "That's Bravo, Subject on the move, eastbound Main."
    "That's Alpha, Lead."

Takeaway: The Trigger is the third leg of the triangle, equally as important as Lead and Back-Up. Together, when all the pieces work in unison, identification by the subject drops exponentially.

May 12: Control Calls (Part Three)

"Language is the roadmap of a culture. It tells you where its people come from and where they are going." —Rita Mae Brown

Surveillance has its own language. Every tight surveillance team develops its own internal dialect—its shorthand, slang, and coded rhythm. At Lynx, we use a structured but flexible set of **control terms**. Call it what it is: the language of surveillance. Here are a few terms:

Heat State (Low, Medium, High): Your Heat State describes how "hot" the follow feels—how much attention you think you have drawn. It's subjective but important. Rookies always think their heat state is hotter than it is. Example: "That's Alpha, Heat State medium."

Take Over: A planned, deliberate transfer of control from one call sign to another. Example: "That's Alpha, request Take Over." "That's Bravo, copy, Take Over."

Off: indicates a call-sign no longer has visual control and is relinquishing responsibility. Example: "That's Alpha, Off."

The Box: is a coordinated procedure for controlling the area around a stationary or slow-moving subject. Example: "That's Bravo, Subject stopped—set the Box."

Checking Drills: When the subject is lost, Checking Drills notify all vehicles to perform controlled searches to re-establish visual. "That's Alpha, Subject Unsighted. Start Checking Drills."

Approaching: Used to warn of hazards, sensitive locations, or potential contact points. Keeps the team aware of upcoming changes. Example: "That's Alpha, Approaching school zone."

Wait: When an operator needs a clear net—whether to verify information or coordinate action—this single word silences all radio traffic. Example: "That's Bravo, Wait..." *(Brief pause, then continues.)* "...Subject just stopped abruptly, stand by." Use it sparingly and with authority.

Bumper: A predetermined location used as a reference or coordination point. Teams can "bumper ahead" to set up a transition or prepare for a likely turn. Example: "That's Charlie, bumping ahead to the Shell station."

Takeaway: Surveillance teams speak their own language. Every team can create its own lingo—but at Lynx, this is the language we speak.

May 13: Operational Discipline

"Discipline is the bridge between goals and accomplishment." —Jim Rohn

Surveillance operations live or die by discipline. Here is a list of pro tips to remember, whether you are a solo operator or part of a 24-person team:

Obey All Traffic Laws: Nothing kills an operation faster than flashing lights in your rearview mirror. I once watched law enforcement officers get pulled over by other officers in an unmarked follow—a surreal moment of professional embarrassment. Always obey the speed limit, use turn signals, and stop completely at stop signs. You can't tail someone from the back seat of a patrol car, explaining why you "had to keep up."

No Loitering Near Sensitive Locations: Never loiter near children's play areas, schools, banks, or jewelry stores. These are high-alert environments where any unusual behavior draws attention. It doesn't matter how legitimate your operation is—if you look suspicious near kids, cash, or valuables, you're one phone call away from a patrol car pulling up behind you.

Don't Be Suspicious (Yes, That's a Thing): "Suspicious" isn't what you're doing—it's how it looks to others. Avoid repetitive head movements, binoculars out the window, or long stares that make bystanders uncomfortable. Engage in believable activities: phone use, reading, eating, or waiting. Act as if you belong. Are you in a grocery store? Grab a cart. At a stadium? Grab a foam finger and an overpriced hot dog.

If Confronted by Staff or Law Enforcement: If a property manager, security officer, or civilian staff member confronts you, you can play dumb. Pretend you're lost, waiting for someone, or just using the parking lot for a call. Keep it calm and short. But if it's law enforcement, identify yourself—especially if you're a licensed private investigator. Keep your license handy, be respectful, and avoid acting defensive. Law enforcement doesn't like surprises, and "playing dumb" with a badge in your pocket only makes things worse.

If You Witness Illegal Activity—Have a Plan: You must decide in advance how to handle illegal activity: report it immediately, record it discreetly, or disengage entirely, based on your legal authority and client direction. One of our private investigators was once doing a workers' compensation case. He followed the subject to an empty parking lot, where the subject got out and argued with his wife. He then smacked her. All on video. The investigator called the police, showed them the video, and the subject was taken into custody. Karma.

Takeaway: Operational discipline isn't glamorous, but it's what keeps you out of jail, off the evening news, and in business.

May 14: Radio Etiquette

"The most valuable of all talents is that of never using two words when one will do."
—President Thomas Jefferson

In surveillance, your radio is your lifeline—and your biggest liability if used poorly. Every operator can key a mic; few can communicate cleanly under pressure. Radio discipline is about how, when, and why you say something.

Before any surveillance mission, conduct radio checks with every operator. It's the simplest habit and the one most often skipped. Confirm everyone can transmit and receive clearly, that you're all on the correct channel, and that backup communication methods are in place—cell, encrypted chat, or satellite if working remotely. A pro tip we use at Lynx: wrap the base station mic wire under your seat belt. It keeps the radio mic near your lap and prevents you from instinctively bringing it to your face—a dead giveaway that you're on comms. Don't worry, the mic can pick you up, and all it looks like is you having a conversation in the car.

Professional operators don't fill the air with chatter. The radio net is sacred ground. When the subject is moving, seconds count—and unnecessary transmissions cost control. Don't step on another person's call. Wait a second before keying the mic; if someone's talking, let them finish. Keep the net clean—no small talk about last night's game or comments about people passing by. This is not CB radio. Emotional or panicked voices cause confusion and draw attention. Urgency does not require volume. Calm voices get copied; loud ones get clipped.

Good radio etiquette has rhythm and respect. Think before you transmit. Speak clearly, pause between key points, and always identify yourself first. Keep transmissions short. Always begin with your call sign. Don't overuse the mic, and acknowledge when you've received a transmission with a simple "Copy," "Affirmative," or "Stand by." A silent radio doesn't mean confusion—it means discipline.

Always have redundant communication methods and at least one admin channel separate from the operational net. The admin channel is where non-essential traffic, like bathroom breaks, fuel stops, or food stops, belongs. Keeping that chatter off the operational net preserves the team's focus. If you're traveling between regions or states, verify that your radios operate legally and effectively in those areas. Don't assume your UHF or VHF handhelds will work everywhere—test them before mission day.

Takeaway: The quietest radio teams are the most effective. Check your gear before roll-out, and keep the net clean.

May 15: Vehicular Surveillance Fundamentals

"The superior driver uses their brakes as little as possible—not because they drive fast, but because they think ahead." —Stirling Moss

Vehicular surveillance. The Hollywood starlet of investigation. Everyone thinks they can follow a car—until they actually try. In vehicular surveillance, you're not chasing—you're managing space and tempo. The goal is to maintain consistent visual contact while remaining unremarkable to everyone else on the road. That means obeying every traffic law, maintaining a safe distance, and blending into the natural flow of traffic. If you're drawing attention to yourself, you have already failed.

Spacing is everything. New operators tend to follow too close, thinking proximity equals control. It doesn't—it equals detection. Maintain natural distance based on environment: farther in rural or open areas, tighter in urban or congested zones. Your vehicle should never look like it's tethered to the subject. The best operators let others fill the space between them and the target, using traffic as camouflage.

Avoid "mirroring." Don't mimic the subject's lane changes, turns, or braking patterns. Nothing flags surveillance faster than a car that moves at exactly the same time you do. Think every movie ever. Instead, use natural delays—signal late, take a different lane, or even allow a vehicle to cut between you. You can always close the distance when it's safe. Professionals understand that losing sight for a few seconds is better than being made for life.

Whenever possible, pre-plan bailout routes and recovery zones. If you lose the subject, don't panic and start darting through traffic—that's how accidents happen, and suspicions start. Announce "Unsighted" calmly and move to pre-determined choke points and commence checking drills to re-establish visual. Teams that plan recoveries in advance rarely lose subjects for long. By the way, any surveillance operator who tells you they have never lost a subject is lying to you. I once served on a 24-person surveillance team, and at times, we temporarily lost the subject. It is okay. Not having a plan is not okay.

If you're operating alone, discipline becomes everything. Use traffic patterns, red lights, and lane changes to mask your movement. Keep a clean vehicle, stay fueled, and always have contingencies for communication and recording. Solo surveillance isn't glamorous—it's grueling—but when done well, it's the mark of true tradecraft.

Takeaway: Vehicular surveillance is an exercise in patience, distance, and discipline. Master it to be the best investigator you can be.

May 16: The Surveillance Box

"Positioning is strategy made visible." —Al Ries

The surveillance box is one of the most effective tools in vehicular operations. It allows a team to maintain control of a subject during stops, extended stays, or slow movement without looking obvious. When used correctly, the box provides 360-degree awareness while minimizing the risk of exposure. When done poorly, it looks like exactly what it is—a bunch of cars trying to look casual in a parking lot.

Imagine the subject as the center of a square. The Lead holds the front corner, managing visual from the subject's direction of travel. The Back-Up or second vehicle controls the rear corner, ensuring escape routes and exits are covered. Additional operators position themselves at the sides—one offset to the left, one to the right—to catch lateral movement and maintain alternate sightlines. If the subject stops in a parking lot or at a business, these positions create a flexible perimeter of observation without clustering together.

The secret to a good box is discipline with movement. Each operator must maintain cover within natural behavior. If one vehicle shifts, another compensates. No one should look like they are watching the same point of interest. Blend with the environment—park near entrances, loading zones, or other vehicles that make sense for the location.

Communication inside a box is short. The Lead or Case Manager will announce, "That's Alpha, Subject stopped—set the Box." Each vehicle acknowledges with a quick confirmation as it assumes its position. Once set, the radio net should go quiet except for necessary updates: "That's Bravo, Subject entering the north door," or "That's Charlie, maintaining visual from the west lot."

Boxes can expand or collapse depending on subject movement. When the subject starts to leave, the Trigger announces, "Subject on the move," and control transitions smoothly back to the Lead and Back-Up positions, which are fluid in the direction of travel. The rest of the vehicles dissolve the box naturally. The goal is to look like the normal flow of life reasserting itself.

In tight areas or when operating solo, a "micro-box" can still be established using fixed positions or observation points. Park at opposing angles, use reflections in windows, or choose elevated vantage points to maintain coverage without constantly shifting. The principle remains the same: maintain eyes without becoming the scene.

Takeaway: The surveillance box is about patience and positioning. A good box keeps the subject contained without ever making them feel surrounded.

May 17: Control & Take Over Procedures

"Get uncomfortable being uncomfortable." —Alex Toussaint

In surveillance, control isn't about who's closest to the subject—it's about who's calm enough to let go. The art of relinquishing control is one of the hardest skills for new operators to master. Everyone wants to stay Lead. Everyone fears being the one to lose the subject. But professionals know that holding on too long is how operations get burned. Smooth handoffs—called *takeovers*—are the mark of a disciplined team.

Relinquishing control happens for one of three reasons: line of sight is compromised, distance has become unnatural, or a new direction of travel favors another team member's position. It's not a sign of weakness; it's the system working. A team that can transition without panic or ego can maintain visual for hours without detection.

A proper takeover begins with communication. The Lead announces clearly: "That's Alpha, loss of visual—Bravo, take Lead." The incoming vehicle responds, "Copy, Bravo, Lead." Everyone on the net now knows the shift has occurred. There's no confusion, no overlap, no unnecessary chatter. It's that simple. The moment control passes, the previous Lead becomes Back-Up, and the operation continues seamlessly. When done correctly, the subject will have no idea that control ever changed hands.

The Case Manager or Navigator monitors these transitions in real time. They track who has Lead, who's Back-Up, and who's staged for the next takeover. In larger teams, this information is logged for after-action review. The cleaner the transitions, the smoother the overall operation. If you ever listen to a seasoned surveillance team on comms, you will notice they sound calm, minimal, and precise. No one rushes to talk because everyone already knows their place.

Sometimes, takeovers happen during moments of stress—heavy traffic, unexpected turns, or visual breaks. When that happens, clarity becomes everything. Avoid overlapping transmissions. Don't step on each other. One voice at a time. A single, calm radio call is always faster than two people talking over each other in a panic.

If you're running solo, you still need a plan. Use turnouts, parking lots, and choke points to reset your position. You may not have a partner to hand off to, but you can hand control back to yourself through deliberate repositioning. Treat every reset like a micro takeover—you're trading chaos for control.

Takeaway: Relinquishing control is not losing control. It's a professional transition designed to preserve the mission, not your pride.

May 18: Checking Drills

"Success depends upon previous preparation, and without such preparation there is sure to be failure." —Confucius

Every surveillance operator, no matter how skilled, will eventually lose the subject. It's not a matter of *if*—but *when*. Losing visual doesn't mean you have failed; it means the operation has entered a new phase that tests your team's discipline. Enter the checking drill. A checking drill is a systematic, preplanned method for re-establishing visual contact after the subject is lost. It's not an improvisation; it's an operational tool. The goal is to regain control without broadcasting that control was ever lost.

The process starts with a clear, calm call: "That's Alpha, Subject Unsighted—start Checking Drills." That phrase immediately signals every operator to execute their predetermined areas of responsibility. Each vehicle or operator runs their assigned pattern—covering logical exit routes, intersections, and choke points based on the subject's direction of travel. These areas should already be mapped during the mission-planning phase, not made up on the fly.

The team must resist the instinct to rush or cluster. Everyone wants to be the first to reacquire the subject, but haste creates exposure. False reports can cause confusion and waste time. When the subject is reacquired, the call should be concise: "That's Bravo, Subject reacquired eastbound on Parker Street."

Once confirmed, the Case Manager resets the team structure, assigns Lead and Back-Up if they didn't seize the opportunity, and resumes normal follow procedures. Checking drills also reveal how well a team knows their area. Operators who have done solid route recon can predict where the subject is most likely to reappear—gas stations, major intersections, or habitual stops.

If the subject remains unsighted after multiple loops, the Case Manager must decide whether to continue coverage with broader patterns or terminate the operation. There's no shame in ending cleanly; there's risk in dragging it out. On the other hand, if you are a private investigator, a client is paying you to be thorough. Give them every penny's worth and justify your termination.

Solo operators face this test alone. When you lose visual, breathe. Don't start driving erratically or circling blocks. Mark the last known location, note the direction of travel, and begin a slow, deliberate pattern toward the next logical destination. If you can't reestablish visual within a reasonable distance or timeframe, disengage and plan a re-contact later based on pattern-of-life data.

Takeaway: Losing visual isn't failure—it's a test of structure. Run your checking drills, stay calm, and let planning guide recovery.

May 19: Extended Stays & Area Control

"Patience is not the ability to wait, but how you act while you're waiting." —Joyce Meyer

Long-term surveillance operations test endurance, discipline, and mental sharpness. It's one thing to follow a moving subject through traffic—it's another to hold position for hours without drawing attention. Extended stays, or "static periods," require the same precision as movement-based surveillance but with far less stimulation. Professionals call this *area control*: maintaining dominance over a fixed environment without becoming part of it.

Extended stays can happen anywhere—a restaurant, a residence, a workplace, or a parking lot. The key is to recognize that stillness doesn't mean inaction. When the subject stops, your focus shifts from following to containing. The team must adjust coverage to form a perimeter, creating a flexible box that provides continuous eyes without bunching or overlap. Lead and Back-Up transition into observation positions, while outer vehicles maintain standoff distance to control escape routes and alternate exits.

Area control also requires situational awareness. Track the subject's possible exits, note any changes in pedestrian traffic, and monitor for signs of counter-surveillance. If someone lingers too long near your vehicles, observe carefully. They might be curious—or they might be the subject's security.

Extended stays are also where time management separates veterans from rookies. Always plan for sustainability: food, hydration, restroom access, and power management. Don't be the one who compromises the operation because you didn't prepare—especially when it comes to the bathroom. Bottles and buckets... professionals think hours ahead, not minutes.

When the subject resumes movement, the transition back to mobile surveillance must be smooth and quiet. The Trigger announces, "Subject on the move," and control shifts to whichever vehicle picks up Lead. Vehicles dissolve the box naturally and re-enter traffic in sequence. No headlights flashing, no synchronized U-turns, no rush to rejoin. Life continues as if you were never there.

Extended operations also reveal team culture. Good teams stay focused and alert. Sloppy teams start chatting, scrolling through their phones, or relaxing too much—and the death sentence: falling asleep. The best operators remain patient but ready. They know the subject always moves again—and when they do, *carpe diem.*

Takeaway: Extended stays aren't downtime—they are tests of discipline. Control the area, manage fatigue, and keep your presence invisible.

May 20: Multi-Vehicle Coordination

"Individual commitment to a group effort—that is what makes a team work, a company work, a society work, a civilization work." —Vince Lombardi

The bigger the surveillance team, the greater the potential for success—or disaster. Multi-vehicle surveillance gives you flexibility, coverage, and recovery options. But it also adds risk. More vehicles mean more movement, more voices on the radio, and more chances for confusion. Without structure and coordination, what should look like traffic starts to look like a convoy. And nothing screams "surveillance" louder than a convoy.

Multi-vehicle coordination begins long before the first ignition key turns. The Case Manager assigns roles, spacing intervals, and call-signs during the mission brief. Lead and Back-Up handle immediate control, while support vehicles stage strategically in adjacent areas—parallel routes, feeder roads, or known choke points. These outer vehicles are your safety net. They don't follow; they anticipate. Their job is to get ahead, not to join the parade.

Deconfliction is the art of managing those moving pieces without stepping on each other. Every operator must know who is where at all times. The Navigator or Case Manager acts as air traffic control—tracking call-sign positions, spacing, and responsibilities. Good teams maintain a mental or written map of the operation: who is in Lead, who is on deck, and who is staged for relief. If two vehicles end up side by side for more than a few blocks, it's time to fix it. That's not teamwork—it's exposure.

Environmental coordination matters too. Urban operations require tight timing through lights, intersections, and roundabouts. Rural operations depend on visibility management—spreading out enough to avoid pattern recognition. In either environment, anticipation beats reaction. If the subject makes a sudden U-turn and you have no spacing, your team's about to make the evening news.

Deconfliction isn't just about vehicles—it's about minds. Every operator must trust the others to do their job. When people start freelancing—making unauthorized lane changes, taking shortcuts, or breaking formation—you lose the rhythm that makes surveillance invisible. Professionals don't compete for Lead; they protect the mission.

When in doubt, simplify. Reduce the number of vehicles actively engaged, reposition others to standby routes, and keep the air clear. Good teams know when to scale down as much as they know when to surge. The goal isn't to flood the field—it's to blend into it.

Takeaway: More vehicles don't make you better—coordination does.

May 21: Practical Exercises & Dry Runs

"Practice does not make perfect. Only perfect practice makes perfect." —Vince Lombardi

Surveillance isn't mastered in the field—it's refined in training. The best teams don't wait for paid operations to discover their weaknesses; they find them during practice. Dry runs and practical exercises are the difference between a team that reacts to problems and one that anticipates them. If your first time running a multi-vehicle handoff, radio call, or area control setup is during a live case, you're not conducting surveillance—you're gambling.

At Lynx, we treat surveillance practice the same way law enforcement and intelligence teams do: deliberately, repetitively, and under controlled stress. The goal isn't to catch anyone—it's to catch mistakes.

Start small. A simple two-car follow on familiar streets is enough to reveal timing, spacing, and communication gaps. Rotate Lead and Back-Up positions after each run so everyone learns both roles. Debrief immediately after: what worked, what didn't, who stepped on calls, who lost visual first. Real feedback, not ego padding.

Once the basics are smooth, increase complexity. Add simulated subjects who make random turns, stops, or short stops to test reaction time. Practice the "unsighted" call and recovery drills. Build in surprise take-overs and extended stays. You can even simulate heat by assigning a "countersurveillance" driver who tries to detect the team. Nothing teaches humility faster than being spotted by someone who knows what to look for.

Dry runs aren't just for teams. Solo investigators should conduct their own drills, too. Pick random vehicles and practice maintaining discreet contact through traffic without tailgating or looking obvious. Use reflections, side mirrors, and timing to naturally track turns. Record yourself making four-part calls while driving, and later critique clarity, tone, and timing. You will be surprised how much you can improve by simply hearing yourself work.

Finally, track performance. Develop measurable standards: time-on-target, communication errors, reaction to loss of visual, and radio clarity under pressure. Treat training like data collection. Numbers don't lie, and improvement only happens when you can measure it.

Takeaway: Rehearse everything until your reactions become muscle memory. A team that trains together thinks together, and that's what makes them invisible.

May 22: Foot Surveillance Basics & Preparation

"You win battles by knowing the enemy's timing, and using timing better than he does." —Miyamoto Musashi

Foot surveillance is the purest form of observation. It is you, your environment, and your ability to blend. Whether following a subject through an urban business district or a residential neighborhood, the same rules apply: move naturally, think ahead, and disappear into the flow of life.

Step One. Dress for the environment, not for the mission. That means matching the local baseline—if it's a downtown area at lunch hour, look like someone on a break. In a rural town, dress like a local. Avoid "tactical casual" —the camo shirt, 5.11 pants, Oakley sunglasses, and boots combo that screams *law enforcement*. Every environment has its own rhythm; blend with it.

Comfort matters as much as concealment. Footwear is critical. You might end up walking miles, so pick shoes that don't draw attention and won't kill your feet. Avoid squeaky soles and heavy tactical boots. The best operators choose neutral styles—something you could wear at work, a coffee shop, or a public park without standing out. If you can't sprint a block in your shoes, they are wrong for the job.

Next comes gear discipline. Carry only what you can manage discreetly. Bulky backpacks, camera rigs, and overstuffed pockets will betray you long before your subject does. Use sling bags, messenger bags, or casual packs to hold essentials: a notebook, a small camera, a phone, water, and a power bank. If you're using a handheld radio, conceal the earpiece wire inside your clothing, or use a wireless system designed for low-profile work. Every piece of equipment should look like something a normal pedestrian might carry.

Route planning and familiarity are vital. Before the operation, walk the area. Know the choke points, blind corners, and natural observation spots, such as bus stops, storefront windows, or benches. If you're following through multiple zones—commercial, residential, or transit—plan your wardrobe layers so you can adjust appearance naturally as the environment changes.

Spacing and pacing are the heart of foot surveillance. Don't shadow too close, but don't lose sight either. Let the crowd and terrain work for you—cross streets diagonally, pause at windows, or use reflections to maintain visual. When the subject stops, don't freeze. Keep moving past, loop naturally, or find a nearby cover position to reorient.

Takeaway: Foot surveillance isn't about how fast you move—it's about how invisible you appear. Dress like you belong and think ahead.

May 23: Appearance & Recognition Avoidance

"Appear weak when you are strong, and strong when you are weak." —Sun Tzu

In surveillance, your biggest threat isn't being seen—it's being remembered. Most operators who get burned don't stand out in the moment; they stand out in hindsight. The subject recalls that same person or vehicle they saw earlier, that familiar gait, that pair of sunglasses, that odd rhythm that didn't fit. Recognition is your enemy, and avoidance is an art.

Surveillance is about managing perception. You can't be invisible, but you can control what people remember. Start with your appearance. Build a flexible wardrobe with layers that can subtly change your look throughout the day. A jacket on or off, glasses swapped, a hat reversed—small differences create big shifts in memory. It's not disguise; it's variability. The goal isn't to trick anyone—it's to avoid pattern recognition.

Avoid extremes. Dressing too casually can look sloppy; dressing too neatly can look official. Match your surroundings. If you're working around college campuses, look like a student or faculty member. In professional districts, lean business casual. Every location has a baseline, and your appearance should fall just above or below it—never at the edge.

Your idiosyncrasies—those small, unconscious habits—can betray you faster than any wardrobe mistake. Investigators have been burned for walking with the same posture, fiddling with earpieces, or carrying themselves like they're "on mission." Your gait, gestures, and movement rhythm must change as naturally as your clothing. If you always stand with your arms crossed, stop. If you scan too wide or pivot too sharply, soften it. In public, mimic how normal people behave: distracted, casual, imperfect.

Surveillance also demands behavioral camouflage. Normal people check their phones, window shop, and get distracted. Use those behaviors deliberately. Pause to tie a shoe, take a phone call, or study a menu. These aren't delays—they are cover moves.

Recognition avoidance extends to vehicles, too. If you transition from foot to vehicular surveillance, avoid driving the same car repeatedly near the subject's common locations. Change vehicles when possible and use your change of clothes in that vehicle to complete your transformation.

May 24: Static Observation Posts

"The details are not the details. They make the design." —Charles Eames

Static observation posts (OP) give you something priceless in surveillance: time. An OP lets you watch without the constant movement, bring in technical gear, and build a controlled, repeatable observation posture.

Begin with site selection. The best OPs offer natural cover, believable occupancy, and superior sightlines. Apartments above a street, a storefront with a front-facing window, a coffee shop with a corner table, or a connecting room inside a public building are all candidates—each with pros and cons. Ask: Can I see the subject's likely approach and exit paths? Is there a high ground or an elevated window? How many alternative exits exist? What is the line of sight at different times of day? If you're law enforcement, connecting rooms or suites used with proper authority can make excellent covert positions that could lead to immediate arrests once an act is caught on camera.

Think like a tenant. If you rent an apartment or storefront, furnish it to make it look lived-in. Avoid sterile setups that scream "stakeout." Use realistic lighting, plausible furniture, a few books, and normal clutter. But also think logistics: power (inverters and UPS for cameras/recorders), reliable Internet or a data plan for real-time feeds, secure storage for cards and drives, and quiet cooling or ventilation so operators aren't forced to open a window and break concealment.

Eyes get tired. No one can stare for hours without losing acuity. Rotate operators on a predictable cadence, and always have a plan for relief that doesn't look like a parade. Remember: coming and going from an OP is one of the biggest giveaway vectors. Stagger arrivals, park offsite when possible, and use multiple approach routes so a single vehicle or person isn't always associated with the location.

Comfort and endurance are operational requirements, not luxuries. Stock the OP with water, food, sanitary supplies, chargers, power banks, and a basic first-aid kit. Plan restroom access without looking obvious—nearby businesses or staggered vehicle relief work best. Power management matters: use smart charging schedules, low-power record modes when the subject is still, and rotate devices to avoid single-point failures.

Finally, think like a Trigger. Most OPs serve as the stationary eyes while the vehicular team waits in orbit. The OP's job is to hold a picture and hand a clean transition back to the moving team.

Takeaway: A good OP multiplies your capability; a bad OP multiplies your exposure. Choose the site deliberately and blend into the environment.

May 25: Clothing Considerations (Part One)

"Dress is a way of saying who you are without having to speak." —Rachel Zoe

Disguise in surveillance isn't Halloween-level costume work. It's subtle, practical, and reversible. The best disguises aren't memorable—they are ordinary. Use this quick checklist before you start a tail; treat it like a pre-op weapon-check.

Shoes: The one thing most people never change. Pick neutral, comfortable footwear that matches the local baseline: sneakers in a college town, loafers in a business district. Break in shoes before the op. Avoid squeaky soles, light-colored soles that show wear, and tactical boots unless they fit the environment. If you must change shoes mid-op, do so in a restroom, a parked vehicle, or another believable cover.

Headgear: Hats, caps, beanies, visors. Headgear is low-effort, high-impact. Use plain styles and avoid logos or team insignia that stand out. A simple baseball cap, reversed or forward, alters silhouette and perceived age. In sun or rain, a hat is a functional cover, not a theatrical one.

Facial hair: One of the fastest identity shifters. Trim, shave, or faux-fill a beard quickly with a pocket razor or beard filler. I once had a student become the class MVP by shaving mid-follow—small change, big effect. Plan for facial-hair transitions; they work.

Glasses: Non-prescription lenses are cheap and useful. Glasses change perceived age and focus. Tinted lenses must match the environment and time of day—don't wear sunglasses at night. Keep a neutral pair in the vehicle for fast swaps.

Jewelry & Watches: Less is more. Flashy rings, necklaces, or large watches become memory anchors. Remove or replace with plain, generic pieces that fit the locale. In affluent areas, wear subtle, plausible accessories—never anything that reads "statement."

Tattoos & Scars: Decide whether to cover or expose based on the neighborhood. Use sleeves, concealer, or light clothing to hide identifying ink. Conversely, in certain environments (biker bars, for example), a visible tattoo can blend you in—use exposure strategically. Scars are conversation starters; plan whether to neutralize or lean into them.

Takeaway: Disguise is modular and reversible. Master small, believable changes—shoes, headgear, facial hair, glasses, jewelry—and you will alter what people remember without turning yourself into a caricature.

May 26: Clothing Considerations (Part Two)

"The joy of dressing is an art." —John Galliano

Continuing the Checklist: The Garments and Props That Complete a Believable, Flexible Appearance System:

- **Shirts**: Layer. A reversible jacket, a button-down over a tee, or a scarf offers immediate options. Watch logos and brand patches—if it's recognizable, swap it. Small patterns can help hide motion; avoid anything loud that becomes a talking point.
- **Trousers/Skirts**: Same rules as shirts. Fit matters: too tight or too baggy draws attention. Pocket placement is useful for concealment and quick access; avoid cargo overload unless it fits the role. Hem length and cuff style change perceived formality—use that to your advantage.
- **Carried Items**: Endless, and highly effective: backpacks, tote bags, coffee cups, umbrellas, grocery sacks, skateboards, strollers. Choose items that look natural in the environment and rotate them. A grocery bag or a stroller in the right context makes you invisible. Beware visible logos—brands are memorable.
- **Quick-change logistics**: Pack "change kits" in support vehicles: basic clothing swaps, a pocket razor, spare glasses, plain jewelry, and a discreet concealer stick for tattoos or scars. Practice quick changes so they're believable and can be done without attracting attention.
- **Advanced training note**: Nation-states and special operations teams sometimes train operatives in character makeup, prosthetics, professional acting, and the fabrication of full identities. These techniques are expensive, time-consuming, and carry legal and ethical risk. They are unnecessary—and usually inappropriate—for most public or private-investigator work. If you ever consider an advanced disguise, weigh the costs, operational necessity, and legality first.

Takeaway: Clothing and props are tools. Build a modular kit you can mix and match quickly, and practice changing convincingly. The best disguise isn't dramatic—it's believable, repeatable, and unremarkable.

May 27: Singleton Tactics

"The secret of getting ahead is getting started." —Mark Twain

Solo surveillance is where tradecraft gets honest. No teammates to rotate, no backup car to relieve you, and no radio net to cover a slip. Solo work forces discipline: you must be planner, navigator, observer, and safety officer all at once.

Start with an honest assessment. Know the limits of what you can do alone—distance, terrain, weather, and hours on task. Set hard thresholds before you begin: maximum continuous visual, maximum hours without relief, where you will disengage, and a clear recovery plan if the subject enters a high-risk area.

Wardrobe and vehicle selection matter more when you're solo. Your clothing must blend for the entire route; you don't have others changing appearance for you. Your vehicle should be ordinary, clean, and plausible in the target area. Vary parking patterns—don't habitually park nose-in at the same lot. If you must change clothes, do it inside the vehicle using a believable cover (curtains, a restroom, or a parked SUV), not on the curb.

Communications are your lifeline. Even operating alone, maintain a check-in cadence with an off-site contact or case manager. Use discreet, scheduled check-ins rather than constant chatter. Always carry redundant comms—a cell with encrypted messaging, a secondary handset, or a personal locator app. Pre-arrange a fail-safe: miss two check-ins, and your partner initiates a preplanned response.

Solo operators must be obsessive about power and storage. Rotate batteries, carry power banks, and schedule short power-conservation periods when the subject is parked. Label and secure media immediately—date, time, operator initials—because when you're the only one who knows what you recorded, sloppy evidence handling is a career-ender.

Safety rules go up a notch when you're alone. Do not engage or confront. If the subject picks up a tail or a hostile third party appears, disengage early and report. Have preplanned safe zones and quick exit routes—public plazas, gas stations, or well-lit commercial areas where your presence looks normal. Never assume you can handle a violent confrontation solo; call for backup or law enforcement where appropriate. Finally, manage yourself. Fatigue, boredom, and overconfidence are your worst enemies. Change your seat, posture, or vantage point to keep yourself fresh.

Takeaway: Solo surveillance is simple on paper and demanding in practice. Plan limits, protect communications, manage power, and evidence.

May 28: Aerial Surveillance (Planes & Drones)

"There are very few men-and they are the exceptions-who are able to think and feel beyond the present moment." —Carl Von Clausewitz

Aerial surveillance has moved from the exclusive domain of governments to an essential capability for law enforcement, private investigators, corporate security teams, and journalists. What used to require fixed-wing aircraft, large budgets, and air-traffic coordination can now be done with a suitcase-sized drone and a licensed pilot. But make no mistake—altitude doesn't equal immunity. Air operations demand precision, planning, and respect for both physics and law. Consider aerial surveillance another tool in your investigative toolkit.

Manned Platforms: Fixed-Wing & Rotary: Traditional aerial surveillance—helicopters, Cessnas, or contracted air units—offers endurance and perspective. It's ideal for wide-area searches, convoy overwatch, or pattern-of-life analysis. But it's expensive, conspicuous, and heavily regulated. The FAA (in the U.S.) requires flight plans, altimeter compliance, and communication with air traffic control. Even in law enforcement, missions need coordination and justification. Fixed-wing aircraft are best used for long-range overwatch or verifying routes and stops that ground teams can't reach quickly. Rotary platforms (helicopters) offer flexibility for hover and zoom but burn through the budget by the minute.

Unmanned Systems: Drones (sUAS): Drones changed the landscape of aerial surveillance. For private investigators, they provide affordable, flexible observation—but they are also tightly regulated under FAA Part 107 or equivalent local law. To fly legally in the U.S., you must be licensed, maintain a visual line of sight, avoid flying over people, and respect airspace restrictions. Violating these can render evidence inadmissible, result in fines, and compromise your credibility in court. Always check NOTAMs (Notices to Airmen) and local ordinances before flight. From a tactical standpoint, small-UAS surveillance works best when planned in advance and integrated with ground operations. Identify take-off and landing zones, flight altitude, battery duration, and signal reliability.

Operational Integration: The key to aerial success is synchronization, not spectacle. Your drone or aircraft is another "call-sign" on the net—it must communicate like one. The Case Manager coordinates flight windows so the air asset supports, not distracts, ground teams. That might mean a brief overhead sweep before a subject leaves a building, then a handoff to vehicular teams. The worst thing you can do is fly just because you can.

Takeaway: Know your airspace, fly with purpose, synchronize with the ground, and collect responsibly.

May 29: Multimodal Surveillance

"Adaptability is not imitation. It means power of resistance and assimilation." — *Mahatma Gandhi*

Subjects don't limit themselves to one mode of transportation, and neither can you. Real surveillance demands fluidity—the ability to adapt from vehicle to foot, from foot to public transport, and back again without hesitation or exposure. This is called **multimodal surveillance**, and it's one of the highest forms of surveillance tradecraft.

Trains and subways: Once those doors close, you're committed. If your subject boards, you must decide instantly whether to follow. Buy a ticket quickly, keep your distance, and enter through a different car if possible. If you lose sight on board, anticipate exits—know which stops are most likely and position team members in advance. Know that only in the movies do radio communications work flawlessly 26 stories below ground. Have a backup comms plan to communicate with the rest of your team so they can be there ahead of time at the subject's final destination for a seamless pickup.

Buses: Bus routes favor patience. They move slowly and make frequent stops, which helps you recover visual if lost. Pay with exact change or a transit card to avoid lingering at the front. Sit diagonally across from, or one seat back from, your subject; never directly behind your subject.

Bicycles & Scooters: Urban mobility tools like bikes and e-scooters can bridge gaps fast, but they also expose you completely. Wear neutral clothing and a helmet—safety gear doubles as a disguise.

Ride Shares & Taxis: When your subject uses Uber, Lyft, Grab, or a cab, things get tricky because the subject doesn't have to park. If you know the route, get ahead rather than follow.

Watercraft & Ferries: In coastal or river cities, ferries and small boats offer both cover and constraints. Board separately, use different decks, and use binoculars subtly if required. Always check schedules in advance—once the boat departs, you're on it until docking.

Air Travel: Track flight bookings, if available, and have operators in both the departure and arrival areas when possible. If the budget allows, put someone on the plane with the subject. Any investigator should always have an active passport, and if you study the patterns of life, you can get visas in advance.

Takeaway: True surveillance mastery is measured by adaptability, whether you're behind the wheel, on the sidewalk, or standing on a subway platform.

May 30: Covert Wearables

"Whenever there's a camera around, a video or film camera, it's a great deal harder for those in power to bury the story." - Peter Gabriel

Technical tools are only as useful as the operator who wears them. Covert wearables—button cams, glasses cams, lapel mics, body-worn recorders—give you a discrete, first-person record that can confirm timelines, actions, and intent. Wearables should be treated like weapons: respect them, train with them, and never deploy one without knowing the law where you operate.

Choose the right platform for the role. Glasses and button/lapel cameras give a natural POV that's great for foot tails and interviews; shirt-pocket or tie-mounted cams work when you need a lower profile. Wearable body cams (chest or shoulder) give stability and hands-free recording, but can be harder to conceal in casual settings. Match form-factor to environment: a visor cam in bright sun, a low-profile button camera in a café, and a chest mount when you expect movement.

Placement and natural movement matter more than resolution. A perfect 4K image is useless if the lens points at your car dashboard or your shoe. Aim the camera at the line of sight you naturally use—slightly off-center for glasses cams, stitched into a seam for button cams. Practice your posture until the camera's frame looks like the scene you want to capture. Don't fuss with the device in public; adjustments draw attention.

Audio. You have heard me say it, and I will say it again. Know your jurisdiction's recording laws before you hit record. One-party consent states allow you to capture conversations you're a part of; all-party consent states require everyone's permission. Recording private conversations inside residences, dressing rooms, or private offices usually crosses a legal line. When in doubt: don't record audio, get consent in writing, or consult counsel. For legal, tactical audio, use directional lavalier mics hidden under clothing, or tie-clip mics routed discreetly to a recorder in your pocket.

Concealment should be believable. Sew camera mounts into ordinary garments, use generic buttons that don't glint, and avoid novelty items that attract stares. If you're using glasses cams, pick frames that match local styles; if you rely on button cams, match shirt fabric and button size to the locale. I want to say I still have not found a glasses camera I like (too thick). For long ops, carry an emergency change-kit (shirt, cap, spare mount) so you can alter your appearance without frantic fumbling. Train with your kit until it becomes invisible.

Takeaway: Wearables give you the world from a different perspective. Pick the right device and hide it believably while staying within the law.

May 31: Counter-Surveillance Awareness

"In war, the truth is so precious that it must always be attended by a bodyguard of lies." —Sir Winston Churchill

Every investigator will eventually follow a subject who knows—or suspects—they're being watched. Some do it instinctively. Others are trained. Either way, counter-surveillance is one of the most dangerous phases of any operation. A single wrong move can expose the team, end the case, or, in some situations, put you in physical danger. Subjects who practice counter-surveillance often display subtle but deliberate actions. They are not random—they are tests. The trained eye can spot the pattern if you know what to look for. Classic tells include:

- **Stair Stepping:** The subject makes a series of right or left turns through a grid of streets. They're not lost—they're checking to see who's following through each intersection. If you mirror those turns, you fail the test. Anticipate and offset by one street or hand off control before the third turn.
- **Channeling:** The subject chooses narrow or single-lane routes like alleys, tunnels, or low-traffic side streets. This funnels followers into predictable positions and limits their options for breaking contact. Maintain distance, use alternate routes, or let them go. A lost target is recoverable; a burned team is not.
- **Unexplained U-Turns or Rotaries:** These are deliberate probes. A sudden U-turn or repeated loop through a rotary (roundabout) isn't indecision—it's a mirror check. Never U-turn immediately after them. Instead, continue straight, take the next turn, or park naturally and wait. Communicate clearly so other vehicles can cover the movement without bunching.
- **Dead Ends:** A favorite move of the suspicious or trained. The subject enters a dead-end road, parking lot, or cul-de-sac to see who follows. If you do, the test is over, and so is your cover. Stop short, divert naturally, and observe from a distance. This is why area fam is so important. Don't get caught in the trap to begin with.

When You're Called Out: It happens to everyone eventually. Maybe you got boxed in, maybe your mirror turn got noticed, or maybe the subject's friend is calling your plate. The key is to stay calm. Have a cover story ready before every operation: who you are, why you're there, and how to say it without hesitation. Keep it simple—delivery driver, real estate scout, or waiting for someone.

Takeaway: Counter-surveillance is the subject's version of self-defense—and your version of danger. Learn the signs and don't take the bait.

June: The Power of Open-Source Intelligence (OSINT)

"The greatest enemy of knowledge is not ignorance; it is the illusion of knowledge."
—Dr. Stephen Hawking

June moves us from the physical to the digital battlefield—the world of Open-Source Intelligence. OSINT isn't about hacking, shortcuts, or social engineering. It's about knowing where to look, how to think, and when to stop. It's the discipline of turning freely available information into actionable intelligence while respecting privacy, legality, and ethics. Most people think information needs to be classified to be valuable, when in reality, if you know where to look, it may already be available.

Every modern investigator, whether in the public or private sector, uses OSINT—even if they don't call it that. It's the map check before a surveillance run, the property search before a background check, or the digital trail that connects an alias to a real identity. The tools evolve constantly, but the mindset stays the same: find what's public, verify everything, preserve integrity, and protect yourself while doing it.

This month, we will explore the full spectrum of open-source techniques. We will begin by building a clean, compartmentalized OSINT environment—secure browsers, virtual machines, VPNs, and burner accounts that separate your research identity from your real one. We will cover search methodology, Boolean logic, and pivoting techniques that turn one clue into ten. You will receive lessons learned on how to investigate people, companies, and assets through public records, social media, business registries, and geolocation tools. We'll walk through reverse image searches, metadata analysis, AI-assisted reconnaissance, and how to document findings for evidentiary use.

We'll also talk about the darker edges of the craft: how to detect deception online, avoid disinformation traps, and recognize digital breadcrumbs that can expose your investigation or your identity. If there's one truth to remember, it's that the Internet never forgets—so part of being an investigator today is learning how to leave the smallest possible footprint.

Technology changes daily. Platforms rise and fall. But the principles behind good open-source work—accuracy, legality, and verification—never change. OSINT is the art of collecting without touching, revealing without being seen, and finding truth hidden in plain sight. And it's not going anywhere. Life won't wait, so let's get going.

June 1: Setting Up Your OSINT Environment

"He who defends everything defends nothing." —Frederick the Great

Before you collect a single byte of data, secure your environment. You need to realize that every investigator leaves a digital footprint—searches, cookies, IP addresses, and metadata that can betray your operation. Whether you're profiling a fraudster or mapping a cartel's digital network, your first line of defense is operational security (OPSEC). You don't want to compromise a multi-year operation because you were careless in researching a subject.

A professional OSINT setup mimics a sterile lab: isolated, controlled, and repeatable. Build virtual machines or use dedicated hardware separate from your personal computer. Create user accounts unlinked to your real identity. Route your traffic through neutral jurisdictions using VPNs or proxies. Remember: privacy tools are not for paranoia—they are for preservation.

Even experienced government investigators forget that defensive OSINT matters just as much as offensive collection. Investigating from your personal email or main IP is like running surveillance in your own car—convenient but foolish.

The private-sector investigator should use burner emails and VoIP numbers tied to their operational persona, not their real credentials. In law enforcement, use your agency's anonymized systems where possible. Metadata hygiene—scrubbing EXIF data from screenshots or PDFs—prevents adversaries from tracing your work back to you.

Think of it like setting up a surveillance post: clean sightlines, concealed position, escape routes planned. You're about to peer into other people's data; make sure they can't peer back. There are dangerous individuals out there who have set up online traps and early warning systems to avoid capture. Don't give them a head start.

Takeaway: A secure OSINT environment isn't optional—it's your badge and body armor in the digital world.

June 2: Browsers: Your Digital Field Vehicle

"Think different. It's more fun that way." —Steve Jobs

Your browser is to OSINT what your vehicle is to surveillance—it gets you everywhere, but it also leaves tracks. The way you configure and drive it determines whether you complete your mission or compromise yourself. Every investigator needs at least two browsers: one for daily admin work and one strictly for investigations.

- **Firefox: The Investigator's Classic**: Firefox remains a favorite among intelligence and investigative communities for its balance between privacy and functionality. Firefox and I have been together for over 20 years since a friend first introduced it to me. It supports a wide range of security add-ons that extend your control of your OSINT environment. Firefox also supports **multi-account containers**, allowing you to isolate sessions—perfect for managing multiple sock puppet personas (more on these later!).
- **Brave: The Modern Minimalist**: A former CIA targeting officer turned me on to Brave. It is built on Chromium but strips out Google's telemetry. It comes preloaded with tracker blocking, script control, and a clean user interface. It's an excellent middle ground for investigators who want Chrome's speed without its data harvesting. Use Brave for quick reconnaissance when you need to move fast while still valuing privacy.
- **Tor: The Cloaked Approach**: When anonymity is mission-critical—such as researching adversarial networks, dark web leads, or foreign influence operations—Tor provides layered routing through volunteer nodes. It's slower, but highly anonymized. Tor is associated with illegal activity, but using it is not illegal. Tor also isn't magic; it's a tradecraft tool.
- **Chrome & Edge: The Necessary Evils**: Chrome dominates the web, which makes it hard to ignore. Some sites render best on it, and certain OSINT plug-ins only exist in the Chrome ecosystem (the power of a multi-trillion-dollar company, I suppose). If you must use it, run Chrome from within your virtual machine and disable every "convenience" feature Google pushes. Edge has improved, but its telemetry and Microsoft account integration make it unsuitable for anything requiring anonymity.

No matter which platform you use, configure each instance intentionally: Disable autofill and password storage. Block location tracking and camera/mic access by default. Set the browser to clear cookies and history on exit.

Takeaway: Your browser is both microscope and mirror—it reveals the world while reflecting you back into it.

June 3: Virtual Private Networks and Shields

"Companies spend millions on firewalls, encryption, and secure access devices, and it's money wasted because none of these measures address the weakest link—the people who use them." —Kevin Mitnick

If June 1 and 2 were about building your lab, today is about fortifying it. Your OSINT environment is only as strong as the digital armor protecting it. Before you type a single search or open a suspicious PDF, you must harden the workspace against the same tactics you investigate.

Every investigator learns that the internet looks back. While you're hunting for information, bots, trackers, and malicious code are quietly hunting you. The right defensive stack—Virtual Private Networks (VPN), anti-malware, antivirus, and browser discipline—keeps you in control of what you reveal.

VPN: A VPN conceals your IP address and encrypts traffic between your device and the wider web. To your target site, you appear to be somewhere else entirely. Choose paid, no-log providers based in privacy-friendly jurisdictions. Free VPNs monetize data; professionals never trade security for cost savings. Rotate exit nodes periodically to prevent your traffic patterns from becoming a signature.

In the private sector, Proton, Mullvad, and Nord are popular because they pair easily with virtual machines. In the public sector, rely on agency-approved tools and policy-compliant gateways. Either way, treat your VPN connection like an unmarked surveillance car—it's there to keep you unseen, not invincible.

Anti-Malware & Antivirus Defense: Investigators open odd links, screenshots, and compressed files every day—the same activities that compromise most users. Keep a reputable antivirus suite running full-time and set to update automatically. Layer that with a dedicated anti-malware utility such as Malwarebytes or Spybot. Take system snapshots before major cases; if your environment is breached, you can roll back to a clean image in minutes.

Handle downloads in a sandbox or quarantined virtual folder. Assume every file is contaminated until you can prove otherwise. A disciplined "click policy" prevents most infections before software ever needs to intervene.

Takeaway: Protect your data, your tools, and your identity with the same discipline you apply to your evidence.

June 4: Sock Puppets & Operational Personas

"Never trust a computer you can't throw out a window." —Steve Wozniak

Every good investigator learns early: sometimes you don't watch the target—you become the target. In open-source investigations, that means creating sock puppets—fabricated online identities designed for collection, not deception for its own sake. Done correctly, they allow you to observe, interact, and infiltrate without exposing your real identity. Done poorly, they compromise your operation and your credibility.

Creating a believable operational persona is part art, part science. Each one must have a purpose, a backstory, and a limited shelf life. Start with the basics: a name, age range, geography, and interests that make sense for the online community you're entering. Build light but real—not a novel, but enough to survive scrutiny.

A professional OSINT sock puppet should be built slowly. Most investigators get burned by impatience—spinning up a new "person" and joining groups the same day. Real accounts have digital history. Create an email, follow a few innocuous topics, and let the account "age." Even better, automate light, benign activity—joining hobby groups, liking posts, or commenting on public threads—to create behavioral depth. Building a sock puppet is like aging a cover identity—the longer and more naturally it develops, the stronger it becomes. Entire teams within state and corporate structures are dedicated to maintaining networks of false personas—treat that as a warning, not a model.

When constructing social media identities, consider cultural context. A Midwest insurance adjuster posting at 0300 hours local time from a Middle Eastern IP doesn't make sense. Mirror time zones, language patterns, and interests consistent with your cover story. If your persona claims to be in Seattle, don't forget the Mariners and coffee posts. Authenticity comes from believable detail.

Photos are the most dangerous part. Never use stolen profile pictures—that's identity theft, not tradecraft. Generate faces using AI tools like This person does not exist, or use your own images modified beyond recognition with filters or composites. Keep these assets in a separate folder and document the source for chain-of-custody purposes if your work ends up in court.

When an operation ends, retire your persona. Log the account creation date, use history, and any data collected. Then deactivate and delete. Never recycle names or content. A burned puppet is a burned bridge.

June 5: Establishing Operational Email Accounts

"Security is not a product, but a process." —Bruce Schneier

E-mail is the plumbing of modern investigation: everything runs through it—alerts, accounts, confirmations, password resets, receipts, and leaks. If your operational emails are sloppy, your entire OSINT posture is noisy and traceable. Creating and managing operational email accounts is a process—one you must treat like evidence handling: deliberate, auditable, and compartmentalized.

Start with purpose. Every persona, campaign, or tool needs its own operational email. Don't reuse one address across multiple personas or projects. That's called being lazy. Segment by function: alerts@toolbox.example. archive@case123.example outreach@cover.example. The habit prevents cross-contamination if one account is exposed.

Choose providers carefully. Use privacy-centric providers (ProtonMail, Tutanota) for personas that need higher confidentiality; they offer end-to-end encryption and stronger metadata protections. For day-to-day tooling, a standard provider inside your VM is fine—but keep it separate from your real accounts. Avoid "burner" providers that log aggressively or sell data—the free option often costs you later.

Harden every account at creation: use a unique password, enable app-based or hardware 2FA, disable recovery links to personal identities, and populate benign, plausible data consistent with the persona.

Maintain an encrypted ledger recording each account's purpose, creation date, recovery path, and retirement plan. This becomes your operational audit trail.

Key Points:

- One email per persona or purpose.
- Prefer privacy-first providers; use hardware/app 2FA.
- Never reuse credentials; store them in a password manager inside your VM.
- Log metadata and retirement dates in an encrypted ledger.
- Preserve headers (.eml) when you need evidentiary value.

Takeaway: An e-mail address is more than a login; it is part of your footprint. Build it with intentionality.

June 6: Establishing Operational Telephone Numbers

"Arguing that you don't care about the right to privacy because you have nothing to hide is no different than saying you don't care about free speech because you have nothing to say." —Edward Snowden

Phone numbers are a tactile link in OSINT: account verifications, two-factor codes, and SMS trails. They are also highly traceable if mishandled. Treat operational numbers as short-term assets with strict compartmentalization.

Define the role first: verification, outreach, or voice. Then choose your platform. Examples include:

- VOIP (Burner, Google Voice): Flexible but logs metadata.
- Prepaid SIMs: Excellent separation, but are still not fully invisible.
- Privacy-oriented virtual numbers: Best for temporary text-based operations.

Tie each number only to its matching operational email. Never link to your personal identity. Prefer authenticator apps or hardware keys instead of SMS 2FA for anything sensitive. Just remember that phone numbers are tough. I was once in a Dark Web Investigations course, and we were all having a heck of a time incorporating telephone numbers into our sock puppets. Stay the course, you will be fine.

Keep physical SIMs catalogued with provider information, activation date, and the assigned persona. Store inactive SIMs in Faraday pouches and record destruction on retirement.

When calling or texting, script interactions in advance. Consistency in tone and language keeps your cover intact. Rotate numbers regularly to avoid pattern analysis.

Key Points:

- Assign each number to a single persona or function.
- Use TOTP/hardware 2FA instead of SMS for critical accounts.
- Catalog physical SIMs and VOIP lines in your encrypted ledger.
- Retire and destroy SIMs securely.
- Observe local laws on telecom registration and use.

Takeaway: A telephone number is a signal flare in the data sky. Control when and how it burns, and never let it mark your real position.

June 7: Virtual Machines

"Talk is cheap. Show me the code." —Linus Torvalds

A virtual machine (VM) is a contained digital workspace that lets you explore, collect, and test without risking your main system or identity. Think of your VM as a portable lab: clean, disposable, and separate from your personal device. Inside that lab, you can browse the web, run tools, or open suspicious files without exposing your real computer to danger.

Choosing and Configuring Your VM: For most investigators, VirtualBox or VMware Workstation will get the job done. Keep it simple. Install only what's needed—your browser, password manager, and analysis tools. The more you install, the more potential vulnerabilities you add. Before you browse, you need to decide how your VM connects to the internet.

Understanding NAT Networking: By default, most VM software uses NAT (Network Address Translation) networking. This means the VM "borrows" your host computer's internet connection instead of connecting directly. To the outside world, all traffic from your VM appears to come from your host's IP address—not from the VM itself. This setup has big benefits for investigators:

- It hides your VM from other devices on the same network (like in an office or hotel Wi-Fi).
- It adds a natural layer of separation; if something inside the VM gets compromised, it can't easily reach your host system.
- It simplifies configuration—no need to manually assign IPs or worry about router settings.

You can think of NAT as a **safe proxy** inside your own machine—the VM stays behind a curtain, speaking to the internet only through your host. The downside? You can't easily run services into the VM (like hosting a web server) or simulate multiple outward connections without extra configuration. But for OSINT research and safe browsing, NAT is the gold standard: contained, controlled, and beginner-friendly.

If you need the VM to appear as a separate device on your network—for instance, to route it through its own VPN or simulate another location—switch to **Bridged Mode.** This makes the VM act like a standalone computer with its own IP. Use it carefully; bridged mode exposes the VM more directly to the network and requires tighter firewall discipline.

Takeaway: Your VM is your containment zone. NAT keeps you safely behind the curtain while you work the case.

June 8: Building Your Web Browser

"Efficiency is intelligent laziness." —David Dunham

Once your virtual machine is ready, it's time to customize the inside of your web browser—the tool you will live in for most of your investigative day.

Bookmarks and Organization: Investigators spend too much time retyping URLs. Stop that. Build a bookmark toolbar with folders that mirror your investigative tasks:

- **Websites**—open-source databases, mapping tools, government portals, and registries.
- **Social Media Accounts**—direct links to advanced search pages (Twitter/X, Facebook, Instagram, TikTok).
- **E-mail Search**—lookup tools, breach databases, and verification services.
- **Phone Numbers**—carrier lookup, OSINT phone databases, and international code references.
- **IP Addresses**—WHOIS, DNS, and traceroute tools.
- **Photos**—reverse image search, EXIF viewers, and image forensics tools.

Arrange the toolbar in the order you investigate—the sequence you naturally move through when starting a case.

Saved Tab Groups and Sessions: Set your browser to open multiple tabs on launch. For example, you can configure a "Morning OSINT" group that opens your core tools automatically: a news aggregator, a social platform search, your email lookup, and your notes dashboard. This workflow keeps your head in the game. Modern browsers like Firefox and Brave allow tab grouping or session saving. Each created profile maintains its own history, cookies, and bookmarks—compartmentalization by design.

Extensions and Add-ons: Install only the extensions that add investigative value. A few high-value add-ons include:

- **uBlock Origin:** removes trackers and ads.
- **NoScript:** controls background scripts.
- **Hunchly:** for case capture and documentation.
- **Wayback Machine:** for archived site retrieval.

Takeaway: Your browser is your cockpit. Build it to your liking, ensuring it has all the tools you need at your fingertips.

June 9: Boolean Logic & Search Discipline

"Information wants to be free." —Stewart Brand

Boolean logic turns an ordinary search engine into a precision instrument, letting you extract what matters. Boolean logic is simply a method for combining keywords and operators (such as AND, OR, and NOT) to control how search engines retrieve and organize information. Once you master it, your searches stop being lucky guesses and start being controlled operations.

Understanding Boolean Basics: At its core, Boolean logic is built on three simple operators:

- **AND** narrows results. "fraud AND indictment" finds pages containing both terms.
- **OR** broadens results. "fraud OR embezzlement" retrieves either.
- **NOT**, or the minus sign **(-)**, excludes noise. "fraud -Ponzi" filters out results you don't want.

Add **quotation marks** for exact phrases ("John Doe") and parentheses to group ideas: ("John Doe" AND "LLC") OR ("J. Doe" AND "Limited")

That single query might surface shell companies, filings, or media articles you would otherwise miss.

Advanced Operators and Filters: Most search engines support specialized syntax that makes your searches far more surgical:

- **site:** limits results to a domain—site:sec.gov "Form 10-K"
- **filetype:** retrieves a specific document type—filetype:pdf "executive order"
- **intitle:** or **inurl:** focuses on words appearing in titles or URLs.
- **cache:** recalls a page that's been taken down or altered.

String them together. For example: ("incident report" OR "police report") site:nyc.gov filetype:pdf 2024. That isn't a guess—it's a targeted search built like a warrant.

Most investigators stop where English stops. Translate your key terms—Spanish, French, Russian, Arabic, Mandarin—depending on your subject. Even small spelling differences (Mohamed vs. Muhammad) change results. Run those variants in new tabs and compare what surfaces; you will often find local reporting, court filings, or leaks invisible to English-only searches.

Takeaway: Boolean logic is the grammar of investigation. When you command it, the web stops hiding from you.

June 10: Boolean Galore

"It is not of the essence of mathematics to be conversant with the ideas of number and quantity." —George Boole

Yesterday, you learned how Boolean logic structures your searches. Today, you will develop muscle memory for it. Every investigator should know these operators thoroughly; they are the alphabet of online discovery.

Operator / Symbol	Purpose	Example
site:	Limit results to a specific domain	site:apple.com
" "	Quotation marks search for the exact phrase	"red rider BB gun"
AND	Show results containing both terms	apple AND orange
OR / |	Show results for term A, term B, or both	gun OR rifle or gun | rifle
*****	Wildcard for unknown words in a phrase	wish * a star
()	Group words or operators together	(gun | pistol) ammo
- (Minus)	Exclude results containing this word	chicago baseball -cubs
$	Search for a specific price	"apple watch" $299
cache:	View the most recent cached version of a site	cache:boston.gov
filetype: / ext:	Find a specific file type	filetype:pdf "confidential" or ext:pdf "confidential"
Advanced Search	GUI version of all these filters	https://www.google.com/advanced_search

Takeaway: Boolean logic isn't just theory—it's your investigative shorthand.

June 11: Seeing the Story

"The true sign of intelligence is not knowledge but imagination" —*Albert Einstein*

Images are data—and like any data, they tell stories when you know how to listen. Every picture, screenshot, or video frame contains layers of intelligence: where it came from, when it was taken, and sometimes even by whom.

Reverse Image Search: Start with the simplest tool in your arsenal: reverse image search. This lets you trace a photo back to its origin, find other places it has been posted, or identify manipulation.

- Google Images: images.google.com—best for mainstream and news content.
- TinEye: tineye.com—excels at finding older or cropped variants.
- Yandex Images: especially strong with facial recognition and non-English web results.
- Bing Visual Search: effective for retail, locations, and product-based imagery.

Upload the photo or paste its URL, then review the results chronologically. Look for first-seen dates, matching backgrounds, or different crops. Those details can reveal origin, authenticity, and manipulation.

Metadata & EXIF Clues: Every digital image may carry hidden data called EXIF (Exchangeable Image File Format)—metadata automatically written by cameras and phones. It can include timestamps, GPS coordinates, device type, and even editing software. Use tools like ExifTool, Jeffrey's EXIF Viewer, or browser plug-ins to inspect these fields.

Always treat EXIF cautiously—many platforms (Twitter/X, Facebook, Instagram) strip metadata on upload, but original files from messages, email, or websites can still retain it.

Visual Verification: Images can lie through omission, cropping, or context. To verify authenticity:

1. Compare shadows and lighting to the claimed time of day.
2. Match architecture, signage, and terrain using Google Earth, Street View, or Mapillary.
3. Zoom into reflections (windows, sunglasses, water) for unintentional reveals.
4. Check file consistency: if compression or edges differ across sections, it may be edited.

Takeaway: Every image tells a story—sometimes the one in front of you, sometimes the one it's trying to hide. Learn to read both.

June 12: Video Verification in OSINT

"It's not what you look at that matters, it's what you see." —Henry David Thoreau

In a world of deepfakes, selective edits, and recycled footage, your credibility depends on knowing how to separate what is real from what is staged. That is where video verification comes into play. As an investigator, your first step is to verify the video's provenance—where it came from, when it was first uploaded, and whether it has appeared elsewhere. First, run the thumbnail or a few still frames through the same reverse image tools you used yesterday:

- **Google Images** or **Bing Visual Search** for common re-uploads.
- **Yandex Images** for foreign-language platforms.
- **Amnesty's YouTube DataViewer** for upload timestamps and channel data.

If you find that a "new" video appeared months or years ago under a different title, you have likely uncovered a recycled or manipulated clip.

Frame Analysis & Metadata: Download the video if legally permissible and safe to do so. Use tools like InVID, Forensically, or FFmpeg to extract frames, inspect compression artifacts, and analyze metadata. Do this by conducting a frame-by-frame review to reveal edits or inserted cuts. Then check pixel distortion or inconsistent shadows. This may indicate splicing or CGI. Then compare audio waveforms. Any mismatched sound could suggest tampering.

If metadata exists, look for creation and modification dates, GPS tags, and camera identifiers. Even a single frame can contain embedded EXIF remnants if the device stored them at capture.

Geolocation and Context: The same visual corroboration rules from still images apply here—just in motion. Freeze critical frames and analyze:

1. **Landmarks and terrain** using Google Earth, Sentinel Hub, or Wikimapia.
2. **Weather patterns** (shadows, cloud cover, rainfall) matching the claimed date.
3. **Voices, accents, and signage** to confirm region and language consistency.

When geolocating video, start broad—continent, country, city—then narrow to exact intersections or buildings using available clues.

Takeaway: When verified properly, video becomes a powerful ally in your investigation. Learn how to verify to enable this tool.

June 13: Data Brokers

"You are not the product; you are the abandoned carcass left behind after the data has been extracted." —Shoshana Zuboff

Every investigator knows that information is power—but in today's digital marketplace, information is also a commodity. Enter the world of data brokers—massive commercial databases that package human behavior, credit records, and public filings into searchable profiles. For investigators, these services can be gold mines—if you know how to use them responsibly.

Data brokers are companies that collect, aggregate, and sell personal information from public, private, and voluntary sources. They scrape court filings, purchase marketing data, analyze online transactions, and buy from credit bureaus. They are the quiet middlemen of the internet economy. If you have ever applied for a loan, ordered something online, subscribed to a service, downloaded an app, or clicked "accept" without reading the fine print—congratulations, you have already participated. As investigators like to joke, how did they get all this info? Well, you gave it to them--- voluntarily. And in some cases, you paid for the privilege.

For licensed private investigators, systems like TLOxp (TransUnion), IRBsearch, and Tracers are industry staples. They consolidate records from credit headers, vehicle registrations, utilities, court filings, and other sources that individuals have consented to share through consumer agreements. These are not "dark web" tools—they are regulated under the Fair Credit Reporting Act (FCRA) and similar laws. Some additional examples include IDI Data, Accurint, and CLEAR.

For public-sector investigators, access may come through interagency agreements or contracted services. Many agencies integrate similar datasets through official portals. In both sectors, these tools are only as good as your understanding of what they are pulling—and how they got it. Most importantly, these tools only serve as a starting point; you must validate the information. Cross-check every data point. A single outdated address or recycled phone number can derail an entire investigation.

Always remember: regardless of whether you work in the public or private sector, you are subject to audit at any time when using these tools.

June 14: Free People-Finder Sites

"The greatest trick the Devil ever pulled was convincing the world he didn't exist." —
Charles Baudelaire

Free people-finder sites feel like magic until you remember where the "magic" comes from: ad-supported business models that monetize your clicks and the data you (and everyone you know) have already scattered across the internet.

Free aggregators gather and piece together fragments from public records, marketing files, social networks, breach dumps, and user-submitted content. The result is a cluttered collage: partial addresses, aliases, relatives, old phone numbers, and guesses about age and location. The data may be outdated, wrongly attributed to someone with a similar name, or influenced by previous residents at the same address. Remember, these sites may start free but quickly lead you to a paywall as they guide you through the available information. Some good examples of "free" include:

- **TruePeopleSearch / FastPeopleSearch / SearchPeopleFree:** Quick pivots for phones ↔ addresses ↔ possible relatives.
- **Whitepages (free tier):** Basic reverse phone/address checks and neighbor lists.
- **Spokeo (free previews):** Cross-platform hints for emails, usernames, and social links.
- **FamilyTreeNow:** Wider "relative" graphs (but heavy on false positives).

When to Stop "Free" and Go Paid:

- You need recency (new number, new address, recent move).
- You need coverage beyond one state or a stronger alias/AKA resolution.
- You need audit trails and usage logs (compliance).

That's when you step up to TLOxp/IRB/Tracers/etc. Free got you the hypothesis; paid helps you confirm it.

Takeaway: Free sites are fast and dirty. Use them to start a trail, never to end one. Verify every lead with primary records or paid, audited sources—and remember: if it's free, **you're** the product.

June 15: Local Public Sources

"Sunlight is said to be the best of disinfectants." —Louis D. Brandeis

If you want reliable, auditable facts, start with the institutions that create them. Local public records—county assessors, recorders, clerks, voter rolls, sex offender registries, and state corporate registries—are the raw data factories for real-world identity, property, and legal status. They are often free and usually authoritative. Some basic places to look:

- County Assessor / Property Appraiser
- Recorder of Deeds / Registrar of Titles
- Clerk of Court / Court Records
- Voter Rolls / Registration
- Sex-Offender Registries / Public Safety Portals
- State Corporate / Business Registries
- Property/GIS Portals & Aerial Imagery
- Chamber of Commerce
- Housing Authorities
- Libraries and Local Archives
- Transit Authorities
- City Council
- Contracts & Procurement Office
- Health Department
- Professional Licensing Board
- Animal Control
- Fire Department Records

Outside the U.S., record systems differ widely. Many countries have centralized land registries and corporate databases (some with English portals); others keep fragmented, paper-based records or restrict access for privacy reasons. Where records are sparse, rely more on local contacts or licensed local professionals. In some places, there is effectively no recourse—no searchable property registry or accessible court archive because records are still kept as if the country were in the Stone Age. Adjust expectations accordingly.

Pro tip for U.S. public investigators: Coordinate with the Regional Security Office at the local U.S. embassy or consulate. Diplomatic Security Service (DSS) Special Agents staff these offices and are at every U.S. Embassy and Consulate. If you are a non-US public investigator, your country might have an equivalent at your embassies and consulates.

Takeaway: Begin your investigation at the source. Local public records give you verifiable facts that form the backbone of any credible investigative report.

June 16: Freedom of Information Act

"The public is lied to every day by the government—transparency is the only antidote to deceit." —Daniel Ellsberg

Every investigator, public or private, eventually hits the wall of official silence. The Freedom of Information Act (FOIA) and its state-level counterparts are how you climb it legally. These laws aren't loopholes—they are deliberate pressure valves built into democratic systems. Used properly, they turn secrecy into data, and rumor into evidence.

At its core, the FOIA gives anyone the right to request access to federal agency records—from the Department of Agriculture to the Department of Veteran Affairs. It doesn't apply to Congress, the courts, or private entities, but it does cover the agencies that generate the most valuable investigative material.

A strong FOIA request is narrow, specific, and focused. Identify the document, date range, and office. Avoid fishing expeditions—they take months and yield frustration. Include your preferred format (digital copies) and explicitly state that you're willing to accept redacted material. That flexibility often saves weeks. If denied, file an administrative appeal. Each agency has a process, and persistence matters. If you hit a wall, you can escalate through litigation or use third-party intermediaries like MuckRock or FOIA.gov to track and manage your requests. Expect delays—the system is often backlogged.

Private investigators aren't always eligible for official fee waivers, but you can still leverage FOIA through partnerships with journalists or attorneys, or by relying on state-level open records laws that mirror FOIA's intent. In other words, what's denied at the federal level might be fair game locally.

Every U.S. state has its own Sunshine Law or Public Records Act. These laws open up property records, business licenses, police logs, 911 calls, and municipal correspondence. They are less bureaucratic and often faster than the federal FOIA. Some states exempt law enforcement records or active investigations; others require proof of identity or residency. But almost all have a public portal or form letter template.

Outside the U.S., access varies. The U.K. Freedom of Information Act (2000) and Canada's Access to Information Act are well-established systems. The European Union has Regulation 1049/2001 for institutional transparency. Australia, New Zealand, and India also maintain national frameworks. Elsewhere, open records may be a privilege rather than a right.

Takeaway: FOIA is lawful transparency in U.S. investigations. Used well, it will give you what rumor can't—official proof.

June 17: Facebook & Instagram

"The truth is not hard to find, but the people in power have a terrible aversion to it."
—Carl Bernstein

People leave more behind on social media than they ever will in a government file. Facebook and Instagram are the modern investigator's neighborhood watch. These platforms are a gold mine for workers' comp investigators trying to prove fake injuries, as claimants routinely place their own damaging photographs online for the world to see (such as them jet skiing when they are supposed to have no use of their legs). Criminals also make it easy by posting confessions of crimes and incriminating evidence to build their reputations. You can use Facebook for:

- **Timelines:** Scroll chronologically. Deleted posts often leave interaction traces—likes, shares, or comment notifications.
- **Friends & Interactions:** Friends lists may be hidden, but comments and reactions expose recurring connections. Look for frequency, timing, and sentiment.
- **Photos & Tags:** Photos tag more than faces—they geotag places, reveal travel patterns, and sometimes include device metadata.
- **Groups & Likes:** Group memberships and page likes identify political leanings, hobbies, or employment sectors.
- **Archived Views:** Use cached versions (Google cache, Wayback Machine) or tools like Social Searcher to recover partial content.

Instagram has exploded in popularity overseas. In the last three countries I have worked, it has effectively replaced traditional websites for restaurants, boutiques, and local services. Want to find a business abroad? You will find it on Instagram before you ever see a formal webpage. Use Instagram for:

- **Visual Timelines:** Posts, reels, and stories create a real-time journal. Save and screenshot story content—it disappears fast.
- **Hashtags:** They act like breadcrumb trails. Combine with date filters to reconstruct activity windows.
- **Location Tags:** Verify authenticity. Cross-check photo backgrounds with Google Maps or Street View.
- **Follower Graphs:** Who interacts repeatedly? Engagement patterns often identify the real inner circle better than the "Followers" list.
- **Image Corroboration:** Use reverse-image searches to see if photos appear elsewhere under other names.

Takeaway: Facebook and Instagram are the investigator's modern canvases—alive, loud, and endlessly revealing.

June 18: X (Twitter)

"The only thing I ever said that made sense was that journalism is the best damn job in the world." —Ben Bradlee

Few platforms rival X—formerly known as Twitter—for its immediacy, chaos, and reach. It's a global sensor network where news breaks first, rumors metastasize, and truth battles to stay alive. Used correctly, X gives you front-row access to the world's unfiltered conversation. Used carelessly, it drowns you in noise and bias. Despite its reputation for volatility, X remains the most open and searchable social platform. Governments, journalists, activists, and criminals all use it to broadcast, bait, or brag—sometimes in the same thread.

No matter your discipline, X offers the fastest public lens into unfolding events.

Search Discipline and Operators- Forget the feed—that's entertainment. The real power lies in advanced search. Combine operators to filter by keyword, date, and geography:

- from: and to: filter sender and recipient.
- since: and until: define timeframes.
- "exact phrase" locates precise statements.
- near: and within: (legacy) pull geo-tagged posts.
- filter:media or filter:links narrow to images or shared URLs. Example: ("explosion" OR "blast") near:"Baltimore" since:2025-03-01 until:2025-03-02

That one line can locate eyewitness accounts within minutes of an incident.

Verification & Context: Every viral post is a test of patience. Screenshots and retweets travel faster than facts. Before citing or saving a tweet:

1. **Check timestamps:** Time zones and UTC differences can distort chronology.
2. **Validate media:** Run attached images through reverse searches (TinEye, Google, Yandex).
3. **Cross-source:** Find at least two independent confirmations.
4. **Archive immediately:** Posts vanish; use tools like nitter.net, Thread Reader App, or archive.ph.

For high-impact investigations, capture the tweet ID, author handle, URL, and time—that metadata may be critical in a report or court filing.

Takeaway: X is the world's fastest rumor mill and its most accessible early-warning system. Scan it constantly and always verify.

June 19: Emerging Platforms (Part One)

"We live in a society exquisitely dependent on science and technology, in which hardly anyone knows anything about science and technology." —Carl Sagan

TikTok is where the world's youngest generations live, laugh, and—often unknowingly—leak intelligence. Like all the platforms listed in this book, it might be toppled and replaced by a new, hot emerging platform. Until then, it's where investigators can observe behavior patterns, community trends, and raw data from places traditional media rarely reaches. TikTok's reach now eclipses every other social network among users under 30.

Unlike Facebook or X, TikTok's algorithm doesn't rely on who you follow; it learns what you linger on. That "For You Page" personalization makes it a mirror of collective interest—and sometimes, collective unrest. Public-sector analysts monitor TikTok for early indicators of protests, emerging subcultures, and disaster footage. Private-sector investigators watch it for counterfeit goods, brand misuse, insider leaks, and reputational threats. Even criminals have embraced it—advertising scams, bragging about fraud, and showcasing lifestyles they cannot afford. Things to look for on TikTok:

- **Audio Cues:** Background sound often reveals location—sirens, dialects, or local radio chatter.
- **Visual Markers:** Street signs, uniforms, storefronts, and license plates can geolocate a clip within seconds.
- **Patterns of Posts:** Posting frequency and timestamps establish time zones and routines.
- **Hashtags & Challenges:** Viral tags tie users together. Tracking a single hashtag can map entire social movements or fraud campaigns.
- **Comments & Stitch Chains:** Replies, duets, and stitches form relationship graphs—who amplifies whom, and why.

Collection & Verification:

- Download or screen-record immediately—videos vanish or change.
- Preserve URLs, usernames, and captions as metadata.
- Run still frames through reverse-image tools to locate duplicates on other platforms.
- Cross-reference speech, accents, and signage for regional confirmation.
- Never trust subtitles or auto-translations; verify with a native speaker when possible.

Takeaway: TikTok and its imitators are the new frontier. They are messy, noisy, and indispensable for your investigations.

June 20: Emerging Platforms (Part Two)

"The social media platforms have taken over the distribution of news globally. They treat a lie the same way you would treat a fact." —Maria Ressa

Continuing our conversation from yesterday, realize that today's TikTok is tomorrow's something else. New networks—Threads, Telegram Channels, Discord servers, BeReal, and even niche forums—regularly emerge and vanish. The principle remains the same: learn the platform's local language, map its social mechanics, and extract only what is openly available. Each ecosystem develops its own norms and vulnerabilities.

Handles and Other Identifiers: People are creatures of habit. If, during the course of your investigation, you find out the name of someone's online handle, chances are it's the same or very similar on other platforms. Once you identify their presence, start your subpoena paperwork and preservation memos—or in the private sector, note the discovery for potential legal request through counsel. The earlier you preserve, the stronger your evidentiary chain later.

Operational Cautions: These environments are engineered for engagement, not truth. Algorithms amplify outrage and emotion, distorting your sense of scale. Use anonymized browsers or sock-puppet accounts created solely for observation; even passive scrolling shapes your feed and reveals your interests to the algorithm. Also note that TikTok's parent company, ByteDance, operates under Chinese jurisdiction—an important privacy and counterintelligence consideration for government users. Assume every click is logged somewhere you can't see.

International Angle: Overseas, TikTok, and other emerging platforms often *are* the news. In regions with restricted media, locals use them to document protests, disasters, or military activity in real time. Those posts can be invaluable—but remember, authenticity drops the further a clip travels. Corroborate with geolocation tools, weather data, and other witnesses before drawing conclusions.

Takeaway: The platform may change tomorrow, but the behaviors they reveal today are timeless—and so is the investigator's need to adapt.

June 21: LinkedIn & Other Job Boards

"The most important thing in the world is honesty... once you can fake that, you've got it made." —Groucho Marx

Job boards and career platforms—LinkedIn, Indeed, Glassdoor, Monster, and others—are treasure troves of self-reported intelligence. They reveal employment history, skillsets, professional networks, and corporate footprints that rarely appear in traditional background checks. For investigators, these sites aren't just about résumés—they are behavioral and timeline tools. I have used them for everything from helping private-sector clients pursue modifications to child support payments to finding associates who worked with the subject when they were committing fraud.

LinkedIn's dominance isn't universal. In parts of Asia and Europe, Xing, Bayt, or Viadeo plays a similar role. Use a neutral or sock-puppet LinkedIn account for viewing. LinkedIn notifies users who check their profiles, and a misstep could tip your hand. Never connect directly with a subject; instead, use open-source tools like RocketReach, SignalHire, or Hunter.io to identify associated professional emails. Some job board tips:

- **Career Verification:** Cross-check dates and titles against public records, corporate filings, or archived company pages. Inconsistencies often indicate résumé inflation or undisclosed employment gaps.
- **Network Mapping:** The "People Also Viewed" and "Mutual Connections" sections are invaluable for identifying business associates, prior supervisors, or undisclosed affiliations.
- **Content Analysis:** Posts, likes, and comments reveal personal interests, client relationships, and even internal company morale. Watch for timing—employees sometimes telegraph changes before official announcements.
- **Company Pages:** Each organization's profile lists key staff, leadership structures, and often physical locations. Historical snapshots from the Wayback Machine can show when major shifts occurred.
- **E-mail & Alias Pivoting:** Many candidates reuse the same contact info across personal sites, professional applications, and social accounts—creating pivots for correlation.
- **Time Markers:** Résumé uploads are timestamped. A "currently seeking" entry from two years ago may indicate unemployment.
- **Company Intelligence:** Employers use these boards, too. Job postings reveal hiring surges and planned expansions—valuable in corporate due diligence or competitor profiling.

Takeaway: A résumé is a person's self-authored biography—polished and deeply revealing. Used properly, it can verify timelines and uncover patterns.

June 22: Dating Sites

"Man is least himself when he talks in his own person. Give him a mask, and he will tell you the truth." —Oscar Wilde

Few places reveal human truth—and deception—quite like dating platforms. Tinder, Hinge, Bumble, Grindr, and their countless clones are digital confessionals wrapped in curated fantasy. They are where people expose more of themselves than they realize: location patterns, relationship history, lifestyle clues, and emotional tells. For investigators, these apps are messy but immensely valuable.

Dating sites sit at the intersection of identity and behavior. Dating data can corroborate relationship claims, reveal undisclosed partners, or show residency patterns through geo-tagged activity. In criminal and civil cases, dating apps have linked suspects to victims, established a presence at a scene, or exposed financial and romantic fraud. Search them early and often. Some tips:

- **Photos:** Look beyond the subject. Backgrounds show apartments, vehicles, pets, and décor—anchors for location or lifestyle verification.
- **Bios & Prompts:** Writing style, humor, and word choice often mirror professional or social-media tone. Compare against emails or texts for authorship confirmation.
- **Activity Timing:** Frequent late-night logins or quick profile edits can signal personal instability, loneliness, or infidelity—patterns that contextualize other evidence.
- **Linked Accounts:** Many profiles tie to Instagram or Spotify. Those links can expose alternate usernames, music preferences, or emotional states that color motive and mindset.
- **Geo-Data:** Apps like Tinder and Grindr are built on proximity. Even partial screenshots can reveal a radius and approximate location history.

Outside the U.S., dating platforms often double as social networks where conventional outlets are restricted. In parts of the Middle East and Asia, investigators may find political dissent, underground commerce, or coded expressions of identity hidden behind dating-app interfaces, which is particularly useful for international human trafficking and narcotics investigations.

Takeaway: Dating apps are paradoxical gold mines—half fantasy, half confession. When people wear masks online, they often tell you exactly who they are.

June 23: Automation, AI, & Scripting

"A computer would deserve to be called intelligent if it could deceive a human into believing that it was human." —Dr. Alan Turing

Automation doesn't replace the investigator—it multiplies their reach. Whether you're scraping public data, mapping digital footprints, or monitoring social feeds, the right code can save hours of manual searching. But like any tool, automation requires restraint and understanding. Modern investigations generate so much data that it cannot be processed by hand. Automation helps you scale collection, but it also forces you to think like a system architect. Each script, crawler, or bot must serve a defined purpose and respect legal limits.

Scripting for OSINT: Languages like Python and JavaScript dominate investigative automation. They integrate with web APIs, parse large text sets, and extract structured data from chaos.

- BeautifulSoup and Selenium scrape websites and social feeds.
- Pandas and NumPy analyze patterns in CSV exports or scraped tables.
- Matplotlib visualizes connections or trends for reports.

Think of scripting as building digital surveillance—passive, repeatable, and controlled.

Artificial Intelligence (AI) in the Investigative Workflow: AI tools (such as GPT-based summarizers or machine vision models) can quickly classify or summarize data, but should never be treated as truth engines. Use AI for triage, not judgment. I remember trying to see how AI would do with scripting and pulling information on a subject (a volunteer fellow investigator). Well, it pulled everything, including the kitchen sink. 800 plus pages of data. Without actually scanning all of it, you could see its limitations where it cross-indexed his name with a similar person and went down the rabbit hole. All of that information was functionally useless. However, it is useful in:

- Summarizing lengthy FOIA dumps or PDF transcripts.
- Detecting duplicate or similar images across platforms.
- Generating leads from clustering text patterns (e.g., common handles, domains, or phrases).

Legal & Ethical Boundaries: Automation must never cross into intrusion. Avoid automated logins, data scraping behind paywalls, or bulk downloads that violate Terms of Service. Many platforms specifically restrict this.

Takeaway: Automation extends your eyes and ears. Use it save time and fine-tune your investigation.

June 24: APIs, OSINT Tools & Toolchains

"The tools are only as good as the hands that wield them." —Neil Armstrong

Open-source intelligence depends as much on craft as it does on code. With hundreds of OSINT tools available—each claiming to automate miracles—the professional must build a personal toolkit that matches their workflow, case type, and comfort level. Rather than give you an exact list of tools that we use, I implore you to examine what is out there and use what works for you and your agency.

A strong OSINT toolchain mirrors a field kit: modular, efficient, and well-maintained.

- **Hunchly:** Automatically captures web sessions, timestamps, and screenshots—ideal for court-admissible collection.
- **Maltego:** Visual link analysis for mapping relationships among people, entities, and domains.
- **SpiderFoot:** Automated reconnaissance combining over 100 data sources.
- **Recon-ng:** Command-line framework for structured OSINT collection.
- **ExifTool:** Extracts embedded metadata from images and documents.
- **Wayback Machine:** Retrieves deleted or modified webpages for historical context.

An API (Application Programming Interface) lets you pull data directly from a service without having to browse it manually. Common examples:

- Twitter/X API for real-time post data.
- Google Maps API for geolocation and route reconstruction.
- Shodan API for scanning exposed devices.
- Have I Been Pwned API for compromised emails.

Using APIs legally means honoring rate limits, access rules, and privacy constraints. Document all retrieved data sources and timestamps for your chain of custody. Clients and attorneys alike will love it, and defense attorneys will hate it.

Takeaway: Your OSINT tools aren't magic—they are multipliers. Master a few deeply instead of collecting dozens you don't understand.

June 25: Geospatial Tools & Satellite Imagery

"The Earth is the cradle of humanity, but one cannot live in the cradle forever." — *Konstantin Tsiolkovsky*

Geospatial intelligence (GEOINT) turns the planet into evidence. From satellite photos to public mapping data, modern investigators can confirm events, locate assets, and measure impact—all without leaving their desk. GEOINT complements OSINT, and you should understand its power, just as governments do. There are some very impressive YouTubers out there using their OSINT and GEOINT skills to put on spectacular displays of locating someone. I suggest you watch some from time to time.

Core Tools:

- Google Earth Pro: Historical imagery, elevation models, and line-of-sight analysis.
- Sentinel Hub & NASA Worldview: Near-real-time satellite data with environmental overlays.
- Mapillary & OpenStreetMap: Crowd-sourced street-level imagery for building verification.
- Caltopo or Gaia GPS: Terrain and land ownership references.

Applications:

- Disaster Verification- Confirm whether alleged property damage coincides with natural events.
- Asset Tracking- Identify undeclared facilities or storage sites through recurring vehicle patterns.
- Environmental Impact- Measure deforestation, illegal mining, or construction over time.
- Location verification- Confirm someone was where they said they were

Analytical Skills:

Learn to read imagery like a witness statement. Shadows, vegetation, and infrastructure tell stories about time and activity. Combine geospatial data with metadata and human reporting to create multi-layered validation. After all, we have come a long way from having to take a train ride to physically count tanks outside a Soviet military base.

Takeaway: Every investigation happens somewhere. Geospatial tools ensure you can find it, prove it, and show it clearly.

June 26: Geo-Forensics

"Science is organized knowledge. Wisdom is organized life." —Immanuel Kant

A single photo can reveal the time, date, and even the direction it was taken—if you know how to read the light. Geo-forensics blends physics with observation, transforming pixels into verifiable evidence. This is a powerful investigative tool for an investigator or an intelligence officer alike. Spend some time mastering this craft, as it will pay dividends.

Shadow Analysis:

Shadows reveal time of day and hemisphere.

- Length & Direction: Compare to sun-angle calculators (Suncalc.org, NOAA Solar Calculator).
- Orientation: North- or south-facing shadows confirm global position.
- Discrepancies: Misaligned shadows often indicate digital alteration or compositing.

Angle Verification:

Structures, terrain, and the sun's elevation form a natural clock. Use local landmarks and elevation data to test whether lighting matches the claimed location or time.

Tools & Techniques:

- Suncalc, Google Earth Pro, and Mapbox for shadow projection.
- EXIF Date vs. Light Position: Confirms authenticity or manipulation.
- Weather Archives: Cross-check overcast conditions that would negate shadow presence.

Applied Example:

In both private and public investigations, shadow and angle analysis have confirmed alibis and exposed false reports. Investigators have proven staged crime-scene photos by showing impossible sun angles, or verified the time of a kidnapping video by matching building shadows to local solar data. Journalists and OSINT professionals use the same techniques to authenticate war footage or environmental imagery. When combined with weather records and geographic context, shadow forensics becomes one of the few tools that can tell you *when* and *where* without a single word of testimony.

Takeaway: Light doesn't lie—but liars forget how it behaves. Understanding natural indicators turns every image into a timestamped testimony.

June 27: The Deep Web

"There are known knowns, known unknowns, and unknown unknowns." —Secretary Donald Rumsfeld

Beneath the Surface Web lies the Deep Web—the vast expanse of online material that search engines don't index. It's used daily by students, businesses, and ordinary internet users without them realizing it. The Deep Web isn't sinister; it's simply the part of the Internet that requires authentication, paywalls, or specialized search tools. Academic databases, subscription archives, legal filings, online banking, and private portals all live here. Some estimates suggest that 85% to 90% of Internet content exists within this layer. Knowing how to navigate it separates the amateur from the professional investigator.

What It Includes:

- Academic and scientific journals (JSTOR, LexisNexis, ProQuest).
- Court and government databases requiring logins.
- Private company registries and data brokers.
- Cloud documents restricted by link privacy settings.

How to Access It Legally: Use institutional or paid access—never credential stuffing, shared logins, or unauthorized methods. Many Deep Web sources are perfectly legal but simply require proper authentication or subscriptions. For investigators, legitimate access sometimes means a formal process. If you identify data crucial to an investigation, you may need to obtain it through a subpoena, court order, or written request under statutory authority.

- **Private Investigators:** Coordinate with attorneys to issue subpoenas for business records, subscriber information, or service-provider logs.
- **Law Enforcement & Government Investigators:** Work through agency counsel or official process to compel production while maintaining evidentiary integrity with preservation memos.

Practical Tips:

- Use Google Scholar and Semantic Scholar for academic leads.
- Query state and federal court portals directly for filings and docket details.
- Explore corporate, NGO, and transparency registries for filings and annual reports.
- When you find paywalled or permission-only material, document the source, URL, and context—it strengthens your subpoena justification.

Takeaway: The Deep Web is where real records live—beyond the reach of Google, but not beyond the reach of lawful curiosity.

June 28: The Dark Web

"We are not now that strength which in old days moved earth and heaven." —Alfred, Lord Tennyson

The Dark Web is the Deep Web's locked basement—a network of hidden services accessible through specialized browsers like Tor. It's where anonymity thrives, and so does risk. It is not inherently illegal to access the Dark Web. However, its anonymity has made it a playground of criminal activity. Investigators should take time to understand how to access it and plan honey pots and other traps to disrupt criminal activity. The Dark Web is a collection of encrypted, decentralized sites ending in .onion that are accessible only through Tor or I2P. The Dark Web hosts both illicit markets and legitimate whistleblower portals operated by the media and governments. Before entering, again, understand that the Dark Web itself is not illegal—what you do there can be. Legitimate access is needed for cybersecurity or investigative purposes.

1. Install the Tor Browser: Download only from the official Tor Project website (https://www.torproject.org). Tor routes your traffic through several encrypted relays worldwide, masking your IP and location.
2. Use a VPN First: Always start your VPN before launching Tor. This adds a privacy layer, hiding Tor usage from your Internet Service Provider (ISP) and reducing your online footprint.
3. Isolate Your Workspace: Access the Dark Web only from a virtual machine (VM) or dedicated system—never your personal device. Disable file sharing, clipboard access, and microphones.
4. Find .onion Sites Safely: Never rely on random "dark web site lists." Use vetted directories like The Hidden Wiki or specialized intelligence feeds. Cross-check all URLs—phishing and spoofing are rampant.
5. Stay Passive: Don't log in, post, or message anyone unless authorized. Most investigative work is observational. Opening the wrong link or accepting a download can expose your system to malware.
6. Record Everything: Screenshots, timestamps, URLs, and notes should be captured through approved tools. In law enforcement or compliance environments, treat every click as evidence.
7. Exit Cleanly: Close Tor, disconnect your VPN, and revert your VM to a clean snapshot when done. This purges cookies, caches, and tracking scripts.

Remember to always access through a secure virtual machine with a VPN. Never download or purchase illegal content. Document every step; the chain of custody applies online, too.

Takeaway: The Dark Web isn't evil—it's unregulated. Approach it like hazardous crime scene: gloves on, eyes open, and every move logged.

June 29: Advanced Persona Linking

"It is a career of make-believe, of masks. We all have masks in life." —Judd Nelson

Every investigator eventually faces the digital hydra: one subject, many identities. Advanced persona linking means connecting usernames, photos, language patterns, and digital breadcrumbs into a single, verifiable individual. Some of the most difficult crimes I have investigated have been identity theft crimes, where you are trying to establish who the "True ID" is.

At a glance, you think these crimes are easy. Then you realize the True ID also might be committing crimes; some of the people using the stolen IDs don't even realize it. Parents sell their children's identity documents, and parents also purchase identity documents for their children. Don't forget to compound the issue if it's a common name. Using OSINT can make things easier on yourself if you find yourself battling a digital hydra.

Core Techniques:

- Username Correlation: Search for handle reuse across multiple platforms using WhatsMyName, Namechk, or Maigret.
- Linguistic Profiling: Writing style, punctuation, and emoji patterns often reveal the same author behind different aliases. AI can help here.
- Photo & Asset Reuse: Cropped selfies or background furniture can confirm continuity across accounts.
- Technical Footprints: IP overlap, metadata, or similar time zones further strengthen links.

Workflow:

1. Start with one verified identifier (email, phone, or username).
2. Map outward through social graphs and data brokers.
3. Document connection strength: confirmed, probable, possible.
4. Validate each link with at least two independent artifacts.

Takeaway: People can change names and faces online—but their habits follow them. True identity isn't found; it's reconstructed.

June 30: Mobile Device OSINT

"The future is already here—it's just not evenly distributed." —William Gibson

Mobile devices are both diaries and tracking beacons. They record where we go, who we talk to, what we buy, and when we sleep. Understanding mobile artifacts is no longer optional—it's the modern investigator's radar. Mobile OSINT techniques could fill an entire book on their own. Many applications like Snapchat actually don't have a traditional web browser interface, which means different interventions are needed. This lesson reminds you that not everything in OSINT is done on a computer.

What to Look For:

- App Footprints: Even deleted apps leave traces in push notifications, screenshots, or shared links.
- Location Artifacts: Photos, map caches, weather apps, and ride-share receipts reveal travel patterns.
- Messaging Apps: WhatsApp, Signal, and Telegram can expose metadata even when content is encrypted (timestamps, file names, or delivery patterns).

Collection Tips:

- Always use consent-based or authorized extraction methods (warrants or client permission).
- Preserve SIM data, cloud backups, and local caches separately.
- Document device make, model, and OS version before acquisition.

Cross-Platform Insight: Many users sync phones with browsers—creating bridges between desktop and mobile footprints. Examine linked accounts, Bluetooth pairings, and photo syncs for continuity.

Android & iOS Emulation: When direct access to a physical device isn't possible, emulation allows investigators to safely analyze app behavior in a controlled environment. Android emulators (such as BlueStacks or Nox) and iOS simulators (such as Xcode's built-in simulator on Mac) can replicate app interfaces without exposing your personal device. These environments are ideal for understanding how an app stores data, verifying geolocation features, or reviewing layout changes that might affect evidence capture. Always isolate your emulator within a virtual machine and keep it disconnected from personal accounts—your test environment should be sterile, not social.

Takeaway: A modern smartphone is a life compressed into a rectangle. Handle it with the precision of evidence collection it deserves.

July: Undercover Work, Confidential Informants, and Field Operations

"All warfare is based on deception." —Sun Tzu

Undercover work, source handling, and field operations are the high-stakes edge of investigation—the place where technique meets temperament and planning meets danger. Despite the Hollywood image, these disciplines are not glamorous; they are serious, methodical tradecraft that protects lives, preserves evidence, and delivers results when other methods fail. Done well, they produce testimony, confessions, and admissions of fact that databases and social media never will. Done badly, they destroy careers, ruin cases, and put officers, sources, and innocent bystanders at risk.

This month's entries will treat these topics as the operational sciences they are: measured, repeatable, and relentlessly safety-first. Expect practical checklists, pre-op templates, legal and ethical red lines, and downloadable workflows you can adapt. We will balance classic human tradecraft (cover stories, source recruitment, face-to-face surveillance) with modern realities (digital footprints, encrypted comms, and safer alternatives to risky in-person contact). Wherever possible, the guidance is jurisdiction-agnostic, but I'll flag United States–specific legal considerations and sensible ways for private investigators and international practitioners to seek counsel or establish local partnerships.

A few framing principles to read this month with:

Plan like an engineer, act like a storyteller. Operational success depends on both precise preparation (timelines, contingency routes, comms, emergency extraction) and believable narrative (cover identity, behavior, cultural fit). Your story must withstand scrutiny from a target and from a judge.

Risk is measurable and mitigatable, not eliminable. Every operation begins with a risk assessment: who could get hurt, how could evidence be lost, and what would happen if the cover is blown? Build mitigations into the plan instead of relying on luck.

Ethics and legality are not optional. Whether you work for government or private clients, know the legal boundaries for deception, entrapment, surveillance, and source payments. When in doubt, pause, consult counsel, and document the decision path.

Sources are people first. Confidential informants and cooperators bring intelligence—and vulnerabilities. Protect them through security planning, trauma-aware debriefing, transparent expectations, and documented agreements. Remember: a well-treated source becomes a long-term asset; a betrayed one becomes a liability. Document everything. Operational logs, preservation memos, chain-of-custody entries, and timestamped comms save cases and careers. Treat documentation as you would evidence at trial: clear, contemporaneous, and auditable.

This month, we will cover:

- Preparing an undercover operation: approvals, cover creation, and rehearsals.
- Recruiting, vetting, and managing confidential informants: safety, compensation, and red flags.
- Low-visibility field surveillance and team choreography.
- Communications plans: secure channels, dead drops, and emergency signals.
- Debriefing, evidence preservation, and psychological aftercare for operatives and sources.
- Cultural competence and international cautions when working abroad.
- When to walk away: operational termination and legal fallout mitigation.

I am not going to tell you everything because not only are some things classified, but we also don't want to risk officer safety in the field. I hope you understand.

Undercover tradecraft is a professional craft—a mix of art, science, and law. Train relentlessly, plan meticulously, and put human safety and legal integrity at the center of every operation. If you keep those as non-negotiables, the intelligence you gain will be usable, defensible, and—most importantly—humanly responsible.

Ready? We begin with pre-op planning and approvals on July 1. You didn't really think we would start with the explosions and martial arts, did you?

July 1: Pre-Operation Planning & Approvals

"In preparing for battle, I have always found that plans are useless, but planning is indispensable." —President Dwight D. Eisenhower

Before the first meeting—or the first alias—comes the plan. Undercover and source operations are not improvised—they are engineered. Every move, every contact, every contingency should be deliberate. In investigations, failure to plan is more than inefficiency; it's liability.

Mission Clarity: The first question is not *how* to do it—it's *why*. Define the objective in plain language: what are you trying to prove, disprove, or discover? Is the undercover role designed to obtain evidence, verify an allegation, or identify participants? Every layer of complexity must serve a documented purpose. For private investigators, this clarity also protects you legally—scope creep and "curiosity collection" are the fastest routes to complaints or lawsuits.

Authorization & Oversight: In the public sector, no undercover operation should proceed without formal written approval. In many agencies, this process requires coordination between investigative and prosecutorial units to ensure compliance with local, state, and federal laws. For private-sector investigators, the same discipline applies in principle. You may not need a supervisor or prosecutor's approval, but you still need client authorization, risk documentation, and insurance coverage review. Operating without documented consent or client clarity can invalidate your findings or expose you to liability.

Risk Assessment & Mitigation: A risk assessment is your blueprint for survival. Identify hazards—physical, digital, legal, and reputational. What happens if the subject recognizes you? If surveillance is compromised? If the informant backs out? Each risk deserves a corresponding mitigation measure: cover stories, emergency contacts, redundant communications, and extraction plans. Always establish a "go/no-go" threshold—conditions under which the operation must stop immediately.

Operational Documentation: Write the plan as though someone hostile will one day read it in court. Include objectives, participants, legal basis, equipment lists, and communication protocols. Attach risk assessments, maps, and any source validation. Date and sign it. After the operation, annotate deviations—what went right, what failed, and what lessons should be carried forward. This document becomes your operational DNA: defendable, teachable, repeatable.

Takeaway: Undercover and field operations begin long before the first contact. Preparation is protection.

July 2: Identity Building

"In a time of deceit, telling the truth is a revolutionary act." —George Orwell

Every investigator—whether government, corporate, or private—must understand how to build and maintain an operational identity that withstands scrutiny. In the field, the line between a well-crafted persona and a blown operation can be as thin as one wrong word.

Purpose Before Persona: A cover story must serve a defined operational purpose. Don't invent a background because it "sounds cool." Build one that logically supports why you're present, how you speak, and what you're asking. Are you posing as a client, contractor, student, or vendor? Every detail must explain your access. An undercover posing as a property investor doesn't need an elaborate backstory about where they went to school—just a credible reason to be there. Simplicity is authenticity.

Grounded Truth: The best cover stories live close to reality. Blend elements of your real background—region, hobbies, slang, or skills—so that natural conversation won't betray hesitation. Never fabricate technical expertise you can't support. A "construction consultant" who doesn't know the difference between rebar and conduit won't last two questions with a foreman. Anchoring in truth reduces cognitive load and keeps your behavior consistent under pressure.

Documentation & Backstopping: Modern covers require more than a name and a business card. They need a believable online shadow. If your persona claims to work in logistics, but a Google search shows nothing, you're already suspect. Create authentic digital scaffolding. For law enforcement, this usually happens under agency authorization. Private investigators must stay within the law—no impersonating government officials, creating unregistered businesses, or forging credentials.

Don't forget that the bad guy can run checks on you to ensure you are who you say you are. I was once speaking with a cop who worked undercover in outlaw motorcycle gangs. He said the first thing they did with your initiation fee was send it to a private investigator to do an initial background check on you. If you didn't match the persona, it wouldn't end well for you.

Behavioral Consistency: Your cover isn't just words—it's conduct. Body language, tone, and timing reveal more than biography. Maintain emotional control and consistent affect. Overexplaining is the first sign of deception.

Takeaway: A good cover story isn't about deception—it's about coherence. The closer your fiction stays to truth, the safer your operation becomes.

July 3: Managing Operational Legends

"The secret of freedom lies in educating people, whereas the secret of tyranny is in keeping them ignorant." —Maximilien Robespierre

A good cover story gets you through the door. A legend lets you live there. In investigative and intelligence operations, a **legend** is a complete, sustainable identity—supported by history, documents, and digital presence—that can withstand deep scrutiny. Building one isn't about lying; it's about engineering credibility so thoroughly that exposure becomes improbable. Legends are essential when operations last weeks or months, or when the investigator needs recurring access to a community, company, or target. A professional legend includes:

- **Identity Layer:** Name, date of birth, address, occupation, and contact channels that can withstand database verification.
- **Documentary Layer:** Supporting records—emails, phone accounts, mailing addresses, business filings, or even utility bills—are legally established and isolated from your real identity.
- **Digital Layer:** A realistic footprint—social media accounts, business listings, minor posts, and interactions that simulate normal life.
- **Behavioral Layer:** The lived-in habits that make the identity consistent— speech patterns, hobbies, work jargon, and local familiarity.

Maintenance & Audit: Treat your legend like a living asset. Review it quarterly: update LinkedIn entries, refresh email logins, or adjust voicemail greetings. Audit for exposure—has anyone tagged the persona, linked it to your real name, or sent phishing attempts? A compromised legend can be more dangerous than no legend at all.

Compartmentation: Each operational legend must exist in its own compartment. Never reuse names, email addresses, or backstops across cases. Maintain a ledger or encrypted database documenting each legend's creation date, purpose, associated tools, and expiration plan. When a legend is retired, close it completely: delete accounts, dissolve entities, and log termination notes for future reference.

Legal and Ethical Lines: Every jurisdiction defines limits differently. In the U.S., law enforcement operations involving fabricated identities require judicial or prosecutorial oversight. For private investigators, the rule is simple: never create a false identity to defraud, misrepresent authority, or access protected systems. A well-documented legend is a professional tool for good.

Takeaway: A cover story gets you through one conversation; a legend gets you through an entire operation. Build it carefully.

July 4: Psychological Preparation

"You have power over your mind—not outside events. Realize this, and you will find strength." —Marcus Aurelius

Undercover operations demand more than disguise—they demand discipline of the mind. The psychological weight of deception, danger, and uncertainty can grind down even seasoned investigators. The difference between a professional and a casualty often comes down to one skill: the ability to manage internal chaos when external control breaks down.

Toughness is endurance. Readiness is awareness. The first lets you survive the moment; the second helps you shape it. Before any operation, visualize stress points: the approach, the conversation, the exit, and the possible compromise. What is your physiological signature under pressure? Heart rate? Voice tremor? Sweat? Learn to recognize those early and practice deliberate control.

Living a cover for hours—or months—requires supreme compartmentalization. You can't fake calm; you must manufacture it through repetition. Practice your legend until it becomes muscle memory, then rehearse responses to confrontation and exposure scenarios. Most compromised agents aren't betrayed by others—they betray themselves through nervous over-explaining, inconsistent details, or emotional leakage. Control the narrative by controlling your internal state. The best undercover operators carry a simple mantra: believability begins with breathing.

Military and law-enforcement programs rely on "stress inoculation" —gradual exposure to simulated fear and ambiguity until the brain normalizes it. Use similar principles: conduct role-plays with unpredictable variables, simulate time pressure, and rehearse in environments that trigger adrenaline spikes. Each repetition rewires your response, teaching your body that fear is information, not paralysis. Document reactions after each exercise—what triggered you, what worked, what didn't. This isn't therapy; it's operational science.

Extended operations distort identity. Sleep loss, moral conflict, and the weight of constant vigilance can cause what psychologists call cognitive dissonance fatigue—the brain rebelling against its own duplicity. Counter it with rituals of self-recovery: physical training, decompression routines, trusted debrief partners, and absolute honesty in post-op psychological check-ins.

Takeaway: You can't control the suspect, the weather, or the chaos of the street—but you can control **yourself.**

July 5: Field Communication Protocols

"Clear communication is the foundation of trust." —Isabel Briggs Myers

Communication in the field isn't about talking—it's about transmitting intent without confusion, interception, or delay. Any fieldwork requires redundant, secure communication systems. When comms break down, so does coordination. And in the field, confusion doesn't just waste time—it gets people hurt, or worse, killed.

Mission-Driven Comms Design: You might be stuck using your agency-selected comms, or you might have free rein. Regardless, you should understand your agency's commo flow: who talks to whom, about what, and how fast it must happen.

Compartmentation & Code Discipline: Every word in a comms plan should serve a purpose. Avoid unnecessary chatter. Field operators must use short, pre-scripted phrases or numeric codes to reduce misunderstanding under stress. If your agency doesn't have a comms plan, then it's up to you to make it.

Analog & Visual Signals: When digital fails, go analog. Prearranged hand signals, radio clicks, or visual cues (like object placement, light flashes, or vehicle patterns) ensure redundancy. Even something as simple as a folded newspaper in a window can confirm safety or compromise. Silent comms demand practice—rehearse until hand gestures and eye contact convey meaning without words.

Redundancy & Failover: Assume your primary system will fail. Build fallback options at every level: multiple networks, battery backups, paper maps, and preplanned check-in times. Establish "loss of contact" timelines—if silence exceeds a set limit, escalation begins automatically. This protects operatives who can't signal distress. If you are not familiar with the term PACE, add it to your arsenal. It stands for primary, alternate, contingency, and emergency channels. Basically, you should have four ways to reach someone during an operation.

Preservation & Legal Accountability: Public-sector teams must preserve communication logs for evidentiary use. Some apps make it very easy to download chat logs like WhatsApp. As a reminder: if you wouldn't say it to mom, don't say it on the radio or the chat. Private investigators should maintain similar standards to defend their findings in court.

Takeaway: Communication is the bloodstream of the operation. Keep it secure, simple, and structured so that everyone comes home.

July 6: Assume You're Being Watched

"Just because you're paranoid doesn't mean they aren't after you." —*Joseph Heller*

Assume you're being watched. Always. That one sentence changes how you plan, where you sit, what you say, and how you leave. Surveillance and countersurveillance are two sides of the same street: while you collect, others—store owners, adversaries, or even the target—may be collecting on you. Recognize the threat vectors—technical, human, and environmental—then design your operation so those vectors can't destroy it.

Technical Threats (the quiet witnesses): Ubiquitous Technical Surveillance (UTS) is here to stay and will only become more pervasive. Shopfront cameras, delivery cams, private CCTV networks, doorbell systems, body cameras, and municipal street cameras record everything with timestamps. Those feeds can preserve a conversation you thought private, show an investigator entering a scene, or document a vehicle's plate. In many courthouses and municipal environments, cameras are omnipresent, and their footage can be obtained by subpoena or public records request. Treat every public-facing lens as potential evidence—and potential prejudice. A casual joke about a shop owner's appearance captured on camera can be a credibility killer in court.

Human & Organizational Countersurveillance: Organized criminal groups, cartels, and other hostile actors run countersurveillance on shipments, stash sites, and meetings. They monitor approaches, record visitors, and watch for patterns that reveal weaknesses in their criminal activities. During deployments in Iraq and Afghanistan, I saw the same dynamic: insurgents filmed coalition patrols to study routes, timings, and tactics for ambush planning. The lesson is universal: if they can film you, they will. Your operational planning must account for adversaries with deliberate intelligence programs and technical capabilities.

Detecting You're Being Watched: Watch for mundane signals: a vehicle that appears too frequently, a person who lingers and always seems "nearby," or staff who suddenly "watch" your every move. There are neighborhoods where people know who lives there, and anyone who doesn't is automatically assumed to be the police (even if you aren't). Technical signs could include people using phones in a conspicuous manner while recording you. Document and Media exploitation (DOMEX) files from captured raids that I have reviewed often showed that what looks ad hoc to you—someone filming with a phone—is part of a deliberate intelligence loop.

Takeaway: The world records more than you think—and adversaries study patterns. Prepare for observation.

July 7: Undercover Operational Security

"Three can keep a secret, if two of them are dead." —Benjamin Franklin

Operational Security (OPSEC) for the undercover investigator begins and ends with the small things. The success of a single meet often hinges not on heroic tradecraft but on whether you remembered to take off a ring, remove an employer badge, or check that a pocket-lint receipt won't reveal your real address.

Start planning long before the meeting. Treat pre-deployment like a mission brief: you will walk through the target's world and your cover's world side-by-side, removing every point of friction that could reveal the truth. That means three simultaneous lines of work: narrative (the cover story and facts you will carry in your head), physical (what you wear, what you carry, what you leave in the car), and technical (what devices, comms, and records exist).

Strip the agent down: Special operators and intelligence officers don't wear jewelry, name-tagged clothing, or items that tie them to a real-life identity. Wedding band? Leave it in the safe. Watch with anniversary engravings? Replace it with a generic watch. The minute you say "I'm single" and your left hand shows a ring, the cover collapses. At the height of the Irish Republican Army's terrorist activities, any newcomer introduced to them would be stripped completely naked and put in a boiler suit to ensure they weren't wearing a wire. All belongings would be searched to ensure they didn't contain devices or that they matched the persona of the person in front of them.

Ditch the real ID: Never introduce yourself as "Don from Baton Rouge" while carrying a driver's license that says "Michael—New Orleans." If you must travel with identification for safety, use documents consistent with the cover (and only if legally and ethically cleared). Otherwise, leave your real ID secured at a safe location and carry no paperwork that contradicts your backstory.

Dress and act the part: Match the physical cues to the story. If your cover is a single contractor, don't arrive with a company polo and ID clipped to your belt. Rehearse your answers to casual questions (where you work, how long you've lived here) until they're automatic and consistent across teammates. Don't say you just got out of Rikers Island after serving time when you can't even explain the cell block. Micro-contradictions sink covers faster than poor acting.

Takeaway: Undercover OPSEC is the art of removing every contradiction before you meet the subject.

July 8: Before the Meet

"Every battle is won before it is fought." —Sun Tzu

Everything that goes right at a confidential informant (CI) meeting happens long before you walk through the door. The meet is a controlled risk: you bring structure to chaos so that, when variables pop up, you already have the answers. Planning is not paperwork—it's the rehearsal of survival. A good plan reduces uncertainty; a great plan anticipates how uncertainty will try to break you.

Start with the mission statement: what is the single, measurable objective of this contact? Is it to obtain a statement, pass a message, confirm identity, measure reaction, or collect evidence? If you can't state the objective in one line, pare it down. Every subsequent decision—venue, timing, cover, and overwatch—flows from that purpose.

Venue selection is tactical. Choose a location that fits the cover, provides predictable lines of sight, and offers discreet exits. Indoor meetings reduce environmental variables (weather, light, noise) but increase the likelihood of recorded audio and CCTV footage, as well as someone recognizing the CI. Outdoor meets can afford anonymity but sacrifice control. A noisy restaurant with multiple exits is different from a hotel lobby with fixed camera angles—know which risk you accept and why.

Do two recon passes: covert and overt. Covert recon maps seat layouts, camera fields, foot traffic, and cellular dead zones at the hour you plan to meet. Overt recon—a plausible visit to confirm staff behavior, parking, and quirks (an hourly delivery, a stock cart that blocks sightlines)—verifies what the covert pass could miss. Identify hard and soft observation points, choke points, and nearby extraction routes. If possible, run a dry approach at the same hour a day or two earlier.

Overwatch and backup are non-negotiable. Assign roles: primary operative, overwatch, extraction lead, and comms officer. Overwatch should be planned, with unobstructed escape options and discreet intervention methods (coded waiter signal, routine phone call). Agree on a single abort trigger and a stronger emergency trigger—and rehearse them until responses are automatic.

Low-tech hazards matter. Decide how you plan to pay for something at the venue. Also, take into consideration where you parked your vehicle. You must avoid linking a personal vehicle to the meet (swap cars if needed). Before you arrive at a venue, remove receipts, loyalty cards, parking stubs, and anything else that could reveal your affiliation as an investigator.

Takeaway: Planning is the quiet weapon that turns risk into a controlled outcome when meeting with a confidential informant.

July 9: During the Meeting

"A good listener is not only popular everywhere, but after a while he gets to know something." —Wilson Mizner

The meeting with a confidential informant (CI) is where planning meets human reality. This is the moment your rehearsal pays off—or doesn't. Your job during contact is deceptively simple: control the dialogue, read behavior, protect the cover, and leave with usable intelligence.

Open the contact on your terms. Arrive on time, calm, and inconspicuous. Begin with short, neutral talk to build a baseline: posture, eye contact, speech cadence, and micro-expressions. Use the first five minutes to set the tone—relaxed, non-confrontational, and routine. This is not interrogation; it's elicitation and verification.

Control the conversation through question sequencing instead of pressure. Start with open-ended questions (like "Tell me what happened that day.") to gather story details, then narrow down with focused closed questions about times, locations, and names. Use prompts like "and then?" and pause quietly—people tend to share more when they fill silence. Avoid leading questions that assume facts you haven't confirmed. When asking for sensitive disclosures, normalize the situation first ("People in that situation often… did that happen here?").

Watch behavior more than words. Speech patterns change under stress: increased filler words, shortened answers, or excessive detail can all signal discomfort or fabrication. Micro-contradictions—a slight hesitation before a name, a hand touching the mouth when denying—matter. If something reads wrong, don't accuse; probe.

Stay in role. Your cover must survive casual scrutiny and hard questions. If the CI abruptly makes a link to your real life or asks a probing legal question, deflect with plausible small talk and return to safe topics. Never volunteer more than the cover requires. If the subject attempts to test you—a staged trap, a loaded question, a request for personal contact info—treat it as an attempt for them to gather intelligence on you. Are they playing both sides?

Manage the CI's motivations implicitly. Many informants trade information for money, safety, revenge, ego, removal of competition, and charges being dropped. Never promise or guarantee anything unless you can back it up.

Takeaway: The best informant contacts are the ones you barely notice afterward because they were handled with discipline and care during the meeting.

July 10: After the Meeting

"Facts do not cease to exist because they are ignored." —Aldous Huxley

The most critical phase of a confidential informant (CI) meeting begins the moment it ends. Once the conversation is over and the adrenaline fades, the small details start slipping—tone, hesitation, pacing, and phrasing. Now documentation comes into play.

Start with the immediate self-debrief. Within minutes of leaving the location, write or record everything while it's still fresh: the CI's demeanor, confidence level, contradictions, or sudden mood changes. Don't edit yet. Raw notes are gold. Capture what stood out, what felt off, and what requires follow-up. The faster you document, the more accurate your observations will be. Memory is a leaking bucket; ink is permanent.

Then move to post-contact verification. Every data point the CI provided should be tested—names, vehicles, addresses, phone numbers, relationships, timelines. Some will check out; others won't. Don't treat errors as failures; treat them as indicators. The more you test and record, the clearer your informant's reliability pattern becomes.

If you're working within a team, hold a hot debrief as soon as possible. Compare observations, reconcile inconsistencies, and identify follow-ups. Move quickly to documentation and evidence handling. Secure everything—audio, video, notes, or physical evidence—under your agency or company's chain-of-custody protocols. Label, timestamp, and file it immediately.

Evaluate source performance and motivation right away. Did the CI's behavior align with previous patterns? Were they cooperative, distracted, nervous, or manipulative? Adjust their reliability rating accordingly. Whether your system uses numbers, letters, or color codes, update it after every contact. Patterns of credibility are only visible if tracked consistently. I have terminated my share of sources when the information or motivations no longer aligned with the organization's objectives.

Don't skip the personal decompression. After tense or high-risk meetings, you need a moment to reset. Take a walk, breathe, and debrief with a colleague if operationally appropriate. Undercover and CI work strains focus and emotional stability. A short pause restores clarity and prevents errors in your next task.

Takeaway: The meet isn't truly over until it's verified, documented, and preserved.

July 11: Managing Confidential Informants

"Trust is earned in drops and lost in buckets." —Kevin Plank

Confidential informants (CIs) are the lifeblood of intelligence-driven investigations, but they are also their greatest vulnerability. A good informant can open doors that surveillance or subpoenas never could.

Recruitment begins with recognition—identifying who has access, motive, and leverage. Some potential informants come forward out of fear, revenge, or self-preservation. Others need a push. You don't recruit with threats; you recruit with logic. The goal is to align their self-interest with your operational objectives. A motivated CI working for mutual benefit is far more reliable than one working under duress.

Before recruitment, conduct a suitability assessment. The Department of Justice calls it "risk evaluation," and for good reason. Examine criminal history, affiliations, substance use, mental stability, and exposure to violence. A CI with unstable behavior or pending felony charges may require heightened supervision or be disqualified entirely. In the private sector, you evaluate reputation, trustworthiness, and motive just as carefully. A company insider motivated by resentment is useful only if their anger doesn't bleed into fabrication.

When recruiting, be clear about roles and limits. Informants often misunderstand their place in the process. They are not partners, officers, or heroes (remember the junior G-man scene in Sopranos?); they are assets—sources of information whose reliability must be continuously tested. Make expectations explicit: what they will provide, how they will communicate, and what they will not do without authorization. Never let a CI believe they can act independently "on behalf" of an investigator.

Establish a communications plan that balances security with accountability. Use recorded, logged, or otherwise documentable means of contact whenever feasible. Every contact should be documented in a contact report, noting date, time, location, and subject matter. Never rely solely on memory or informal exchanges. The most catastrophic CI failures in both public and private sectors stem from undocumented promises, unclear instructions, or verbal side deals.

Takeaway: Managing a CI is managing risk. The best investigators balance empathy with control, trust with verification, and opportunity with oversight.

July 12: Source Vetting & Validation

"Trust starts with truth and ends with truth." —*Santosh Kalwar*

Every investigator has heard something that felt right—a story that fits the case theory a little too neatly. But intelligence without validation is just noise. The difference between a tip and a lead is verification.

Vetting starts as soon as a source begins speaking. Every detail they share—such as names, locations, vehicles, and relationships—should be quietly checked for consistency and plausibility. You're not just evaluating the information but also the person giving it. Are their facts steady? Do timelines match up? Does their body language change when asked for specifics?

Validation separates what a source believes from what they know. The Department of Homeland Security standard is simple: corroborate, cross-check, and compare. Verify each claim through at least one independent means—surveillance, record checks, open-source data, or another informant. Never rely solely on one human source, no matter how long you've worked with them.

In the private sector, the same rules apply. Before you act on insider information—whether from a whistleblower, employee, or competitor contact—ask yourself: Can I prove this without them? If the answer is no, you have not verified it yet. Acting on untested claims can expose you or your client to liability, reputational harm, or worse. A credible source enhances your reputation; an unchecked one can destroy it overnight.

Documentation is the backbone of validation. Record how information was obtained, what was verified, and what didn't check out. If one source confirms another, document that link. If they conflict, track both. Discrepancies reveal motives and manipulation patterns. In intelligence work, contradictions are as valuable as confirmations—both map the boundaries of truth.

Assess source reliability continuously. Track how often a source's information has proven accurate, timely, or self-serving. Many agencies use reliability and validity codes; you can apply the same concept mentally. Keep a log of what they have gotten right and wrong, and adjust your confidence level accordingly.

Beware of confirmation bias. Investigators naturally want the world to confirm their theories. Validation requires humility—the willingness to be wrong. If the data fits too perfectly, it's time for another round of checks.

Takeaway: Vetting and validation protect both sides—they preserve integrity, credibility, and, ultimately, the mission.

July 13: Handling High-Risk Sources

"Government is not reason, it is not eloquence—it is force. Like fire, it is a dangerous servant and a fearful master." —President George Washington

You want to know what else is like fire? High-risk sources. Some of the most valuable informants are also the most dangerous. They live in unstable worlds—organized crime, narcotics, corruption, or violence—and they bring that volatility into every contact. Handling high-risk sources demands precision and humility. You can't extinguish the fire; you can only control it.

A high-risk source is one who poses danger to themselves, the handler, or the integrity of the investigation. That can mean active criminal participation, violent associations, substance abuse, or simply the potential for retaliation. Before accepting such a source, conduct a full risk assessment. Ask yourself: Is this person controllable? is the information unique? is the safety plan sufficient? If the answer to any of those questions is uncertain, pause. Sometimes walking away is the most professional move you can make.

When working with active offenders, never forget who you're dealing with. They are not partners; they are opportunists operating under pressure. They will test boundaries and manipulate sympathy. Federal law enforcement agencies stress strict oversight for good reason—high-risk informants often blur the line between cooperation and crime. Limit them to clearly authorized actions.

Develop a source control plan before the first meeting. Conduct meetings in secure, controlled locations. Rotate sites, times, and personnel to reduce predictability. Use overwatch whenever safety or surveillance conditions warrant it. The higher the risk, the tighter the leash.

Prioritize safety and separation. Protecting an informant's identity isn't just policy; it's life insurance. Compromise it once, and you will never get it back. Share their identity only on a strict need-to-know basis. Establish emergency protocols for extraction or contact if the confidential informant senses a threat. Even in the private sector, that may mean encrypted communication, alternate contact points, or legal relocation assistance.

Never lose sight of ethics and legality. You cannot authorize, ignore, or rationalize illegal activity in pursuit of progress. If a source commits a crime outside the parameters of an approved operation, document it and report it immediately.

Takeaway: Handling high-risk sources is managing controlled danger. Like fire, they can illuminate the path forward—or burn down the case.

July 14: Documentation & Payments

"Trust is good. Control is better." —German Proverb

Every investigator loves the adrenaline of a meet—the tension, the dialogue, the reveal. But long after that excitement fades, what keeps your work defensible isn't what you heard—it's what you wrote. A properly managed confidential informant (CI) program runs on accountability. Every contact, payment, and piece of information must be traceable. In law enforcement, this means a control file—a comprehensive record of the informant's identity, risk assessments, suitability reviews, and reporting history. In the private sector, it may take the form of a secure source file, locked behind digital and physical controls.

Financial control is equally critical. Every payment to a CI—whether cash, credit, or consideration—must be documented with the same rigor as evidence handling. Law enforcement agencies use serial-numbered receipts, witnessed signatures, and dual-approval systems. Private investigators should mirror that discipline. Maintain a clear paper trail for all funds distributed or reimbursed. Never rely on verbal agreements or IOUs. Informant payments may buy information, but they should never buy ambiguity. Always link payments directly to results. Compensation should match measurable contributions—intelligence quality, cooperation, or specific assistance rendered.

Periodically review your CI's financial relationship and motivation. Money can distort behavior. A source who once cooperated out of fear or conscience may become transactional. When that happens, step back and reevaluate the relationship. Are you paying for information or performance? Every dollar spent should serve an operational goal, not maintain dependency. Protect the confidentiality of documentation as fiercely as the informant's identity.

Audits and administrative reviews aren't nuisances—they are safety nets. A well-documented CI file can survive scrutiny from prosecutors, inspectors general, or defense attorneys because it tells a simple story: the investigator followed the rules.

Takeaway: Documentation and payments are the twin pillars of control. They don't make headlines, but they make careers.

July 15: Managing Informant Motivation

"Everyone has a weakness. The trick is to find it." —Victor Cherkashin

Undercover work and confidential informant (CI) operations are sustained by motivation, not paperwork. For decades, intelligence and law enforcement have relied on **MICE**—Money, Ideology, Compromise (Coercion), Ego—to explain why people spy or cooperate. Another variation over the years: **CRIME**—Cooperation/Coercion, Revenge, Ideology, Money, Ego. These frameworks help identify leverage. But leverage is not the same as longevity. An informant motivated purely by money will constantly calculate risk versus reward. A source pressured into cooperation may comply, but rarely commits. Revenge burns intensely—then fades. Ego requires continual reinforcement. The most stable informants are those whose cooperation aligns with identity.

External vs. Internal Motivation: External motivation requires maintenance. Internal motivation sustains itself. If a source cooperates because charges were reduced, you must continually reinforce that incentive. If a source cooperates because they believe they are protecting their community, correcting injustice, or striking back at corruption, their discipline increases. Internal motivation produces consistency. External motivation produces transactions.

The "True Believer": In intelligence history, the most formidable penetrations were often "True Believers" —individuals driven by ideology. They believed they were serving a higher mission. Risk, money, and pressure mattered less because their identity and their actions were inseparable. Nothing is more powerful—or more dangerous—than belief. In the CI world, the scale is smaller, but the principle remains the same. When a source sees cooperation as morally justified or personally meaningful, resilience increases. When they view themselves as part of something significant rather than merely "working off a case," performance stabilizes.

A Lesson from the Cold War: When Aldrich Ames first approached the Soviet Embassy in Washington, D.C., money was the entry point. But his KGB handler, Viktor Cherkashin, did not treat him like hired help. He treated him as a valued partner. Cherkashin reinforced Ames' sense of importance and framed the relationship in terms of mutual protection and shared purpose. Money opened the door. Identity kept it open. The same principle applies to the handling of informants. If you treat a source as a paid asset, they will behave like one. If you treat them as a meaningful contributor to something larger, many will rise to that expectation.

Takeaway: Managing informant motivation is not about pressure—it is about alignment. When you and your informant align, you are unstoppable.

July 16: Recruitment Strategies

"The greatest ability in business is to get along with others and to influence their actions." —John Hancock

Recruiting a confidential informant (CI) isn't a game of luck—it's a disciplined process built on observation, judgment, and timing. Every recruitment follows the same intelligence cycle known as SADR: Spot, Assess, Develop, Recruit. Mastering that cycle turns random contacts into reliable sources.

Spot is where it begins. You identify potential informants based on access, opportunity, and motivation. Who sees what you can't? Who lives in the world you're trying to penetrate? In criminal investigations, it may be a low-level associate, a family member, or someone on the fringe looking for a way out. In private investigations, it might be an employee, contractor, or insider with access to proprietary information. Spotting isn't about desperation—it's about placement. A CI without relevant access is just a spectator.

Assess comes next, and it's the foundation of safety and control. Evaluate the potential CI's motivation—fear, greed, revenge, or ego—and whether it aligns with your operational needs. Conduct a suitability assessment early: criminal background, reliability, stability, and risk of exposure. If the CI is motivated by self-preservation, can you deliver on what they expect?

Develop is where the groundwork of trust is laid. You're not manipulating—you're building a professional relationship. Keep the tone consistent, calm, and respectful. The CI needs to see you as stable, not emotional, or unpredictable. Early development meetings aren't about information; they are about credibility. Be honest about your role, your limits, and what cooperation looks like. Don't bluff safety, payment, or immunity you can't authorize. Overpromising destroys trust faster than confrontation ever could.

Recruit is the final step—the point of commitment. Here, the CI agrees to cooperate formally under defined conditions. Set clear boundaries on conduct, communication, and expectations. Outline what is authorized and what isn't—no unsupervised contact with targets, no independent "investigating." In law enforcement, this stage includes documentation, control numbers, and acknowledgment of responsibilities. In the private sector, it's the point where legal and ethical standards must be made explicit because institutional safeguards don't really exist. A CI who understands their role is far less likely to compromise it.

Takeaway: Recruiting a CI isn't about persuasion; it is about you showing them how your goals are in sync for the benefit of you both.

July 17: Clandestine Exchanges

"Secrecy is the beginning of tyranny." —Robert A. Heinlein

Every investigator eventually faces the problem of secure communication—how to move information, money, or evidence without being seen together. Whether you're managing a confidential informant (CI) or operating undercover, there comes a time when physical contact is too risky. That's when you turn to the oldest form of covert communication: the clandestine exchange.

Dead drops and live drops serve the same purpose: separating people from the information they share. A dead drop is a prearranged location where one-party leaves material for another to retrieve later, minimizing the risk of exposure. A live drop is an in-person handoff that's brief, discreet, and controlled. Both require discipline, precision, and an understanding that the smallest deviation can compromise security. For the purposes of this lesson, we will only focus on the dead drop.

A good dead drop follows three rules: concealment, timing, and deniability. The site should blend naturally into the environment—a hollow tree, loose brick, magnetic container, or piece of public infrastructure that won't draw attention. The location must be accessible without obvious detours or suspicious behavior. Timing is critical. Staggered arrival windows ensure neither party crosses paths. Finally, deniability: nothing at the drop site should link either party to the material if discovered.

When dealing with CIs, dead drops serve as lifelines for high-risk sources who can't risk face-to-face meetings. The material being exchanged might be physical or digital. Whatever the format, the handler must keep the process sterile. Never reuse a location once it's been employed. Predictability kills security.

Modern adaptations of these methods exist in both government and private work. Digital "dead drops" —encrypted cloud folders, one-time use communication apps, or shared virtual drives—follow the same principle: separation and security. But technology adds new vulnerabilities. Metadata, IP logs, and timestamps can expose users. The best practice is still compartmentation: isolate devices, accounts, and channels. A single slip in digital hygiene can reveal what a thousand covert meetings never did. A parting tip for those in the private sector. Remember: without government backing, tread extremely carefully to avoid illegal territory. In every case, remember that safety outweighs secrecy. If a source appears compromised or surveillance is suspected, abort immediately. No piece of evidence is worth a life.

Takeaway: Use clandestine exchanges to gather information from CIs and undercover investigators safely.

July 18: Interagency Coordination

"The fewer men know, the fewer mistakes we shall make." —Duke of Wellington

When multiple teams, agencies, or contractors operate in the same space, the biggest threat is not the target—it's each other. Deconfliction and interagency coordination are not bureaucratic niceties; they are safety and mission preservation. Two well-meaning teams who don't talk can collide, ruin evidence, expose sources, or, worse, create a violent, avoidable outcome.

Start with a clear point of authority: a Single Point of Contact (SPOC) or operations desk that owns situational awareness. The SPOC's job is simple and critical—know who is doing what, where, and when, and route coordination requests through a single, auditable channel. Multiple coordinators create multiple failure points. Centralize awareness; decentralize execution within defined boundaries. Obviously, you won't have this luxury in the private sector, but if you aren't doing it on the public side, start.

You can also designate liaison officers for high-touch coordination between agencies. A vetted liaison—someone who understands both operational needs and administrative limits—can brief partners without spilling sensitive tactical detail. Use vetted liaisons to bridge cultures: federal, local, military, private security, or corporate investigative teams don't share the same policies. This is where your liaison can shine.

Protect sources during cross-briefs. Before sharing any CI-derived intelligence, confirm your partner's legal authority and operational need-to-know. Don't swap a name for convenience. If a partner's request would expose a CI, propose alternatives—surveillance confirmation, physical corroboration, or an anonymized summary. Never mortgage a human life to convenience.

A deployed colleague shared a good example of why we deconflict. The source had been "shopping" his fake story across multiple military bases—repeating the same tale to anyone who would listen. When other units grew suspicious, they apprehended him and searched his vehicle. Investigators found dozens of notebooks, each page bearing the same narratives written repeatedly. The source had rehearsed the disinformation, refining it to sell in hopes of influencing U.S. decisions in the area. That single discovery not only exposed the source but also compromised every lead connected to him. The lesson is clear: uncontrolled sources, even those that seem cooperative, can be a risk for intentional or accidental contamination across multiple investigations.

Takeaway: Deconfliction is not red tape—it's good practice for any agency to avoid duplicative or disastrous efforts.

July 19: Undercover Safety

"No plan survives first contact with the enemy." —Helmuth von Moltke the Elder

Undercover operations rarely go as planned. The best strategies don't predict the future—they prepare you to adapt when circumstances change. Safety and extraction aren't afterthoughts; they form the backbone that keeps an investigator alive when chaos erupts. If you don't plan your escape before you go in, you're relying on luck in a profession that doesn't believe in it.

Before any meeting, develop two exit plans—one deliberate, one emergency. The deliberate plan is the usual closeout: you disengage smoothly, check in, and leave unnoticed. The emergency plan is the one that keeps you safe if something goes wrong. Set clear abort triggers—small, unmistakable signals that mean "end the meeting now." These triggers should be simple, repeatable, and pre-approved: a phrase in conversation, a text that doesn't belong, or a time-overdue check-in. Everyone involved—overwatch, extraction, or command—must know them thoroughly.

Map primary and secondary extraction routes. Your primary path should match your cover's routine; the secondary should look nothing like it. Know every choke point, every traffic pattern, and every place where you could disappear. When possible, plan to exit through natural crowds or neutral facilities—places where you can change your look, vehicle, or behavior without drawing attention.

Account for medical and legal contingencies. Every operation should include a route to a nearby hospital and a plan for first response. My first law enforcement supervisor worked narcotics with the NYPD. They were conducting some standard buy-bust deals, and an undercover officer was shot because the perp thought he was a cop. No evidence, just a thought. They had to rush to the hospital using their preplanned hospital route. That officer is alive today because of basic contingency planning. Having emergency medical supplies on hand is mandatory in any field operation.

Rehearse extraction drills until they feel ordinary. Practice what to do when the car is blocked, comms die, or a CI panics. Walk through every role—who covers, who drives, who confirms extraction complete. Familiarity under stress is survival.

Takeaway: Undercover work rewards preparation, not perfection. The plan may not survive first contact, but the investigator who planned for failure will.

July 20: Protecting your CI in Court

"Trust is built when someone is vulnerable and not taken advantage of." —Bob Vanourek

If you work long enough as an investigator, you will eventually face the hardest confidential informant (CI) question of all: *what happens if the case goes to court?* Protecting a CI during an investigation is one thing. Protecting them once litigation begins—when discovery rules, motions, and testimony come into play—is something else entirely. The first principle is simple: you protect a CI long before court is even on the horizon. That starts with documentation. CI agreements matter. They establish expectations, scope, confidentiality language, and your intent to fully protect the informant's identity, as allowed by law.

Next are legal protections. In many jurisdictions, courts recognize some form of **informant privilege**, allowing the withholding of identifying information when disclosure would endanger the informant or chill future cooperation. Motions, protective orders, and in camera reviews—where a judge privately examines sensitive material—are common tools. Courts balance disclosure against safety and fairness, and that balance matters.

Identity minimization is equally critical. Use pseudonyms, anonymized identifiers, and redacted reports whenever possible. Avoid unnecessary descriptors that allow a motivated party to triangulate an informant's identity. Occupation, location, timing, and relationships all compound risk. Protecting a CI often means removing details that feel harmless—but aren't. Digital hygiene also cannot be overlooked. Secure storage, encryption, access controls, and compartmentalization are mandatory when dealing with CIs.

Testimony strategy matters. A case does not always require a CI to testify. Often, the investigator's testimony—supported by documents, financial records, surveillance, or independent verification—can carry the evidentiary load. The goal is to make the CI useful without exposing them.

There is, however, a hard truth every investigator must accept: if an informant becomes central to a party's ability to confront evidence, disclosure may be ordered. Courts ultimately balance justice against risk. Law enforcement may have access to witness protection mechanisms that private investigators do not, making close coordination with counsel essential. Never promise a CI what the court may not allow you to keep. Finally, law enforcement agencies have formal CI units, statutory privileges, and institutional safeguards. Private investigators operate differently—but the obligation is the same. If you ask someone to take personal risk by sharing information, you owe them appropriate protections.

Takeaway: Protecting a CI isn't about secrecy for its own sake. It's about trust, safety, and integrity.

July 21: Cross-Border Cooperation

"Diplomacy is the art of letting someone else have your way." —David Frost

Operating across borders tests every part of an investigator's discipline—tradecraft, judgment, patience, and humility. Laws shift, cultures collide, and priorities rarely align perfectly. In domestic work, control is an illusion you can at least manage; overseas, it's a privilege you negotiate.

Start by understanding the landscape. Every country has its own legal thresholds, privacy expectations, and political sensitivities. Before you deploy, study host-nation laws, liaison structures, and status-of-forces or mutual-assistance agreements. Ignorance abroad isn't just embarrassing—it's criminal.

Cross-border cooperation thrives on personal rapport, not paper. The most productive exchanges come from officers, attachés, and investigators who have already shared coffee, not crisis. Introductions through embassy security offices, INTERPOL desks, or vetted private-sector partners build trust that formal cables alone can't. If you are in U.S. law enforcement, the Diplomatic Security Service should be your first call after coordinating with your supervisor. Courtesy and patience go farther than demands. Remember: you may represent your country, but you are also representing your own credibility.

When operating with foreign partners, oversharing can compromise both the mission and your source. Limit what you disclose to what is necessary for mutual objectives. Many foreign agencies run internal intelligence services with separate agendas; they treat every partner as cooperative but not cleared.

Timelines, communication styles, and even what "urgent" means differ globally. Western investigators often expect linear progress; other systems move through consensus and protocol. Impatience is misread as arrogance. Adapt your rhythm to the environment. That doesn't mean lowering standards—it means packaging requests in the way your counterparts can accept and act on.

Private-sector investigators face the same frictions, amplified. A multinational fraud case, missing-persons case, or corporate espionage probe can span legal systems that don't recognize one another's subpoenas or privacy rules. Working through counsel in each jurisdiction, securing translators under nondisclosure, and ensuring data-handling complies with local law are not optional.

Takeaway: Diplomacy isn't weakness; it's the art of moving others to your purpose while letting them believe it was their idea.

July 22: Tactical Planning for Warrants

"You can't build a reputation on what you are going to do." —Henry Ford

A warrant isn't a moment of action—it's a test of preparation. Tactical planning for a warrant is about controlling the chaos before it starts: protecting people, preserving evidence, and proving professionalism under pressure. Verify the warrant's validity, address, and scope. Everyone must understand the objective—what is being sought, where it's authorized, and why it matters

Move next to the pre-raid checklist. It's simple, repeatable, and lifesaving. Confirm the most current intelligence: number of occupants, possible weapons, known threats, and the building layout. Identify approach routes and fallback points and assign a medic with access to trauma supplies and a clear evacuation route to the nearest hospital.

Scene safety starts the moment the team arrives. Secure the perimeter quickly and calmly. Never allow unsecured individuals to linger near doorways or driveways—that's where surprises live. Inside, move deliberately. Loud commands should be short and clear, chaos breeds panic. Once the scene is stable, transition from control to containment: separate occupants, identify them, and document everyone present. Don't forget the technical and surveillance threats we discussed earlier in the year.

Children, elderly residents, or uninvolved roommates must be removed from immediate areas of operation and kept safe, ideally in a designated "clear zone" under supervision. Speak to them professionally, not with adrenaline. How you treat bystanders will be remembered long after the case is closed.

Animals are often the forgotten threat. A large or aggressive dog can end a career in seconds and spark public outrage. Anticipate pets from intelligence or neighbor tips. If feasible, use barriers, leashes, or animal control. Avoid escalation; retreat and contain before considering any higher-risk option.

Once the location is secure, document immediately. Assign an evidence officer to control photos, logs, and item recovery. Record who found what and where. When the last room is cleared, conduct a quick "hot wash" before anyone departs—confirm safety, count personnel, and anything else needed.

While private investigators don't serve warrants, they can participate in contractual searches. They must apply the same rigor when they do. Scene safety, documentation, and respect for occupants are universal standards.

Takeaway: A warrant operation is judged less by what happens at the door than by what happens before it. Plan, prepare, and execute.

July 23: Arrest Procedures

"Speak softly and carry a big stick; you will go far." —President Theodore Roosevelt

Arrest is the moment theory becomes reality—and reality is where mistakes get people hurt, evidence lost, and careers ruined. Whether you wear a badge or run a private investigative firm, the rules are simple: safety first and ego last.

Public sector first: We are not talking about standard police work where a single officer is on patrol, witnesses a crime, and then takes action. We are talking about investigators who build cases, then make arrests in an organized manner. Therefore, treat every arrest like a team evolution. Use **contact and cover** investigators deliberately. The contact investigator controls hands and voice, and oversees the primary compliance sequence; the cover investigator observes threats, monitors exits, and neutralizes surprises. Roles must be rehearsed until they are instinctive. A sloppy handoff between contact and cover is how people get punched, shot, or panicked into resisting.

Know both dominant-hand and support-hand techniques so you can cuff a suspect in tight spaces or when adverse angles force you off your trained side. Carry your cuffs on your person; leaving restraint tools in a belt bag because you "want to travel light" sacrifices safety for convenience. I have worked with investigators who refused to wear cuffs to "keep weight down." If you get into a scuffle, and the other investigator's pair is lost, what now? Read your agency's Miranda warning from an agency-issued card to prevent any misinterpretations or claims of rights deprivation. If the suspect doesn't speak English, have another investigator read it in a translation of that language.

For private investigators: I will make it simple for you. **Do not perform citizens' arrests as policy.** The legal and practical downsides are severe: mistaken identity, false imprisonment, assault, kidnapping allegations, and crossing statutory lines that differ from state to state. If you are an employee of a private investigator firm, ask not to be involved in these matters. If you own a private investigation company, make a written policy forbidding employees from effecting arrests.

Instead, train them to observe, document, preserve scene integrity, and call law enforcement. It is much easier and safer for private investigators this way, and they usually can hand the evidence over on a silver platter via surveillance video. If immediate intervention is unavoidable to prevent imminent serious harm, ensure your teams understand the narrow legal standard and that every action is justified, proportionate, and documented.

Takeaway: An arrest has no room for ego. It is a procedure that requires the investigator's safety before, during, and after the event.

July 24: Elicitation for the Undercover Officer

"Whether you're in Moscow, Tehran, or Miami, club girls are a good source of information. Men say things to a beautiful woman. They give out phone numbers and hotel keys. They let down their guard." —Michael Westen, Burn Notice

Elicitation is the quiet work of the undercover investigator: getting strangers to share what they should not, without ever appearing to ask for it. It's not interrogation—it's influence disguised as conversation. Done well, it yields usable intelligence; done poorly, it exposes your cover.

Start by owning the environment. Your cover should place you where natural conversation flows: a bar stool with a view of the room, a service counter, a social event where people naturally overshare. Use props—a drink, a phone call, a joke—to create realistic reasons to be noticed and to notice others. Remember: plausibility is your armor. If your presence makes sense, people lower their guard faster.

Open with harmless, open invites. "Tell me about your trip" or "How do you know the host?" invites narrative; people reveal identity, associations, and routines in stories. Follow with neutral follow-ups such as "And then?" —and let silence do the heavy lifting. People dislike gaps and will often fill them with details the investigator can later verify.

Master the art of indirect questions. Rather than asking, "Do you traffic in X?" try, "What's the busiest night for deliveries around here?" or "Where do people go when they want discretion?" Questions framed around routines or norms let informants describe behavior without feeling accused. Normalize admissions: "A lot of people in that business tend to do Y—is that true here?" It removes stigma and encourages candor.

Listen more than you speak. Active listening—paraphrasing, mirroring, and minimal encouragers—builds rapport without committing you. When someone says a name, repeat it back casually: "So, Marco's the driver?" Small confirmations make the speaker feel understood and often yield corrections that reveal more detail.

Guard against entrapment and legal exposure. Never manufacture a crime to induce disclosure. Elicitation is about letting people reveal what they already will; it is not about creating reasons for them to act.

Takeaway: Elicitation is subtle work: patient, methodical, and ethical. The best undercover investigators can gather information without the subject realizing it.

July 25: Managing Split Loyalties

"It's easier to fool people than to convince them that they have been fooled." —Mark Twain

Every investigator eventually meets a source who seems too good to be true—because they are. Dual-role sources work both sides of the table: they feed you information while serving another master. That could be a rival agency, a criminal network, or their own ego. These individuals can destroy cases, expose operations, or worse, get people hurt.

Start with awareness of motive drift. Even reliable sources can change sides over time. Pressure from prosecution, revenge, greed, or fear can alter allegiances overnight. Monitor for changes in tone, new demands for information, or evasiveness about who else they are talking to. When loyalty shifts, it's rarely announced—it's inferred from behavior.

Operational testing is the cornerstone of detection. Slip harmless but traceable details into conversations—a date, a false meeting location, a minor operational name—and monitor where that information reappears. If another agency or adversary references the same data, you have confirmed a leak. Use compartmentalized information—what intelligence officers call "canaries in the coal mine" —to isolate breaches without tipping your hand.

Run periodic credibility audits. Cross-check the CI's reporting with independent sources and surveillance. If patterns show they only deliver when under pressure, they may be fabricating to maintain favor. Vetted handlers conduct "truth testing" through follow-up interviews and third-party corroboration.

Watch for emotional play. The most dangerous double agents are not the desperate ones—they are the charming ones. Flattery, sympathy, or appeals to friendship are tools of manipulation. Maintain empathy but not attachment. The moment you start believing you're the exception, you're the next mark. I knew an intelligence officer who did pre-briefs and debriefs with his officers before their meetings with sources. He would often say, *"Don't fall in love with your source,"* and *"Who is running whom?"*

In the private sector, this problem often takes a subtler form. A corporate insider might share legitimate data while also feeding competitors. Treat every whistleblower as both an asset and a risk until verification confirms loyalty. Use structured communication channels, strict data-handling protocols, and access logs. Every informant—no matter how trusted—must remain auditable.

Takeaway: A double-dealing source is a test of your discipline. Consistently operationally test your source to flush out dual loyalties.

July 26: Shadow Work

"Great things are done by a series of small things brought together." —Vincent van Gogh

Every successful undercover operation has two stories: the one unfolding in front of the target, and the one unfolding quietly behind it. The second story belongs to the shadow team—the unseen professionals who keep the undercover investigator safe, the operation on track, and the chaos contained when things go sideways. They don't get credit, but they make survival possible.

Shadow work is everything that happens offstage. It's the surveillance units that track the investigator's route in and out. It's the overwatch officer in a parked car who notices a tail, the analyst watching digital comms in real time, the technical specialist running GPS trackers and encrypted radios. These are the safety nets beneath the tightrope. When an undercover investigator is out front, the shadow team is the lifeline that turns risk into a calculated risk.

Start with situational coverage. Every undercover meet should have eyes on approach routes, contact points, and exit corridors. Overwatch isn't just someone parked nearby with binoculars; it's a deliberate, layered safety perimeter. One observer watches the subject's vehicle, another monitors the environment for new arrivals, and a third tracks the undercover's position via discreet signals or coded comms. If any part of that triangle fails, the entire operation becomes a blindfolded walk.

Shadow work also means technical overwatch. Today's operations use encrypted messaging, covert GPS beacons, and panic signals built into devices. The digital team must monitor not just the operative's safety but also the integrity of the network—if a signal stops, they should know whether it's a loss of coverage or a loss of control.

Contingency response separates professionals from amateurs. The shadow team rehearses what happens if contact fails. Who drives in first? Who monitors exfil routes? No one improvises those steps on the fly. The best units practice time-on-target drills—"If comms drop for 90 seconds, we move" —so hesitation doesn't become tragedy.

For private investigators or protection teams, shadow work might look different—discreet overwatch from a second vehicle, a nearby safe location, or remote comms monitoring. Regardless of scale, the principle is the same: the undercover or field operator should never be alone, even when it appears that way.

Takeaway: Behind every undercover walking into the unknown is a quiet network of professionals watching, guiding, and ready to pull them out.

July 27: The Handler's Burden

"Leadership is not about being in charge. It is about taking care of those in your charge." —Simon Sinek

The handler carries the quiet weight of every confidential informant (CI) and undercover investigator in their orbit. They are equal parts mentor, supervisor, therapist, and firewall—the one person who sees both the mission and the human cost beneath it.

Every CI and undercover asset tests their handler in different ways. Some push boundaries; others seek validation or connection. The handler's first responsibility is control—not dominance, but structure. Federal law enforcement guidelines emphasize the same truth: unsupervised informants drift toward chaos. Regular debriefs, scheduled contact, and documentation are not bureaucracy; they are survival measures.

Emotional detachment is essential. A handler who becomes a friend loses objectivity; a handler who becomes a tyrant loses trust. The balance is professionalism with empathy—showing enough humanity to maintain rapport without being manipulated by it. Informants will often test handlers through sympathy plays, guilt, or manufactured crises. The seasoned handler recognizes these for what they are: attempts to shift control.

Operationally, the handler is also the system's conscience. They ensure that the mission doesn't cross into entrapment, that approvals are documented, and that every action can withstand courtroom light. Supervisory review, legal consultation, and command notification may slow the tempo, but they also prevent careers and cases from burning together. In the private sector, this same burden falls on owners and lead investigators who must protect employees from overreach, ethical lapses, or psychological collapse.

Documentation is the handler's mirror. Every meeting, every payment, every decision belongs in the record. Written accountability isn't about mistrust—it's about institutional memory. If the handler fails to document it, it never existed.

Finally, the hardest truth: sometimes the handler must end a relationship that once worked. A CI becomes unreliable, an undercover crosses ethical lines, or the emotional toll grows too high. Ending it isn't betrayal; it's leadership. The handler's burden is knowing when to close a door before someone walks through it and doesn't come back.

Takeaway: A handler's job isn't to control outcomes—it's to stay emotionally detached and gather information that otherwise could not be gathered.

July 28: Lessons from Failed Operations

"Failure is simply the opportunity to begin again, this time more intelligently." — *Henry Ford*

Every investigator has a story about an operation that didn't go as planned. The best learn from it; the worst hide it. Despite the tragedies connected to them, failed undercover and informant operations can make us better. Here are three:

Case 1: Operation Fast and Furious. Between 2006 and 2011, the Bureau of Alcohol, Tobacco, Firearms, and Explosives launched an operation intended to trace firearms from U.S. gun dealers to Mexican cartels. Agents allowed hundreds of weapons to "walk" in hopes of later tracking the networks. Instead, most guns vanished. At least two turned up at crime scenes, including the murder of U.S. Border Patrol Agent Brian Terry. What went wrong wasn't just policy—it was ego and lack of interagency coordination. Field agents acted without clear command authority or continuous oversight. Intelligence sharing failed, surveillance collapsed, and no one had a working retrieval plan. The lesson: if you can't control the risk, you don't own the operation—it owns you.

Case 2: The Louisiana Informant Assault. In 2021, a female informant working with a Louisiana narcotics unit was allegedly raped twice during a sting while her handlers waited "down the street." The operation had no live monitoring, no overwatch, and no pre-planned emergency extraction. Command treated it as routine, and routine became complacency. This case shows how operational neglect becomes moral failure. Informants, particularly those without training or backup, depend entirely on their handlers' foresight. Federal and state guidelines require constant supervision, communication checks, and post-contact debriefs precisely to prevent tragedies like this. The moment an agency treats a CI as disposable, it has already failed the mission.

Case 3: The Death of Andrew Sadek. In 2014, a North Dakota college student named Andrew Sadek was caught selling small amounts of marijuana. Law enforcement recruited him as an informant under threat of severe prosecution. He received little training, no protective measures, and minimal oversight. Weeks later, he disappeared. His body was found in a river with a gunshot wound to the head; his informant status wasn't even publicly acknowledged until after his death. Sadek's case reflects systemic blind spots: coercive recruitment, poor documentation, and absent aftercare. The investigation failed before it began because no one asked whether the risk was proportionate to the offense or whether the CI was emotionally or operationally equipped to handle it.

Takeaway: Undercover and informant operations fail not because they are risky, but because people forget why the rules exist in the first place.

July 29: Source Deactivation & Exit Strategy

"The greatest mistake you can make in life is to be continually fearing you will make one." —Elbert Hubbard

Every confidential informant (CI) relationship has a beginning, a middle, and—if managed properly—a purposeful end. The problem is that most don't end well. Handlers become attached, sources grow dependent, and programs keep them alive well past their usefulness. In intelligence and investigations, failing to close a source properly is like leaving a door unlocked during a storm: eventually, everything you built can be blown open. The goal is to end the relationship without jeopardizing the case, the agency, or the person. According to federal guidelines, termination begins when continued cooperation no longer serves a clear investigative purpose—whether because the information has dried up, credibility has eroded, or the risk outweighs the benefit. The handler must recognize this decline early, document it, and initiate the exit plan before the relationship descends into chaos.

Start with a risk assessment. Ask three questions: Is the source still manageable? Are they still productive? And is continued use justifiable? If the answer to any is no, initiate the off-ramp. High-risk sources are never simply "turned loose." They go through a structured process: final debrief, payment reconciliation, documentation of all unresolved issues, and a closure memo signed by command.

The final debrief serves both operational and psychological purposes. It's where the handler collects remaining intelligence—names, patterns, rumors—and clarifies with the source what the next steps are. Be straightforward: the relationship is ending, they are no longer assigned tasks, and unauthorized contact will not be allowed. Record this conversation exactly as spoken. Ambiguity increases the risk of re-contact and liability.

For high-profile sources, aftercare is essential. Law enforcement may coordinate relocation or sealed-record procedures, while private investigators might arrange legal counsel or corporate non-disclosure protections. The goal is to contain the situation, ensuring the source does not endanger themselves or reveal the operation out of resentment or fear.

In the private sector, deactivating a source usually involves cutting ties with insiders, whistleblowers, or subcontractor informants. Follow the same process: document the termination, immediately restrict data access, and provide a written acknowledgment of non-disclosure obligations.

Takeaway: A good handler knows when to recruit; a great one knows when to let go.

July 30: The Secret Weapon

"Experience is a hard teacher because she gives the test first, the lesson afterward."
—Vernon Law

Every investigator eventually learns that the field is the world's most honest classroom. It teaches through failure, humbles through friction, and rewards the disciplined. Manuals, policies, and training academies prepare you for the job; the field completes the education. Every contact, every mistake, every decision you survive becomes part of your tradecraft if you're willing to study it. There is one thing you might be surprised to learn in the world of confidential informants (CI), which we call the secret weapon: Be Nice.

Why? Most criminals or people who have been in trouble continuously are used to a heavy-handed approach. You can literally disarm them mentally. I once supervised a Soldier who grew up in the infamous Cabrini-Green projects of Chicago. In and out of institutions his whole life (even told me he went to Scared Straight three times). My predecessor employed a heavy-handed approach with him for minor issues and said he was untrainable.

When I took him in, I treated him like a person and gave him second chances. One time, he failed a weigh-in, and he told me, *"I know I have been losing weight,"* so I had another NCO tape him. He was still over the allowance, but better than before. He told me that no one had ever done something like that for him before in his entire life. He changed from volunteering for nothing to volunteering for everything first whenever I asked for volunteers.

I can't stress this lesson enough. My friend's first CI recruitment involved him offering the CI a snack, a drink, and some basic conversation about the CI. Once the guy agreed, he called my friend later that day. He told my friend that there was a guy at a gas station with PCP and a gun. He then told my friend exactly where these items were on the suspect's person. My friend made contact shortly after, patted down the suspect, and the PCP and gun were exactly where the CI said they would be. One phone call, and within 15 minutes, my friend had an arrest with two felony charges. Be nice.

Being nice is not about being a pushover. It is about being kind but assertive. Private investigators should take this same lesson to heart. You don't need to be in law enforcement to get the benefits of being nice. The standards are the same whether your credential card reads "Special Agent" or "Licensed Investigator".

Takeaway: Be nice. It might make or break your case.

July 31: The Investigator's Compass

"In matters of style, swim with the current; in matters of principle, stand like a rock."
—President Thomas Jefferson

Every investigator who spends enough time in the field eventually learns that tradecraft keeps you alive, but values keep you sane. The longer you work undercover or manage confidential informants, the more you realize the true battle isn't against the suspect—it's against erosion.

A compass isn't just about ethics. It's the discipline of knowing who you are when no one is watching. It's how you behave when things go wrong, when the case stalls, or when your integrity is your only remaining asset. Investigative work, especially undercover, requires deception for a purpose—but that deception must never define you. If you start believing the role more than the reason, you have crossed the line.

Every handler, source, and undercover investigator eventually feels the weight of blurred identity. You pretend long enough, and it's easy to forget what's real. A friend of mine left undercover work because he said his undercover life became his real life. That is why regular reflection and debriefing matter as much as surveillance logs and case reports. Many training courses stress self-assessment, but in truth, it's deeper than that—it's moral maintenance.

One of my mentors once said, "If you ever stop feeling something after a good or bad operation, it's time to come in from the cold." He was right. Numbness is not toughness—it's corrosion. The best investigators learn to stay human without becoming fragile. They know that compassion doesn't weaken discipline; it strengthens judgment.

In the private sector, the compass matters just as much. Without an institutional code or badge, your reputation becomes your credential. Ethics aren't a slogan— they are the invisible uniform you wear in every boardroom, every deposition, and every surveillance van. Lose that, and you're just another wannabe chasing a paycheck.

Takeaway: The compass is what remains when the adrenaline, cases, and recognition fade. Don't let yours go off course.

August: Investigative Photography and Videography

"You don't take a photograph. You make it." —Ansel Adams

An investigation lives and dies by its ability to see. Witnesses forget, suspects lie, and reports can be misread—but the camera doesn't flinch. It captures the truth as it exists, not as someone remembers it. Photography and videography are more than documentation tools; they are the silent witnesses that testify when memory fails and words collide. For the investigator, understanding how to use a camera is not art for art's sake; it's serious business.

Every camera, whether digital or film, works on the same principle: controlling light. The difference between a clear evidentiary photo and an unusable one comes down to a few small settings—aperture, shutter speed, ISO, and white balance. These terms might sound like something from an art school syllabus, but in the hands of an investigator, they determine whether a photograph is admissible or irrelevant. A well-balanced exposure can show the faint bruising that proves force, the license plate at twilight, or the subtle handoff that would otherwise be missed.

Aperture controls depth of field—what is sharp and what is blurred. Shutter speed dictates motion—whether a moving subject is frozen or streaked. ISO adjusts sensitivity—how the camera responds to light and darkness. White balance corrects the color cast of an image, keeping daylight from looking blue or tungsten from looking yellow. Each setting is a decision, and each decision changes what truth looks like. A professional investigator must understand not only how to operate a camera but why those choices matter in context.

Then there's the histogram—a misunderstood but vital tool. It's not an art graph; it's your exposure audit trail. It tells you whether you've captured detail in shadows and highlights or whether evidence is hiding in overexposed glare. A camera with a histogram is like a heart monitor for your images; ignore it, and you might not know your evidence flatlined until it's too late.

Videography adds an entirely new dimension: time. Still photos freeze a fact; video tells its story. For surveillance, controlled interviews, or operational documentation, the ability to capture motion with clarity, stability, and sound integrity can make or break credibility. Frame rate, resolution, and audio discipline matter. A shaky, handheld recording with poor sound quality can raise as many doubts as it resolves.

Yet, for all its technology, investigative imaging is not about the equipment—it's about the operator. Cameras don't testify; people do. Knowing how to capture what matters and when to stop recording are both acts of judgment. Poor camera discipline can compromise privacy, violate policy, or introduce bias into evidence. A camera pointed at the wrong time can destroy as much as it preserves.

In the private sector, photography often serves as the bridge between surveillance and substantiation. For corporate, insurance, or domestic investigations, clean, clear, and properly timestamped images carry the same weight as sworn statements. In the public sector, the same images must meet evidentiary standards for chain of custody, authenticity, and contextual neutrality. In both, the difference between "useful" and "useless" evidence often comes down to the investigator's mastery of light, time, and restraint.

This month, we will take a deep dive into the mechanics and mission of investigative imaging—how to make your camera work as hard as you do.

We will break down aperture, shutter speed, ISO, and white balance, study how to compose and expose scenes under stress, and explore videography from static surveillance to mobile recording. We will examine editing, storage, courtroom presentation, and the ethics of recording others. By the end of the month, you will not only know how to take a picture—you will know how to tell the truth through one. Ready to have some fun?

P.S. I have worked with countless investigators in the public and private sectors. Given how little attention these skills normally get, I thought it would be fun to change the entries up and give you a simple exercise to do each day. You will thank me later when you have the $10,000 money shot.

August 1: The Investigator's Eye

"Vision is the art of seeing what is invisible to others." —Jonathan Swift

The difference between a professional and an amateur isn't what they see, but how they see it. Investigative photography begins long before the shutter clicks; it begins when you learn to frame reality with purpose. The untrained eye looks for subjects. The trained investigator looks for relationships—between light and shadow, subject and background, fact and context. The human eye naturally adapts to changing conditions, correcting for light, distance, and focus. A camera doesn't. It records exactly what's there, flaws and all. That's why understanding what the lens sees is fundamental to documentation.

Every image you capture should serve one of four purposes: identify, prove, preserve, or persuade. Identification photos establish who or what. Proof photos connect actions to evidence. Preservation images maintain the scene for analysis. Persuasive images tell the story clearly to a jury, a supervisor, or a client. If a picture doesn't serve one of these purposes, it doesn't belong in the case file.

Composition—how elements are arranged within the frame—determines whether a photograph reads as evidence or confusion. That's where the **Rule of Thirds** becomes your compass. Imagine your frame divided by two horizontal and two vertical lines into nine equal boxes. The points where these lines intersect are where the human eye naturally lands first. Placing your subject or evidence at these intersections draws attention without distorting it.

In investigative use, this principle is critical. During an interview, frame your subject on one of the vertical third lines, leaving space in the direction they're facing. At a crime scene, place the main piece of evidence—a weapon, a broken lock, a footprint—slightly off-center, leaving room to show its relationship to the surrounding area. In surveillance, use the rule to balance your subject against environmental markers for scale and location context. Centered shots feel posed; off-center shots feel observed. In this work, authenticity often persuades more than perfection.

Exercise: Spend ten minutes with your camera or phone today. Photograph a single object—a badge, notebook, or piece of equipment—five times: centered, left third, right third, high angle, and low angle. Study which image best tells the story. Ask yourself: Which one would I trust if I were the jury?

Takeaway: Seeing like an investigator means composing with purpose. The lens records what you show it—nothing more, nothing less.

August 2: Understanding Exposure

"Good composition is merely the strongest way of seeing." —Edward Weston

Exposure is the language of light, and understanding it separates the professional from the hopeful. Every investigator with a camera, whether a high-end DSLR or a phone, must know how to balance light, motion, and sensitivity to reveal the truth clearly. Exposure isn't about guessing—it's about control. It determines whether a firearm glints in shadow, a license plate remains legible at dusk, or a subject's face is recognizable under streetlights.

Three settings control this balance: aperture, shutter speed, and ISO. Together, they make up what photographers call the **exposure triangle.** Learn them, and you will no longer have to rely on luck with your evidence using auto mode.

Aperture is the size of the lens opening. It controls how much light enters the camera and how much of the scene is in focus. A wide aperture (low f-stop, such as f/2.8) isolates a subject against a blurred background—ideal for interviews or surveillance shots where you want the focus on one person. A narrow aperture (a high f-stop, like f/8 or f/16) keeps everything sharp—perfect for documenting crime scenes or property damage.

Shutter speed controls how long the camera's sensor is exposed to light. A fast shutter (1/500s or faster) freezes motion—a fleeing suspect, a passing vehicle, or a handoff caught mid-action. A slow shutter (1/30s or slower) brightens low-light scenes but risks motion blur. Blur might look artistic in photography; in investigations, it's just lost evidence. When the environment is dark, stabilize the camera or raise the ISO before lowering the shutter speed.

ISO measures the camera's sensitivity to light. Lower ISO values (100–200) produce crisp images but require more light. Higher settings (800–1600 or higher) brighten dark scenes but add digital "noise" —a grain that can make a clear image look unreliable. The key is balance. Too much ISO makes things look artificial; too little hides details in the dark. Keep ISO low unless conditions demand it, and use artificial or auxiliary light when possible.

Exercise: Go outside during golden hour—the hour after sunrise or before sunset. Photograph a single object at three apertures, three shutter speeds, and three ISO settings. Review which combination gives you the most balanced exposure. Note how the light changes the story the photo tells.

Takeaway: The camera doesn't lie—but it doesn't forgive, either. Control the light, and you control the investigation.

August 3: Aperture & Depth of Field

"The eye should learn to listen before it looks." —Robert Frank

Aperture isn't just a number on your lens—it's the gateway between light and focus. In photography, it decides what's sharp and what fades away. In investigative work, it decides what is understood. Mastering aperture and depth of field means learning how to direct attention—how to show what matters and let the rest fall away.

Aperture is measured in f-stops, such as f/2.8, f/4, f/8, and beyond. The smaller the number, the larger the lens opening, and the shallower the focus. The larger the number, the smaller the opening, and the deeper the focus. In plain terms: wide aperture, less in focus; narrow aperture, more in focus. This balance of focus and blur is called *Depth of Field.*

For investigators, depth of field isn't an aesthetic choice—it's functional control. A shallow depth of field (low f-stop) isolates a subject from its surroundings. It's useful for interviews or surveillance where you need to emphasize a face or an object while blurring out distractions. In contrast, a deep depth of field (a high f-stop) is essential for crime scenes, evidence photography, or accident reconstruction—moments when every corner of the frame might hold a clue.

Imagine photographing a drug buy in a parking lot. At f/2.8, the suspect's handoff is crisp, but the license plate in the background disappears into blur. At f/11, both are visible—context and detail together. The right choice depends on what the photograph must prove. The seasoned investigator doesn't pick settings for beauty; they pick them for meaning.

Depth of field also helps in covert documentation. When you can't move closer, increasing your aperture (higher f-stop) ensures detail across the scene, even from a distance. For example, photographing a target in a crowded environment requires maintaining context—who they were with, what they were holding, and where they stood. Shallow focus may look cinematic, but it loses facts.

Exercise: Place three objects in a line—one close, one mid-distance, one far. Photograph them at f/2.8, f/5.6, and f/11 (or your camera's closest equivalents). Study the difference. Which image reveals the full story? Which isolates the subject? Then repeat the exercise outdoors, where light changes the equation.

Takeaway: Aperture isn't about artistry; it's about attention. What you choose to keep in focus determines what the viewer sees.

August 4: Shutter Speed & Motion Control

"It is more important to click with people than to click the shutter." —Alfred Eisenstaedt

If aperture decides what's in focus, shutter speed decides what survives the moment. It's the heartbeat of photography—the time between light and record. A slow shutter reveals motion; a fast one stops it. For investigators, it determines whether a moving subject becomes a blur of color or a usable piece of evidence.

Shutter speed is measured in fractions of a second: 1/30, 1/125, 1/500, and faster. The smaller the fraction, the quicker the exposure. A fast shutter freezes motion—the handshake during a handoff, a suspect stepping from a car, the precise instant a key turns in a lock. A slow shutter collects light over time, letting movement smear across the frame. In surveillance or field documentation, that smear isn't artistic—it's uncertainty.

The key to control is anticipation. You don't react to the event; you predict it. In an operation, motion is constant—vehicles, people, changing light. A fast shutter speed (1/250–1/1000) provides clarity in daylight and dynamic scenes, but it requires plenty of light. Indoors or at night, you'll need to slow the shutter (1/60 or slower) or compensate with aperture and ISO. The danger is motion blur from your own hand. Even the smallest movement—heartbeat, breath, or nervous tension—can destroy detail. That's why professionals brace themselves or use tripods, window mounts, or vehicle supports whenever possible.

For interviews or controlled settings, a slower shutter speed can serve you well. It adds light, keeps noise low, and allows smaller apertures for greater depth of field. The trick is balance—just enough motion to suggest reality, not enough to erase it.

One often-overlooked factor is camera shake. Investigators working long hours in vehicles or static surveillance positions must respect fatigue. As muscles tire, control weakens. A practical rule: your shutter speed should never be slower than the focal length of your lens. If you're shooting with a 100mm lens, stay above 1/100 of a second. Below that, even the steadiest hands tremble.

Exercise: Stand near a moving roadway and photograph passing cars at five shutter speeds: 1/1000, 1/500, 1/250, 1/60, and 1/30. Then repeat the test at night or in low light. Notice how motion, light, and sharpness change. Which speed gives you the most usable image?

Takeaway: Shutter speed isn't just a setting—it's timing and awareness to get the shot that matters at the speed that matters.

August 5: ISO & Low-Light Photography

"Light makes photography. Embrace light. Admire it. Love it. But above all, know light." —George Eastman

Low light is where investigators earn their craft. It is where evidence hides—in alleys, dim motel rooms, parking lots, and back seats of vehicles. A well-handled camera in darkness can capture what the naked eye forgets. ISO measures your camera's sensitivity to light. The lower the number (ISO 100–200), the less sensitive the sensor is—perfect for bright scenes and daylight documentation. Higher ISO settings (ISO 800–3200 or higher) increase sensitivity in darker environments. The trade-off is noise—a grainy, speckled distortion that creeps into images as ISO rises. Too much, and your evidence looks altered or untrustworthy.

Think of ISO as light amplification. It brightens the scene without adding external illumination. In surveillance or undercover work, this is invaluable—you can photograph discreetly without using a flash that compromises position or safety. But that same gain exaggerates color, contrast, and edge detail, often making an image appear artificial. The best investigators learn the sweet spot for their camera—the highest ISO they can use before quality degrades.

ISO also affects shutter speed and aperture. Raising sensitivity lets you shoot faster or narrower, balancing the exposure triangle. When photographing in near darkness, use the lowest ISO that achieves clarity while maintaining a usable shutter speed. A photo that is slightly underexposed is recoverable in editing; one drowned in noise is not. Noise doesn't just ruin beauty—it ruins credibility. In court, digital grain can appear to be tampering. A defense expert might claim image manipulation, even if it's just high ISO.

Practical tools help. Use ambient light sources—streetlamps, dashboard glow, even moonlight. Position yourself where light naturally falls, rather than fighting darkness head-on. I promise you this is a critical skill. I recall doing it on surveillance in the South Bronx, and it was very dark, except for the streetlights. Adjusting settings for low light made all the difference in photographing the subject. Low-light mastery is patience, not magic. Let your camera acclimate. Take a test shot, review it, and gradually increase the ISO.

Exercise: Photograph a dark scene—a garage, alleyway, or interior room—at ISO 200, 800, 1600, and 3200. Keep aperture and shutter constant. Compare results side-by-side under bright light. Identify the highest ISO where the detail remains crisp without heavy grain. That is your camera's low-light ceiling.

Takeaway: ISO is the investigator's night vision—use it to see what others can't, and use it to separate you from the rookie investigator.

August 6: White Balance & Color Accuracy

"Color is my daylong obsession, joy, and torment." —Claude Monet

Investigators rarely think about color until it betrays them. In courtrooms and reports, color carries meaning—the shade of a bruise, the tint of a vehicle, the hue of a pill or stain. Yet color is subjective. What looks "white" under one light can look yellow, blue, or green under another. White balance is the camera's way of telling the truth about light.

Every light source has a temperature measured in Kelvin. Daylight hovers around 5500K—neutral and balanced. Tungsten bulbs glow warm and orange at 3200K. Fluorescent lights cast a sickly green tone around 4000K, and overcast skies lean cold and blue above 6000K. Your camera sees these variations far more dramatically than your eyes do. Left uncorrected, they distort reality—turning neutral tones into misleading evidence.

That's why white balance exists. It tells your camera what "true white" is in any lighting condition, so all other colors align naturally. Most cameras offer presets—daylight, cloudy, tungsten, fluorescent, or shade—but professionals set it manually. In the field, a simple trick works: Photograph a white card or neutral gray object in the same light as your subject, then use that frame to calibrate.

White balance errors can undermine credibility. A blue-tinted image of a red bruise might make it appear purple, suggesting an older injury. A yellow cast could make a suspect's shirt look different than what witnesses described. Even a mild shift can create reasonable doubt in court. During nighttime or mixed lighting, white balance becomes a moving target. Streetlights, neon signs, and interior bulbs mix together unpredictably. The best approach is consistency—pick one light source to balance from.

Many investigators rely on auto white balance—and it works most of the time. But auto mode guesses based on averages, not evidence. In critical conditions, take control. If you're indoors under tungsten lighting, set the camera to tungsten. Outside under clouds, switch to cloudy. In a car interior with dashboard light and streetlamps, test both tungsten and auto—whichever yields truer skin tone is your baseline.

Exercise: Photograph a white sheet of paper under three light sources—indoor lamp, daylight, and fluorescent. Set your camera to auto, then to the matching preset for each condition. Compare results side-by-side. Learn what "white" truly looks like through your lens.

Takeaway: White balance isn't just about aesthetics—it's about accuracy. Color tells stories in investigations, but only if you let the light tell the truth first.

August 7: The Histogram

"Photography is the story I fail to put into words." —Destin Sparks

Every photograph tells a story, but not every story is honest. A photo that looks fine on your camera's screen might be hiding critical details in shadow or glare. Enter the histogram. The histogram is the investigator's polygraph for light, the visual audit trail that shows what the camera actually captured.

A histogram is a graph that represents the brightness of every pixel in your image. The left side shows dark tones (shadows), the right side shows bright tones (highlights), and the middle represents midtones—the natural balance between the two. The shape of that graph reveals where the photo will sit.

If the graph is pushed hard to the left, your photo is underexposed—important details are lost in the darkness. If it's jammed to the right, it's overexposed—highlights are blown out, and information is gone forever. A balanced image usually shows a smooth curve that tapers near both ends, meaning you have captured a full range of tones without losing either side of the story.

For investigators, this is more than technical trivia—it's quality control. The histogram ensures your evidence survives translation between devices, lighting conditions, and courtroom projection. What looks bright on your phone might print dark on paper; what looks fine under fluorescent office lights may appear washed out on a monitor. The histogram ignores all of that and tells you what is actually there.

Modern cameras often display two versions: one for overall brightness and another for color channels (red, green, blue). The color histogram helps identify subtle imbalances—a red spike in tungsten light, or a blue dip in shade. For evidence photography, color accuracy matters just as much as brightness. A distorted color channel can alter the perception of injuries, substances, or materials. Learning to read histograms also sharpens your investigative mindset. It teaches you to verify rather than assume, to check the record rather than trust your impression.

Exercise: Photograph a scene with strong contrast—half in sunlight, half in shade. Review the histogram after each shot. Adjust exposure until both light and dark areas show visible data on the graph without either side clipping. Compare results.

Takeaway: The histogram does not lie—it only reports. Investigators who learn to read light like evidence see more and miss less.

August 8: Exposure Compensation

"Where there is light, one can photograph." —Alfred Stieglitz

Cameras don't see the world the way we do. The human eye adapts instantly to darkness and glare, while a camera struggles to balance both. That limitation—called **dynamic range**—is the span between the darkest and brightest details a sensor can capture simultaneously. Understanding and controlling that range through **exposure compensation** is how investigators turn impossible lighting into usable imagery.

Dynamic range determines what survives in your photo. When you photograph a subject standing under a bright doorway, your camera must choose: Expose for the subject and lose the background to white, or expose for the background and lose the subject to shadow. Investigators can't afford that compromise. Every detail matters. Exposure compensation lets you override the camera's guess and reclaim control.

Most cameras measure light using internal meters that average brightness across the frame. But meters get fooled—especially in scenes with strong contrast, like a suspect standing under a streetlight or evidence photographed near a reflective surface. The result is overcorrection: the scene looks balanced overall, but the subject is either washed out or hidden. Exposure compensation, usually marked as "+/-" on your camera, allows you to adjust brightness in small steps, typically in thirds of a stop. Increasing (+1 or +2) brightens; decreasing (−1 or −2) darkens.

In surveillance, dynamic range is your silent ally. Streetlights, headlights, and neon signs can easily overpower faces or actions. Dial down exposure slightly to preserve definition—it's better to lighten a dark image later than to recover what's been burned away. In field or evidentiary photography, you rarely need more than **±2 EV** of adjustment per shot. The goal is consistency, not creative dynamic range. Extreme compensation (±4 to ±5 EV) is mostly useful for:

- Backlit subjects (e.g., person in front of a window)
- Very dark or bright environments where flash is prohibited
- Bracketing multiple exposures for later comparison

Exercise: Photograph the same subject—such as a parked car—under bright midday light. Take one image at your camera's recommended exposure, one at -1 stop, and one at +1 stop. Compare the details in each. Which reveals more?

Takeaway: Cameras guess; professionals decide. Exposure compensation and dynamic range aren't about brightness—they are about control.

August 9: Metering Modes

"To photograph truthfully and effectively is to see beneath the surfaces." —Ansel Adams

Exposure compensation corrects the result—metering determines the cause. Every modern camera uses a built-in light meter to decide how bright or dark a scene should be. But that "decision" depends entirely on which metering mode you choose. For an investigator, understanding metering isn't creative theory—it's how you make sure the camera's reading matches the truth of the scene. Most cameras offer three main metering modes: **evaluative (matrix)**, **center-weighted**, and **spot**.

Evaluative (Matrix) metering divides the frame into zones and analyzes brightness, contrast, and color across the entire image. It's reliable for evenly lit scenes, outdoor shots, or large areas like parking lots or building exteriors. However, it can fail when small bright objects—such as flashlights or reflective evidence—dominate the frame.

Center-Weighted metering focuses primarily on the center of the frame while still considering the surroundings. This mode is ideal for interviews, suspect documentation, or medium-range evidence work, where the subject is central and lighting is uneven but controlled.

Spot Metering reads light from only a small portion of the frame—often 2–5%. It's surgical precision. Investigators use it to expose for the most critical detail: a face under a hood, a tattoo, a license plate in shadow. Spot metering ignores everything else, so accuracy depends on where you aim it. Miss the target, and the entire image swings bright or dark.

Understanding **how** the meter "thinks" helps prevent mistakes in complex light. Most meters assume the scene should average to mid-gray (18% reflectance). That's fine for neutral subjects, but misleading for extreme ones—snow appears gray, and asphalt looks lighter than it should. Compensate deliberately: add +1 EV for bright, high-reflective scenes, and subtract -1 EV for dark ones. In surveillance or crime-scene conditions, metering choices dictate the clarity of evidence. A blown-out glare on a car hood or an underexposed entryway can erase identifiers.

Exercise: Find a scene with strong contrast—half shadow, half sunlight. Take three shots: one in evaluative, one in center-weighted, and one in spot mode (aiming at the subject's face). Compare. Which one gives you the best result?

Takeaway: The camera's meter doesn't see context—only light. Your job is to interpret that light with intention.

August 10: Focal Length & Field of View

"Look and think before opening the shutter. The heart and mind are the true lens of the camera." —Yousuf Karsh

For an investigator, understanding focal length means knowing how to reveal—or conceal—relationships among subjects, surroundings, and evidence. Measured in millimeters (mm), focal length defines how much of a scene the lens captures and how magnified the subject appears. A short focal length (wide-angle, such as 18–35mm) captures a broad field of view—great for documenting rooms, vehicles, or outdoor environments. It exaggerates distance and depth, making foreground objects appear larger and backgrounds recede. A long focal length (telephoto, such as 85–200mm) compresses space—useful for surveillance or isolating a subject from afar. The trade-off: less depth, narrower view, and higher sensitivity to camera shake. Lengths include:

- **Wide-angle (18–35mm):** Ideal for tight interiors and scene overviews. Use it to document crime scenes or property inspections where spatial relationships matter—doorways, footprints, or the distance between objects. Be cautious of distortion near edges, especially with faces or straight lines.
- **Standard (35–70mm):** The lens that sees most like the human eye. It's balanced and discreet, perfect for interviews or general documentation where accuracy outweighs dramatics.
- **Telephoto (85mm and beyond):** The investigator's distance tool. It compresses perspective, making distant subjects appear closer together. In surveillance or covert observation, this lets you maintain cover while still recording usable detail. Remember: the longer the lens, the steadier your hand must be. Even a heartbeat can blur a distant shot.

Field of view—how much you see—shrinks as focal length increases. This means you can control attention by choosing what to include and what to exclude. A narrow frame isolates; a wide frame contextualizes. Depth of field also changes with focal length. Telephoto lenses naturally blur backgrounds, helping you separate subjects from clutter. Wide lenses keep everything sharp but risk putting unnecessary content in the frame.

Exercise: Photograph a single subject—a parked car, a piece of evidence, or a person—from the same distance at three focal lengths: wide (24mm), standard (50mm), and telephoto (100mm). Observe how space compresses, how the background changes, and how the subject's proportions shift. Which focal length best serves clarity and context?

Takeaway: Focal length is the control of perspective. Pick the right lens for the right job.

August 11: Zoom vs. Prime

"The camera sees more than the eye, so why not make use of it?" —Edward Weston

Investigators must understand the trade-off between zoom and prime lenses. The decision between zoom and prime lenses defines how your picture will appear.

A **zoom lens** covers a range of focal lengths, such as 24–70mm or 70–200mm. It allows quick adaptation without changing lenses—essential in surveillance, mobile operations, or rapidly changing environments. Zoom lenses often have smaller maximum apertures, which means less light in dark conditions, and subtle distortion or softness at the extreme ends of their range. For covert documentation, that can mean the difference between a readable license plate and a useless blur. When I first started getting serious about photography, I was all about the zoom lenses. However, a prime lens can get sharper images (and more client satisfaction) than any zoom lens I have used.

A **prime lens**, by contrast, has a fixed focal length—35mm, 50mm, 85mm—and no zoom capability. It demands physical movement to change composition but rewards discipline with sharper images, wider apertures, and greater low-light performance. For interviews, evidence stills, or controlled environments, a prime lens delivers unmatched optical purity. It also enforces intentionality: when you can't zoom, you must think. Magnification adds another layer of complexity. **Optical zoom** changes focal length through lens mechanics, preserving image quality. **Digital zoom**, however, simply crops and enlarges the image—magnifying pixels, not detail. In court or internal review, digital zoom can raise questions of manipulation. If your device only offers digital zoom, it's better to record wide and crop later, preserving the original file as evidence.

Investigators must weigh practicality against precision. Surveillance operators often rely on high-quality zoom lenses or camcorders because repositioning may break cover. Crime-scene or forensic photographers, on the other hand, prefer primes to ensure detail, control depth of field, and maintain optical consistency across frames. Each choice reflects the mission's priorities. In hybrid operations—such as undercover documentation—both approaches are combined.

Exercise: Photograph the same subject using a zoom lens at three focal points (wide, mid, telephoto), then repeat with a prime lens of similar focal length. Compare sharpness, brightness, and color consistency. Which setup captures better detail? Which one would you want to see in court?

Takeaway: A zoom lens gives you options; a prime lens gives you performance. Consider optical and digital zoom when selecting lenses.

August 12: Distortion & Perspective Control

"Photography is truth. The cinema is truth twenty-four times per second." —Jean-Luc Godard

Distortion happens when straight lines curve or proportions shift, depending on the lens used. Barrel distortion—common in wide-angle lenses—causes straight edges to bulge outward, making walls or doors appear bowed. Pincushion distortion—often found in telephoto lenses—pulls lines inward toward the center. Both can subtly misrepresent scale, distance, or alignment, especially in architectural or forensic documentation. In investigative photography, distortion is more than a cosmetic flaw; it can alter interpretation. A footprint photographed with a wide lens too close to the ground can appear longer than it is. A bent wall line might suggest forced entry where none occurred. Knowing your lens's optical tendencies lets you correct or prevent these errors before they reach the case file.

Perspective distortion is different—it's not a lens flaw but a function of distance. Move too close with a wide-angle lens, and subjects appear exaggerated; step too far with a telephoto, and the scene looks unnaturally flat. This matters when documenting relationships—how far a person stood from a vehicle, or the distance between two objects. Keep your camera parallel to the subject whenever possible and use a normal or slightly telephoto focal length (50–85mm) to preserve proportional accuracy.

Modern cameras and editing software offer in-camera correction profiles or post-processing tools to reduce barrel and pincushion distortion. Use them cautiously. For evidentiary images, document every correction you apply. Courts care more about procedural integrity than technical perfection. If you alter geometry, even to fix distortion, note it in your photo log or metadata.

When working in confined spaces—like hallways or small rooms—distortion becomes unavoidable. The best defense is consistency. Use the same lens and angle for all shots so any optical bias remains uniform. Investigators often place a reference scale or ruler within the frame to anchor dimensions against distortion.

Exercise: Photograph the same object (a doorframe or brick wall) at three focal lengths—24mm, 50mm, and 100mm—maintaining the same center point. Observe how lines bend, and shapes compress. Then, step back and retake the 24mm shot at a greater distance to see how perspective correction improves without digital editing.

Takeaway: Distortion is inevitable; deception is optional. The professional investigator learns to recognize the difference and correct it.

August 13: Stability & Support

"The single most important component of a camera is the twelve inches behind it."
—Ansel Adams

Whether you're documenting a crime scene, recording surveillance footage, or photographing evidence, stability separates usable proof from wasted effort.

The physics are simple: even the slightest vibration translates into motion blur, especially at slow shutter speeds, long focal lengths, or high magnifications. The solution is equally simple—reduce motion by any means necessary, which often means accessories. Also, to be clear, blur is an artistic technique that looks cool. It is just not one that belongs in investigative photographs.

Tripods are the gold standard for stability. A solid, adjustable tripod provides consistent framing and allows long exposures without shake. For indoor evidence photography, use one whenever possible. Extend the legs fully, lock them firmly, and level the head before shooting. If the tripod is too bulky for confined spaces, use a mini-tripod or ground plate to get low and steady shots.

Monopods offer mobility with partial support. They reduce vertical shake while allowing quick repositioning—ideal for surveillance or mobile documentation. When planted correctly, a monopod provides two points of contact: one on the ground and one in your hand. That third point—your body—completes the triangle of stability.

Then there is the investigator's secret weapon: the beanbag rest (which you can thank my neighbor, a professional photographer at NASA, for). A small, flexible support you can shape to any surface—a car window (absorbing vibration), fence post, wall, or ground—it provides stability without attention. Other field tricks make a difference, too:

- **Use your environment:** Lean against a wall, rest your elbows on a car roof, or brace your arms against your torso.
- **Control your breathing:** Exhale slowly and press the shutter at the bottom of the breath.
- **Trigger smart:** Use a remote release or timer to eliminate finger-induced shake, especially in long exposures.

Exercise: Photograph a stationary object at 1/30 second handheld, then repeat with a tripod, monopod, and beanbag support. Compare sharpness at 100% zoom. You will quickly see why "good enough" isn't.

Takeaway: Stability is invisible when it works and unforgivable when it doesn't. A steady image proves intent, control, and professionalism.

August 14: Framing & Composition

"A good photograph is knowing where to stand." —Ansel Adams

Every investigation begins with perspective. In photography, that perspective is literal—where you place yourself relative to the subject determines not just what the camera sees, but what the viewer believes. Framing and composition are how you turn observation into communication. Composition is the arrangement of visual elements within the frame—the structure that guides the viewer's attention. Techniques like the Rule of Thirds and leading lines can help.

Start with **the Rule of Thirds**. Remember it from earlier in the month? Imagine your frame divided by two horizontal and two vertical lines, forming nine equal sections. The points where the lines intersect are visual anchors. Placing your subject or evidence at these intersections draws natural focus. In investigations, that means positioning the most relevant detail—a weapon, footprint, or suspect—off-center, where the viewer's eye instinctively lands first. Perfectly centered images feel staged; slightly offset images feel real.

Leading lines—paths, walls, fences, or road markings—direct the viewer's gaze. Use them to guide attention toward the subject or connect evidence within a scene. For example, a tire track that visually points toward a footprint or a line of sight from a window to a suspect's position builds narrative coherence without words.

Framing also defines emotion. A **low angle** can make a scene or object appear dominant or imposing, useful when documenting forced entry or damage. A **high angle** provides an overview—ideal for showing layout and object relationships. Eye-level shots, on the other hand, feel neutral and objective, best suited for witness interviews or identification photos.

The investigator's goal is not aesthetic perfection; you're in the information and fact-finding business after all. Every object in the frame must earn its place. Remove clutter, reposition yourself, or change perspective until the story reads instantly. Consistency matters, too. When photographing a series—multiple rooms, pieces of evidence, or angles of a suspect's vehicle—keep framing and height consistent.

Exercise: Choose a familiar room or workspace. Photograph it three ways: (1) centered and straightforward, (2) using the Rule of Thirds, and (3) with leading lines guiding toward a specific object. Show the images to someone unfamiliar with the space. Ask which image told them the most.

Takeaway: A well-framed photograph doesn't just show evidence; it explains it before a single word is spoken.

August 15: Lighting & Flash Control

"It is the photographer's job to bring light to the shadows." —*Teju Cole*

Photography begins and ends with light. How light hits a surface determines what the camera records, what details emerge, and how evidence is interpreted. Light has three qualities you must control: intensity, direction, and color. Each changes how a scene reads. Soft, diffused light reduces shadows and brings out texture; harsh, direct light emphasizes edges and contrast. In investigative photography, light control divides into two worlds: forensic documentation and surveillance.

- In crime scene investigation and forensic settings, you own the environment. Use external light sources—strobes, flash units, or continuous lamps—to control every shadow and reflection. A properly used flash can freeze motion, expose fine details, and neutralize mixed lighting. Use diffusers or bounce cards to soften light and avoid glare on reflective surfaces like glass, blood, or metal.
- In surveillance or covert work, flash is a liability. It reveals your position, alerts your subject, and destroys operational discretion. Instead, learn to use available light—streetlamps, signage, moonlight, or ambient glow from vehicles. Boost ISO or widen aperture as needed, but always maintain image integrity over exposure perfection.

Flash has its place. Document every flash exposure, especially in controlled environments where reflective evidence can create misleading glare. At a crime scene, for instance, you might photograph a weapon with and without a flash to capture both its contours and reflective surfaces. If flash introduces distortion or hotspots, take alternate exposures at reduced power or use off-camera positioning to shift angles.

- **Front lighting** (light from behind the camera) provides clarity and even exposure—best for evidence.
- **Side lighting** reveals texture, fingerprints, tool marks, or surface irregularities.
- **Backlighting** outlines form, useful for photographing fluids, dust, or transparent evidence.

Exercise: Photograph the same object twice indoors—once with only ambient light, once using a flash bounced off a white ceiling or wall. Compare surface texture, shadow depth, and color accuracy. Then take a third shot outdoors at dusk using only natural light. Which is closest to the real thing?

Takeaway: Whether under the glare of a flash or the dim glow of a streetlight, your job is to make the truth visible with your relationship to light.

August 16: Reflections & Glare Management

"When the photograph is a mirror of the man and the man is a mirror of the world, then Spirit might take over." —Minor White

In investigative photography, glare and reflection aren't just aesthetic distractions—they can conceal critical detail, misrepresent evidence, or even compromise operational safety. A reflective surface doesn't care what's being recorded; it shows everything within reach of light, including the photographer.

The professional's job is to control what the light reveals. Reflections occur when light bounces cleanly off smooth surfaces like glass, polished metal, or water. Glare happens when that reflection overwhelms the camera sensor, producing white-hot spots and lost data. Both are enemies of clarity. A single reflection can erase a fingerprint, distort the appearance of a wound, or make a surface look wet when it isn't.

The first solution is angle discipline. Change your position, not the evidence. Even a few degrees up, down, or to the side can eliminate a reflection completely. When documenting through glass—such as photographing inside a vehicle or display case—never shoot straight on. Move off-axis at about a 30- to 45-degree angle so the reflection deflects away from your lens.

Filters can assist. A circular polarizer, used sparingly, can help manage reflections on glass, paint, or water. However, investigators should avoid overreliance on post-processing or hardware corrections—the first defense is awareness. When possible, document how lighting and angle affect visibility. Courts value transparency more than technical polish.

In surveillance, reflections become tactical hazards. A bright lens glint or a window reflection can reveal your position to a suspect. Survey your environment for reflective threats—parked cars, windows, or polished signage—and reposition accordingly.

Exercise: Photograph an object behind a reflective surface, such as a glass window or picture frame. Take one image straight on, one at a 45-degree angle, and one with indirect light or bounced flash. Compare how each treatment changes clarity, color, and reflection intensity.

Takeaway: The skilled investigator learns not to fight reflections, but rather, to control them.

August 17: Shadows & Contrast Control

"In the right light, at the right time, everything is extraordinary." —Aaron Rose

Shadows are the silent counterpart of light. Where light reveals, shadow defines. The same scene photographed with different lighting can tell very different stories. Your role is to ensure the story remains accurate.

A well-placed shadow adds depth and texture, making objects appear three-dimensional and helping viewers judge distance and shape. However, uncontrolled shadows can conceal essential details—like a fingerprint impression, a mark on the ground, or a weapon's edge against a dark background.

Contrast is determined by tonal range—the span between the darkest and brightest parts of an image. High contrast emphasizes shape and definition but risks losing midtone detail. Low contrast softens the scene but may flatten critical textures. The key is balance: keep enough difference to define edges without losing subtle transitions.

In forensic or evidentiary photography, side lighting (also called raking light) is often used to reveal surface irregularities such as indentations, tool marks, or impressions. Position your light source low and at a sharp angle to the surface; this enhances shadows and emphasizes contours. For general scene documentation, diffuse or overhead lighting maintains neutral contrast, ensuring an accurate representation.

In surveillance or field photography, you often work with available light. Late afternoon or nighttime conditions create deep shadows that can obscure faces and vehicles. Whenever possible, reposition so the main light source (like a streetlamp, sign, or window) is behind you, providing even illumination on the subject. If that's not possible, adjust the exposure or ISO settings to recover shadow details—but be cautious not to over-brighten, as this can introduce noise.

Exercise: Capture images of a textured surface, such as a wall, shoe print, or coin, under three conditions: overhead light, side light, and backlight. Compare how shadows either reveal or conceal details in each shot. Which lighting setup shows the most accurate form?

Takeaway: Mastering shadows and contrast involves knowing how to use both light and darkness to tell a compelling story.

August 18: Macro & Close-Range Photography

"A small detail can be the key to the whole mystery." —Agatha Christie

Macro photography involves capturing images at life-size or larger magnification, but in investigative terms, it emphasizes precision and control. The closer you get, the smaller your margin for error becomes. Depth of field decreases significantly; even a slight shift in focus can blur the critical detail. Lighting, focus, and stability are essential requirements.

Begin with distance discipline. Don't depend solely on autofocus—it searches in tight spaces. Switch to manual focus and move the camera physically until the subject's sharpest edge becomes clear. A tripod or copy stand works best; even slight body sway can shift focus when you're working inches from the subject.

Lighting defines texture. Use diffused, angled light to emphasize surface depth—side lighting will reveal ridges on a tool mark, striations on a bullet casing, or residue on a piece of tape. Direct flash tends to flatten surfaces and create glare, while raking or ring lighting evenly wraps illumination around small objects. In field conditions, a small LED panel or flashlight with diffuser film can substitute for lab gear.

Scale transforms your photos. Always include a measurement reference—like a forensic scale, ruler, or coin—in at least one shot. Place it on the same plane as the subject to avoid parallax distortion. Without a scale, an image is just a photo; with it, it becomes data.

Focus stacking, if your camera supports it, is another helpful technique. By capturing multiple images at slightly different focus points and combining them later, you can achieve full-depth clarity across uneven surfaces.

In surveillance or private-sector documentation, "macro" often means getting close discreetly—photographing a lock, keypad, or small label without alerting anyone. Use compact lenses, quiet shutters, and natural light whenever possible. Avoid casting shadows across your subject; position yourself slightly to the side or above to keep illumination even.

Exercise: Photograph a small object—like a key, coin, or printed logo—from six inches, three inches, and one inch away. Observe how focus, lighting, and perspective shift. Then include a scale in the shot and notice how it changes the image from artistic to analytical.

Takeaway: Close-range photography is where the investigator becomes the lens. Practice distance discipline to elevate your photography game.

August 19: Long-Range Photography

"The more you look at the world, the more you realize everything is connected." — *Diane Arbus*

Distance changes everything. It alters light, motion, and even perception. In surveillance and long-range photography, the investigator must bridge that distance. Heat waves, humidity, wind, and vibration can all distort an otherwise perfect shot. Knowing your equipment's limits is a hallmark of professionalism.

Start with optics. A telephoto lens (85mm and beyond) compresses space and magnifies detail, but the longer the lens, the narrower your field of view—and the greater your vulnerability to shake. Image stabilization helps, but mechanical support is essential. Use a tripod, monopod, or vehicle brace. Even a rolled-up jacket or the trusty beanbag rest absorbs vibration from engines or wind. At long distances, movement you can't even feel becomes a visible blur.

Atmospheric distortion is the invisible enemy. Over long distances, air movement bends light, creating shimmer or "mirage" effects that ruin fine detail. Early morning or late evening typically offers the cleanest air and best contrast. Midday heat introduces distortion and glare.

Composition and concealment are your next priorities. Position yourself where natural cover breaks your outline—behind vehicles, foliage, or architectural edges. Reflections from windows, lenses, or even watches can betray your presence. Blackout cloth or matte lens hoods reduce reflection.

Depth and distance judgment also change at range. A compressed scene may make two subjects appear closer than they are. Counter this by including contextual elements—road markings, vehicles, or environmental features—to establish scale and orientation. Investigators documenting from a distance must show both where and who. If you must shoot toward a light source, reduce exposure slightly to preserve outline detail, then capture a secondary shot from a different angle for verification.

Exercise: Set up your camera or camcorder to photograph a stationary subject—such as a person or object—from 50, 100, and 200 feet away. Use a stable rest, adjust focal length, and note how atmospheric conditions affect sharpness and color. Review the images side-by-side and assess where detail begins to fade.

Takeaway: Distance photography is about patience and knowing your equipment inside and out.

August 20: Covert Cameras & Concealment Techniques

"The best camera is the one that's with you." —Chase Jarvis

Covert cameras are a useful supplement in the camera world. Technique matters from selection to retrieval: lens choice, placement, power, signal, and most of all, testing.

Start with equipment selection matched to mission tempo. For short-duration undercover meets, body-worn devices (button cams, pen cams, glasses) offer perspective and plausible concealment, but their sensors are small, and their battery life is short. For prolonged observation, choose concealed, weatherized modules with external battery options or hardwired power. For vehicle work, use purpose-built dash or mirror housings with vibration-damped mounts; for interior overwatch, select devices with low-light sensitivity or discreet IR that won't produce telltale glints.

A camera must belong to its environment. A clock on a nightstand, a fake air vent, or a utility box are obvious choices—but only if they fit the scene. Think like everyone else in the room: what object would naturally be there and not attract handling? Mounts should be secured out of reach, angled for the target's primary position, and tested for reflections. Tiny changes in angle change proof value; a lens that only captures forearms misses faces and license plates.

Power and heat management are practical tradecraft. Batteries drain faster in cold weather, and compact modules can overheat in cars or enclosed fixtures. Staggered duty cycles—record bursts timed to the objective—extend life and reduce detectable heat signature. For long-duration surveillance, concealed mains (where lawful) or magnetically connected external packs give endurance; design retrieval plans that don't require repeated exposure of the device. Signal and storage strategy must assume failure. Wireless transmission is convenient but creates a trail that can be intercepted and often draws attention when signals appear on scans. Minimize detectability by addressing optical and acoustic signatures. Lenses reflect. Matte housings, deep-set lenses, and anti-reflective baffling reduce glints.

Exercise: Choose one concealed camera you have access to (or simulate with a small camera/phone). Deploy it in three different concealment spots in the same room. Record a 10-minute session at each location, then review for angle, reflections, audio clarity, and detection risk from multiple approach vectors.

Takeaway: Covert cameras succeed where regular cameras can't. Match device to mission, conceal it naturally, power it reliably, and test it thoroughly.

August 21: Autofocus vs. Manual Focus

"The ability to concentrate and to use time well is everything." —Lee Iacocca

The difference between a usable frame and a useless one is often a fraction of a second. For home videos, autofocus is fine. For evidentiary video, it's a liability. If you want the "money shot" that survives courtroom scrutiny, you need to understand—and actually use—your camera's manual focus.

Automatic focus sounds appealing: let the camera's software handle it. Modern systems use contrast or phase-detection to hunt for sharp edges and lock onto whatever they think the subject is. That hunting costs processing power and battery life, which matters during long surveillance operations. Worse, the camera doesn't know what *you* care about. It just looks for the closest, most obvious thing in the frame. If someone walks between you and your subject, autofocus will instantly jump to the wrong person. Through glass, rain, or reflections, it will pulse in and out, trying to lock onto a focus point in glare or droplets. In the courtroom, that constant "breathing" comes across as unprofessional and can make it harder to identify the subject.

Manual focus solves these problems because the best focusing device available is still the human eye. The tradeoff is that manual focus requires practice. Investigators generally use two types of manual focus: deep focus for anything beyond a few inches, and macro focus for extreme close-ups.

For **deep manual focus**—the bread and butter of surveillance—set the camera to manual focus, then zoom in tight on the most distant object you want in focus for the shot. That might be the right angle of a business's front door frame, text on the door, or a feature on a nearby wall. Manually adjust focus until that point is as clear as possible. Then zoom back out to your working composition and start recording. As long as your subject stays near that focal plane, they will be sharp.

For **macro manual focus**—serial numbers, documents, phone or GPS screens, fingerprints, and other fine details—start with the camera in manual focus and the lens at its widest angle. Move the camera so the lens is only a few inches from the object. Adjust focus at the lens's shortest focal length until the detail snaps into clarity, then make small movements toward or away from the object until it's perfect. Record your close-up. Macro focus, done correctly, will give you a crystal-clear evidentiary video of objects at extremely close range.

Exercise: Record a short video of a person walking toward and away from the camera using autofocus, then repeat manually. Compare sharpness and consistency. Which method delivers more usable detail?

Takeaway: Use autofocus for family vacations. Use manual focus for evidence.

August 22: Low-Light & Night Surveillance Techniques

"Fear is the darkroom where negatives are developed." —Michael Pritchard

Most investigative work doesn't happen under perfect light. It happens in alleys, parking lots, or back roads. Mastering low-light and night surveillance techniques means learning how to see when others can't.

Light at night behaves differently. Artificial sources—streetlamps, signage, headlights—create unpredictable zones of brightness and shadow. These contrast extremes can fool your camera. The goal is control, not brightness. To preserve detail and avoid overexposure, you can start with stabilization. At night, slower shutter speeds are inevitable, which means motion blur becomes your biggest enemy. Use tripods, monopods, or vehicle mounts whenever possible. If handheld, brace your elbows against your torso, control your breathing, and shoot in bursts.

Next, optimize your exposure triangle. Widen your aperture (low f-stop) to pull in more light, but be mindful of shallow depth of field. Increase ISO gradually to the edge of acceptable noise—learn your camera's ceiling. A slightly grainy image is better than an unreadable one. Shutter speed should be as fast as the light allows without losing detail.

Leverage ambient light. Streetlights, moonlight, or reflections from nearby structures can illuminate your subject without a flash. Flash use is rarely appropriate during surveillance; it breaks cover and draws attention. Instead, let available light define the scene. A nearby illuminated sign can act as a natural key light, while taillights or passing cars can briefly reveal motion without exposing position.

Operational awareness remains the investigator's greatest tool. Darkness conceals the observer as much as the observed—use that advantage. But remember, it also hides hazards, such as uneven ground, obstacles, or bystanders. I was doing a video surveillance exercise in a cemetery once, and my partner tripped over a gravestone. It could have ended in an injury. Always have a flashlight available and consider a red-light lens for it.

Exercise: Record short clips under three lighting conditions: streetlight, near-complete darkness, and mixed sources. Review which combination of ISO, aperture, and shutter delivered the most recognizable detail while staying hidden.

Takeaway: Learn to balance exposure, movement, and concealment in low light until darkness becomes an ally.

August 23: Drone & Aerial Photography

"Once you have tasted flight, you will forever walk the earth with your eyes turned skyward." —Leonardo da Vinci

Drones give investigators a perspective previously reserved for helicopters and expensive charter time. From scene overview and search operations to roofline inspection and route reconstruction, aerial imaging is here to stay. The success of an aerial operation depends on operational planning and equipment selection.

Mission planning is where good imagery is won or lost. Define the objective in a single line: is this mapping, surveillance, search-and-rescue, or documentation for court? That objective drives altitude, overlap, and sensor choice. For mapping or orthomosaics, fly nadir (camera straight down) with 60–80% front and side overlap to ensure stitchability of photographs later.

Sensor and lens choices matter. Higher-resolution sensors increase ground sample distance (GSD) fidelity—the smaller the GSD, the more detail per square meter. For forensic work, aim for a GSD that renders the minimum necessary detail (license plates and small markings require a low GSD and a lower altitude). Remember that altitude multiplies errors: double the height and you halve the detail. Use neutral-density filters to control shutter speed in bright daylight and to avoid rolling-shutter artifacts during fast maneuvers.

You may not have a plane or drone at your agency. You may have to rent or borrow one. Regardless, safety and contingency protocols are non-negotiable. Pre-flight checklist: batteries, prop nuts, firmware, compass/calibration, NOTAMs/airspace checks, and a clear, secured launch/recovery zone, and fuel. Remember that scene in the movie Casino? Also, for drones, always establish a loss-of-link procedure and a safe fallback altitude.

Exercise: Plan and execute a two-part mission (operational planning and the operation) on a property you have legal access to. Try for a nadir mapping pass at a predetermined altitude with 70% overlap using a drone or small plane. Download flight logs, export raw images, and create a simple mosaic or labeled stills showing your work product.

Takeaway: A drone and an airplane are modern investigative marvels. Plan deliberately, fly within the law, and capture great photos and video.

August 24: Interview Recording

"Sound is the vocabulary of nature." —Pierre Schaeffer

For investigators, mastering audio capture means more than hitting "record." It means preserving the full context. Begin with the microphone. The microphone is your lens for sound. You may recall some of this from earlier in the year:

- **Lavalier (lapel)** microphones clip to clothing and capture clean voice recordings during interviews or undercover operations. They are discreet but sensitive to clothing rustling.
- **Shotgun** microphones focus tightly, ideal for directional pickup during surveillance or standoff documentation. They require careful aiming but will eliminate any noise from sides.
- **Omnidirectional** mics record all ambient sound—useful in rooms or vehicles to capture both speaker and environment.
- **Parabolic** microphones amplify distant speech by focusing sound waves into a receiver dish.

Microphone placement matters as much as type. For interviews, mount lavaliers six to eight inches below the mouth, centered on the sternum. Keep cords secure and avoid jewelry or fabrics that create friction. For ambient documentation, use stands or stable mounts to minimize handling noise.

Wind and background noise are your enemies. Use foam windscreens or dead cats (synthetic covers) for outdoor interviews. Indoors, turn off fans, silence phones, and humming electronics. Noise reduction begins before recording, not after. If you must record near traffic, choose directional mics and position them so the target voice faces away from the noise source.

Chain of custody applies to audio, too. Save recordings in uncompressed formats like WAV or AIFF, not MP3, which discards data. Label files immediately with date, time, case number, and participants. Backup to secure, redundant storage, and restrict access to logs just as you would with photographs.

Exercise: Record yourself speaking for thirty seconds in three environments: a quiet office, a car beside traffic, and outdoors in the wind. Review each sample for clarity and noise. Adjust the mic distance and direction until your voice remains intelligible in all conditions.

Takeaway: Audio is the unseen half of evidence collection in videography. Master it to master the fundamentals of videography.

August 25: Video Handling

"Cinema is a matter of what's in the frame and what's out." —Martin Scorsese

Video captures what still photography cannot: continuity. Movement, timing, pacing, hesitation, behavior—all unfold in real time. For investigators, video documentation bridges the gap between observation and proof. But video is unforgiving. Every angle, every second, and every unintended sound becomes part of the evidentiary record.

I once attended a video surveillance course where the instructor demonstrated this truth perfectly. First, he flashed a single image: a woman appearing to hand something off. Then he showed a still photograph of the exact moment from a different angle—ambiguous, open to interpretation. Finally, he played the full video. With context and continuity, the entire exchange became clear: it was a drug buy. Video did not just show the act—it removed doubt, neutralizing any attempt by a defense attorney to reframe the moment. Every recording must serve one of three investigative goals:

Observation—discreet, real-time monitoring of behavior or activity. Observation footage is often longer, wider, and less polished; its job is to capture *patterns* rather than pretty images. You are building a timeline: who arrived, who left, what they did, and how often it happened.

Documentation—accurate capture of conditions, scenes, or interactions. This is your walkthrough of a vehicle, a room, a crime scene, a worksite, or an interview setting. The standard here is clarity and completeness: a reasonable person should be able to understand what it looked like without ever having been there.

Presentation—footage designed for prosecutors, supervisors, or juries. This is the video you expect others to scrutinize frame by frame. It should be stable, concise, and immediately understandable, with minimal distractions or unnecessary movement, so the viewer focuses on the conduct, not your camera work.

Before you hit record, decide which of these three goals you are serving and frame accordingly. Purpose should drive how you move, where you stand, and what you choose to show—or leave out.

Exercise: Film a three-minute walkthrough of a room or vehicle. Use stable framing, slow pans, and natural light. Review it twice—once silently, once with audio. Note where your technique unintentionally added confusion or bias.

Takeaway: Video is accuracy in motion. Treat each frame as testimony.

August 26: Continuity & Sequence (Part One)

"To make a great film, you need three things: the script, the script, and the script."
—Alfred Hitchcock

In investigative video work, continuity is your script. Still photographs freeze a moment; video builds a narrative. But without proper continuity, even factual footage becomes confusing, disjointed, or vulnerable to courtroom attack. Continuity answers the three questions the human brain asks when interpreting visual information:

1. **Where am I?**
2. **What is here?**
3. **What is happening?**

If your video answers these questions clearly, you have achieved functional continuity. Professional videographers—and investigators who follow best practices—structure every sequence with three foundational shots:

- **The Establishing Shot:** This orients the viewer. It shows the entire scene: the parking lot, storefront, roadway, or room. It removes doubt about location and anchors everything that follows.
- **The Medium Shot:** This bridges the gap between the environment and the subject. It includes enough context to maintain orientation while focusing attention toward relevant action.
- **The Close-Up Shot:** This is where evidence becomes clear—faces, hands, objects exchanged, locks tampered with, tools, injuries, or identifiers. Close-ups answer: *"What exactly am I supposed to see?"*

A well-made investigative video moves through these three shots in logical order, creating a clean, intuitive flow of information. Human brains need approximately four seconds to interpret a frame fully. Anything shorter looks like an error or manipulation. Therefore, each shot—establishing, medium, close-up—should run at least four seconds unless operationally impossible. A longer duration is preferable if the action continues. Before you take your establishing shot, ensure you have a slate (handwritten or typed) that documents which agency you are from, your name, subject/case, location, and the date.

Exercise: Record a simple sequence—such as walking from your vehicle into a building using the flow above. Afterwards, review it. Does someone unfamiliar with the location understand the sequence without your explanation?

Takeaway: Continuity isn't just a filmmaking concept. A properly structured sequence removes confusion and prevents misinterpretation.

August 27: Continuity & Sequence (Part Two)

"The moving image is the most powerful instrument of seeing." —Maya Deren

A few more tips and lessons learned about continuity to make you a better investigator when recording video.

Stop-and-Start vs. Continuous Recording: Contrary to myth, investigators do not need to record continuously. A properly sequenced set of establishing, medium, and close shots—with clean transitions—is more effective than aimless continuous video. Each cut must represent a change in information, not a break in narrative logic. Transitions are the glue of continuity. You don't jump directly from wide to close. You *transition*. Two reliable transitions:

Re-establishing Shots: Before moving to a new point of interest, show the previous subject from a medium or long distance, then move the camera toward the new subject. This reassures the viewer that nothing has been cut or altered.

Pan Transitions: Used sparingly. A controlled pan (ideally left-to-right in Western audiences) visually connects two areas without implying a time or location jump. Key rules with panning:

- Don't overuse pans—viewers get motion fatigue.
- Face your body toward the *end point* of the pan and twist to the start so you can "untwist" smoothly.
- Pan in one direction only—no "paintbrush" back-and-forth.

Sequence Integrity: Every shot must relate to the previous one. If a viewer ever asks, "How did we get here?" continuity has failed.

Sequence Examples:

- Establishing →Medium → Close → Re-establish → New Medium → New Close
- Establishing → Pan → Medium → Close
- Establishing → Series of Medium shots → Final Close-up

Exercise: Incorporate transitioning into your shots from yesterday. Do they remain as smooth?

Takeaway: Using transitions and maintaining sequence integrity helps you get the money shot, whether you work in the public or private sector.

August 28: Pole Cameras

"Observation more than books, and experience more than persons, are the prime educators." —Amos Bronson Alcott

A pole camera is any static, fixed-location camera system mounted on a pole, utility box, rooftop edge, or disguised structure. These cameras are typically PTZ (Pan-Tilt-Zoom) capable or equipped with long lenses, infrared, or onboard recording. Some agencies deploy them for weeks or months at a time; private investigators may use smaller, commercially produced variants for corporate surveillance or insurance cases. Regardless of manufacturer, pole cameras exist for one purpose: to capture sustained behavioral patterns without exposing the investigator.

Site Selection Is Strategy: Choosing the location matters far more than camera features. A pole camera must blend naturally with its environment. Streetlight poles, utility boxes, traffic-control housings, and existing security hardware all offer natural concealment. Before installation, conduct a pre-survey: identify the subject's pathways, vehicles, entry points, and habitual movements. Whenever deploying near electrical infrastructure, follow your jurisdiction's utility-safety rules. Some power-line poles require high-voltage certification or coordination with local utility providers.

Concealment Principles: Effective concealment makes the camera invisible to three audiences: the subject, the public, and vandals. Manufacturers now produce covert housings disguised as streetlight components, junction boxes, landscaping fixtures, and even birdhouses. Some units resemble "high-voltage transformers," which helps them fade into industrial environments. Placement should never alter the pole's normal silhouette; anything that looks new draws suspicion. You have to get creative with concealment. Investigators that I speak with who work gangs and narcotics report that in high-crime neighborhoods, criminals identify and deface pole cameras to prevent their illicit activities from being recorded.

Recording Strategy: Unlike body-worn or handheld recording, pole cameras often capture everything. This creates massive data volume and legal exposure. Always maintain a log: installation time, operator identity, camera settings, and retrieval procedures. Document who had access and complement pole cameras with mobile surveillance when needed.

Exercise: Survey a location you have legal access to. Identify three possible fixed-camera vantage points that would blend naturally into the environment.

Takeaway: Pole cameras trade mobility for persistence while capturing everything. Survey your site, conceal them, and use a solid recording strategy.

August 29: Internet Protocol Cameras

"To see clearly is poetry, prophecy, and religion all in one." —John Ruskin

Internet Protocol (IP) cameras have transformed modern investigations. Unlike traditional analog CCTV, IP systems don't just record—they communicate. They send footage across networks, integrate with analytics, alert investigators in real time, and create a digital surveillance ecosystem that can be monitored from across a city or across the world.

An IP camera is essentially a small computer with a lens. It captures video digitally and transmits it over a network—wired Ethernet, Wi-Fi, or cellular. Image quality varies widely, from basic 720p feeds to forensic-level 4K systems with optical zoom, infrared, and onboard processing. Because they are networked, IP cameras enable remote monitoring, zooming, and retrieval. They integrate into DVR/NVR systems, cloud storage, and analytics platforms.

Unlike pole cameras, which require concealment, IP cameras often rely on legitimacy. A camera placed naturally on a building, warehouse, parking lot, or office interior is most effective when it appears to belong there. Placement must cover entry/exit points, choke points, and areas of recurring behavior. Wide Dynamic Range (WDR) is essential for mixed-light environments—loading docks, warehouses with skylights, and storefronts with bright exterior lighting. A camera without WDR will either overexpose the background or underexpose the subject, losing detail either way.

Because IP cameras depend on networks, the network becomes a vulnerability. A camera that drops connection irregularly creates gaps that a defense attorney can exploit. Use hardwired Ethernet whenever possible. IP cameras excel at:

- Long-term monitoring of facilities, warehouses, or parking lots
- Confirming employee behavior in corporate investigations
- Capturing comings and goings at stash houses or fraud targets
- Monitoring assets or restricted-access areas
- Providing remote overwatch during field operations

Their weakness is predictability: once installed, their angle rarely changes. Subjects familiar with the environment may deliberately avoid coverage zones.

Exercise: Access an IP camera system you legally control. Review its field of view at three times of day—morning, afternoon, and night. Note how shadows, glare, IR illumination, or traffic flow change the clarity of the scene.

Takeaway: IP cameras expand your investigative arsenal. They are not "set-and-forget" devices; instead, they are tools that rely on the power of legitimacy.

August 30: Content Editing Techniques

"The camera is no more an instrument of preservation; the image is." —Susan Sontag

Editing in investigative work is not about creativity. It is about clarity, accuracy, and the preservation of the chain of custody. Every cut, enhancement, or redaction must serve one purpose: revealing the relevant facts without altering the underlying evidence. Acceptable edits include:

- **Trimming** irrelevant dead time
- **Sequencing** clips in chronological order
- **Enhancement** (brightness, contrast, noise reduction) done minimally
- **Redaction** of faces, identifiers, or sensitive material
- **Annotation** such as timestamps, labels, or arrows

What is never acceptable is altering meaning: removing actions, adding elements, or manipulating visuals beyond defensible enhancement. The rule is simple: editing clarifies; alteration deceives. To protect yourself, always preserve the original, unmodified file in a secure location and generate a forensic hash (MD5/SHA-256) whenever possible. Work only on a duplicate.

An investigative video must tell a clear story. Start by cutting only what is necessary—long moments of inactivity, accidental recording before the scene begins, or irrelevant transitions. Sequence clips logically: establishing → medium → close-up → re-establishing → secondary details. Use fade cuts sparingly. Hard cuts are preferred in investigations because they do not imply missing content.

Sometimes raw footage is too dark, too bright, or too noisy. Enhancement should improve visibility without altering what occurred. Follow these rules:

- Adjust exposure gently (±10–20% at most).
- Avoid extreme sharpening—it creates halos and artifacts.
- Use noise reduction conservatively; too much erases detail.
- Document every enhancement with the settings used.

If challenged, you must be able to show that enhancements clarified, not altered, the event.

Exercise: Edit a short, legally recorded video. Trim dead time, adjust brightness slightly, and add a timestamp. Document your changes. Are they defensible?

Takeaway: A properly edited video is clear, truthful, and defensible. A poorly edited one is a liability waiting to happen.

August 31: Redaction Techniques

"Privacy is not something that I'm merely entitled to, it's an absolute prerequisite."
—Marlon Brando

Redaction protects privacy and shields the identities of minors, uninvolved persons, undercover officers, or sensitive assets. It is essential to video and photography work in investigation. Common methods include:

- **Face pixelation** (preferred—maintains motion without revealing identity)
- **Blurring** (less secure; sometimes reversible in low-quality software)
- **Black-box masking** (clear but visually intrusive)
- **Audio redaction** (muting, bleeping, or low-pass filtering sensitive speech)

Always ensure redactions cannot be reversed—this is a common failure with cheap or automated tools.

Subtitles & Captions: If adding captions, do not paraphrase. Transcribe verbatim. Misquoting in subtitles can be as damaging as altering footage.

Exporting & Delivery: Export edited clips in high-quality formats (MP4/H.264, ProRes, or similar) and retain metadata whenever possible. Provide:

- Original file
- Edited file
- Enhancement/redaction log
- Hash values for integrity
- Explanation of editing purpose

Attorneys, clients, and judges appreciate clarity—but they demand accuracy, so ensure you master redaction techniques.

Exercise: Edit a short, legally recorded video. Trim dead time, adjust brightness slightly, and add a timestamp. Document every change you made. Could you defend those edits in testimony?

Takeaway: A properly edited video is clear, truthful, and defensible. A poorly edited one is a liability waiting to happen.

September: Legal Aspects and Compliance

"The law is the witness and external deposit of our moral life." —*Oliver Wendell Holmes Jr.*

Investigative work lives at the intersection of truth and authority. Whether you operate in the public sector, private sector, or somewhere in between, your success is measured not only by what you uncover but by **how** you uncover it. Skill without legality is liability. Evidence obtained improperly does not merely weaken a case—it can destroy it. A brilliant investigation can collapse under a single unlawful recording, an unlogged file, or a poorly executed disclosure. September is dedicated to preventing that collapse.

This month focuses on the legal frameworks that govern all the investigative skills you use, including modern investigative photography, video, audio recording, digital surveillance, and case management. These frameworks are complex, varied, and continually evolving. A technique that is perfectly legal in one state may be a felony in another. A surveillance practice acceptable in one country may be tightly restricted on the other side of the border. Even within the United States, the rules governing consent, privacy, retention, and disclosure differ between federal law, state law, administrative policy, and judicial precedent.

The goal of this month is not to turn you into an attorney—it is to give you the legal awareness that protects your case, your client, and your career.

This month's entries will give you a comprehensive legal foundation across investigative disciplines. Topics will include:

- Consent laws for audio and video recording
- Expectation of privacy in public and private spaces
- Search-and-seizure considerations (public sector vs. private sector)
- Chain of custody, data integrity, and evidence logs
- Retention laws for digital media
- Redaction, disclosure, and production requirements
- The legal status of drones, GPS tracking, pole cameras, and modern tech tools
- Cross-border and international considerations (e.g., GDPR, PIPEDA)
- Civil liability hazards and how to avoid them

By the end of the month, you will have a working understanding of the legal landscape that governs modern investigations—not only what the law says, but how investigators in the real world apply it. You will see that legality is not an obstacle to good investigative work; it is the foundation that supports it. One more thing, I am not an attorney and can't give legal advice. I can only share my opinions and experiences. Check with your legal counsel early and often during your investigation to ensure you stay in compliance with the law.

September 1: Understanding Legal Authority

"The law is reason free from passion." —Aristotle

Every investigation, no matter where it begins, eventually encounters a legal system that decides what becomes of your work. That system may be an American courtroom, a foreign tribunal, an administrative hearing, or an internal review board in a multinational corporation. Regardless of the venue, investigators must understand the framework of authority that governs the evidence they collect, the methods they use, and the decisions that follow.

Investigators often make the mistake of assuming their work speaks for itself. It doesn't. It speaks through laws—constitutional principles, statutes, regulations, case precedent, and international agreements. These determine what you're allowed to do, what you cannot do, and what happens when you cross the line. Whether you're a state investigator citing your statutory authority, a private investigator relying on civil permissibility, or a government agent bound by constitutional limits, your actions are justified (or condemned) by a set of rules bigger than the case at hand.

Understanding legal authority begins with knowing who grants power in the first place. In the U.S., investigators operate under a layered system: the Constitution, federal and state statutes, administrative regulations, and judicial interpretation. Those layers control everything from search authority to surveillance laws to the admission or exclusion of evidence.

Internationally, that picture shifts. Some countries operate under civil law systems with codified statutes and limited judicial interpretation. Others follow common law, like the U.S., where precedent shapes rules over time. Some nations place greater weight on privacy, others on state security. A corporate investigator working in Europe feels the pull of GDPR. A government investigator deployed abroad works under treaties, host-nation agreements, or Status of Forces Agreements. Even private-sector investigators—conducting workplace inquiries or internal interviews—must navigate cross-border data transfers, local employment laws, and varying consent standards.

The point is simple: your investigation doesn't exist in a vacuum. It exists inside a structure of authority that you must understand if you expect your work to survive contact with attorneys, judges, oversight bodies, or foreign regulators. When you know the court—or tribunal, or board—you know the standard your work must meet.

Takeaway: You don't investigate for yourself—you investigate for the legal system your work will enter.

September 2: Civil vs. Criminal Investigations

"The power to investigate must never be confused with the power to accuse." — *Robert H. Jackson*

Most investigators learn early in their careers that civil and criminal cases "feel" different. What many fail to appreciate is that the difference isn't just procedural—it's foundational. Civil and criminal investigations operate under various legal authorities, standards of proof, evidentiary expectations, and consequences. Understanding these distinctions isn't optional for professionals.

Criminal investigations answer to the state. Their purpose is to determine whether a crime occurred and whether the government can prove it **beyond a reasonable doubt**. Because liberty is at stake, criminal investigations are weighed down by constitutional protections: the Fourth Amendment, Miranda requirements, due process, and the exclusionary rule. Public-sector investigators must justify every intrusion into privacy, every search, every seizure, and every custodial interview. Failure to do so doesn't just damage the case—it can violate a person's rights and expose the investigator or agency to liability.

Civil investigations operate in a very different ecosystem. These cases involve disputes between private parties—companies, employees, landlords, insurers, or individuals. The objective is not punishment but resolution: compensation, injunctions, or compliance. The standard of proof is lower **(preponderance of the evidence)**, and the rules governing what you can collect or observe are often broader. But broader does not mean unlimited. Private-sector investigators must still navigate privacy laws, surveillance restrictions, consent standards, contract obligations, and tort exposure. You can easily commit a civil wrong while trying to fix one.

The distinction becomes even more critical when cases cross over. A workplace theft investigation may begin as a civil matter, only to evolve into a criminal referral. A domestic investigation may reveal evidence of fraud, exploitation, or abuse. When this happens, the original investigative path comes under scrutiny. What you collected, how you collected it, and how you documented your decisions will now be evaluated under criminal standards—not civil expectations.

Public-sector investigators aren't immune to crossover risk either. When they gather evidence that becomes relevant in a civil lawsuit—wrongful termination, discrimination, use of force, or misconduct—their work is examined under civil procedure and employment law rather than criminal rules.

Takeaway: Civil and criminal investigations follow different rules and carry different risks. Know which one you are operating in and when they cross over.

September 3: Burdens of Proof and Elements

"Proof is the soul of justice." —Sir Edward Coke

Investigators quickly learn that a case isn't built on hunches, suspicions, or instincts—it's built on meeting elements. Every criminal offense has defined elements that must be proven. Every civil action has threshold requirements that must be satisfied before a claim can survive challenge. No amount of good investigative work can compensate for failing to establish the legal building blocks of the issue you're examining.

This is where burdens of proof collide with the realities of case construction. A prosecutor cannot pursue charges unless each element of the crime—every single one—is supported by evidence that meets the "beyond a reasonable doubt" standard. A civil attorney can't advance a case unless the facts satisfy the legal threshold for standing, damages, and the cause of action under a "preponderance of the evidence."

Even an internal inquiry, though less formal, requires evidence that meets a policy-defined standard such as "substantial evidence" or "more likely than not." Investigators who ignore elements work twice as hard for half the result. They gather impressive volumes of information—but not the correct information. Surveillance captures activity, but not intent. Interviews gather narratives, but not corroboration. The essential question is always the same: *Does this evidence satisfy an element?*

International matters complicate this even further. Some jurisdictions define offenses differently or require specific documentation to substantiate claims. A corporate investigator dealing with cross-border fraud may contend with varying thresholds for financial loss. A government investigator deployed overseas may need evidence that meets both U.S. standards and host-nation legal requirements. It's not enough to know the facts—you must understand what those facts must legally prove.

Takeaway: Strong investigations begin with the elements. Know what must be proven, what threshold the case must meet, and what evidence satisfies each requirement.

September 4: Reasonable Expectation of Privacy

"A person's rights must not be judged by the quality of their shelter." —Justice Thurgood Marshall

Most legal mistakes made by investigators—public or private—stem from a misunderstanding of where privacy actually exists. The concept of a "reasonable expectation of privacy" is the cornerstone of lawful surveillance, search authority, and evidence collection. It governs everything from covert cameras to GPS trackers to dumpster dives. And if you get it wrong, your entire investigation starts on a cracked foundation.

In the United States, the reasonable-expectation-of-privacy test comes from *Katz V. United States*, which asks two questions: Did the individual expect privacy? And is that expectation one society is prepared to recognize as reasonable? That simple framework determines whether government investigators must obtain a warrant and whether private-sector investigators risk civil liability for intrusion.

But the test applies far beyond police work. A corporate investigator who monitors employee communication without proper notice may violate privacy laws or employment regulations. A private investigator who plants a camera in what turns out to be a protected space may commit a tort, even if no criminal law was broken. Even internal workplace inquiries must account for e-mail monitoring policies, consent requirements, and the limits of "authorized use."

Privacy expectations also shift dramatically across borders. Some countries recognize robust data-protection rights that exceed anything in the U.S. Others place minimal emphasis on personal privacy and allow broader investigative monitoring. An action that is lawful in one jurisdiction—such as observing someone through their apartment window from a public street—may be illegal in another that treats the home's interior as universally protected. Investigators working abroad or handling multinational cases must understand that privacy isn't just a local issue; it's a legal landscape that varies by geography.

Even within the U.S., the boundaries are more nuanced than people realize. Always keep in mind the steps the individual took to maintain privacy. This will separate the amateur from the professional.

Takeaway: Privacy isn't defined by convenience—it's defined by law, location, and expectation.

September 5: Curtilage & Open Fields

"The house of everyone is to him as his castle." —Sir Edward Coke

Every investigator who works outside an office—surveillance, interviews, scene assessments, neighborhood canvassing—inevitably runs into the ancient but still-relevant concept of **curtilage**. It's one of the most misunderstood boundaries in investigative work, and it's where both public- and private-sector investigators most often drift from lawful observation into unlawful intrusion.

In simple terms, curtilage is the area immediately surrounding a home that enjoys the same privacy protections as the home itself. For a government investigator, entering curtilage without the appropriate legal authority can violate the Fourth Amendment. For a private investigator, it can create civil exposure for trespass or intrusion upon seclusion. The porch, the back patio, the driveway, the fenced yard—these are not "gray areas." The law treats them as extensions of the home because they are tied to the intimate activities of living.

Beyond curtilage lies what the law calls **open fields**—areas where expectations of privacy shrink dramatically. A wooded property line, a large rural lot, a pasture, or unfenced terrain may belong to the subject, but they typically do not carry the same privacy protections. Observing someone in an open field is generally permissible; entering curtilage is not. The challenge is that real life doesn't draw the boundaries for you. Investigators often find themselves in that awkward middle zone where the land "looks" open but isn't legally open.

Even the front door can present a trap. The law recognizes the "knock and talk" doctrine in the U.S., allowing investigators—government or private—to approach a front door the same way any member of the public could. But once you deviate from the normal route a visitor would take, you may be stepping into protected space. Walking around the home, peering through windows, opening gates, or entering side yards without permission can turn lawful presence into unlawful intrusion.

There is the practical reality of surveillance: sometimes the best vantage point is also the riskiest one legally. Cutting corners by "just stepping inside the fence line" or "walking a few feet up the driveway" can destroy the integrity of an otherwise solid investigation. Experienced investigators know that observational boundaries are not inconveniences—they are guardrails that protect the case's credibility.

Takeaway: Curtilage is protected; open fields are not. Know the difference and never let a few extra feet of access cost you the legality of the entire investigation.

September 6: The Electronic Communications Privacy Act

"The right to be let alone is the most comprehensive of rights and the right most valued by civilized men." —Justice Louis Brandeis

Few areas of investigative law create more confusion—or more liability—than digital communication. The Electronic Communications Privacy Act (ECPA) was enacted in 1986, but its reach now extends to every e-mail, text message, cloud file, chat app, server log, and electronic transmission investigators encounter. If you misunderstand ECPA, you don't just risk exclusion of evidence. You risk civil penalties, criminal exposure, and professional disaster. ECPA is not one law—it's three interconnected laws that govern access to digital communications:

- The Wiretap Act (real-time interception)
- The Stored Communications Act (accessing stored data)
- The Pen Register/Trap and Trace Act (non-content dialing/routing information)

For government investigators, these laws define when a warrant is required, when consent is enough, and when an action constitutes unlawful interception. Installing monitoring software without proper authority, capturing content in real time, or obtaining stored data outside the statutory process can all violate federal law—even when done for legitimate investigative purposes.

Private-sector investigators face a different but equally dangerous landscape. Many assume ECPA only restricts law enforcement. It doesn't. The Wiretap Act broadly prohibits the interception of electronic communications by *anyone* without proper consent or a statutory exception. That includes recording Zoom calls, capturing the contents of chat messages, installing spyware for a client, or accessing an employee's email account without authorization. A single misstep can trigger federal civil liability with statutory and punitive damages.

The most dangerous misconception is that consent solves everything. It doesn't. ECPA distinguishes between one-party consent for recording and the separate, higher standard required to intercept electronic communications in transit. Recording a phone call may be legal in a one-party state. Intercepting a text message in transit is not. The technologies investigators use today carry risks that didn't exist when the law was written, but the penalties remain.

Takeaway: Digital communications are protected by some of the strictest laws in the investigative world. Know what you can access, when you can access it, and what requires consent or legal process.

September 7: Handling Minors and Vulnerable Persons

"The measure of a society is found in how it treats its weakest and most helpless citizens." —President Jimmy Carter

Few investigative situations carry more legal and ethical weight than those involving minors and vulnerable persons. Whether you work in the public sector, private sector, or a hybrid environment such as corporate security or regulatory enforcement, the moment a juvenile, elderly individual, or vulnerable adult enters the case, the rules change.

In the public sector, investigators are bound by strict constitutional and statutory protections. Interviewing minors without proper consent, conducting custodial questioning without the presence of a guardian, mishandling digital evidence involving juveniles, or failing to recognize mandatory reporting obligations can jeopardize both the case and the investigator. Courts scrutinize these interactions intensely, often viewing a minor's statements, consent, and understanding through a protective lens.

Private-sector investigators face different but equally serious responsibilities. Corporate, insurance, domestic, and workplace investigations often encounter minors indirectly—through witnesses, victims, family members, or digital evidence. Obtaining statements, collecting photographs, monitoring online activity, or securing consent from a parent or guardian must be handled with caution. Many states impose civil and criminal liability for improper contact with minors, even in the context of legitimate investigations. Recording or photographing a minor without proper authorization—however innocent—can expose an investigator to claims of intrusion or regulatory violation.

Elderly and vulnerable adults introduce their own complexity. Many jurisdictions have mandatory reporting laws for suspected elder abuse, exploitation, or neglect. Investigators—public or private—can face penalties for failing to report concerns, even when the evidence appears preliminary. In addition, cognitive impairment, diminished capacity, language barriers, and mental health considerations require heightened professionalism in interviews and documentation.

The consistent theme across all these environments is caution. Professional investigators slow down when a minor or vulnerable person is involved.

Takeaway: Any case involving minors or vulnerable persons demands heightened care. Know the laws, obtain proper consent, document everything, and err on the side of protection.

September 8: The Gramm–Leach–Bliley Act

"Trust is built with consistency." —Lincoln Chafee

Pretexting has long been part of investigative tradecraft, but it is also one of the fastest ways an investigator can cross from lawful information-gathering into criminal conduct. The Gramm–Leach–Bliley Act (GLBA) draws a bright line around financial privacy, and many investigators—public and private alike—still underestimate how unforgiving that line is.

GLBA prohibits obtaining someone's financial information through false pretenses. That means no pretending to be the customer, no pretending to be a bank employee, no pretending to be a service provider, and no calling a financial institution under any identity other than your own. The law was enacted in response to private-sector abuses, but it applies broadly to anyone seeking account information, including investigators, attorneys, skip tracers, insurance adjusters, corporate compliance teams, and even government personnel operating outside their lawful authority.

The danger is that pretexting often feels harmless and was mainstay investigative technique for years. Calling a bank to "verify" an account, asking a lender for confirmation of a loan, or trying to obtain a subject's financial records through a third party may seem like clever investigative shortcuts. Under GLBA, they are federal offenses. Courts have repeatedly upheld that even attempted pretexting—when no information is successfully obtained—can still create liability.

Private-sector investigators face additional pitfalls. Many states have their own financial-privacy or consumer-protection laws, some of which impose harsher penalties than GLBA. Insurance investigations involving claims verification, corporate inquiries into employee misconduct, and domestic investigations involving marital assets all risk GLBA violations if financial information is obtained improperly.

International work expands the risk further. Many countries maintain financial privacy laws even stricter than GLBA, and cross-border investigations may involve banking systems with their own reporting requirements, disclosure limitations, or criminal penalties for improper access. Investigators who assume U.S. standards apply globally may find themselves violating foreign law without realizing it.

Takeaway: Pretexting around financial information is not clever—it's illegal. Know what GLBA prohibits, avoid deceptive practices, and treat financial data with the highest level of legal caution.

September 9: Civil Liability for Investigators

"You can't talk your way out of something you behaved your way into." —Stephen R. Covey

Investigators often picture lawsuits as something that happens to other people—usually the subjects of an investigation, the employer who hired them, or the attorneys running the case. The truth is far less comforting: investigators themselves are frequent defendants in civil actions. Surveillance mistakes, interview errors, documentation gaps, and overstepping legal boundaries all carry civil consequences. A single misjudgment can cost an investigator years of work, reputation, and financial stability.

Civil liability usually falls into predictable categories. The most common is **trespass**. Stepping onto private property, even unintentionally, can expose a private-sector or corporate investigator to damages. Public-sector investigators may be protected by qualified immunity, but only when acting within clearly established legal authority. Protections can be erased instantly if you are not careful.

Intrusion upon seclusion is another frequent claim. Even lawful surveillance becomes unlawful when it intrudes upon an activity in which a person has a reasonable expectation of privacy. Filming through a partially closed window, using overly intrusive lenses, or capturing audio without proper consent can all create liability—even if the investigator never sets foot on the property.

Investigators operating in corporate, insurance, or regulatory environments face an additional risk: **vicarious liability**. Even when an investigator follows instructions, the organization that hired them may be pulled into litigation because of their actions. Conversely, the organization may attempt to shift blame onto the investigator to protect itself. Policies, contracts, and scopes of work matter, especially when working internationally. They determine not only authority but also who carries the financial risk when something goes wrong.

Finally, do not forget **professional liability insurance** (often called errors and omissions insurance). Whether you're a private investigator, a corporate security professional, or a government employee moonlighting in off-duty details, insurance is not optional. Professional liability insurance provides legal defense, settlement protection, and peace of mind. Even public-sector investigators benefit from supplemental coverage; agency indemnification often ends the moment an investigator steps outside policy, authority, or training.

Takeaway: Civil liability is part of the investigative landscape. The best time to prepare for a lawsuit is before one arrives.

September 10: Criminal Liability for Investigators

"It is more honorable to repair a wrong than to persist in it." —President Thomas Jefferson

Civil liability is costly. Criminal liability is career-ending. Investigators sometimes forget that the very tools they use—surveillance, interviews, access to data, impersonation, digital monitoring—can cross into criminal conduct if misapplied. The law does not give investigators a free pass simply because they were "working a case." A violation is still a violation, and investigators who cross the line can face charges ranging from misdemeanors to federal felonies.

The most common area of criminal exposure involves unlawful interception of communications. Recording a phone call without proper consent, capturing digital content in transit, installing monitoring software, or accessing communications under false pretenses can violate state wiretap laws or the federal Wiretap Act. A single unauthorized recording can lead to criminal penalties in two-party consent states—and ignorance of the law is never a defense.

Impersonation and fraudulent representations also create significant risk. Pretending to be a police officer, government official, bank employee, utility worker, or service provider to obtain information can violate impersonation statutes, identity theft laws, or fraud provisions. Even "routine" investigative pretexts can become criminal when they deceive protected entities such as financial institutions or telecommunications providers.

Investigators also expose themselves to criminal liability when they misuse their authority. Public-sector investigators risk charges for obstruction of justice, tampering with evidence, unlawful detention, or exceeding statutory powers. Private-sector investigators can face similar charges if they interfere with a law enforcement investigation, destroy evidence, or coerce a witness.

International work magnifies the risk. Many countries have strict criminal penalties for unlicensed investigation, unauthorized surveillance, photographing individuals without consent, or mishandling personal data. An act lawful in the U.S. may be a criminal offense abroad—and foreign criminal exposure can follow investigators long after the case concludes.

The best investigators operate under a simple principle: **If you have to justify it to yourself, you probably shouldn't do it.**

Takeaway: Investigative work does not shield you from criminal law. Know the limits and remember that one unlawful act can undo an entire career.

September 11: The Driver's Privacy Protection Act

Investigators rely heavily on vehicle information. License plates, registration records, VIN lookups, accident histories, and driver details often unlock critical leads. But accessing Department of Motor Vehicles (DMV) data is not as simple as running a plate or calling a contact. The Drivers Privacy Protection Act (DPPA) is one of the most tightly enforced privacy statutes in the United States, and violations—intentional or accidental—can carry civil and criminal penalties.

DPPA restricts the disclosure and use of personal information contained in motor vehicle records. That includes a driver's name, address, photograph, medical information, Social Security number, and in many states, even vehicle details tied to an identifiable individual. It applies to all investigators—public, private, corporate, insurance, and regulatory. If the information originates from DMV records, DPPA governs it.

The law recognizes specific permissible uses, and investigators must fit squarely into one of them. Common permissible purposes include use by government agencies carrying out official functions, use in connection with litigation or legal proceedings, use by insurers investigating claims, and use for matters of motor vehicle safety and theft. Private investigators may rely on certain permissible uses when working for attorneys, insurers, or government entities—but only when the investigation's purpose directly aligns with the statutory allowance. Often, many database aggregators require you to justify your DPPA reason before allowing a search.

DPPA also prohibits secondary use, meaning that even if the data was obtained legally, it cannot be used for a purpose outside the one for which it was originally accessed. For example, an insurance investigator who lawfully accesses DMV data for a claims investigation cannot later use that same data in a separate case or skip-trace unrelated to the original permissible purpose.

Foreign investigators may assume U.S. vehicle information is freely accessible, only to find themselves violating the DPPA when the records originate from a state DMV. I have worked with some UK private investigators who would tell me how difficult it was to obtain vehicle data in the UK, so they had to turn to more labor-intensive alternatives. All I could do was cringe hearing their woes.

Takeaway: Vehicle records may look routine, but DPPA treats them as highly protected personal information. Know your permissible purpose.

September 12: Legal Privilege

"A lawyer's duty is to protect his client's rights; your duty is to protect your work."
—Attorney General Robert F. Kennedy

One of the most powerful legal protections available to investigators is the attorney–client privilege, specifically when their work is conducted at the direction of an attorney. This relationship can significantly limit what becomes discoverable in litigation, and when properly structured, it creates a protective barrier around interviews, notes, work product, and analysis. But this shield is not automatic. It must be earned, maintained, and understood.

Attorney–client privilege protects confidential communications between an attorney and their client for the purpose of seeking or providing legal advice. When an investigator is brought in to support that purpose—gathering facts so the attorney can give informed counsel—their work can fall under the same privilege. But only when the relationship and purpose are crystal clear.

For investigators, the first rule is simple: **you work for the attorney, not the client.** Whether the client is a corporation, a private individual, or a government agency, your chain of communication runs through counsel. If you start reporting directly to the client, adjusting your scope on your own, or drifting into non-legal objectives, you risk destroying the privilege. In private investigation, it is okay to work directly for a client, especially if you don't think the matter is going to court. Just know that you lose certain protections when you do, and I still advise you to work under the attorney.

A common misconception is that privilege covers everything an investigator does. It does not. Privilege protects *communications*, not *facts*. If a fact exists independently—an e-mail, video footage, personnel file, or financial record—it can still be discoverable even if you obtained it under the attorney's direction. Privilege protects the flow of information, not the underlying evidence itself.

International matters create additional challenges. Some countries do not recognize the attorney–client privilege the same way the U.S. does, particularly in corporate settings. In certain jurisdictions, in-house counsel communications are not privileged at all. Investigators supporting multinational organizations must understand which legal protections apply where—and which do not travel across borders.

Takeaway: Privilege is powerful, but it is not automatic. Work through counsel, maintain confidentiality, and document your purpose clearly.

September 13: The Work Product Doctrine

"Preparation is the foundation upon which success is built." —Alexander Graham Bell

If attorney–client privilege protects communications, the work product doctrine protects the engine behind those communications—the notes, impressions, strategies, and analysis created in anticipation of litigation. For investigators, this doctrine can be just as crucial as privilege because it shields the thinking behind the investigation, not just the conversations surrounding it.

Work product protection covers materials prepared by attorneys or their agents, which includes investigators, analysts, and subject-matter specialists working under counsel's direction. Unlike attorney–client privilege, which focuses on confidentiality, work product protection focuses on the purpose: Was the material created because litigation was expected or underway?

When investigators operate under that purpose, their drafts, notes, timelines, interview outlines, mental impressions, and investigative strategies receive heightened protection. But, as with privilege, the shield isn't automatic. Courts distinguish between **opinion work product** (your thoughts, interpretations, and mental impressions) and **fact work product** (raw observations, summaries, and collected information). Opinion work product is challenging to overcome; fact work product may be discoverable under certain conditions, especially if the opposing party shows a clear need.

International investigations further complicate this area. Many countries do not recognize the work product doctrine, and some provide no comparable protection for investigator-created materials. A multinational corporation may have strong protection for work done in the U.S., but those same documents may be fully discoverable or seizable by foreign regulators. Investigators supporting global organizations must understand which jurisdictions recognize work-product protections and which do not.

The most skilled investigators safeguard work product by working closely with counsel, keeping factual and analytical materials separate, labeling documents appropriately, and maintaining strict control over distribution.

Takeaway: Work product protects the investigator's mind, not just their materials. Work closely with counsel to maximize your protections.

September 14: Subject Representation

"A person who represents themselves has a fool for a client." —President Abraham Lincoln

Once a subject becomes represented by an attorney, the entire investigative landscape changes. What you can say, what you can ask, how you can communicate, and what leverage you possess all shift immediately.

In the public sector, this boundary is enforced by constitutional and ethical rules. Once a subject has asserted their right to counsel, investigators cannot initiate custodial questioning without the attorney present or a clear, voluntary waiver. Even seemingly harmless engagement—small talk, "just clarifying something," or asking logistical questions—can violate constitutional protections and result in suppressed statements. Courts view violations of the right to counsel harshly, and prosecutors will abandon statements rather than risk a tainted case.

Private-sector investigators face a parallel challenge. When a subject is represented—whether in a workplace dispute, civil action, or regulatory matter— you cannot contact them directly about the issue under investigation. The "no-contact" rule exists to preserve fairness and prevent investigators from sidestepping legal representation. Any communication must go through the subject's attorney unless explicit permission has been granted.

Representation also changes the dynamics of interviews. If a subject's attorney permits the interview, they may attend, influence the tone, or attempt to control the scope. This can be frustrating, but professional investigators understand that an attorney's presence is not an obstacle—it is a guardrail. A well-managed interview with counsel present can still produce valuable information.

Investigators must also recognize the **signals** of representation. Formal notice is ideal but not always provided. An email signature, a letter of intent, a verbal claim, or even a mention that "my lawyer told me..." may indicate representation. The safest approach is to treat any ambiguity as a stop sign until representation status is confirmed.

International work requires even greater caution. Some countries require an attorney's presence for any investigative inquiry involving employees. Others have strict labor-law rules about contacting represented individuals or union members. In some jurisdictions, violating representation boundaries can carry not just civil penalties but criminal consequences. Investigators must understand the cultural and legal expectations of the operating environment they are in.

Takeaway: Representation is a legal boundary, not a suggestion. Once a subject has an attorney, adjust your approach and communicate through counsel.

September 15: Consent to Monitoring

"Liberty cannot be preserved without general knowledge among the people." —John Adams

Few areas of investigative law are as widely misunderstood—or as easy to violate—as audio recording and electronic monitoring laws. The United States is split between **one-party consent** jurisdictions, where only one participant must consent to the recording, and **two-party consent** (or "all-party consent") jurisdictions, where everyone involved must consent. Crossing this line, even unintentionally, can carry criminal penalties.

In one-party consent states, an investigator who is part of the conversation may record it without informing the other party. This rule applies to phone calls and in-person interactions. But it does *not* allow hidden microphones in environments where the investigator is not present. Once you step outside your role as a participant—such as bugging a room, intercepting communications between third parties, or placing a recording device without being present—you enter territory governed by federal wiretap laws, not state consent statutes.

In two-party (all-party) consent states, every person being recorded must be informed of and consent to the recording. Violating this rule can lead to criminal charges, statutory damages, and suppression of critical evidence. Investigators working near state borders must be especially careful; a call from a one-party state to a two-party state defaults to the stricter rule. Many seasoned investigators memorize the map of consent laws precisely because one wrong phone call can ruin a case.

Private-sector investigators face additional considerations. Many states require *employee notice* for workplace monitoring—whether e-mail, phone, or electronic systems. A company may legally record calls for training or quality assurance, but only if employees (and sometimes customers) have been informed. Investigators conducting internal interviews or digital reviews must ensure proper notice has been provided. A lack of notice can turn a lawful inquiry into unlawful surveillance.

Public-sector investigators must also tread carefully. Even when operating within their authority, constitutional and statutory protections still apply. Government agents cannot sidestep two-party consent laws just because they are conducting an investigation. Consent requirements vary widely across agencies and jurisdictions, and federal agents may be subject to different rules than state or local counterparts. When in doubt, legal guidance—not assumptions—should lead the way.

Takeaway: Know your consent laws before you ever hit "record." One-party and two-party states draw very different lines.

September 16: Covert Recording Laws

"Big brother is watching you." —George Orwell

Covert recording tempts many investigators because it feels like a shortcut: a way to capture the truth without interference, influence, or performance. But secret audio or video recordings are among the most heavily regulated areas of investigative practice.

The first rule is understanding privacy expectations. Recording is generally lawful in places where there is no reasonable expectation of privacy, such as public streets, common areas, storefronts, or open spaces. But bathrooms, dressing rooms, private offices, homes, hotel rooms, and any enclosure designed to shield personal activity are treated as protected spaces. Hidden cameras in these environments aren't just unethical—they are often criminal.

The second rule is knowing the difference between audio and video. Video alone is governed primarily by privacy-location rules. Audio is governed by wiretap and eavesdropping laws, which carry far stricter penalties. Many states treat covert audio recording as a felony, even when the investigator's intent is legitimate. Adding a microphone to a video device can instantly transform a lawful recording into an unlawful interception.

For public-sector investigators, agency policy and constitutional protections add another layer of complexity. Many agencies require supervisory approval, legal review, or documented justification before any covert recording is attempted. A legally permissible recording can still violate internal policy—and internal violations can ruin careers as quickly as criminal ones.

For private-sector investigators, the risks often stem from misunderstanding boundaries. Hidden audio in a workplace, camera placement inside private residences, or recording third-party conversations without being present can lead to criminal charges, civil lawsuits, and regulatory sanctions. Covert recording is one of the top reasons PIs lose their licenses.

International work can be even more dangerous. Some countries prohibit secret recording entirely. Others allow it only for personal documentation, not investigative use. In many jurisdictions, covert audio—regardless of consent or location—is treated as unlawful surveillance with severe penalties.

Takeaway: Covert recordings may feel like power—but they are a legal minefield. Know the rules, respect privacy, and never deploy a hidden recorder unless you are certain the law allows it.

September 17: GPS Tracking Laws

"The most important trip you may take in life is meeting people halfway." —*Henry Boyle*

GPS trackers are one of the most powerful—and most dangerous—tools available to investigators. They provide real-time location data, confirm behavioral patterns, and uncover movements that would take days of manual surveillance to document. But they also sit at the intersection of privacy, property rights, constitutional protections, and state-level criminal statutes.

Public-sector investigators operate under the U.S. Supreme Court's decision in *United States v. Jones*, which held that attaching a tracker to a vehicle constitutes a search under the Fourth Amendment. That means government agents cannot place a tracker without a warrant supported by probable cause, unless a narrow exception applies. This requirement extends to prolonged monitoring, which courts have increasingly scrutinized as potential violations of reasonable-expectation-of-privacy standards. Even minor procedural missteps—poor documentation, expired warrants, or lack of supervisory oversight—can lead to suppression of evidence and civil liability.

Private-sector investigators face an even more complicated landscape. No federal statute directly governs private use of GPS devices, leaving regulation to the states—and the states do not agree. Some treat unauthorized GPS placement as a misdemeanor. Others classify it as felony stalking or unlawful surveillance. A few states allow limited placement when a vehicle is jointly owned, but even then, only under strict conditions. Some states have made minor exceptions for private investigators.

The biggest mistake investigators make is assuming that the vehicle's owner always controls consent. In several jurisdictions, ownership is irrelevant; the person being tracked must consent.

Internationally, GPS laws differ even more dramatically. Some countries treat vehicle tracking as a form of personal surveillance requiring government authorization. Others allow tracking only for asset protection. In the EU, GPS monitoring often implicates the GDPR, requiring data minimization, documented necessity, and strict retention limits.

Takeaway: GPS tracking is not just a tactical decision—it's a legal one. Know your authority, and never place or access a tracker unless the law allows it.

September 18: Stalking & Harassment Laws

"Where the law ends, tyranny begins." —William Pitt the Elder

Surveillance seems straightforward—follow, observe, document. But in the eyes of the law, surveillance that crosses the line from professional observation into persistent, unwanted, or intimidating conduct can become a criminal offense. Stalking and harassment statutes were not written with investigators in mind, yet they frequently ensnare investigators. The challenge is simple: what looks like legitimate surveillance to you may look like stalking to a neighbor, a subject, or responding officers who don't yet know the details of your case.

Most states define stalking as a course of conduct that causes a reasonable person to feel fear, intimidation, or emotional distress. Surveillance—by definition—involves repeated observation, following, and documentation. When subjects notice surveillance, misunderstand it, or feel targeted, investigators can suddenly find themselves on the wrong end of a police contact. Harassment statutes are often even broader, capturing behaviors that "annoy," "alarm," or "interfere," even without fear of harm. This means an investigator can unintentionally satisfy the statutory elements of a crime simply by doing their job improperly.

Public-sector investigators typically operate under clear authority, but that authority is not a blank check. Surveillance must support a legitimate investigative purpose and be conducted within policy. Repeated contact, aggressive tactics, prolonged presence outside a residence, or failing to disengage when safety or policy demands can all expose agents to administrative action—or criminal exposure if the conduct appears excessive or threatening. Courts expect government surveillance to be reasonable and proportional.

Private-sector investigators face even greater vulnerability. They have no governmental authority, making their presence and actions easier to misinterpret. Many states explicitly include "tracking or monitoring" within their stalking statutes. Sitting outside someone's home too long, following too closely, conducting mobile surveillance repeatedly, or allowing surveillance to escalate into confrontation can trigger stalking allegations.

The risk increases when subjects confront the investigator or call the police. Always, and I mean always, have a services agreement between you and your client to show the police why you are doing what you are doing. Even then, if not in compliance with the law, the agreement is not worth the paper it is printed on.

Takeaway: Poorly executed surveillance looks like stalking. Know the laws and conduct surveillance the way you'd want it defended in court.

September 19: Trespass

"Good fences make good neighbors." —Robert Frost

Nothing derails an investigation faster—or more dramatically—than a physical-access violation. Trespass, unlawful entry, and breaking and entering are not abstract legal concepts; they are charges that investigators face every year for crossing physical boundaries they had no legal right to cross.

Trespass is the most common violation because it is also the easiest to commit. Stepping onto private property without permission—even a few feet—can create criminal and civil liability. Investigators often miscalculate property lines, mistake open gates for implied permission, or assume that a lack of signage equates to lawful access. It does not. For private-sector investigators in particular, trespass claims are among the most frequently filed lawsuits, and many are filed simply because the investigator "looked suspicious" while standing somewhere they had no right to be.

Breaking and entering escalates the consequences. An unlocked door, unsecured garage, or propped-open gate does not grant investigative permission. Entering enclosed structures without consent—even without causing damage—meets the legal threshold for B&E in many jurisdictions. The test is not whether the investigator intended to steal or harm, but whether they crossed a protected physical boundary without lawful authority. Too many investigators have justified these actions to themselves by saying they were "just checking," only to find out that the law does not recognize curiosity as a defense.

Public-sector investigators must follow Fourth Amendment doctrine and statutory authority. Even when acting under color of law, entry into private spaces requires warrants, consent, exigent circumstances, or specific statutory authorization. Mistakes here have steep consequences: cases suppressed, evidence excluded, administrative discipline, civil suits, and loss of public trust. Government investigators who push physical boundaries without proper justification can do more damage to their agency than to the subject they're pursuing.

Professional investigators keep themselves safe by adopting a simple rule: **If you're not certain you can be there, you can't be there.** They verify boundaries, confirm consent, document authority, and err on the side of distance rather than closeness.

Takeaway: Physical access is a bright line. Respect property boundaries, obtain proper authority, and never assume permission where none exists.

September 20: Records Retention & Evidence

"Everyone is entitled to his own opinion, but not his own facts." —Daniel Patrick Moynihan

Investigations live or die on documentation. But it isn't enough to simply collect records—you must preserve them, store them properly, and retain them for as long as the law, policy, or litigation requires. Evidence preservation is one of the most overlooked responsibilities in investigative work, yet it is among the most legally consequential. Spoliation—the improper destruction, alteration, or mishandling of evidence—can cripple a case faster than two shakes of a lamb's tail.

Public-sector investigators operate under strict constitutional, statutory, and agency-specific retention rules. Digital media, body-worn camera footage, forensic extractions, interview recordings, and physical evidence all carry mandatory retention periods. Losing or altering any of it—even unintentionally—can result in case dismissals, Brady violations, internal discipline, or civil liability. Courts expect government investigators to anticipate litigation and preserve everything relevant from the moment they "reasonably should have known" it may be needed. That standard is far broader than most realize.

Private-sector investigators face a different but equally dangerous landscape. Civil litigation, insurance disputes, HR matters, regulatory inquiries, and corporate compliance investigations all impose their own preservation obligations. When a client is facing potential litigation, a litigation hold must be put in place—and investigators must preserve every note, recording, photograph, message, and file associated with the matter. Destroying evidence after a litigation hold is in place, even as part of routine cleanup, can lead to sanctions, adverse inference instructions, or catastrophic financial penalties.

Digital evidence adds yet another layer of complexity. Videos, text messages, GPS logs, social media captures, and cloud-based files degrade or disappear faster than many investigators expect. Platforms auto-delete, metadata changes, and systems overwrite data unless properly preserved. Failing to capture original metadata or relying solely on screenshots can render evidence unreliable in court.

The professionals who excel in evidence preservation share one habit: they build preservation into their workflow from day one. They assume the case will end up in court, even if most never do.

Takeaway: Evidence is only as strong as its preservation. Retain it, protect it, and document it.

September 21: Mail Tampering and Postal Laws

"Gentlemen do not read each other's mail." —Secretary Henry Stimson

Mail is a deceptively sensitive area of investigative work. Letters, parcels, courier shipments, and interoffice envelopes may appear mundane, but the laws governing them are strict, unforgiving, and aggressively enforced. Opening, delaying, interfering with, or even touching the wrong piece of mail can escalate an otherwise routine investigation into a federal crime.

In the United States, mail delivered through the U.S. Postal Service is protected under federal law—specifically 18 U.S.C. § 1702–1708. Mail tampering includes opening sealed letters, diverting delivery, removing items from mailboxes, or obtaining postal contents without authorization. For investigators, this means one thing: if the subject does not consent and the mail is not addressed to you or your client, it is off limits.

Private-sector investigators often stumble here, especially in domestic, workplace, or fraud cases. A suspicious package on a porch, an envelope left on a desk, or interoffice mail sitting in a shared workspace may tempt an investigator to "peek." But unless you have explicit permission from the addressee or a lawful basis to inspect it, you may be committing a crime.

Public-sector investigators are not immune from restrictions. Law enforcement must obtain proper warrants or statutory authority before seizing or inspecting mail. Even postal inspectors—who have the most specialized authority in this arena—operate under strict rules requiring probable cause, documented reasons for detention, and supervisory approval.

A brief word on mail covers: A U.S. Postal Service mail cover is a long-standing investigative technique allowing law enforcement to record external information on mail—names, addresses, postmarks—but never the contents. Mail covers require formal written requests, supervisory approval, and a legitimate criminal or national security purpose. No private investigator can lawfully request one, and no investigator—public or private—may attempt an informal version by examining mail left in a subject's mailbox. Anything outside the official USPS mechanism is simply mail tampering by another name.

The safest investigators follow the same rule here that applies to physical entry: **if the item is addressed to someone else and you don't have explicit legal authority, do not touch it.** Document what is visible, photograph what is in plain view, and seek legal counsel before action.

Takeaway: Mail—whether personal, corporate, domestic, or international—is legally protected property. Treat every envelope and package as such.

September 22: Data Access Laws

"Knowledge without justice ought to be called cunning rather than wisdom." —Plato

Modern investigations live in a world of data—bank records, phone logs, subscriber information, medical files, employment records, social media content, and cloud-stored communications. But investigators often forget a simple truth: **just because data exists does not mean you are legally permitted to obtain it.** Accessing protected information without proper authority can violate federal law, state law, civil statutes, professional licensing rules, and—in some cases— criminal codes.

Financial records are among the most heavily protected. Bank account information, transaction histories, and credit reports fall under the Gramm– Leach–Bliley Act (GLBA), the Fair Credit Reporting Act (FCRA), and a patchwork of state privacy laws. Obtaining financial data through deception, pretext, or misuse of a business relationship is illegal for both public and private investigators.

Communications data is equally restricted. Phone subscriber information, call detail records, text content, email access, and IP logs all fall under federal frameworks like the Stored Communications Act (SCA) and the Electronic Communications Privacy Act (ECPA). Law enforcement may access certain records with warrants, court orders, or administrative subpoenas. Private-sector investigators, however, cannot. No client—no matter how compelling their story—can authorize you to access another person's phone or email account.

Medical, educational, and employment records are governed by their own specialized regimes: HIPAA, FERPA, and state labor codes. These laws sharply restrict third-party access to personal information, often requiring signed releases or formal legal process.

Internationally, restrictions grow even tighter. The EU's General Data Protection Regulation (GDPR) imposes strict rules on accessing, transferring, and processing personal data. Some nations criminalize unauthorized access entirely, regardless of purpose. Investigators conducting cross-border assignments must ensure compliance not only with U.S. law but also with the laws of every country whose territory the data touches.

The recurring theme is caution. Professional investigators rely on proper legal processes—such as subpoenas, court orders, or requests through counsel—or obtain written consent from the data owner.

Takeaway: Data access is governed by some of the strictest laws in the investigative world. Know what you are and aren't allowed to touch.

September 23: Surveillance Conduct Standards

"Authority without wisdom is like a heavy axe without an edge." —Anne Bradstreet

Surveillance is one of the most common investigative techniques. It looks simple from the outside: sit, watch, record. But the legal and ethical standards governing surveillance differ sharply between public-sector and private-sector investigators. Failing to understand those distinctions is one of the fastest ways to compromise a case, violate someone's rights, or expose yourself to liability.

Public-sector investigators work under constitutional constraints. The Fourth Amendment, case law, departmental policies, and statutory authorities define what government agents may observe, when they may observe, and for how long. Surveillance must support a legitimate investigative purpose, be proportionate to the suspected offense, and avoid tactics that would create a privacy intrusion requiring a warrant. Even something as basic as following a subject into semi-private spaces can cross constitutional boundaries. Courts expect government surveillance to be reasonable, documented, and subject to supervisory review.

Private-sector investigators operate under a different framework—civil law, tort exposure, licensing rules, and state privacy statutes. They lack constitutional authority, so they cannot claim law enforcement powers or an implied governmental privilege. Their surveillance must be conducted from lawful vantage points, avoid trespassing, and avoid conduct that resembles harassment, stalking, or intimidation. A private investigator who lingers too long outside a residence, follows too closely, or uses aggressive mobile techniques risks not only losing the case but also losing their license, reputation, and freedom.

Both sectors share a critical responsibility: professional conduct. Surveillance is not an excuse for reckless driving, confrontations, or tactics that escalate risk. Good investigators understand that surveillance is as much about restraint as it is about persistence. Blending in, staying unobtrusive, and avoiding actions that draw attention are not just best practices—they are legal safeguards.

International work complicates surveillance further. Many countries impose strict limitations on following individuals, filming in public, or monitoring movements without explicit legal authority. In some jurisdictions, private surveillance is effectively illegal unless conducted by licensed entities under narrow statutory conditions. The investigator who assumes "U.S. rules apply everywhere" will quickly find out otherwise.

Takeaway: Surveillance is not defined by what you can see—it is defined by what the law allows. Know the rules for your sector and stay within legal limits.

September 24: Entrapment

"The greater the power, the more dangerous the abuse." —Sir Edmund Burke

Few investigative errors are more damaging than crossing the line into entrapment. While most investigators think it is something "only undercover cops worry about," the truth is far broader. Entrapment, inducement, coercive prompting, and manufactured opportunity all carry legal risks that can collapse public-sector cases and expose private-sector investigators to civil liability.

In the public sector, entrapment carries constitutional and procedural weight. The classic definition centers on government agents inducing a person to commit a crime they would not otherwise have been predisposed to commit. Courts look not only at what investigators said or did, but at the entire context: Was the opportunity overly persuasive? Did the investigator apply pressure, encouragement, or repeated requests? Did the suspect show reluctance? If the government manufactures criminality rather than uncovering it, entrapment becomes a defense—and sometimes a scandal.

Inducement is subtler but just as dangerous. Suggesting a criminal idea, escalating a subject's willingness, or offering benefits—financial, personal, or emotional—to push conduct forward can transform a legitimate operation into an improper one. Investigators must ensure that any opportunity presented aligns with an existing predisposition. You are allowed to provide a chance; you are not allowed to create the desire.

Private-sector investigators face a different—but equally critical—boundary. Although "entrapment" is legally a government-focused doctrine, private investigators can still face civil liability or criminal charges for inducing misconduct. Encouraging an employee to break company policy, prompting a spouse to violate court orders, or coaxing a claimant into dishonest statements can all trigger claims of interference, defamation, or bad-faith investigation. A PI who manufactures wrongdoing risks not only losing the case but also being held responsible for the harm that follows.

The strongest investigators follow a consistent principle: they observe more than they influence. They document behaviors that already exist. They avoid suggestive questions, avoid shaping narratives, and avoid prompting misconduct.

Takeaway: Entrapment destroys cases. Inducement destroys credibility. Stay on the observation side of the line, present opportunities only where lawful and justified, and never push a subject toward wrongdoing.

September 25: Undercover Legal Considerations

"He who permits himself to tell a lie once finds it much easier to do it the second time." —President Thomas Jefferson

Undercover work carries an aura of excitement, but in reality, it is one of the most legally constrained and professionally hazardous techniques an investigator can use. Whether in the public sector, private sector, or corporate environment, operating under a false identity—however mild—raises issues of legality, ethics, admissibility, safety, and credibility. Investigators cannot simply "go undercover" because the situation feels appropriate. Cover must be lawful, justified, and controlled.

Public-sector undercover operations are governed by strict rules—constitutional boundaries, departmental policies, Attorney General guidelines, and sometimes, judicial oversight. Law enforcement agents must articulate a legitimate investigative need, receive supervisory approval, and maintain detailed documentation of every covert interaction. The law recognizes the necessity of deception in specific investigations. Still, it also draws clear boundaries: undercover operations cannot induce crimes, coerce conduct, or violate rights that would be protected in any other context.

Private-sector investigators face an even narrower path. While some forms of pretext are lawful—such as posing as a customer in a retail setting—others quickly become criminal acts. Impersonating a government official, utility worker, bank representative, medical provider, or an employee of a regulated industry can violate impersonation statutes or consumer protection laws. Even using a simple alias on the phone can trigger liability if it deceives a protected entity or gains access to restricted information. Many states explicitly prohibit pretexting for financial, telecommunications, or personal data. A private investigator who assumes a false identity without legal authority risks not only the case but also their license and livelihood.

In international environments, the stakes rise dramatically—many nations criminalize false identities entirely, and undercover operations may require special licensing or government sanction. If you are not a citizen of the host country you are operating in, your actions could be construed as espionage; something you don't want to be accused of internationally because the penalty is often death.

Takeaway: False identities may serve investigative purposes, but they carry serious legal consequences. Use cover only when lawful, plan every detail, and document every action.

September 26: Confidential Informant Rules

"The weakest link in a chain is the strongest because it can break it." —*Stanislaw Jerzy Lec*

Every jurisdiction treats confidential informants (CI) differently, but the themes are universal: oversight, documentation, and due-process integrity.

According to federal and state guidance, CI agreements must avoid any structure that incentivizes unreliable or manufactured testimony. Courts have repeatedly warned that reward structures tied directly to convictions or specific targets violate due process. For example, agreements promising a percentage of forfeited assets have been struck down or heavily criticized because they can distort an informant's motivation, undermining credibility, and legality.

Even permissible agreements require caution. Payments to informants are legal, but investigators must ensure the compensation is reasonable, capped, and authorized at a higher supervisory level—safeguards designed to prevent undue influence and preserve reliability. According to the NCJRS manual Use of Informants and Undercover Investigations, "Just because an agreement is legal does not guarantee that the informant will be believed," especially if the terms risk compromising credibility or suggest inducement.

Where cooperation is ongoing, written agreements must clearly set expectations: honesty requirements, prohibited conduct (such as committing crimes during cooperation), and compliance checks, such as daily reporting or adherence to supervision protocols. Handling agencies must also avoid "undue pressure," since aggressive tactics can push informants toward perjury, fabrication, or entrapment-adjacent behavior—each of which carries legal consequences for the investigator and the organization Private-sector investigators face different statutes, but many of the same risks. Payments, promises, or coercive recruitment can expose PIs to civil liability or criminal exposure. The principle remains consistent across sectors: your job is to gather truth, not manufacture it.

Fundamentally, documentation is key for all informant work. Control files, suitability assessments, payment logs, and corroboration records form the backbone of defensibility. Every payment, contact, and statement must be traceable to withstand prosecutorial, judicial, or internal review.

Takeaway: CI work isn't dangerous because informants are unpredictable—it's dangerous because the law demands precision. Clear agreements, capped compensation, strict oversight, keep investigations on the right side of the line.

September 27: International Law

"Laws control the lesser man. Right conduct controls the greater one." —*Mark Twain*

Modern investigations rarely remain confined to a single jurisdiction. Data moves globally, companies operate across continents, and subjects may live in one country while storing their records in another. But the moment an investigation reaches beyond U.S. borders, the legal terrain changes.

The most well-known example is the European Union's General Data Protection Regulation (GDPR), which governs how personal data is collected, processed, stored, and transferred. GDPR applies not only to European entities, but to **any investigator anywhere** who touches EU resident data. Basic investigative acts— pulling server logs, reviewing corporate email, or exporting case files to a U.S. server—may require explicit consent, legitimate interest analysis, or formal data-transfer safeguards such as Standard Contractual Clauses. Violations can produce fines far beyond anything found in U.S. law.

But GDPR is only one piece of a much larger global privacy puzzle. Canada's PIPEDA, Brazil's LGPD, Singapore's PDPA, South Africa's POPIA, and dozens of national privacy statutes impose their own restrictions. Some countries restrict employee monitoring, some limit surveillance in public, and others prohibit cross-border transfer of certain personal or financial data entirely. Privacy is not a universal concept—its definition changes with culture, law, and local expectations.

Public-sector investigators face even more complexity. U.S. government agencies and law enforcement must comply not only with U.S. constitutional rules, but with host-nation law, SOFAs, treaties, and diplomatic agreements. Many nations prohibit unilateral investigative activity by foreign agents, restricting interviews, surveillance, digital forensics, or source operations unless coordinated through designated authorities. A poorly timed knock on a door can become a diplomatic event.

This is where Mutual Legal Assistance Treaties (MLAT) become essential. MLATs are formal agreements allowing countries to request evidence, records, or investigative assistance from one another through official channels. When U.S. investigators need foreign banking records, subscriber information, cloud data stored overseas, or testimony from a foreign resident, they often must proceed through the MLAT process. MLATs are deliberately slow and bureaucratic—but they are the only lawful avenue in many cases.

Takeaway: International laws are different. Know the privacy laws, respect borders, use proper channels, such as MLATs for foreign evidence, and never assume U.S. rules apply abroad.

September 28: Use of Force Law

"Force always attracts men of low morality." —Dr. Albert Einstein

Investigators are not supposed to be warriors. They are fact-gatherers. But in the real world, investigations occasionally collide with situations involving physical danger, resistance, or self-defense. In those moments, knowing the legal boundaries is not optional—it is survival.

For public-sector investigators, the guiding doctrine is clear: Graham v. Connor. Under Graham, an officer's use of force must be **objectively reasonable** based on the totality of the circumstances. Courts do not assess force with hindsight or emotional framing—they look at what a reasonable officer on the scene would have done. That assessment hinges on three core factors:

1. The severity of the crime at issue,
2. Whether the subject poses an immediate threat to the safety of the officer or others,
3. Whether the subject is actively resisting or attempting to evade arrest by flight.

Public agents must also follow agency policy, local statutes, and training standards. The use of force can be legally justified yet still violate policy, and careers often end on policy violations.

For private-sector investigators, the reality is entirely different. Private investigators do **not** have arrest powers (beyond what any citizen possesses), do not operate under Graham, and cannot use force except under ordinary civilian self-defense laws. This means:

- You cannot use force to detain someone unless citizen's arrest statutes explicitly allow it—and many don't.
- You cannot use force to protect property except in extremely narrow circumstances.
- You may only use force to defend yourself or another from an imminent, unlawful threat.
- The level of force must match the threat; disproportionate force becomes criminal, even if you didn't start the confrontation.

Many private investigators ruin careers by forgetting this: You are not law enforcement (even if you once were). Use of force used beyond what an ordinary citizen is allowed can lead to criminal charges and license revocation.

Takeaway: Public investigators act under Graham. Private investigators act under civilian self-defense law. Know your authority and your alternatives.

September 29: Preparing for Court

"Truth is proper and beautiful in all times and in all places." —*Frederick Douglass*

Most investigators will someday find themselves in a courtroom—civil, criminal, administrative, military, or regulatory. When that day comes, the outcome rarely depends on how exciting the investigation was. It depends on how clearly, truthfully, and professionally the investigator can present what they did.

Preparing for court starts long before a subpoena arrives. Reports must be written as if every sentence will be enlarged on a screen and picked apart by opposing counsel. That means factual language, chronological structure, careful citations, and absolutely no personal opinions unless explicitly required by policy. Investigators who treat reports as casual summaries create their own impeachment material. Courts reward precision.

Exhibits must also withstand scrutiny. Photographs require metadata preservation. Videos need clear timestamps and a documented chain of custody. Digital evidence must be exported in formats that preserve original integrity. Every exhibit should allow a judge or jury to follow the investigator's logic without needing explanation or interpretation. Exhibits are supposed to support your testimony—not rescue it.

Public-sector investigators must prepare for Brady/Giglio challenges. Any inconsistency, disciplinary history, or documentation issue may be used to undermine credibility. Private-sector investigators face parallel risks through civil discovery, where opposing counsel may explore inconsistencies, bias, scope creep, or faulty methodology.

International work adds another level of preparation. Some courts require certified translations, legalized documents, or country-specific formats for evidence. Data collected abroad may require proof of compliance with foreign privacy laws before a court will accept it. Failing to meet these procedural demands can exclude otherwise solid evidence.

The best investigators rehearse with their counsel—not to memorize testimony, but to organize it. They review their notes, re-read reports, examine exhibits, and meet with counsel to understand the theory of the case. They know their limitations and stay within them. Court is not a stage for performance; it is a venue for professional communication.

Takeaway: Courtroom success is built long before you raise your right hand.

September 30: Serving as an Expert Witness

"An expert is a person who has made all the mistakes that can be made in a very narrow field." —Niels Bohr

More investigators today find themselves asked to serve as expert witnesses, not just fact witnesses. The difference is profound. A fact witness says what happened. An expert explains what it means. With that power comes ethical responsibility, legal consequences, and a level of scrutiny far greater than most investigators have ever experienced. Expert testimony in the U.S. is governed by two major frameworks: the Frye and Daubert standards.

- **Frye (1923)** asks whether your methods are generally accepted in your professional field.
- **Daubert (1993)** asks whether your methods are reliable and scientifically valid, tested, peer-reviewed, with known error rates and clear standards.

Your résumé alone is not enough—your methodology must withstand legal and scientific scrutiny. An expert cannot simply advocate for the side that hired them. Once under oath, they serve the court—not the client. Their opinions must remain objective, even if inconvenient.

Preparation is more demanding than ordinary testimony. Experts must be fluent not only in the facts of the case but in the technical standards governing their field. For investigators, this may include surveillance protocols, digital forensic practices, interview methodology, background investigations, workplace inquiries, or regulatory compliance. Opposing counsel will test your knowledge relentlessly: definitions, best practices, exceptions, and scientific or procedural foundations. You are not preparing for cross-examination; you are preparing for academic debate under oath. Also, the court does not want jargon-filled lectures. It wants clarity, simplicity, and fairness.

Private-sector experts must understand marketing boundaries. Selling yourself as an "expert" can backfire if your credentials are exaggerated or if past cases reveal shaky foundations. Public-sector experts—especially law enforcement—must prepare for challenges to training, internal policy deviations, and prior disciplinary findings.

Ultimately, expertise is not about knowing everything—it is about knowing your field deeply, admitting your limits honestly, and presenting your opinions responsibly.

Takeaway: Expert testimony is a privilege that carries weight. If you only recall one thing, remember this: you serve the court before you serve anyone else.

October: The Big Picture: Investigative Analysis

"Analysis is the art of separating the whole into its parts." —Aristotle

If September teaches investigators the legal boundaries, October teaches them how to think. Investigative analysis is where information becomes understanding—where facts are arranged, compared, tested, and transformed into conclusions that withstand real-world scrutiny. No case succeeds on evidence alone.

Investigative analysis is not a single skill. It is a process, a mindset, and a toolkit. It begins with collecting raw information—surveillance logs, interview notes, financial records, digital artifacts, timelines, phone dumps—and asking the most important question in the analytical world: what does this actually mean? Raw material is not the truth. It is the starting point from which truth is extracted.

Modern investigators—law enforcement, corporate, private-sector, insurance, regulatory, or military—rely on the same foundational concepts. Information becomes intelligence when it has been evaluated for reliability, relevance, and context. Analysis breaks complex problems into components. Techniques give structure to thinking. Tools give structure to data. And the process—screen, analyze, integrate, produce—ensures that nothing important is overlooked and nothing unsubstantiated is allowed to slip through.

October covers the full spectrum of analytical practice: building timelines, mapping relationships, constructing matrices, linking people to actions, and actions to consequences. You will see methods familiar to intelligence analysts— link charts, event trees, association matrices, commodity flow diagrams—but each has a direct application to investigations at any scale. These are not theoretical exercises. They are practical tools for building cases, identifying gaps, validating hypotheses, and avoiding tunnel vision. Private investigators use them to organize domestic cases and fraud files. Public-sector analysts use them to dismantle criminal networks and support prosecutions. The techniques are identical—the stakes differ, but the process remains the same.

This month also introduces the importance of process maps—a structured way to visualize how a case unfolds, from lead intake to investigative action to analytical review. Process mapping forces clarity. It reveals gaps, redundancies, inefficiencies, and missed opportunities. Strong investigators do not stumble through cases; they build analytical frameworks that guide them.

Investigative analysis is also an exercise in humility. It requires the discipline to challenge assumptions, the patience to follow the evidence rather than emotion, and the courage to abandon a favored theory when the facts contradict it. The best investigators do not rely on instinct—they rely on structure. They know that a properly built timeline can break an alibi. A well-constructed matrix can reveal hidden connections. A link analysis can expose an overlooked accomplice. A simple process map can prevent months of wasted effort.

The goal of this month is to give you the mental tools to think like a professional analyst, regardless of your role. You will learn to see patterns, identify gaps, weigh competing explanations, and build conclusions that are defensible—not just persuasive. October is when your investigative thinking becomes sharper, deeper, and more reliable.

Investigative analysis is the backbone of case-building. Master the process, use the tools, and think critically—or the strongest evidence in the world won't matter.

October 1: The Investigator as Analyst

"It is the mark of an educated mind to be able to entertain a thought without accepting it." —Aristotle

Most investigators think of themselves as collectors of information—interviewers, observers, researchers, and technicians. But the truth is far simpler and far more demanding: Aside from being fact finders, every investigator is an analyst, whether they realize it or not. Cases are not built on the information you gather; they are built on the meaning you extract from it. That comes from analysis.

Analysis is the bridge between fact and conclusion. It transforms disconnected pieces of information into coherent findings. It determines what matters, what doesn't, and where the investigation must go next. Without analysis, investigators are simply hoarding data.

Analysis begins with critical thinking, not tools. Software can assist—link-analysis programs, mapping tools, timeline software, and visual diagramming platforms—but tools cannot replace thought. The core responsibilities remain the same:

- Recognize relevant facts.
- Organize information logically.
- Identify gaps and inconsistencies.
- Challenge assumptions.
- Generate and refine hypotheses.
- Corroborate before concluding.
- Communicate clearly and objectively.

These skills are universal. They apply equally to homicide detectives, OSINT researchers, insurance investigators, corporate compliance teams, federal agents, defense investigators, and international due diligence professionals. If you work with facts, you work with analysis.

Takeaway: An investigator who cannot analyze is just an information custodian.

October 2: Building the Analytical Mindset

"Facts are the air of scientists. Without them, you can never fly." —Linus Pauling

The difference between an average investigator and an exceptional one is not experience, equipment, or even intelligence. It is mindset. Analytical thinking determines how investigators approach information, interpret events, and adapt when the picture shifts. And make no mistake: in real investigations, the picture always shifts.

The analytical mindset begins with humility. Investigators who believe they "already know what happened" stop thinking. They stop listening. They stop testing their assumptions. Confirmation bias sets in, and from that moment forward, every fact is filtered through belief rather than evidence. The strongest investigators resist this trap by treating every hypothesis as provisional until corroborated through independent sources.

It also requires curiosity. Analytical curiosity asks: What does this mean? What am I missing? What else could explain this? Curiosity expands investigative thinking, revealing angles others overlook. Equally important is the willingness to revise conclusions when evidence contradicts them. This is harder than it sounds. Investigators grow attached to their theories. They build mental models and expect the world to fit inside them. But professional rigor demands the opposite: the model must fit the world, not the other way around. If new facts undermine your original conclusion, you adjust. You do not force the facts into alignment through interpretation or omission.

Finally, the analytical mindset requires patience. Analysis cannot be rushed. The first explanation is rarely the best one, and the last piece of information may reverse your understanding entirely. Professional investigators slow down at critical moments because they know speed is the enemy of accuracy. Across public, private, corporate, intelligence, and international environments, the formula remains constant: investigators who think clearly produce better cases, fewer errors, and findings that withstand scrutiny.

Takeaway: Analysis is not what you do—it is how you think. Build a mindset grounded in curiosity and critical thinking so you will see what others miss.

October 3: Information vs. Intelligence

"All knowledge is uncertain; the future is the most uncertain of all." —*Karl Popper*

Every investigation begins with information—raw, unprocessed, unfiltered material gathered from interviews, documents, databases, surveillance, digital records, and human behavior. But information alone cannot solve a case. What matters is intelligence: information that has been evaluated, verified, contextualized, and transformed into insight. The distinction is not academic. It is the difference between collecting facts and understanding what those facts mean.

Investigators who fail to distinguish between information and intelligence drown in data. They gather more and more without ever moving closer to a conclusion. They mistake volume for progress. This trap affects public- and private-sector investigators alike. It is why some cases expand unnecessarily, timelines get cluttered, and critical leads get buried in noise.

- Information is abundant; intelligence is scarce.
- Information is a witness statement. Intelligence is determining which parts are credible, corroborated, and relevant.
- Information is a list of calls on a phone bill. Intelligence is identifying which calls matter, to whom, and why.
- Information is surveillance footage. Intelligence is extracting behavioral patterns, opportunities, and contradictions from it.

The transformation from information to intelligence requires **analysis**.

Public-sector investigators have long institutionalized this distinction. Intelligence-led policing, threat assessments, fusion centers, and criminal intelligence guidelines all revolve around converting data into actionable insights. Their challenge is often too much information—large databases, vast digital collections, and endless reports, which can lead to analysis paralysis.

Private-sector investigators face the opposite challenge: too little verified information and too much unreliable or unstructured material. OSINT, corporate data, third-party reports, social media, and client-provided information must be vetted before becoming intelligence. A single unverified claim can misdirect an entire case, waste finite resources, or expose the investigator to liability.

Takeaway: Information is what you collect. Intelligence is what you understand.

October 4: Analytical Standards

"In seeking truth, you have to get both the facts and the meaning right." —Walter Lippmann

Information is never the end of an investigation; it's the beginning. What sets professional investigative work apart from rumor, assumption, or guesswork is the analytical standards applied to every piece of information that enters the case file. Reliability, validity, and corroboration are the three pillars of solid investigative reasoning.

Reliability addresses the source. Can this person, platform, device, or document be trusted? It doesn't mean you believe everything a source says; it means you understand who they are, what they saw, what they had access to, and what motivations or limitations may shape their account. Public-sector investigators often use formal source-rating systems. Private-sector investigators rely on professional judgment. Both must critically evaluate vantage point, consistency, competency, and potential bias. A reliable source can still be wrong—but they are wrong for human reasons, not deceptive ones.

Validity addresses the information itself. Does the detail make sense and align with reality? A source may be reliable, but their information might still be incomplete, misremembered, outdated, or incoherent. Validity analysis requires investigators to test the information's coherence with known facts, physical evidence, timestamps, digital footprints, and context. An employee may misremember an incident; a log file may be partial; a camera angle may distort perspective. Validity is the process of evaluating whether the information stands on its own.

Corroboration is the gold standard. Can another independent source confirm this? Corroboration protects investigators from being misled by a persuasive witness, a convincing lie, or a single piece of evidence that seems definitive but is not. The best investigators never rely on a single source. They test statements against surveillance, link charts, time-event sequences, digital forensics, financial records, or other witnesses. Corroboration doesn't just strengthen findings—it reveals deception, exposes fabrication, and uncovers gaps that might otherwise be missed.

Takeaway: Truth in investigations is not self-evident. It must be earned. Apply the standards of reliability, validity, and corroboration for a solid analysis.

October 5: Chronologies (Timelines)

"Clarity comes from the sequence of events." —Marcus Aurelius

Every investigation, no matter how complex or chaotic, has a story buried inside it. The fastest way to uncover that story is through a chronology, aka timelines. They are the backbone of investigative clarity—they impose order on disorder, reveal patterns that narrative summaries hide, and expose inconsistencies that witnesses never intend to reveal. If analysis is the skeleton of a case, a well-built timeline is its spine.

Timelines do more than record dates; they create structure. They show what happened, when it happened, who was involved, and how each event connects to the next. This sequencing transforms scattered facts into a coherent picture. Without a timeline, investigators operate in fog. Public-sector investigators rely on timelines for everything from homicide cases to financial crimes to national security inquiries.

Investigators use them to narrow windows of opportunity, test alibis, and link movements between suspects and victims. Private-sector investigators benefit just as much. In workplace cases, timelines reveal whether misconduct was isolated or progressive. In insurance investigations, they contrast reported events with objective timestamps—receipts, digital logs, phone metadata, surveillance footage, or card-use histories.

Well-constructed timelines also challenge assumptions. When investigators place events side by side—statements, surveillance, phone records, badge swipes, financial transactions, vehicle data—the inconsistencies jump out. A claimed meeting doesn't fit the travel time. A reported injury predates the incident. A suspect's alibi overlaps with digital activity miles away. Timelines reveal what narrative summaries conceal. The most effective timelines include:

- **Date and exact time** (down to seconds when available)
- Event description
- **Source of information** (statement, video, log, OSINT, physical evidence)
- **Confidence level** (high/medium/low)
- Notes on gaps or contradictions

Timelines also serve as communication tools. They help supervisors understand the case (and military commanders love demonstrative material). They help clients grasp the facts. They prepare investigators for interviews, revealing what questions remain unanswered. They are helpful all around to your case.

Takeaway: A timeline turns scattered details into a coherent story. Build them early and often to ensure you are building a comprehensive picture of events.

October 6: Time Event Charts

"Order is the shape upon which beauty depends." —Pearl S. Buck

If timelines tell you when things happened, time–event charts tell you how they happened. They are the next level of chronological analysis—an investigative technique that places multiple sequences side by side, allowing the investigator to compare actions, reactions, gaps, and overlaps across people, systems, and events. When timelines reveal the story, time–event charts reveal the relationships within it.

A time–event chart is a structured matrix. Down the left column are key actors, entities, systems, or evidence sources. Across the top is the timeline. In the cells between them are the actions each actor took—or failed to take—at each moment in time. It is simple in design and powerful in effect. Time–event charts expose inconsistencies that a linear timeline cannot. They reveal coordination, opportunity, deception, and absence. They show when someone is lying, not from what they said, but because of how it presents on the chart.

Public-sector investigators rely on this tool constantly. For example, homicide detectives use time–event charts to compare suspect statements with surveillance footage, vehicle movements, and digital footprints. Private-sector investigators use time–event charts just as effectively. In insurance and domestic investigations, they align the claimant's version of events with objective data—receipts, toll records, social media activity, or vehicle tracking. In corporate investigations, they allow security, HR, and compliance to see how a policy failure unfolded across departments. Time–event charts reveal several categories of insight that investigators often miss:

- **Overlap:** When two actors claim not to have interacted, but their timelines intersect.
- **Gaps:** Periods where no data exists—often the most important parts of the investigation.
- **Contradictions:** A person's actions do not match their statements.
- **Dependencies:** When one event was only possible because of another.
- **Sequencing errors:** A witness describes events in an order that contradicts physical reality.
- **Patterns of movement or behavior:** Repetition that suggests planning, opportunity, or routine.

The power of a time–event chart lies in forcing information to live in a shared space. When sources conflict, the conflict becomes visible.

Takeaway: A time–event chart doesn't just show what happened—it shows how events intersect. Use them to visualize truth and expose deception.

October 7: Link Analysis

"The connections between things are often more important than the things themselves." —John Muir

Every investigation—criminal, civil, corporate, or intelligence-driven—hinges on relationships. People, places, events, objects, companies, digital accounts, financial transactions, and communications rarely stand alone. Link analysis is the discipline of mapping these relationships to reveal structure, hierarchy, influence, and hidden connections that linear narratives fail to capture.

At its core, link analysis involves visualizing nodes (people, entities, or data points) and the links between them. Some links are obvious—family ties, business affiliations, co-workers. Others are far more subtle—shared phone numbers, overlapping travel, synchronized transactions, mutual associations, common devices, or digital interactions that suggest coordination. What investigators cannot see in text, they often see instantly in a visual map. The analytical value of link analysis comes from three insights it produces:

1. **Hidden centrality**: Sometimes the most important person in a network is not the loudest or most visible—it's the one who sits quietly at the intersection of multiple actors. Link charts make these central figures impossible to miss.
2. **Missing links**: Gaps in a network can be as meaningful as the connections. A sudden lack of communication, an unexplained intermediary, or a missing data point often indicates deception, operational security, or an undiscovered actor.
3. **Strength of connection**: Not all links are equal. Some are weak (one-off transactions). Others are strong (regular communication, shared assets, long-term associations). Professional link analysis weighs these connections and prioritizes those most relevant to motive, means, or opportunity.

Relationship mapping also highlights convergence through the links—moments when multiple actors share time, location, or behavior. These convergence points often reveal planning, coordination, or opportunity windows critical for prosecutorial or civil argument.

Tools can assist—i2 Analyst's Notebook, Maltego, OSINT mapping platforms—but software does not replace judgment. A cluttered chart is as useless as no chart at all. The investigator's responsibility is in deciding what to include, what to exclude, and arranging it meaningfully for a judge, jury, client, or attorney.

Takeaway: Link analysis transforms disconnected data points into a networked picture of reality. Use it to expose hidden relationships, identify key actors, and understand the structure of anything.

October 8: Pattern Recognition

"To understand is to perceive patterns." —Isaiah Berlin

Pattern recognition is one of the most powerful analytical abilities an investigator can develop—and one of the least formally taught. Patterns reveal behavior. Behavior reveals motive. Motive reveals opportunity. And when investigators combine all three, cases that once felt complex suddenly become clear. Patterns emerge when you compare actions over time, across locations, or between individuals. They show consistency—habits, routines, and methods of operation. They also show deviation—changes, anomalies, or behaviors that do not fit established norms. The key is learning to see both.

Public-sector investigators rely heavily on pattern recognition. Investigators identify modus operandi across multiple incidents. Intelligence analysts track pre-operational indicators across threat actors. Financial-crimes teams flag repetitive account activity, timing anomalies, or transaction structuring that signals fraud. Behavioral analysts examine escalation patterns, triggers, and routines to predict future actions or identify risk.

Private-sector investigators encounter patterns in different forms. Corporate investigators identify procurement irregularities, vendor collusion, or conflicts of interest through repetitive or synchronized actions. Even domestic investigations rely on behavioral patterns—social media activity, messaging rhythms, financial habits, or location routines of someone cheating. Patterns fall into three broad categories:

1. **Temporal patterns:** Events repeating at similar times, intervals, or sequences. (Examples: recurring travel times, repeated login windows, weekly cash withdrawals, synchronized communication spikes.)
2. **Spatial patterns:** Behavior tied to specific locations or movement routes. (Examples: consistent surveillance paths, repetitive store visits, triangulated meeting points, vehicle routes that form predictable loops.)
3. **Behavioral indicators:** Actions that reflect underlying motives, habits, or concealment strategies.

The most dangerous mistake investigators make is ignoring anomalies. Patterns matter—but so do breaks in those patterns. A subject who always behaves one way but suddenly changes may be signaling stress, deception, or opportunity. The hallmark of a strong investigator is the ability to spot patterns early and test them continuously—never assuming they are correct.

Takeaway: Patterns reveal the truth through behavior. Learn to recognize, track, challenge, and use them to understand your subject's actions.

October 9: Association Matrices

"The obvious is often the last thing we see." —Edward R. Murrow

Some investigative tools help you see what happened. Association matrices help you understand how people, objects, evidence, or events relate to one another. They are among the simplest yet most powerful analytical tools—especially when dealing with multiple actors, complex fact sets, or conflicting statements. Where link charts show relationships visually, association matrices show them logically.

An association matrix is a grid that compares one set of variables against another. Along the top may be people. Down the side may be events, evidence types, locations, or behaviors. The intersections show the nature of the connection: involvement, access, influence, proximity, possession, benefit, or opportunity. With each cell filled in, patterns of association emerge that are impossible to see in narrative form.

Public-sector investigators use association matrices to decode networks in organized crime, terrorism, fraud, and significant cases. Analysts populate cells with levels of confidence (high, medium, low), types of involvement (direct, indirect, unknown), or behavioral indicators (present, absent, inconsistent). Private-sector investigators use association matrices differently but just as effectively. Corporate security teams use matrices to compare vendors, transactions, or internal actors during procurement fraud investigations. Insurance investigators map claimants, witnesses, service providers, and financial flows to identify collusion. The keys to these matrices are:

1. **Concentration of association:** Some individuals appear repeatedly across key moments, evidence types, or decision points. The matrix reveals this concentration instantly.
2. **Unexplained connections:** An actor who should have no affiliation with an event or data point suddenly appears in the cross-section. That unexplained link often becomes the investigative pressure point.
3. **Missing associations:** Absences can be just as meaningful as presences. When an individual claims involvement but appears nowhere in the matrix, or claims non-involvement but shows up everywhere, you need to investigate!

Association matrices also expose investigative gaps. Empty cells tell investigators where to look next, who to interview again, or what evidence remains uncollected. These gaps often guide the next phase of inquiry more effectively than any single piece of evidence.

Takeaway: Association matrices reveal who is connected, how they are connected, and what those connections mean. Use them wisely.

October 10: Avoiding Cognitive Bias

"We don't see things as they are; we see them as we are." —Anaïs Nin

If analysis is the engine of investigative work, cognitive bias is the grit in the gears. It slows thinking, distorts judgment, and quietly pulls investigators toward conclusions that feel right but are wrong. The danger is not that investigators are careless—it's that bias operates invisibly, shaping interpretation long before the investigator realizes it.

Bias creeps into investigations in predictable ways. The most common is confirmation bias, the tendency to seek or favor information that supports an existing theory while discounting evidence that contradicts it. Once investigators form an early impression of guilt, innocence, motive, or sequence, they unconsciously reorganize the world to fit that impression. Excellent investigators counter this by treating early theories as hypotheses, not conclusions. They test them, challenge them, and welcome contradiction as a sign of progress, not error.

Availability bias causes investigators to overvalue the information that is easiest to recall—dramatic events, recent cases, personal experiences—even when those examples are irrelevant to the facts at hand. Public-sector investigators may default to familiar crime patterns. Private-sector investigators may lean on anecdotal experience. True analytical rigor demands that each case be treated uniquely, not squeezed into the shape of the last one.

Expectancy bias occurs when investigators subconsciously steer observations toward what they expect to see. This is especially dangerous during surveillance, interviews, or digital analysis. Expectation filters perception. Investigators must train themselves to see what is, not what they assume *should be*. More subtle forms of bias—hindsight bias, groupthink, halo effects, and overconfidence bias—can also rot the investigative foundation if left unchecked. Some helpful tips to combat bias:

- Use peer review or supervisory review to challenge your assumptions.
- Explicitly list alternative explanations before choosing one.
- Build timelines and association matrices that force all facts into a structured environment.
- Separate raw data from interpretation in reports.
- Regularly revisit and revise hypotheses in light of new information.

Takeaway: Bias is inevitable, but its influence is optional. Build solutions that challenge your assumptions.

October 11: Process Maps

"A good system shortens the road to the goal." —Ralph Waldo Emerson

Investigations feel chaotic when the investigator cannot see the process. Process maps fix that. They transform an investigation from a collection of actions into a structured workflow—revealing inefficiencies, dependencies, decision points, and failure risks that are invisible in narrative form.

At its core, a process map visualizes the steps of an investigative activity from start to finish. Unlike timelines or time–event charts—which sequence facts—process maps sequence actions. They show what the investigator must do, who does it, when decisions occur, and where the case can branch in different directions. They answer questions that investigators often ignore, such as:

- Are you following a logical path?
- Are you skipping critical steps?
- Are you doing work twice?
- Are there bottlenecks slowing the case?
- Are there compliance or authorization points you have neglected?

A strong process map includes:

1. **Inputs:** What starts the process? (complaint, referral, OSINT lead, supervisor directive)
2. **Actions:** The specific investigative steps taken, in order.
3. **Decision points:** "If yes, go here. If no, go there."
4. **Responsibilities:** Who performs each step? (investigator, analyst, supervisor, counsel)
5. **Compliance points:** Legal or policy moments that must be met before proceeding.
6. **Outputs:** What completes the process? (report, referral, closure, escalation)

Process maps also expose organizational vulnerabilities. Repeated backtracking, excessive handoffs, unclear roles, and unmonitored decision points often reveal where mistakes occur. Process map audits uncover whether investigators are deviating from policy—and whether policy itself needs updating.

Takeaway: Process maps bring order to the complexity of investigations. By visualizing each step, investigators can make a structured, defensible process that stands up to scrutiny.

October 12: Analytical Flowcharts & Modeling

"The most dangerous thing about human beings is our ability to believe almost anything." —Charles Murray

If process maps show *how* an investigation should unfold, analytical flowcharts show *how investigators should think.* They translate reasoning into a visual sequence—laying out options, branching paths, decision points, and possible outcomes. Flowcharts and decision models prevent investigators from relying on instinct or habit when the situation demands structure.

Investigators make hundreds of decisions over the life of a case: whom to interview first, what evidence to prioritize, which leads to pursue, whether a finding is supported, and whether a case should be escalated, closed, or referred. Flowcharts force those decisions into the open, revealing the logic behind them. Flowcharts begin with a central question—often a decision point. Examples:

- Does the evidence meet the threshold for administrative action?
- Is the subject lying or misinformed?
- Do we have sufficient corroboration to proceed?
- Is the next step surveillance, interview, or document recovery?

From those questions, branches emerge. Each branch represents an option, and each option leads to another decision point or an action. When done correctly, the flowchart lays bare the investigator's reasoning path—and in doing so, exposes flaws.

The discipline of decision modeling strengthens the investigator's thinking. It forces clarity, reduces error, and reveals when a case is drifting off course. No matter the environment—public, private, corporate, regulatory, or international—flowcharts and decision models help investigators make consistent, defensible, and evidence-based decisions.

Takeaway: Flowcharts turn reasoning into structure. Use them to guide choices and ensure every conclusion rests on a clear, defensible path of analysis.

October 13: Gap Analysis

"What you see depends on what you look for." —John Lubbock

As an investigator, you must develop the ability to see what isn't there. Facts rarely present themselves neatly; they appear in fragments—statements, timestamps, videos, logs, receipts, behaviors, or observations. The investigator's job is not merely to assemble what exists but to identify what *should* exist and doesn't. That discipline is called gap analysis, and it separates methodical investigators from those who rely on luck.

Gap analysis is the structured process of identifying missing information, contradictions, incomplete sequences, unverified claims, or unexplained events. It takes the products of earlier analytical tools—timelines, time–event charts, association matrices, link diagrams—and asks the most important question in analysis: *what don't we know yet?* Practical gap analysis typically reveals:

1. **Missing Time:** Unexplained intervals, inconsistent timestamps, downtime in logs, or periods where no corroborating evidence exists. Missing time often hides action.
2. **Missing Evidence:** A camera that should have captured an event but didn't. A record that should exist but is absent. Documents that should be present in a process but aren't.
3. **Missing Behavior:** When someone should have acted—but didn't. Failure to report, failure to log in, failure to follow procedure, or missing reactions that contradict normal behavior.
4. **Missing Witnesses or Statements:** People who should have been present but were not interviewed. Employees who had access but were overlooked. Bystanders who were not identified.
5. **Missing Corroboration:** Claims supported only by a single source. Events described without evidence. Assertions inconsistent with physical, digital, or financial data.

Gap analysis is robust because it shifts the mindset from passive acceptance of information to active interrogation. It reveals deception, exposes fabrication, and uncovers investigative blind spots. Equally important, it guides next steps: who to re-interview, which records to subpoena or collect, where to refocus surveillance, and which new hypotheses to test.

Takeaway: Gap analysis gives structure to the unknown, transforming absence into direction and uncertainty into action.

October 14: Source Reliability

"The greatest enemy of knowledge is not ignorance, it is the illusion of knowledge."
—Daniel J. Boorstin

Every investigation depends on people—witnesses, victims, complainants, subjects, informants, employees, neighbors, analysts, or third parties who "saw something." But people are imperfect instruments. They misinterpret, misremember, exaggerate, downplay, conceal, or get it wrong. The professional investigator knows that the question is never, *"What did they say?"* But, should *"I believe what they said"* —and to what degree?

Source reliability and credibility assessment is a structured method for evaluating whether a statement deserves weight. It prevents investigators from building cases on sand—unverified statements, emotional accounts, or confident but inaccurate narratives. And make no mistake: confidence is not credibility. Reliability evaluates the source. Credibility evaluates what the source said. Treating these as identical has led to more investigations being collapsed than deliberate deception ever has.

A dramatic real-world example illustrates the danger. In the early 2000s, Western intelligence services relied heavily on a single source known by the codename CURVEBALL. His claims about mobile biological weapons labs in Iraq were persuasive, detailed, and timely—but they were also false. Analysts later learned that his reliability had not been properly vetted, his access to the information had been overstated, and his statements lacked independent corroboration.

Yet because the information "fit" an existing narrative, the usual rigor of reliability and credibility assessment broke down. While not the only reason the U.S. invaded Iraq, the consequences from CURVEBALL's actions were global, leading to the deaths of thousands of Iraqis and coalition service members. One unreliable source, not malicious intelligence agencies, not flawed technology, became a key pillar in the justification for a major international conflict. Investigators in every field should remember CURVEBALL whenever a single source appears too central, too perfect, or too convenient.

Takeaway: Investigators should never fully trust a source—only the evidence that supports them. Evaluate both the source and the statement, or you may find yourself repeating the same mistake the world made with CURVEBALL.

October 15: Analyzing Digital Footprints

"The smallest deed is better than the grandest intention." —John Burroughs

In the modern era, nearly every investigation leaves a digital shadow. People advertise their behavior without realizing it—through phones, apps, vehicles, social media, GPS systems, logins, transactions, and metadata that record far more than users ever intended to reveal. For investigators, digital footprints are not just helpful—they are often the difference between theory and proof. Digital footprints fall into two categories: **active** and **passive**.

Active footprints are the deliberate actions a subject takes: posts, messages, photos, emails, searches. Passive footprints are generated automatically: geolocation pings, metadata, device logs, wireless connections, browser cookies, fitness trackers, app history, cloud-sync timestamps, and a modern favorite—data exhaust left behind by "background" apps a subject forgot they installed.

Digital footprints tell investigators four critical things:

1. **Where the subject was:** GPS data, IP addresses, tower dumps, app location histories, digital payments, toll passes, vehicle trackers.
2. **What the subject did:** Search histories, message logs, social media activity, cloud sync events, access attempts, and app usage patterns.
3. **What the subject tried to hide:** Deleted files (and their metadata), factory resets, missing logs, sudden inactivity, mismatched timestamps, encryption changes, or gaps that point to concealment.
4. **Who the subject interacted with:** Contacts, tagged photos, shared devices, overlapping IP locations, mutual followers, message threads, and digital proximity indicators.

Digital footprints do not lie, but they can mislead the untrained. Location data has a margin of error. Metadata can be altered through editing software. Social media can be spoofed or staged. Phones can be shared. VPNs can mask origins. Investigators must validate and corroborate before drawing conclusions.

Takeaway: Digital footprints reveal movement, behavior, intent, and deception. Use them to illuminate the story—but always validate before acting.

October 16: OSINT as an Analytical Tool

"Information is a source of learning. But unless it is organized, processed, and available to the right people, it is a burden, not a benefit." —William Pollard

I wanted to take a day to talk about OSINT as an analytical tool. Some people think it means "looking things up online," but true OSINT is systematic, disciplined, and analytical. It is the art of extracting actionable insights from publicly available information: social media, databases, corporate records, geospatial imagery, forums, news archives, public filings, leaked datasets, and the unending stream of digital exhaust humans generate each day. Used properly, OSINT is not just research—it is intelligence, and intelligence is evaluated information from analysis. To use OSINT analytically, investigators must understand four principles:

1. **Attribution matters:** The investigator needs to determine who controls a profile, post, or account—without assuming identity based solely on names or photos.
2. **Context matters:** A post made at 2:00 a.m. may reflect emotion, not fact. A "like" is not a confession. A tagged location may be delayed, inaccurate, or spoofed.
3. **Verification matters:** Screenshots can be altered; metadata can be missing. OSINT often requires corroboration from independent sources before drawing conclusions.
4. **Bias matters:** Investigators often find what they expect to see. Structured OSINT collection prevents selective attention and confirmation bias from shaping the narrative.

OSINT analysis is key in international work. Differences in naming conventions, multilingual content, foreign corporate registries, offshore financial structures, and region-specific social networks reveal information unavailable in U.S.-centric databases. But OSINT abroad also requires caution: privacy laws, data-protection rules, and cultural interpretations of online behavior vary dramatically. Keep this in mind during your search.

Takeaway: OSINT is not just online searching. Use OSINT analysis to illuminate patterns, confirm facts, and expose deception.

October 17: Metadata Analysis

"The truth is rarely pure and never simple." —Oscar Wilde

Most investigators focus on the content of information—photos, documents, messages, audio, or video. But in the digital age, the most revealing part often isn't the content at all—it's the metadata. Metadata is the data about the data. It tells you when a file was created, where a photo was taken, who accessed a document, what device recorded a video, and how many times a message was forwarded or edited.

Metadata shows facts that subjects cannot easily manipulate, even when they alter or delete the content itself. That makes metadata one of the most powerful—and underused—investigative tools available. Metadata typically answers four categories of questions:

When did this occur? Timestamps from files, photos, text messages, GPS pings, email headers, and cloud sync logs often provide the first crack in a false narrative. A claimant says they were injured at 2 p.m., but the photo they posted was taken at 4:17 p.m. A subject claims they weren't home, but a device log shows the door-camera synced at precisely the wrong time.

Where did this originate? EXIF data from photos, IP addresses from emails, geolocation tags from apps, and metadata embedded in videos can reveal where someone was—even if they never directly stated it. An image sent from a mobile device can carry latitude and longitude precise enough to undermine an alibi.

How was it created or altered? Metadata can show whether a file was edited, saved under a new name, moved, taken as a screenshot, or run through software. Investigators routinely uncover fraud or fabrication when underlying metadata contradicts the purported authenticity of a document or recording.

Who interacted with it—and when? Access logs, version histories, audit trails, and cloud-based metadata reveal who opened, modified, or shared a file. In corporate and public-sector investigations, these trails expose unauthorized access, insider threats, and tampering attempts.

Professional investigators treat metadata as a primary evidentiary layer—not an afterthought. They preserve it, analyze it, document its significance, and use it to anchor the larger timeline.

Takeaway: Content can lie. Metadata rarely does. Use it to validate claims, including what the subject never intended you to see.

October 18: Geographic & Spatial Profiling

"The map is not the territory." —Alfred Korzybski

Geography is one of the most underrated analytical tools in investigative work. Every event happens somewhere, and that "somewhere" carries meaning—opportunity, access, risk, routine, concealment, or convenience. Geographic and spatial profiling allow investigators to transform locations, movements, and distances into insight. When done correctly, this analysis reveals patterns of behavior that no interview or document ever could.

Geographic profiling begins with a simple premise: human movement is rarely random. People tend to operate within familiar zones, travel predictable routes, and choose locations that reflect comfort, opportunity, or necessity. Criminals, fraudsters, employees, insiders, and corporate actors all leave spatial signatures behind. Spatial profiling typically examines four layers:

1. **Anchor Points:** These are locations that define a person's life—home, work, social hubs, family residences, storage units, gyms, or favored areas. Repeated behaviors often radiate outward from these anchor points.
2. **Travel Paths**: People rarely take arbitrary routes. Their travel patterns follow roads, traffic conditions, habits, or concealment strategies. Comparing a subject's claimed travel route to GPS logs, tolls, license-plate readers, or telematics often reveals deviations that indicate deception.
3. **Activity Nodes:** These are locations where events cluster—repeated purchases, recurring meetings, frequent digital logins, synchronized movements, or repeated phone pings. Activity nodes often reveal planning, logistical hubs, or coordination with others. In international cases, activity nodes highlight border crossings, offshore jurisdictions, or foreign business centers linked to shell activity.
4. **Spatial Anomalies:** Just as in pattern analysis, deviations are often more important than routines. A sudden stop in an unusual place, a detour that contradicts the stated purpose, a device ping far outside normal range, or a cluster of activity in an unexpected area all raise investigative red flags. These anomalies point to meetings, hidden objectives, or concealed behavior.

Geographical and spatial profiling can reveal whether a claimant was too far from the alleged incident location or whether an employee could have physically been where they claimed to be.

Takeaway: Geographic profiling and spatial profiling expose routines, opportunities, and deception, but are rarely used. Change that dynamic now.

October 19: Financial Analysis (Part One)

"Money behaves like light—it illuminates everything it touches." —Amelia Barr

If information builds a case, money explains it. Financial pattern analysis is one of the most powerful investigative tools available because nearly every human action has a financial echo—a purchase, a withdrawal, a transfer, a subscription, a bill, or a digital payment that leaves a trace. Whether operating in the public or private sector, investigators know that money reveals truth long before statements do. Financial patterns are not accounting or spreadsheets—they are behavioral intelligence. Financial patterns reveal behavior such as:

- Where someone goes (card swipes, tolls, ATM logs)
- What they value (recurring payments, spending habits)
- How they operate (structured withdrawals, cash-heavy behavior)
- What they hide (new accounts, prepaid cards, sudden cash use)

Investigators rely on these trails to identify opportunities, capabilities, and motives. Financial crime units use spending sequences and transaction timing to identify structuring or layering. A claimant reports disability, but large recreational purchases or high spending on physical activities prove otherwise. In both public and private sectors, financial contradictions are often the most decisive evidence in a case. These patterns also expose possible motive and intent, such as:

- Incentive to commit fraud
- Conflicts of interest
- Hidden income streams
- Kickbacks
- Bribery
- Embezzlement
- Internal theft
- Lifestyle inconsistent with income

The old adage "follow the money" exists because it works. Many a transnational criminal organization and terrorist organization have been taken down by doing just that.

Takeaway: Money is a behavioral map. Analyze the patterns—not just the transactions—and the financial trail will reveal motive, contradiction, and truth.

October 20: Financial Analysis (Part Two)

"Where borders complicate truth, money simplifies it." —Gabriel García Márquez

Domestic financial analysis is powerful. International financial analysis is indispensable. Once money crosses borders—through wires, transfers, shell entities, offshore accounts, crypto exchanges, or foreign business structures—investigators enter a world shaped by sovereignty, secrecy, and complex legal regimes. But the principle remains the same: money moves according to human needs and human motives. Some tools that strengthen financial analysis are:

- Transaction chronologies
- Heat maps of spending
- Cluster analysis of repeated vendors
- Anomalous activity detection
- Link charts connecting persons, accounts, and entities

Timeline overlays comparing financial activity to behavioral claims

Public-sector investigators have legal processes—such as subpoenas, warrants, and administrative orders—to obtain financial records. Private-sector investigators must rely on client consent, open-source financial intelligence, public filings, corporate records, lawful behavioral indicators, and subpoenas when permitted. Internationally, foreign financial systems create layers that obscure ownership, control, and purpose. Investigators frequently encounter:

- Shell corporations
- Layered holding companies
- Offshore jurisdictions
- Correspondent banking
- Nominee directors
- Trusts with minimal transparency
- Multi-currency movement
- Crypto tumblers or cross-chain swaps

Remember that a transaction that is accessible through subpoena in the U.S. may be fully shielded in another country. Finally, know that international financial work requires an understanding of GDPR and EU data-protection rules, FATF recommendations, EU Anti-Money Laundering Directives (AMLD), local bank secrecy laws, Sanctions regimes (OFAC, EU, UN), MLATs, and treaty-based information requests, as well as differences in evidentiary standards and reporting obligations.

Takeaway: In-depth financial analysis turns borders into clues rather than obstacles. Leverage this capability to catapult your investigation.

October 21: Surveillance Analysis

"The world is full of obvious things which nobody by any chance ever observes." —
Sir Arthur Conan Doyle

Surveillance doesn't solve cases—analysis does. Investigators often think of surveillance as a collection task: follow, watch, record. But raw footage is not evidence until the investigator gives it meaning. Surveillance analysis is the concept of transforming observation into finalized intelligence.

Every surveillance event carries analytical value. Movements reveal habits. Habits reveal priorities. Priorities reveal motive. Even the absence of movement—unexplained gaps, prolonged pauses, unusual detours—can be as revealing as what the camera captures. The investigator's challenge is to interpret these behaviors without either overstating or underestimating them.

Public and private sector investigators have long used surveillance analysis to test alibis, reconstruct movements, identify co-conspirators, or evaluate pre-operational steps. Footage is compared against interviews, time–event charts, digital footprints, cell-site records, and financial transactions. In each domain, surveillance analysis is less about catching a single moment and more about evaluating a subject's consistency across time. When surveillance contradicts a narrative, it enables the investigator to explore the lead more thoroughly.

The greatest analytical value often comes from correlation. Surveillance aligned with metadata, financial activity, digital logs, or witness statements creates a stronger evidentiary picture than any source alone. A trip to a location matters more when paired with a payment made minutes earlier, a phone call placed on the way, or a lie told in an interview afterward. Surveillance analysis is not about the footage—it is about the connections the footage enables.

Takeaway: Surveillance is only the beginning. The investigator's task is to read behavior, interpret movement, compare timelines, and merge observation with other evidence.

October 22: Motive, Means, & Opportunity

"Character is far more easily kept than recovered." —*Thomas Paine*

Motive, means, and opportunity (MMO) is one of the oldest analytical frameworks in investigative work. Some investigators treat MMO as a checkbox exercise, something to reference in a report or mention in passing. But when used properly, MMO is a powerful analytical engine that filters suspects, tests theories, and reveals which explanations are plausible and which are impossible.

Motive answers the *why.* Means answers the *how.* Opportunity answers the *when and where.*

Motive is often the most misused element. Investigators sometimes mistake speculation for motive or assume that emotional friction automatically predicts wrongdoing. In reality, motive must be grounded in evidence: financial stress, workplace grievances, personal conflicts, lifestyle inconsistencies, or documented behavioral changes.

Means is the most objective of the three. It refers to whether the subject had the capability, access, resources, tools, knowledge, or physical capacity to commit the act. Means often reveal the difference between suspicion and possibility.

Opportunity is the filter that removes impossible scenarios. It focuses on time, place, and presence. Did the subject have access to the relevant location? Were they physically capable of being there when the event occurred? Do surveillance, digital footprints, badge data, or independent witnesses support or contradict opportunity? Opportunity testing frequently disproves theories that seem compelling at first glance. An investigator may believe a subject had a strong motive and clear means—but if the timeline shows they were across town at the critical moment, the hypothesis collapses.

The true strength of MMO lies in the interaction among the three elements:

- A person with motive but no means becomes less relevant.
- A person with means but no motive may be an administrative concern, not a suspect.
- A person with opportunity but neither means nor motive is usually a coincidence, not a threat.

But a subject who demonstrates all three—supported by timelines, digital data, or corroboration—deserves immediate attention.

Takeaway: Motive, means, and opportunity are not checkboxes—they are analytical filters. Use them to bring structure to complex investigative decisions.

October 23: Event Trees

"Logic will get you from A to B. Imagination will take you everywhere." —Dr. Albert Einstein

Event trees are among the most versatile analytical tools available to investigators. They are a favorite of major-case squads, intelligence units, and specialized corporate risk teams. An event tree structures uncertainty. It takes a single incident, allegation, or claim and branches outward—mapping every possible explanation, outcome, or contributing factor. Event trees force investigators to think methodically rather than instinctively by laying out all plausible scenarios, even the uncomfortable ones. Public-sector investigators use event trees in complex incidents such as:

- Officer-involved shootings
- Industrial accidents
- Intelligence failures
- Serial offenses
- Aviation, maritime, or transportation incidents

These trees break an event into sequential nodes: first action, reaction, turning points, failures, alternative possibilities, and eventual outcomes. At each node, multiple branches represent different explanations—ranging from the obvious to the improbable. Evidence then supports or eliminates each branch, narrowing the tree until only a defensible explanation remains.

Private investigators use them to analyze process breakdowns, internal theft, data breaches, or compliance failures. In domestic and civil cases, an investigator can use event-tree thinking to evaluate alternative explanations for behavior, timing, or communication patterns. Event trees help investigators avoid three common analytical traps:

1. **Assuming intent without evidence:** A branch must be supported, not assumed.
2. **Ignoring alternative explanations:** A scenario may seem "correct" until a tree reveals a competing explanation that fits the evidence better.
3. **Overlooking contributing factors:** Human error, environmental conditions, system flaws, or third-party actions may all appear as separate branches that ultimately converge.

The true power of event trees lies in their ability to identify missing evidence. When a branch cannot be closed without additional information—another interview, a financial record—the tree directs the next investigative step.

Takeaway: Event trees structure uncertainty. Use them to map all possible explanations and follow the branches until the facts appear.

October 24: Fraud Indicators and Red Flags

"The easiest person to deceive is yourself." —Edward Bulwer-Lytton

Fraud indicators fall into four broad categories: behavioral, transactional, documentation-based, and process-related. The strongest investigations emerge when indicators appear across multiple areas—not just one.

Behavioral Indicators: Fraud almost always begins with behavior. Common warning signs include sudden lifestyle upgrades, unusual defensiveness or secrecy, refusal to delegate or take vacations, frequent "innocent mistakes" that benefit the same person, isolation from coworkers, or avoidance of oversight.

Transaction Indicators: Money creates patterns, and fraud disrupts them. Watch for round-dollar amounts, duplicate payments, or recurring "errors", unexplained refunds, credits, or reversals, transactions occurring just below approval thresholds, and vendor payments inconsistent with historical activity.

Documentation Indicators: Fraud thrives where records are manipulated or incomplete including missing documents or inconsistent versions, altered files or metadata discrepancies, delayed submissions, supporting documents that appear overly polished or uniform, itemized lists that do not match receipts, logs, or physical evidence.

Process Indicators: Fraud exploits structural weaknesses. Key vulnerabilities include single-person control over a financial process, weak separation of duties lack of audits or supervisory review, informal shortcuts becoming standard practice, and employees resisting procedural changes that increase transparency

A red flag does not prove misconduct—it signals the need for deeper inquiry. One indicator may reflect carelessness. Two may show coincidence. A pattern of indicators across categories demands further inquiry.

Takeaway: Fraud exposes itself through signals. Recognize the red flags early.

October 25: Using the Process of Elimination

"When you have eliminated the impossible, whatever remains, however improbable, must be the truth." —Sir Arthur Conan Doyle

Most investigators are trained to look for confirming evidence—facts that prove a theory, support a suspect, or validate a complaint. But some of the strongest cases are built not only on what fits, but on what has been carefully ruled out. The process of elimination is an analytical method that narrows possibilities until only the most defensible explanation remains. The process of elimination begins with a straightforward acknowledgement: at the start of a case, multiple explanations are possible.

An incident might be accidental, negligent, intentional, staged, or misreported. A data breach might be an external attack, an insider threat, a misconfiguration, or simple human error. A financial anomaly might be fraud, incompetence, policy failure, or a systemic glitch. The best investigators resist the urge to pick a favorite early.

The key is evidence-based elimination, not assumption-based elimination. You do not eliminate a theory because "it seems unlikely" or "the person doesn't fit the profile." You eliminate it because specific facts make it impossible or highly implausible. That might include:

- Physical impossibility (location, time, capacity)
- Technical impossibility (no access, no capability, no system path)
- Documentary contradiction (records that logically exclude a scenario)
- Corroborated alibis or verified third-party accounts

The process of elimination also protects against confirmation bias. When used correctly, it forces the investigator to hold competing hypotheses side by side and test each. If your preferred theory survives only because you ignored evidence that supports an alternative, you have not used elimination—you have used rationalization. Strong investigators are willing to admit when the evidence eliminates their favorite theory.

Takeaway: The process of elimination is not about proving you were right—it is about demonstrating what cannot be true until only a defensible explanation remains.

October 26: Intelligence Gaps

"The absence of evidence is not evidence of absence." —Carl Sagan

Every investigation begins with what you know, but the real work starts with what you don't know. Intelligence gaps are the missing pieces of information that prevent an investigator from forming a complete, defensible understanding of an event, allegation, or subject. Requirements setting is the structured discipline of identifying gaps, prioritizing them, and directing subsequent investigative steps to close them. Without this process, investigations drift, stall, or chase irrelevant leads. Intelligence gaps appear across every domain—public, private, corporate, insurance, fraud, digital forensics, and international cases. Gaps typically fall into four categories:

1. **Missing Facts:** Information that should exist but has not yet been collected: key witnesses, documents, metadata, financial records, surveillance, timestamps, or technical logs.
2. **Missing Context:** Facts that exist but are meaningless without additional explanation: a log entry with no associated event, a payment with no known purpose, a suspicious behavior with no patterns behind it.
3. **Missing Corroboration:** Statements or evidence supported by only a single source. Without independent confirmation, these details remain unverified and vulnerable to challenge.
4. **Missing Alternatives:** When investigators assume a single explanation, they fail to explore competing hypotheses. A gap in alternative explanations is one of the most dangerous weaknesses in an investigation.

Once gaps are identified, investigators must set requirements—precise, actionable tasks designed to close those gaps. Requirements differ from general to-do lists because they are tied to an analytical purpose. A good requirement answers a specific question, such as:

- Where was the subject during the unaccounted time window?
- What device generated this metadata entry?
- Who else had access to the compromised account?
- What financial pattern explains the anomaly?
- What alternative explanation could match the physical evidence?

Ultimately, requirements setting turns uncertainty into direction.

Takeaway: You cannot analyze what you do not have. Identify the gaps, convert them into requirements, and let those requirements drive the investigation forward.

October 27: Probability

"Doubt is not a pleasant condition, but certainty is absurd." —Voltaire

Investigators are expected to deliver clear conclusions, but the truth is that most cases contain uncertainty. Witnesses contradict each other. Digital data has gaps. Financial records stop at jurisdictional borders. Surveillance captures angles but not intent. In these moments, professional investigators rely on structured probability, likelihood assessments, and confidence levels—not instinct or guesswork. Analytical confidence is the study of saying how sure you are and why. Probability in investigations is not about mathematical formulas—it's about evaluating the strength of competing explanations.

Public-sector investigators formalize these concepts through intelligence ratings, probability scales, and structured analytic techniques. Intelligence analysts may label findings as "high," "medium," or "low" confidence depending on corroboration, source reliability, and data completeness. Homicide detectives routinely assess which version of events is most consistent with physical evidence, timelines, and behavioral indicators. Counterintelligence and national security teams use probability language to avoid overstating conclusions drawn from partial information.

Private-sector investigators need this technique just as much—sometimes more. Corporate investigations involve incomplete logs, partial interviews, and uncooperative subjects. Insurance cases feature conflicting accounts, ambiguous timelines, or injuries that could be legitimate or staged. Domestic cases include emotional narratives that distort objectivity. In these environments, assigning likelihood helps prevent hasty conclusions. Instead of claiming certainty, the investigator explains:

- The most likely explanation
- The plausible alternatives
- The explanations the evidence rules out

Probability assessments also guide next steps. When multiple explanations remain viable, the investigator asks: What evidence would increase or decrease the likelihood of each scenario? Requirements are then set to confirm or eliminate specific hypotheses. This prevents wasted effort and keeps the investigation aligned with the facts rather than with intuition.

Takeaway: Certainty is rare. Probability is universal. Continuously evaluate why what is being presented in front of you is probable.

October 28: Building the Investigative Narrative

"Facts do not speak for themselves; we speak for them." —Paul A. Samuelson

Every investigation ultimately leads to a story—but not the kind built on emotion, persuasion, or creative writing. The investigative narrative is an evidence-driven explanation of what happened, why it happened, and how the investigator knows it happened. It is the final analytical product: the bridge between raw facts and a defensible, coherent conclusion. A professional investigative narrative is built on five pillars:

1. **Chronology and structure:** A narrative must follow a logical sequence—often chronological, sometimes thematic—so the reader can understand the progression of events. Timelines, time–event charts, and association matrices provide the skeleton. The narrative provides the connective tissue.

2. **Evidence-supported statements:** Every assertion must trace back to evidence: surveillance, logs, interviews, documents, financial records, or metadata. Unsupported statements, even if true, weaken the entire case. Public-sector investigators expect cross-examination. Private-sector investigators expect litigation risk. Every sentence must survive either.

3. **Neutral, objective language:** Investigators must avoid characterizing people or motives without evidence. Phrases like "he acted suspiciously" or "she was clearly lying" are replaced with:

   - "Subject avoided answering direct questions,"
   - "Statement conflicts with digital logs,"
   - "Behavior deviated from established routine."
   - Objectivity is a shield—it protects credibility.

4. **Addressing contradictions and alternatives:** A credible narrative openly acknowledges conflicting evidence and explains why certain interpretations are more defensible. By showing the reader how competing explanations were tested and eliminated, the investigator strengthens the conclusion and demonstrates analytical fairness.

5. **Logical conclusions, not emotional ones:** The final section of a narrative should answer the core investigative question: What happened? Why? Who was responsible? How is this supported? It should avoid exaggeration, overconfidence, or speculation. The investigator must show the path from evidence to conclusion without skipping analytical steps. If the story cannot be told clearly, the investigation was not analyzed clearly.

Takeaway: A professional investigative narrative transforms evidence into understanding.

October 29: Red Teaming Your Own Case

"We are never so defenseless against error as when we trust our own judgment too much." —Georg C. Lichtenberg

Similar to the murder boards we discussed earlier in the year, red teaming in this capacity is challenging your own investigation before someone else does. It is the structured practice of adopting an adversarial perspective—stepping into the shoes of defense counsel, opposing experts, regulators, auditors, or hostile reviewers—and asking: Where is this case weak? Where am I making assumptions? What would a critic attack first? Red teaming typically focuses on five areas:

1. **Assumptions and blind spots:** Red teaming starts with identifying hidden assumptions—beliefs you accepted without fully testing. Did you assume a witness was truthful because they seemed cooperative? Did you assume a timestamp was accurate? Did you assume a timeline was complete because no contradictions surfaced?
2. **Alternative explanations:** A red team mentality forces you to build competing hypotheses and test them against the same evidence. What if the subject's explanation is true? What if the behavior interpreted as deception has an innocent cause? What if the financial anomaly reflects policy failure rather than fraud?
3. **Evidence weaknesses and vulnerabilities:** Red teaming requires asking how your evidence will be attacked. Is metadata complete? Is surveillance interpretable or ambiguous? Are financial records authenticated? Are statements corroborated or single-source?
4. **Logical inconsistencies:** A red team looks for breaks in reasoning: leaps, gaps, circular logic, and unsupported conclusions. If the narrative requires the reader to "fill in the blank," that blank becomes a liability.
5. **Documentation and defensibility:** A case is only as strong as its documentation. Red teaming tests whether each conclusion is tied to evidence, excluded scenarios were documented and justified, timelines and logs are complete, and analytical decisions are traceable

Done properly, red teaming reveals whether your case rests on solid evidence or on comfortable assumptions.

Takeaway: Challenge your own conclusions before anyone else does, and your investigations will become stronger and far more resilient under scrutiny.

October 30: Tools & Automation Support

"A tool is anything that saves your time—and doesn't cost you your judgment." —
Adam Osborne

Modern investigations are increasingly shaped by the tools we use to collect, organize, and analyze information. But tools don't make investigators—investigators make tools useful. Software can accelerate workflow, visualize patterns, and surface hidden correlations, but no automation can replace critical thinking. Across public and private-sector environments, investigators rely on a growing ecosystem of analytical tools. These tools fall into several categories, but the ones related to analysis are analytical tools, automation, and validation:

Analytical Tools: Programs that help investigators understand what the data means: link-analysis software, geospatial/mapping platforms, metadata analyzers, financial-pattern detection tools, and behavioral-analysis platforms. One of the most widely used tools in U.S. government link analysis is i2 Analyst's Notebook (from i2 Group). While license pricing varies by scope and term, publicly reported figures start around $7,160 per year for a single-user annual subscription. That figure helps illustrate that deploying high-end analytical tools requires both budget and training and may be out of reach for your agency. Other strong alternatives in the market include Kaseware, Maltego, Visallo, and Lampyre—each with its own strengths and varying cost structures.

Automation & AI Assistance: Machine-learning tools can flag irregularities, summarize documents, identify anomalies, and suggest connections, including pattern-recognition models, automated transcription, keyword extraction, workflow automation (alerts/triggers/dashboards), and predictive analytics for fraud, risk, or compliance. Automated insights require verification. Overreliance on AI without human oversight leads to false positives, missed nuance, and untested assumptions.

Validation & Corroboration Tools: Tools that confirm, authenticate, or disprove information: metadata-verification suites, image-forensics utilities, geolocation-confirmation platforms, version-history tracking, audit logs, and system-integrity checkers. These tools act as truth-testing mechanisms—critical for court, compliance, or counterintelligence environments.

Tools save time. Automation expands capability. But neither replaces the investigator's judgment, ethics, or analytical mind. A poorly trained investigator with advanced tools creates sophisticated errors. A skilled investigator, armed with simple tools, produces defensible results.

Takeaway: Tools enhance investigations—but they do not think for you. Use automation to accelerate your work—but interpret it on your own.

October 31: Analysis & Recommendations

"Knowledge is of no value unless you put it into practice." —Anton Chekhov

Analysis is only useful when it produces action. Investigators can create impeccable timelines, precise link charts, refined association matrices, and elegant flow models—but without actionable recommendations, the case stops short of its purpose. The final responsibility of the investigator is not just to explain what happened, but to guide what should happen next.

Recommendations give direction. A strong recommendation converts analytical insight into a clear, defensible, and proportional next step. A weak recommendation is vague, overly cautious, or disconnected from evidence. Actionable recommendations are built on four pillars:

Clarity and Specificity: A decision-maker should be able to act immediately without guessing the investigator's intent. Examples include: "Initiate disciplinary action for confirmed policy violations." "Refer the matter to outside counsel for legal review." "Notify law enforcement based on evidence of criminal conduct," or "Implement access restrictions on high-risk accounts."

Evidence Alignment: Every recommendation must flow logically from the findings. Public-sector investigators tie recommendations to statutes, policies, or evidentiary thresholds. Private-sector investigators tie them to liability risks, regulatory obligations, contractual requirements, or organizational priorities.

Proportionality and Risk Awareness: Effective recommendations match the severity of the issue and the strength of the evidence. Investigators weigh legal exposure, financial consequences, operational impact, reputational risk, and safety implications when presenting their recommendation.

Preventive Value: The best recommendations do not simply resolve what occurred—they prevent recurrence. Examples include strengthening internal controls, revising procedures, enhancing authentication or access security, clarifying policy language, improving training, or reporting mechanisms.

Investigators are not policymakers, but they are uniquely positioned to identify where systems failed. A strong recommendation should stand on its own: clear, defensible, and tied directly to evidence.

Takeaway: Convert analysis into clear, proportional, evidence-backed recommendations that help leaders make informed, defensible decisions.

November: Specialized Investigative Techniques

"A good investigator is limited not by authority, but by imagination and discipline."
—Anonymous

Most investigators learn to work with the tools their agency, company, or unit has always used. Interviews, records checks, surveillance, timelines, digital footprints—these form the backbone of every case. But the professional investigator understands another truth: investigative breakthroughs come from other techniques outside your usual toolbox.

Specialized investigative methods—whether legal, technical, forensic, psychological, or procedural—open doors that routine techniques cannot. And while not every investigator can personally execute every method, every investigator must understand them. Knowing what is possible helps you ask the right questions, request the proper assistance, and recognize when a case demands a different approach.

November is about expanding your operational imagination.

Some techniques originate in federal law enforcement or intelligence work. Others come from private-sector investigations—insurance, corporate compliance, digital forensics, fraud examination, or domestic cases. Many cross boundaries. A method developed for counterintelligence may apply to workplace theft. A tool used in domestic investigations may uncover procurement fraud. A forensic technique used in cybercrime may solve a civil dispute.

This month, we will explore a broad spectrum of specialized investigative methods, including but not limited to:

- Mail covers
- Grand jury subpoenas and court orders
- Pen registers & trap-and-trace
- Constructive possession & asset forfeiture mechanisms
- Administrative subpoenas
- Pretexting
- Undercover letters, ruses, and authorized deception
- Trash pulls/refuse analysis
- Controlled deliveries
- Wiretaps, intercepts, and Title III basics
- Psychological profiling
- Statement analysis
- Polygraphs (strengths, limits, and legal pitfalls)

Across the public, private, and international arenas, these techniques share a common purpose: to extract truth from complexity. Not every technique is available in every environment, and each carries legal boundaries, ethical considerations, and jurisdiction-specific restrictions. But understanding them expands what is possible.

Throughout November, investigators will be shown how these techniques work, when to use them, how they cross-apply between investigative fields, and how they fit into a professional, legally sound investigative strategy.

Your power as an investigator is not defined by the tools you currently have—but by the techniques you understand, the options you can recognize, and the discipline you bring to choosing the correct method at the right moment. Let's get started.

November 1: Asset Forfeiture

"Follow the money, and you will find the truth." —Sherron Watkins

Asset forfeiture is first up. For some investigators, it feels like a legal hammer—something reserved for federal organized crime cases or drug task-force operations. But the principles behind forfeiture investigations apply far more broadly: tracing ownership, documenting illicit gain, following financial trails, and identifying assets connected to wrongdoing. Even when forfeiture isn't the end goal, the analytical techniques behind it strengthen almost every type of case. At its core, asset forfeiture is about removing the profit from misconduct. If you eliminate the financial incentive, you eliminate the behavior.

Public-sector investigators use forfeiture to dismantle criminal enterprises, recover stolen funds, and disrupt the financial pipelines that enable ongoing criminal activity. While the U.S. has roughly 12 primary federal law enforcement agencies with asset-forfeiture authorities—DSS, FBI, DEA, HSI, ATF, IRS-CI, USSS, and others—the real frontline is far larger. Over 18,000 state, county, and local police departments exist across the country, many with access to state forfeiture statutes or task-force partnerships that allow them to participate in asset-tracing investigations. These agencies seize vehicles, currency, weapons, and property tied to narcotics, fraud, organized retail theft, cybercrime, corruption, and other offenses. If your agency isn't getting in the action, see how you can make it happen. Asset forfeiture rests on three pillars:

1. **Identification:** Recognizing assets connected to misconduct: bank accounts, vehicles, real estate, shell companies, digital wallets.
2. **Tracing:** Following the money across platforms, accounts, businesses, or jurisdictions.
3. **Attribution:** Proving the connection between the asset and the underlying act.

Private-sector investigators cannot seize assets, but they frequently build **forfeiture-grade tracing packages** for attorneys, insurers, corporations, and civil litigants. Asset tracing reveals embezzlement, vendor kickbacks, concealed wealth, marital assets, and internal theft. And sometimes the private side offers unexpected opportunities. In South Korea, the government recently launched a program encouraging citizens—and even private investigators abroad—to report tax evasion in exchange for rewards sharing payouts when funds are recovered. It's a reminder that asset-tracing skills can generate financial opportunity globally, not just within formal law-enforcement channels.

Takeaway: Asset forfeiture is not just about seizing property—it's about understanding financial motive and eliminating the behavior.

November 2: Trash Pulls

"What people discard tells more truth than what they keep." —Mignon McLaughlin

Trash pulls are one of the oldest and most overlooked investigative techniques—simple in concept, powerful in practice, and legally viable when executed correctly. In both public and private investigations, what a subject throws away often reveals what they never intended anyone to see.

Trash pulls rest on a fundamental legal principle: once property is abandoned, there is usually no expectation of privacy. In the U.S., the Supreme Court has repeatedly upheld this concept in the context of garbage placed for collection. Public sector investigators use trash pulls for narcotics cases, corporate fraud, counterfeiting, document forgery, identity theft, threat investigations, gang intelligence, and pre-operational terrorism indicators. Private-sector investigators use trash pulls far more than most people realize. In infidelity, fraud, and workplace-related cases, discarded material can reveal all kinds of pattern of life information. A single trash pull might reveal:

- Drug packaging, precursors, or ledgers
- Mail addressed to aliases
- Handwritten notes or planning materials
- Shredded documents (which can often be reconstructed)
- Financial clues—receipts, money transfers, prepaid card packaging
- Evidence of counterfeiting or document manipulation
- Items indicating motive or stressors (eviction notices, bills, warnings)

Even more valuable is pattern development. Multiple trash pulls create a behavioral timeline: what the subject buys, consumes, reads, plans, or hides.

- Burner phone packaging
- Receipts contradicting alibis or evidence of double lifestyles
- Business records removed from an office
- Product packaging suggesting undisclosed employment or activity
- Notes, calendars, or lists tied to misconduct
- Discarded IDs, credentials, or access materials

Not all jurisdictions interpret abandonment the same way. Apartment complexes, shared dumpsters, private-property boundaries, and gated communities impose constraints. Investigators must be careful not to trespass, violate local ordinances, or create liability. Documentation is crucial. Always photograph location, access, condition, and chain of custody for overall success.

Takeaway: Trash doesn't lie. Done legally and professionally, trash pulls reveal patterns, contradictions, and evidence that no interview or database ever will.

November 3: Mail Covers

"The truth is often delivered quietly, in envelopes no one notices." —Secretary Henry Stimson

Mail has always been a source of intelligence. Long before digital forensics, metadata analysis, or OSINT existed, investigators learned to read envelopes, senders, postmarks, and patterns of correspondence to understand a subject's network, activities, and priorities. In the modern era, physical mail techniques remain underutilized. Maybe you can change that.

A mail cover is an investigative technique that records the outside of mail—names, addresses, postmarks, return labels, sender information, postage type, and routing data—without opening the correspondence. In the U.S., authorized mail covers must be formally approved and executed through the U.S. Postal Inspection Service (USPIS). The technique dates back over a century and remains essential in cases involving fraud, narcotics, organized crime, terrorism, financial crimes, threat cases, and major conspiracies.

Mail covers reveal valuable investigative information without intruding on the contents of the communication. They can identify undeclared business relationships, alias identities, co-conspirators or associates, financial patterns (bills, payments, subscription services), shell companies or front entities, indicators of foreign influence or international ties, and behavioral patterns such as late-night mailing, high-volume correspondence, and unusual routing.

The power of a mail cover is not in any single envelope—it's in the patterns that emerge over time. A public sector investigator might map narcotics activity by tracing packages back to source cities. Private-sector investigators cannot request formal mail covers, but they can use postal intelligence techniques that rely on legally available information and pattern analysis. These include observing mail patterns delivered to shared mailrooms, examining discarded envelopes found during trash pulls, identifying forwarding addresses through lawful means, using OSINT to match return labels, business entities, or sender identities, and documenting delivery frequency to uncover undisclosed relationships.

Mail may seem old-fashioned, but its investigative value remains timeless. People reveal more through what they send and receive than they realize—and envelopes cannot lie about who sent them, when, or from where.

Takeaway: When appropriately analyzed, mail covers and postal intelligence techniques expose networks, corroborate timelines, and reveal hidden patterns.

November 4: Subpoenas

"The law cannot compel the truth—only the opportunity to find it." —Benjamin Cardozo

Subpoenas, summonses, and grand-jury tools are not interchangeable, and misunderstanding their differences leads to delays, denials, or even compromised cases. While private-sector investigators generally cannot issue subpoenas themselves, they must understand these tools because attorneys, regulators, or partnering agencies will use them to drive information collection. At the highest level, subpoenas come in three primary categories:

Administrative subpoenas are issued directly by certain government agencies under authority granted by Congress. They are faster than court subpoenas, require no judge, and are often used for records such as financial documents, subscriber information, travel data, and transactional logs. Agencies traditionally holding administrative-subpoena power include the standard three-letter federal agencies. Many state-level regulatory agencies—labor departments, health agencies, and insurance commissioners—have similar authority.

Court-ordered subpoenas are issued by a judge, magistrate, or clerk acting under court authority. Local and state police departments routinely work with prosecutors to obtain these subpoenas during criminal investigations. They compel production of documents, testimony, or both. Court subpoenas carry judicial oversight, making them more resistant to challenge but also slower to obtain. Public-sector investigators rely on these subpoenas to obtain phone records, business documents, surveillance video, and other materials that require formal process.

Grand-jury subpoenas are among the most powerful tools in American criminal procedure. They come in two forms: subpoenas *ad testificandum* (to testify) and *duces tecum* (to produce documents). Grand-jury secrecy rules protect the integrity of sensitive investigations, particularly in cases involving organized crime, corruption, financial fraud, trafficking, homicide, and national-security matters. Federal and state-level grand juries both use these tools, though procedures vary. Their broad investigative mandate allows prosecutors and investigators to compel nearly any non-privileged material needed to determine whether charges should be filed.

Private investigators cannot issue subpoenas—but they work with attorneys who can. Effective private investigators organize evidence, identify specific records needed, prepare subpoena-ready lists, and ensure counsel requests the right documents from the right custodians, making them invaluable to the team.

Takeaway: Subpoenas are the backbone of formal information-gathering. Understanding their limits allows investigators to access the evidence they need.

November 5: Communications Record Tools

"The wires carry more truth than the voices that speak through them." —Laurence J. Peter

Pen registers, trap-and-trace devices, and other communication-record tools are non-content surveillance methods that reveal patterns of contact without capturing the substance of communication. Many investigators misunderstand these tools, believing they function like wiretaps. They do not. They collect metadata—the who, when, and how often—not the "what was said." Understanding these tools is essential for modern investigative analysis, whether you ever deploy them or not.

A **pen register** captures outgoing dialing or signaling information. A **trap-and-trace** device captures incoming numbers or connection attempts. In practice, investigators typically request a combined order that logs non-content communication metadata in both directions. Communication-record tools extend beyond PR/T&T, including subscriber information, call-detail records (CDRs), historical cell-site logs, IP connection records, and other metadata obtainable through lawful process.

Public sector investigators use PR/T&T under the Pen Register Act (18 U.S.C. §§ 3121–3127) or state equivalents. These orders require a court finding of relevance, not probable cause, making them one of the least intrusive but most analytically valuable surveillance tools.

Metadata often exposes relationships that no witness will disclose, and no suspect will admit. It is also a critical preliminary tool for determining whether a more intrusive step—such as a Title III wiretap—is justified. Private investigators **cannot** deploy pen registers or trap-and-trace devices under any circumstances. But understanding these tools remains crucial because PIs routinely analyze the products of communication-record requests obtained legally through civil subpoenas, corporate internal records, and client-authorized phone logs.

Private investigators also need to educate clients about legal boundaries, given how much Hollywood has distorted what they can actually do. No one can authorize a PI to run a pen register—not a spouse, employer, or attorney. What PIs can do is interpret metadata, identify anomalies, map communication networks, and correlate contact patterns to timelines and financial activity.

Takeaway: Understand the legal limits of these tools to continue on your investigative mastery journey.

November 6: Pretexting

"Half the harm that is done in this world is due to people who want to feel important."
—T. S. Eliot

Pretexting is one of the oldest investigative techniques in existence. It is best defined as an attempt to lawfully obtain information by assuming a role, identity, or scenario that encourages someone to speak or act differently than they otherwise would. Pretexting is about elicitation, not deception for deception's sake. It leverages human behavior, conversational dynamics, and natural tendencies to fill silence or answer seemingly harmless questions.

Law enforcement and regulatory agents may use undercover identities, ruses, or scenario-based interactions—but only within the bounds of policy, legal authority, and case strategy. Public investigators must never use pretexting to obtain protected financial information without legal process (GLBA), medical information (HIPAA), educational records (FERPA), communications content (ECPA/SCA), Credentials, passwords, or access codes, or anything that requires a warrant or subpoena.

Ruses are permissible—for example, posing as a delivery driver to verify residence or as a customer to observe business practices—but impersonation of federal officers or regulated professionals is criminal.

Private investigators rely more heavily on pretexting, but their boundaries are even narrower. Courts and regulators treat improper pretexting as fraud, identity theft, or unlawful access. Legal pretexting includes things like calling as a customer to verify business hours, contacting a workplace to confirm employment status (where permitted), and using benign identities to schedule interviews or appointments.

Examples of illegal pretexting include pretending to be a bank employee, police officer, insurer, or government official. Attempting to obtain financial, medical, or account information through disguise and using pretexts to access non-public databases or systems. Even when legal, pretexting must be defensible. Juries and judges scrutinize intent. Clients misunderstand the limits and it is up to you to educate them. When in doubt, seek counsel before executing.

Takeaway: Use pretexting sparingly, lawfully, and ethically. A case is never worth your license, reputation, or freedom.

November 7: Controlled Deliveries

"Control is not something you own; it is something you exercise." —*John Keegan*

In its simplest form, controlled delivery involves allowing a suspect package, shipment, or item of interest to continue its journey under the investigator's supervision. The goal is not just to intercept contraband—it is to identify networks, reveal end-users, document co-conspirators, and establish evidentiary chains that reach farther than a single seizure ever could.

When appropriately executed, controlled deliveries are intelligence multipliers. When executed poorly, they become liability traps. A controlled delivery involves timing, coordination, planning, and effective surveillance measures. Controlled deliveries are well-established in federal, state, and local law enforcement being conducted routinely. Local police may conduct controlled deliveries through task-force partnerships or under state authority. Typical use cases include narcotics counterfeit goods, and weapons trafficking.

A successful controlled delivery requires surveillance teams covering the delivery area, a preplanned arrest/interdiction window, risk assessments for officer safety, legal authority (warrant, anticipatory warrant, or statutory exception), coordination with postal inspectors or private carriers, and clear rules of engagement.

Private investigators **cannot** conduct controlled deliveries in the traditional law-enforcement sense. They cannot place trackers, infiltrate the mailstream, intercept packages, ride along with carriers, etc. But private-sector investigators do conduct controlled delivery–adjacent operations in civil, corporate, and insurance contexts—legally and ethically, such as:

- Controlled returns of stolen or counterfeit goods
- Coordinated delivery observations with corporate security
- Monitoring package receipt in workplace investigations
- Documenting who retrieves fraudulent shipments
- Working with counsel to coordinate evidence collection.

International drug-trafficking and money-laundering investigations often rely on multinational controlled-delivery frameworks, where each country must approve the operation at each border crossing. It is an intense exercise in liaison and coordination, but well worth the trade-off of shutting down criminal networks.

Takeaway: Controlled deliveries are high-value, high-risk techniques. When done right, they reveal networks and expose end-users for prosecution.

November 8: Constructive Possession

"We are the sum of our choices, even the ones we try to distance ourselves from." — *José Saramago*

Newer investigators sometimes assume you must physically hold contraband to "possess" it. But in most jurisdictions—criminal, civil, or administrative—possession also includes situations where a person has knowledge of and control over an item, even if it's not in their hands. Constructive possession concerns dominion, control, intent, and access, and understanding it enables investigators to build stronger, more defensible cases. **Actual possession** is simple: the item is on the person. **Constructive possession** is more complex: the item is in a place the person controls, or the person exercises authority over the location, container, or circumstances. To establish constructive possession, investigators must show two things:

1. **Knowledge:** The person knew the contraband existed.
2. **Control**: The person had the ability and intent to exercise authority over it.

Courts look at "totality of the circumstances" —a holistic evaluation of facts rather than one decisive factor. Indicators of constructive possession include having exclusive control of a vehicle, room, locker, or digital device; Having the contraband located within the driver's reachable area; and having keys, access codes, or account control. You can also look at attempts to hide, distance, or disclaim ownership during the course of your investigation.

Public-sector investigators see constructive-possession cases constantly: narcotics, firearms, stolen property, digital contraband, financial records, or identity-theft materials found in vehicles, residences, or shared spaces. On the private side, the concept still applies. Corporate investigations, HR cases, internal theft, digital forensics, and workplace-misconduct matters often hinge on proving someone **knew about** and **could control** a file, device, asset, or credential.

Criminals often use rental cars to transport narcotics or weapons, believing that distance from ownership will shield them. They claim, "It's not my car," or "Someone else must have left it there." But if they are the sole renter and driver, and the keys are in their possession—and the contraband is located in areas only the driver could access—courts routinely find constructive possession. The suspect's attempt to create distance instead becomes circumstantial evidence of knowledge.

Takeaway: Physical possession is not the standard. Knowledge and control are.

November 9: Polygraphs

"The eye sees only what the mind is prepared to question." —Robertson Davies

Polygraphs occupy a strange space in investigative work—trusted by some, dismissed by others, and misunderstood by many. A polygraph is **not** a lie detector. It is a physiological stress-measurement tool, and like any tool, its value depends entirely on how, when, and why it is used. When properly understood, polygraphs can elicit confessions, uncover contradictions, and guide investigative strategy. When misunderstood, they introduce bias, create liability, and mislead decision-makers.

A polygraph measures changes in respiration, cardiovascular activity, and galvanic skin response while a trained examiner asks structured questions. The underlying assumption is that deception produces measurable stress. But stress is not synonymous with lying—fear, anxiety, trauma, medication, or misunderstanding can all trigger similar reactions. This makes polygraph results **informational** rather than **determinative**. Public-sector agencies use polygraphs in settings where they function as investigative aids rather than conclusive evidence. Examples include:

- Sex-offense cases
- Internal-affairs matters
- Counterintelligence and national-security vetting
- Post-conviction supervision programs

The actual investigative value of a polygraph often lies in what happens **before** and **after** the exam. The pre-test interview reveals inconsistencies, and the post-test conversation usually prompts admissions.

Agencies should treat polygraphs as investigative tools, not evidence. Most courts reject them as scientifically unreliable. For private investigators, polygraphs are far more restricted. The Employee Polygraph Protection Act (EPPA) prohibits most private employers from requiring or requesting a polygraph. There are only narrow exceptions for armored-car companies, security companies protecting sensitive facilities or property, and pharmaceutical manufacturing or distribution. Even when an exception applies, the employer must provide written notice to the employee, describe the specific incident under investigation, use a licensed examiner, avoid disciplinary action solely based on the result, and corroborate any adverse findings with independent evidence.

Takeaway: Polygraphs can inform an investigation, but cannot prove the truth. Use them sparingly, legally, and as only one component of your investigation.

November 10: Technical Surveillance Countermeasures

"The price of liberty—and even of common humanity—is eternal vigilance." — *Aldous Huxley*

Technical Surveillance Countermeasures (TSCM) sweeps—commonly called "bug sweeps"—are a specialized investigative technique. Movies portray them as magic wands that instantly detect hidden transmitters. Real TSCM work is far more limited and technical. Investigators must understand this technique regardless of whether they plan to be technicians themselves.

TSCM is about detecting, verifying, and mitigating unauthorized surveillance, whether in audio, video, digital, or electromagnetic forms. It combines physical inspection with electronic scanning to identify anomalous devices, signals, wiring irregularities, or compromised spaces. Public-sector investigators (especially federal agencies) use TSCM for safe-house preparation, counterintelligence cases, executive protection, and preparing the environment for sensitive interviews involving cooperating sources. State and local agencies may rely on regional task forces or contracted specialists. Most lack internal TSCM teams due to cost, training requirements, and complexity.

Private investigators usually do not have all the same government-grade tools. Still, they often conduct TSCM sweeps for corporate espionage concerns, domestic investigations, insider-threat investigations, pre-interview room checks, and executive-protection environments. A proper sweep includes:

1. **Physical inspection:** Outlets, vents, fixtures, furniture, wiring, ceilings, walls, and vehicles.
2. **Electronic detection:** Wideband receivers, spectrum analyzers, non-linear junction detectors (NLJDs), and thermal analysis.
3. **Signal mapping:** Identifying unknown transmissions or unusual RF activity.
4. **Device tracing:** Determining whether a discovered device is active, abandoned, a decoy, or part of legitimate infrastructure.

TSCM does **not** guarantee a space is "clean." Advanced devices may be dormant, frequency-hopping, or piggybacking on existing infrastructure. Even expert sweeps provide confidence—not certainty. You may not be the TSCM technician, but you will be responsible for what happens in a compromised environment. If a meeting is leaked, or a witness is exposed, investigators must assess whether technical surveillance played a role.

Takeaway: TSCM is about finding bugs AND controlling the environment.

November 11: Storefront Operations

"Strategy is about making choices; tactics are about making things happen." —Peter Drucker

Storefront operations are among the most resource-intensive—but also most revealing—investigative techniques available. In essence, a storefront is a controlled physical location established to observe, detect, or interact with a target or environment without revealing investigative involvement. Though often associated with federal undercover operations, storefront techniques have a long history across local law enforcement and, increasingly, the private sector.

A storefront can be a rented office, a vacant retail space, a workshop, a warehouse bay, or even an apartment. The point is not the building—it is the **proximity**. When investigators position themselves near a subject's known patterns, behavior reveals itself. Movement becomes predictable. Associates appear. Contradictions emerge. Storefront operations compress distance, allowing investigators to monitor routine without suspicion.

Public sector agencies have deployed storefronts in all kinds of investigations, from narcotics distribution to prostitution to disrupting organized theft retail networks. Local agencies often repurpose seized property, abandoned storefronts, or city-owned units to reduce cost. Federal task forces sometimes subsidize long-term leases to build durable undercover credibility. Always follow agency policy regarding how and under what name or entity (LLC, corporation, the department, etc.) you would rent or buy these properties under.

While private investigators have no undercover law-enforcement authority, wealthy clients, corporations, and insurance companies often use "storefront-adjacent" strategies—legally and effectively. I have seen it with our high-net-worth clients at Lynx. One rented an apartment for us adjacent to the apartment where his children lived with his ex. This provided our surveillance team with a clear vantage point for a trigger alert. We were able to monitor the pattern of life and child custody activity. Storefront operations style techniques can also be used for infidelity and cohabitation documentation, residence verification, and vehicle activity monitoring. Just use your imagination.

Takeaway: A storefront operation is not about the building—it is about controlled proximity. This stable vantage point can reveal things other techniques cannot.

November 12: Controlled Buys

Whether in narcotics, human trafficking, stolen property, counterfeit goods, or organized retail crime, a controlled buy allows investigators to document an illegal transaction in real time, link a suspect to contraband, and establish facts that no interview or surveillance alone could produce. A controlled buy is precisely what its name implies: a purchase conducted under investigative supervision. The investigator—often through an undercover officer or cooperating individual—purchases an illicit item while surveillance, recording devices, and documentation create an evidentiary package around the transaction. A controlled buy provides several critical elements:

1. **Direct evidence**: A recorded, supervised transaction confirms illegal conduct.
2. **Identification**: Visual, audio, or digital documentation ties the seller to the act.
3. **Chain of custody**: The item purchased becomes an exhibit, often with forensic value.
4. **Corroboration**: It supports surveillance, digital analysis, or confidential informant statements.
5. **Operational leverage**: The buy may justify search warrants, arrests, creation of a confidential informant, or broader conspiracy investigations.

Public-sector-controlled buys must comply with agency policy, legal requirements, and safety protocols. These usually include pre-operation briefings, audio/video monitoring, funds documentation ("serializing" buy-money), direct surveillance coverage, arrest criteria, disengagement plans, medical considerations, safety considerations, and formal supervisory approval. No controlled buy should ever be improvised. Improvisation is how cases—or people—get hurt.

Private investigators **cannot** conduct controlled buys involving illegal narcotics, prostitution, contraband firearms, or any item where participation would itself be a crime. I have stories from PIs purchasing counterfeit merchandise and conducting retail "mystery shop" integrity checks. Again, your imagination is the limit. The goal is always the same: obtain proof of misconduct that can withstand legal scrutiny.

Takeaway: Controlled buys are powerful because they transform theory into proof. Through strong corroboration, the technique provides clear evidence of crime.

November 13: Wiretaps and Title III Basics

"Power without restraint invites ruin." —Tacitus

Wiretaps are one of the most powerful—and most misunderstood—surveillance techniques in modern investigations. Movies and television make them look routine. In reality, lawful wiretaps in the United States are extraordinarily rare, tightly regulated, and available only to a narrow group of public-sector agencies under strict judicial oversight. Investigators must understand the dos and don'ts for this specialized technique.

A wiretap is the interception of communication content—the words spoken in a phone call, the text of a message, or the substance of a digital transmission. Under federal law, this is governed by Title III of the Omnibus Crime Control and Safe Streets Act of 1968. Title III authorizes real-time interception for serious offenses, but only when all other investigative methods have been tried and failed, or are reasonably unlikely to succeed. To obtain a wiretap, public-sector investigators must meet a criterion far higher than probable cause. Title III orders require:

- Probable cause of a qualifying offense (often major drug trafficking, conspiracy, violent crime, corruption, or organized crime)
- Probable cause that the communication facility is being used for that offense
- A showing of necessity—that normal investigative techniques have been exhausted or are inadequate
- Minimization requirements, ensuring non-relevant communications are not intercepted
- Strict time limits, usually 30 days
- Supervisory and prosecutorial approval
- Detailed progress reports to the court

Federal judges review Title III applications with intense scrutiny. Many agencies go years without ever seeking one. Some investigators complete entire careers without participating in a wiretap. Private investigators **cannot** conduct wiretaps. Not with client consent, not with employer permission, not with a spouse's authorization, and not through third-party technical services. Attempting to intercept communications without lawful authority violates the Wiretap Act and state eavesdropping laws. What PIs can do is analyze metadata, interpret communication patterns, and assist attorneys in preparing material for lawful requests—nothing more.

Takeaway: Wiretaps are not routine—they are extraordinary. They require necessity, judicial oversight, and strict compliance with the law.

November 14: Cryptocurrency Tracing

"Every choice we make leaves a trace—especially the ones meant to disappear." — *Joan Baez*

Cryptocurrency once appeared to be the perfect hiding place for illicit funds—anonymous, unregulated, and invisible to traditional financial systems. Today, that myth is gone. Crypto is not anonymous; it is pseudonymous, and pseudonymity can be pierced. Modern investigators—public and private—must understand how blockchain analysis works, why it matters, and how subjects use crypto to conceal assets, move value, or obscure financial motives.

Cryptocurrency tracing is the practice of following transaction flows across a public or semi-public ledger. Bitcoin, Ethereum, and most major coins operate on blockchains that record every transfer ever made. This transparency gives investigators a unique advantage: cryptocurrency leaves a permanent trail. Even when criminals try to hide it, the ledger remembers. Crypto is attractive because it moves fast, crosses borders instantly, and can be held in wallets that exist only as strings of characters. But every wallet has a digital fingerprint.

Law enforcement agencies worldwide have built robust crypto-tracing capabilities. Even small local agencies now encounter cases involving Bitcoin ATMs, dark-web markets, stolen credentials traded for crypto, and more. Tools like Chainalysis, TRM Labs, CipherTrace, and Elliptic allow federal, state, and international investigators to identify wallet clusters (multiple wallets controlled by one actor), to follow funds across exchanges and blockchains, flag transactions tied to sanctioned or high-risk entities, correlate blockchain events with real-world timelines, and produce affidavits for seizure warrants or forfeiture actions Most breakthroughs occur when cryptocurrency touches a regulated exchange, because exchanges hold something priceless: KYC data (Know Your Customer information).

Private investigators cannot subpoena exchanges, but the attorney working with them can. PIs still play a critical role in asset tracing for clients. Lynx recently assisted in a divorce case in which the soon-to-be ex-husband thought he could hide wealth in crypto. Well, he thought wrong because he had bragged to his soon-to-be ex-wife for years about where he was keeping it. PIs can still use many of the same techniques as public sector investigators. If you aren't already incorporating crypto investigative techniques in your arsenal, start today. It is the future, and the future is here.

Takeaway: Cryptocurrency does not eliminate the money trail—it moves it. Investigators must understand blockchain mechanics to be able to trace funds.

November 15: Psychological Profiling

"Behavior is the mirror in which everyone shows their image." —*Johann Wolfgang von Goethe*

Psychological profiling has long held a strange place in investigative work—part science, part art, part myth. Popular culture portrays profilers as mind-readers who can divine motive from a single photograph. Real investigators know better.

Psychological profiling is the structured analysis of behavior, not personality. Investigators look at actions, choices, routines, anomalies, stressors, and risk indicators to understand how a subject is likely to act—not who they are as a person. Profiling is never a conclusion; it is a hypothesis generator. Public-sector investigators use behavioral analysis extensively in threat assessment, serial crime analysis, prediction of domestic violence escalation, workplace violence prevention, assessment of terrorism radicalization indicators, counterintelligence vetting, and analysis of missing-persons behavior patterns.

Private-sector investigators use psychological insights differently, and I have seen it for everything from insider-threat identification to executive protection risk assessments to high-risk employee behavioral monitoring. Lynx had a case where the company was concerned that an executive was going to snap, so the board authorized private investigator surveillance for early warning, and they also asked a psychologist to review his behaviors caught on surveillance video. He never did anything wrong, but the company's legal team insisted on due diligence. Given the dangers of workplace violence, I applaud their efforts.

Profiling helps identify who might escalate risk, who fits an opportunity structure, or who matches observed patterns—but only as a starting point for further evidence-driven inquiry. Just remember, many wrongful convictions and botched investigations grew from misplaced reliance on profiling. Investigators then developed tunnel vision, failing to review the evidence before them. A subject who "fits the profile" has done nothing wrong. A subject who fits the evidence deserves attention and further inquiry.

This isn't Hollywood. Corroborate your evidence against other methods before going down a rabbit hole. Your agency may not have a full-time psychiatrist or psychologist on the books, but you can always ask for them to contract with one or your client to pay for one if the investigation might make use of this method.

Takeaway: Profiling is a perspective tool. Use it to expand your thinking, not narrow it.

November 16: Honeypots

"The trap always tells you more than the mouse ever will." —John le Carré

Honeypots are deliberate traps—controlled environments designed to attract, observe, and identify subjects who engage in misconduct. Unlike an intelligence "honey trap," which relies on seduction or emotional manipulation (and is generally unethical or illegal for investigators), a honeypot in investigative work is a technical or physical lure that allows subjects to reveal their own behavior without prompting. Honeypots must be passive, not provocative. The subject must self-select into misconduct. Investigators cannot push, prompt, pressure, or coerce anyone into taking action.

Honeypots exist in two major forms: digital and physical. In both, the guiding principle is identical—create a controlled asset that only a wrongdoer would interact with, then observe what they do. Digital honeypots are tools used to detect unauthorized access, credential theft, insider threats, or cyber intrusion. They range from simple to highly sophisticated and include, but are not limited to, decoy login portals, fake file shares, false credentials seeded into systems, unused email accounts monitored for activity, and Canaries (documents embedded with tracking mechanisms).

Physical honeypots are just as common, including the famous "bait cars" for auto theft units, marked or serialized items placed in theft-prone areas, decoy shipments used in retail or supply-chain investigations, strategically placed cash drawers in internal-theft cases, and even fake packages left for porch-piracy interdictions. The private sector uses physical honeypots more than most people realize. Retailers place bait items to identify habitual offenders. Warehouses place serialized tools to test internal theft. Private investigators may coordinate with clients to leave controlled items in a workplace environment to see who interacts with them and under what circumstances.

In both the physical and digital world, honeypots cannot create artificial opportunities that would not naturally exist, induce crime by suggestion, place investigators in the role of participants, or violate privacy, trespass, or entrapment standards. Other than that, you are only limited by agency policy and your imagination.

Takeaway: Honeypots are investigative mirrors—subjects reveal themselves through their interaction with the trap.

November 17: Operational Ruses

"Deception, when it is lawful, is merely another form of observation." —E. Phillips Oppenheim

Operational ruses are among the oldest investigative tools in the profession. They allow investigators to obtain information, test reactions, verify facts, and observe behavior without revealing investigative intent. A good ruse is subtle, legal, and necessary. A bad ruse is reckless, coercive, or unlawful. A ruse is a non-intrusive, legally permissible deception used to gain information or create an observation opportunity—never to coerce cooperation or induce criminal behavior.

Public investigators have long used ruses to verify residency or occupancy, identify who answers the door, determine whether a suspect is home before warrant service, observe reactions under controlled conditions, confirm employment or business activity, and assess risk before executing a warrant. Some of the common and lawful ruses I have seen over the years include posing as a delivery driver to confirm a person's presence, leaving a door hanger or flier to gauge who retrieves it, and using a benign pretext to initiate a non-custodial conversation. If you want a scalable example, look into Operation Flagship, a 1985 Washington, D.C., Metropolitan Police operation in which officers invited dozens of wanted fugitives to a fake party by telling them they had won free NFL tickets and prizes. When the suspects arrived at the convention center to claim their winnings, they were peacefully arrested en masse without incident.

Neither public nor private investigators can impersonate attorneys, doctors, journalists, or clergy, mislead someone about their rights, use ruses to obtain protected records (financial, medical, educational), or create opportunities that push subjects toward criminal conduct. Ruses must not cross into coercion, inducement, or entrapment.

Private investigators face tighter limits than law enforcement. Legal ruses typically include calling as a customer to verify basic business information, using a neutral identity to schedule an interview or appointment, or approaching a workplace under a benign pretext to confirm employment or hours, and conducting neighborhood canvases using non-deceptive identities.

The key question is always: Would this ruse be seen as fraud, impersonation, or unlawful access if scrutinized? Once you answer that negatively, you can start planning your ruse.

Takeaway: Ruses are an investigative scalpel, not a hammer. Use them sparingly, legally, and ethically to verify facts or observe behavior.

November 18: Controlled Encounters

"Speech is the mirror of the soul; as a man speaks, so is he." —Publilius Syrus

Controlled encounters—often called "knock-and-talks" are voluntary communication initiated by an investigator at a time and place chosen for strategic effect. It is not an interrogation, a detention, or a search. Its value lies in what the subject chooses to reveal—verbally, nonverbally, or behaviorally.

In law enforcement, controlled encounters are a staple. Investigators knock on a door, identify themselves, and request a consensual conversation. Legally, the encounter remains voluntary as long as the occupant is free to decline, no coercion is used, and investigators do not imply authority they do not possess. Uses include verifying timelines, assessing demeanor, clarifying inconsistencies, or observing surroundings in plain view. These encounters become unlawful when investigators imply a warrant, restrict the subject's movement, block exits, or convey—intentionally or unintentionally—that cooperation is mandatory.

Private investigators use controlled encounters differently but with equal caution. They cannot imply governmental authority or fabricate credentials. Acceptable purposes include verifying a witness's or subject's residence, confirming employment, or gathering context for civil investigations, such as determining whether someone has camera footage of an incident. The encounter must end the moment the subject withdraws consent. For PIs, legality hinges on voluntariness, honesty, and non-coercion. Some strategies when approaching someone for a controlled encounter:

1. **Timing:** Approach when the subject is most likely home, calm, and not engaged in conflict or chaos. Early morning or late-night approaches appear coercive and are often counterproductive.
2. **Positioning:** Stand slightly offset from the door to avoid appearing aggressive and so the occupant can open the door without feeling blocked or cornered. Maintain a relaxed posture; hands visible.
3. **Purpose Clarity:** Decide beforehand what you need: a simple verification, a short conversation, or an assessment of the subject's demeanor. Enter without excessive expectations.
4. **Team Roles:** If a second investigator is present, define roles. One speaks; the other simply observes and provides security. Multiple voices confuse subjects and appear confrontational.
5. **Exit Strategy:** Plan your exit before you knock. If the encounter becomes confrontational, ends abruptly, or the subject refuses to speak, leave immediately. Overstaying creates legal exposure.

Takeaway: Controlled encounters succeed when they are voluntary, respectful, and strategically executed.

November 19: Tactical Diagramming

"The line between disorder and order lies in logistics." —Sun Tzu

Tactical diagramming is one of the most underrated investigative tools available. Investigators tend to view floor plans, building diagrams, and architectural features as the domain of SWAT teams or specialized tactical units. In reality, understanding the physical layout of a structure is essential for any investigator preparing for a high-risk operation—especially when undercover placement, confidential-source briefings, or surreptitious access are impossible. Proper diagramming can prevent surprises, reduce risk, accelerate mission execution, and dramatically increase the success of warrant service.

Tactical diagramming is the structured process of mapping a building, property, or operational environment to anticipate hazards, movement routes, vantage points, and choke points before investigators ever set foot inside. It relies on combining open-source information, architectural cues, surveillance observations, and external features to create a defensible pre-operational plan. Tactical diagramming typically incorporates five categories of information:

1. **Exterior Architecture & Approaches:** Driveways, alleys, choke points, terrain, lighting patterns, vegetation, parking layouts, potential countersurveillance positions, and angles of observation. Drone imagery or aerial OSINT often can provide substantial detail as well.
2. **Structural Layout:** Approximate room placement derived from windows, HVAC protrusions, rooflines, stairwells, utility meters, and architectural symmetry. Even without a floor plan, investigators can often infer layout using external cues.
3. **Entry & Breach Points:** Front doors, side doors, basement access, sliding doors, garage entries, fire escapes, and shared-wall vulnerabilities. Identifying reinforced structures or upgraded locks prevents surprises.
4. **Human Factors:** Likely sleeping areas, kitchen activity hubs, home-office setups, or rooms consistent with illegal activity (growing, processing, storage, computing). Subjects behave predictably within built environments.
5. **Risk Zones:** Blind corners, fatal funnels, narrow hallways, elevated positions, or interior spaces that complicate movement. These areas dictate tactical sequencing and timing.

You can also make your life easier by checking county records and, if available, pulling floor plans before hitting a structure. These blueprints can easily help you avoid being surprised by architecture or environmental features.

Takeaway: Buildings tell stories—if you learn to read them. Tactical diagramming transforms walls, doors, and windows into intelligence for operations.

November 20: Computer Forensics

"Technology is anything that wasn't around when you were born." —Alan Kay

Many investigators hear words like imaging, hash values, or artifact recovery and assume the process belongs exclusively to digital forensics labs or high-end federal units. The truth is more straightforward: investigators don't need to perform computer forensics, but they absolutely must understand what it means for their cases.

Computer forensics is not "looking through a laptop." It is the process of recovering, preserving, and analyzing electronic evidence to ensure it survives courtroom scrutiny. Whether the investigation is criminal, civil, corporate, insurance-related, or internal to an organization, computer forensics provides answers that no interview or paper record can match. A forensic image is an exact, sector-by-sector copy of a storage device—a hard drive, SSD, phone, USB drive, cloud directory, or server. It is **not** a drag-and-drop copy. It captures deleted files, system files, slack space, residual, fragmented data, metadata, and timestamps. Investigators must know this principle: once an image is taken, analysis occurs on the image—not on the original device. This protects the chain of custody and prevents contamination.

Every forensic image receives a hash value—typically MD5, SHA-1, or SHA-256. A hash is a unique numerical signature generated from the data. If a single bit changes, the hash changes. Hash values verify integrity, confirm the absence of tampering, and enable laboratories and attorneys to verify authenticity. Investigators don't need to compute hashes, but they must understand why reports include them and why courts demand them.

Digital artifacts are the traces of user activity—browser history, registry entries, link files, auto-saves, app logs, cloud sync traces, deleted items, remnants of prior installations, and fragments stored in unallocated space. Artifacts answer questions such as what files were opened? Which USB devices were connected? What websites were visited? What accounts were accessed? What was deleted?

Forensics cannot recover everything. Encryption, cloud-only data storage, overwritten blocks, or secure-delete programs make recovery attempts more difficult. SSDs complicate analysis because of wear-leveling algorithms. Reviewing cloud activity often requires legal process. Recognizing limits keeps investigators realistic and prevents overpromising to clients or prosecutors.

Takeaway: Computer forensics is not magic—it is a method. Understand it so you know what digital evidence can (and cannot) prove.

November 21: Open-Source Facial Recognition

"A false conclusion, once reached, is the most stubborn of errors." —Johann Wolfgang von Goethe

Facial recognition feels deceptively simple: upload a photo, compare it to a database, and watch the technology do the work. But in real investigative environments—public, private, corporate, or international—open-source facial recognition (OSFR) is far more complex and constrained. OSFR refers to comparing images using publicly available platforms, algorithms, and datasets—not law-enforcement biometric systems. These tools can be powerful, but they are also inconsistent, opaque, and easily manipulated. OSFR assists with:

- **Corroboration** of social media profiles, burner accounts, or aliases
- **Linking subjects** across platforms by matching profile pictures, frame-grabs, or group photos
- **Locating digital footprints** tied to the same individual under different usernames

Image-verification workflows—such as reverse image searches, metadata extraction, cross-platform comparisons, and contextual OSINT—are often more reliable than algorithmic matching alone. OSFR often fails in predictable ways:

- **Low-resolution or compressed images** distort facial landmarks
- **Aging, weight changes, and facial hair** degrade match accuracy
- **Lighting, angle, and partial obstruction** produce false positives
- **Twins, siblings, or look-alikes** can trigger algorithmic misfires
- Edited, filtered, or AI-generated images sabotage authenticity

Investigators must treat OSFR results as leads, not evidence. Public-sector investigators may use OSFR only within policy and must recognize that courts view facial-recognition hits as non-probable-cause indicators unless corroborated. Private investigators must be even more cautious. They should not access law-enforcement biometric systems, use scraping tools that violate a platform's terms of service, or present OSFR suggestions as verified identifications to clients or courts.

I don't think we're at Minority Report levels yet, and civil liability is real. Misidentification has led to defamation suits, wrongful termination, and claims of investigatory malpractice. OSFR is never the final word—it is the starting point of a verification chain.

Takeaway: OSFR is a lead, not a conclusion. Use OSFR cautiously and verify through multiple independent methods before making a claim.

November 22: Vehicle Telematics

"The road reveals more than the traveler intends." —Arab Proverb

Vehicles are among some of the richest sources of investigative insight. Think about how many times a day people are in and out of them. Many investigators view mobility data solely through the lens of GPS trackers, but modern vehicles generate far more information than most realize. Telematics, automated license plate readers (ALPR), OBD-II forensics, toll records, and fleet-management data can map behavior, confirm timelines, and expose deception without ever placing a device on a target vehicle.

Public-sector investigators may obtain telematics through subpoenas, warrants, or voluntary consent. Private investigators cannot directly subpoena telematics providers but can analyze client-owned fleet data, employer-issued vehicle logs, consumer telematics information provided with consent, and app-based data from rideshare, delivery, or rental services (when obtained through counsel).

ALPR systems capture plate numbers, timestamps, and geolocation from fixed cameras, patrol vehicles, toll systems, and commercial providers. Public-sector investigators rely on ALPR for suspect-vehicle tracking, historical route reconstruction, patterns of life, identification of associates, and counter-surveillance detection. Private-sector investigators cannot directly access law-enforcement ALPR systems, but many jurisdictions allow access to commercial ALPR databases, often used by repossession companies or private fleets.

The On-Board Diagnostics (OBD-II) port stores far more than just maintenance codes. Specialized extraction tools allow trained forensic analysts to retrieve speed, RPM, and throttle data; hard braking or acceleration; information on crash events; airbag deployment; and engine-on/engine-off cycles. Public-sector investigators use this after crashes, hit-and-runs, vehicular assaults, or fraud cases. Private investigators generally analyze OBD-II data only with vehicle owner consent—often in insurance investigations.

Regarding fleet intelligence, don't forget that companies and governments that operate vehicle fleets generate enormous volumes of mobility data. That can include driver logs, hours-of-service data, fuel-card activity, geofencing and route deviations, and idle-time abnormalities. Corporate investigators routinely use this to identify policy violations, time theft, internal fraud, or misuse of company assets. Proper analysis of fleet data often reveals behaviors employees never expected anyone to notice.

Takeaway: Vehicles are investigative goldmines. Use telematics and other fleet intelligence to corroborate timelines, map patterns, and expose deception.

November 23: Biometrics

"What we call identity is merely the story our body tells." —Salman Rushdie

Biometrics have become central to modern investigative and security work. They promise certainty: a match, an identity, a verification that cuts through aliases, forged documents, and deceptive statements. But like every powerful investigative tool, biometrics come with limitations, risks, and consequences that extend far beyond the moment of collection. Public-sector investigators rely on them extensively, such as:

- **Fingerprints** for criminal databases
- **Iris and facial scans** for border security
- **Voice analysis** for threat assessments
- **DNA profiling** for major crimes and unidentified remains

Private-sector investigators encounter biometrics through corporate access-control logs, authentication systems (fingerprint or face unlock), biometric timekeeping, mobile-device biometric locks, behavioral biometrics used by banks, and fraud-detection systems. While private investigators typically cannot collect biometrics directly, they can analyze biometric-derived logs and access events with proper authorization.

Biometrics are not infallible. Facial-recognition systems continue to misidentify people. Voice recognition can be fooled by high-quality recordings or AI-generated voices. Gait patterns change with injury. Fingerprints degrade with damage or age. DNA matches require careful laboratory controls. Biometrics are powerful—but not perfect. And because biometrics cannot be "reset," compromised biometric data becomes a lifelong vulnerability.

Perhaps the clearest illustration of this risk comes from Afghanistan. During the U.S. mission, biometrics were widely used to vet personnel, verify identities, and prevent insider threats. Thousands of Afghan soldiers, police officers, interpreters, and government workers were enrolled through fingerprint, facial, and iris systems to validate access and prevent infiltration. When the U.S. withdrew rapidly in 2021, control of biometric databases and equipment fell into the hands of the Taliban. Reports quickly emerged that Taliban fighters were using biometric devices and captured records to identify individuals who served the Afghan government. They started a campaign of house-to-house targeted killings. The very technology designed to protect lives became a roadmap for retribution. Keep this in mind, especially when you serve in government.

Takeaway: Biometrics can clarify identity—but they can also endanger it. Use them wisely and remember that once collected, they can be compromised.

November 24: Digital Traplines

"Machines take me by surprise with great frequency." —Dr. Alan Turing

Investigators often struggle with bandwidth. Cases sit idle while awaiting developments, subjects go quiet and leads fade over time. But in the modern digital ecosystem, information doesn't go still—it updates, shifts, posts, syncs, records, and reveals itself over time. Digital traplines harness this reality. They are recurring, lawful, structured checks across online and public-data environments that alert an investigator the moment something changes.

A trapline is a scheduled review cycle, often automated, that continuously monitors open sources for new activity. In the past, investigators had to manually recheck social media, court filings, business registrations, or public databases. Today, automation tools and structured routines allow investigators to keep dozens of cases alive simultaneously—quietly waiting for the next digital breadcrumb to appear. Digital traplines span four categories:

OSINT Platforms & Social Media: Monitoring new posts, follows, photos, connections, contact changes, or digital movements. This can be useful for everything from infidelity cases to insider-threat monitoring.

Public Filings & Court Records: Civil suits, criminal filings, evictions, liens, protective orders, corporate updates, or probate actions. Many investigators underestimate how often cases break open because a subject quietly filed something that contradicts their story.

Business & Corporate Records: New LLC formations, dissolutions, mergers, registered agents, addresses, or licenses. These traplines help reveal shell companies, side businesses, concealed income, or conflicts of interest.

Digital Activity & Breach Monitoring: Username, phone number, or e-mails that appear in data breaches, on new platforms, on dark-web dumps, and in leaked credential lists. Private investigators can use legal breach-monitoring tools and client-provided authorization to track exposures relevant to a case.

Traplines must rely on **public** or **permissioned** data. Anything else risks violating laws. Instead of working a case reactively, investigators build an automated early-warning system. The moment the subject does something traceable—files a lawsuit, changes an address, posts a photo, starts a business, renews a license, joins a platform—the investigator gets a hit.

Takeaway: Digital traplines let investigators track evolving facts in real time, saving you time and money in your investigation.

November 25: Cell-Site Simulators

"The greatest dangers to liberty lurk in insidious encroachment by men of zeal." — Justice Louis Brandeis

Cell-site simulators—often called Stingrays, Triggerfish, Hailstorms, or IMSI catchers—have an outsized presence in public imagination and an equally oversized misunderstanding among investigators. These devices are among the most tightly controlled surveillance tools in the U.S. They are capable of extraordinary things, but they also carry significant constitutional, statutory, and ethical constraints. Knowing what they can and can't do is essential.

Cell-site simulators impersonate a legitimate cell tower. When powered on, nearby phones attempt to connect, revealing identifying information such as the IMSI (International Mobile Subscriber Identity), ESN/MEID, or device-specific data that can help investigators locate or track a handset. Critically, modern U.S. usage policies prohibit the collection of content. These devices cannot be used to capture calls, texts, or recordings. Their lawful function is limited to device identification and location, not interception. Federal agencies—FBI, DHS components, U.S. Marshals, and military investigators—operate under strict DOJ and DHS policies that require:

- A warrant supported by probable cause (except in rare exigent circumstances)
- Immediate deletion of any non-target device identifiers
- Supervisory and sometimes headquarters-level approval
- Documented minimization procedures

Many states impose even stricter requirements. Some mandate explicit disclosure of cell-site simulator use in warrant applications. Others have barred their use without explicit legislative authorization. Improper deployments have led to evidence suppression and civil litigation.

Private investigators **cannot** legally use cell-site simulators under any circumstance. Not with client consent, not overseas, and not through commercial "IMSI catcher" devices marketed online. These tools operate by manipulating radio frequencies licensed by the federal government and by forcing connections from devices that did not consent. Using one as a civilian constitutes unlawful interception, unauthorized access, FCC violations, and often federal felonies. PIs can analyze historical cell-site records, tower dumps, and geolocation inconsistencies from legally obtained records. Understanding the limitations helps PIs avoid overstating what a tower hit means—and avoid being misled by imprecise location data.

Takeaway: When it comes to cell-site simulators, public-sector investigators must follow strict legal frameworks. Private investigators must not use them.

November 26: Mesh Networks

"In the midst of chaos, there is also opportunity." —*Sun Tzu*

Most investigators think of networks in terms of offices, routers, or cellular towers. But in high-risk, high-tempo operations—crime scenes with no infrastructure, disaster areas, rural tactical deployments, secure perimeters, or large special events—traditional networks fail precisely when you need them most. That is where mesh networks come in.

A mesh network is a decentralized, self-healing communications system in which each device serves as both a user and a relay. Instead of depending on a single tower or access point, the network spreads like a web, radio-to-radio or node-to-node, giving investigators communication resilience when everything else breaks down. Mesh networks are not limited to SWAT teams, tactical units, or federal special-response groups—they are rapidly becoming tools that skilled investigators and security professionals use to maintain situational awareness and preserve command and control in environments where regular communications fail or are compromised.

Mesh networks thrive where traditional communication struggles, which include areas with no cell coverage, signal congestion at large events, damaged infrastructure during disasters, dense urban environments with dead zones, and rural crime scenes with no commercial towers. They can enhance:

- **Crime scene management:** Units can deploy secure nodes across the perimeter, enabling real-time updates without relying on overburdened public systems.
- **Tactical responses:** Mesh-linked devices allow teams to share video, location, and sensor data across an ad hoc network.
- **High-profile events:** VIP protection details, counter-surveillance teams, and mobile response units benefit from congestion-proof comms.
- **Disaster operations:** When hurricanes, earthquakes, or conflict zones wipe out infrastructure, mesh networks reestablish comms quickly.

The key advantage of mesh networks is having encrypted communications isolated from public networks. However, mesh networks are not magic. They still require someone to place nodes and keep line-of-sight considerations in mind. There are also power, encryption, and legal concerns. The system is only as strong as its weakest configured node.

Takeaway: Mesh networks provide investigators with communication resilience when traditional systems fail, ensuring continuity and control.

November 27: Victimology

"The victim's story is the first chapter of the offender's." —Patricia Cornwell

Investigators often begin by trying to understand the offender. It feels natural—after all, the offender is the one who caused the harm. But seasoned investigators know a quiet truth: cases rarely start with the offender. They start with the victim. Who the victim is, how they live, what risks they face, and what vulnerabilities intersect with their daily life often explain more about the offender's decision-making than the first ten interviews combined.

Victimology is the discipline of understanding victims to understand offenders better. It asks: "Why this victim, at this moment, in this way?" When investigators can answer that, they begin to see the shape of the offender—sometimes even before identifying them by name. Victimology explains selection. Offenders almost never choose randomly. Even so-called "random" crimes often follow invisible lines of opportunity, access, or perceived vulnerability. A victim's lifestyle, routines, relationships, employment, online presence, financial pressures, and recent changes often reveal:

- Why did the offender focus on them
- How the offender gained access
- Whether the offender had prior familiarity
- What precipitating factor triggered the event
- Whether the victim was targeted, opportunistic, or collateral

Victimology can possibly show what happens next by:

- **Locating offenders:** Certain victim characteristics suggest offender familiarity.
- **Preventing additional harm:** If the offender selected based on a pattern, investigators can disrupt the next opportunity window.
- **Identifying accomplices:** The victim's connections often illuminate overlooked links to offenders or facilitators.
- **Sharpening interviews:** Knowing the victim's world allows investigators to ask targeted, strategic questions that expose contradictions.

Victimology also serves as a safeguard against bias. It forces investigators to move beyond instinct and into structured thinking. When you understand the victim's life, the offender's behavior begins to make sense.

Takeaway: Investigators who study the victim as much as the offender achieve the clearest picture of what happened.

November 28: Crime-Scene Processing

"The first rule is: Do not touch." —Agatha Christie

Most investigators—public or private—will eventually arrive at a scene before trained technicians. It might be a break-in, workplace event, domestic incident, or location tied to surveillance. In those moments, the biggest risk isn't missing evidence—it's damaging it. Crime-scene processing is a specialized skill, but the earliest decisions are universal: secure the area, preserve what exists, disturb nothing. A single step can move trace material, a single touch can erase prints, and a single adjustment can distort blood patterns or physical relationships. Even well-intentioned actions—closing doors, turning lights on, "checking" items—rewrite the scene. Your job is not to "solve" anything. Your job is to stabilize and protect. The rule is simple: **secure first, examine later.**

Non-CSI investigators can make a significant positive impact by capturing clean documentation:

- Photograph the scene *as found*—wide, medium, detail.
- Record time, conditions, lighting, and who entered.
- Note sights, sounds, odors, and transient elements.
- Capture spontaneous witness statements.
- Identify fragile evidence verbally, not physically.

If something must be moved for safety—rendering aid or preventing further damage—document exactly what changed and why. Many investigators assume they understand crime-scene work because they have observed professionals or taken a short course. True processing involves specialized expertise: bloodstain pattern interpretation, trace collection, impression evidence, digital artifact preservation, biological handling, fire-pattern reading, and scene geometry. These tasks require training and equipment outside the scope of most criminal investigators. Attempting them risks contamination, suppression in court, or civil liability. An investigator's initial responsibilities are:

- Keep people out.
- Keep the scene stable.
- Keep your hands off everything.
- Capture what you see, not what you think it means.

Crime scene professionals can interpret patterns; you can ensure those patterns survive long enough for them to analyze.

November 29: Forensic Statement & Video Sync

"The camera never lies, but it can be misunderstood." —Roland Barthes

In complex investigations, the most decisive breakthroughs often come from comparing what people *say* happened to what the evidence shows *actually* happened. Forensic statement and video synchronization is the technique of aligning recorded statements—verbal, written, or transcribed—with time-stamped video, telematics, metadata, and other digital logs. Synchronization is not just watching a video and reading a statement. It is a frame-by-frame, second-by-second process that places every claimed action against objective reality. Let's talk about four things related to this technique:

1. **Matching Statements to Physical Movement:** The heart of synchronization is comparing what a witness claims they did to what the camera captures them doing. Small discrepancies matter. For example, a suspect denies contact with another person, but the footage shows interaction.
2. **Detecting Omission, Fabrication, and Rehearsal:** Inconsistent timing often reveals deception more clearly than inconsistent language.
3. **Accounting for Timestamp Drift:** Video systems are imperfect. DVR clocks drift. Body-camera clocks drift. Phone timestamps may run minutes ahead or behind. Vehicle telematics may sync from the cloud, while surveillance systems sync from outdated local servers.
4. **When Synchronization Becomes Evidentiary Gold:** Courts, juries, HR panels, arbitrators, and corporate decision-makers respond strongly to synchronized timelines. They make evidence **intuitive**. With synchronization, the investigator can clearly demonstrate:

   - What the subject said
   - What the video shows
   - Where the timelines diverge
   - And how those divergences reveal truth or deception

Public-sector investigators use synchronization in officer-involved incidents, major crimes, fraud investigations, and intelligence cases. Private-sector investigators use it for workplace-misconduct cases, insurance claims, corporate incidents, and domestic disputes. Regardless of context, synchronization forces a witness's timeline to coexist with the recorded fact.

Takeaway: Synchronization transforms digital evidence into clarity. Use it to home in on deception and uncover any pertinent facts for the investigation.

November 30: Fusion Analysis

"No single piece of intelligence ever tells the whole story—it is the mosaic that reveals the truth." —Sir William Stephenson

The most skilled investigators are not defined by their mastery of any single technique, but by their ability to combine techniques into a coherent, strategic whole. Fusion analysis is the process of weaving together disparate investigative methods—financial tracing, digital forensics, behavioral profiling, surveillance, metadata interpretation, statement analysis, OSINT, communication records, biometrics, and countless others—into a unified picture of what actually happened. It is the culmination of everything explored throughout the month: specialized methods do not stand alone; they reinforce one another.

Fusion analysis begins with a simple recognition: no evidence source is complete in itself. Every tool captures a different dimension of human behavior. Surveillance shows movement. Financial records show motive. Metadata shows timing. Statements show perception or deception. Digital footprints show habits. Biometrics show identity. Physical surveillance shows capability and opportunity. When investigators fuse these strands, weaknesses in one source are strengthened by the others.

Public-sector investigators rely on fusion analysis in nearly every major case. Task forces—local, state, and federal—exist precisely because no single discipline can answer every question. A narcotics investigation might begin with a controlled delivery, shift into financial-pattern analysis, integrate cell-site data, and end with a Title III wiretap. A threat case might merge psychological indicators, OSINT patterns, digital traplines, and surveillance logs.

Private investigators also apply fusion analysis. An insurance investigation might combine video synchronization, medical record metadata, social media indicators, and financial anomalies. A domestic investigation might combine surveillance, OSINT, digital footprints, pattern-of-life insights, and pretext-based contact. Even small PI firms with limited budgets can fuse techniques: the power lies in analysis, not equipment.

Fusion analysis also prevents investigators from over-relying on a "favorite" method. A compelling statement means little without corroborating metadata. A strong surveillance clip is vulnerable without a timeline and context. Fusion analysis forces the investigator to ask: How does each piece of evidence reinforce, contradict, or refine the others? The final product—the fused case—becomes more defensible, more resilient, and more persuasive.

Takeaway: A great investigation is never the result of one technique. It is the result of many techniques working together.

December: Training & Professional Development

"The more you know, the more you realize how much you don't." —Aristotle

When I was younger, like most juveniles, I knew everything. Then you quickly realize that as an adult and the older you get, the more you realize how little you do know. This applies to all of someone's life. For investigation professionals, experience alone does not create skill. Repetition does not guarantee improvement. Longevity does not equal professionalism. What separates exceptional investigators from average ones is the deliberate, lifelong commitment to developing their craft.

Professional development is not a course, a certificate, or a box to check. It is the recognition that every skill—interviewing, surveillance, analysis, digital forensics, operational planning, report writing, courtroom testimony, and decision-making—decays without constant reinforcement. This month is about building the investigator behind the investigation. The goal is to show that training is not something you attend; training is something you become.

Both public and private-sector investigators face a similar truth: the cases we work evolve faster than the training available. Technology outpaces doctrine. Criminal networks innovate more quickly than policy. And the global investigative landscape—digital, physical, legal, and geopolitical—changes every year, whether we prepare for it or not.

That is why professional development must be intentional. Investigators must learn to build their own training pipelines, fill their own knowledge gaps, and create systems for skill maintenance that do not depend on agency budgets or employer priorities. A professional investigator cannot wait for training to come; they must go find it. As my first Regional Security Officer would often say: *"You can control little outside your sphere of influence, but you can master your skill, will, fitness, and gear."*

This month focuses on three core themes:

1. **Training as Skill:** How to build, refine, and sustain technical abilities through deliberate practice, scenario work, repetitions, and post-event learning.
2. **Training as a Career:** How to pursue certifications, advanced courses, professional networks, mentoring, and cross-disciplinary learning that expands your value.
3. **Training as Mindset**: How to develop judgment, reduce cognitive bias, strengthen resilience, sharpen analytical habits, and build the internal discipline that defines excellence.

Training is not a luxury. It is an ethical obligation. Poorly trained investigators miss evidence, misinterpret behavior, violate rights, and weaken the justice system. Well-trained investigators prevent harm, elevate truth, and earn trust. Every case is a reflection not just of skill, but of preparation.

This month, we explore diverse topics such as:

- Training standards across public and private sectors
- Selecting the right courses and certifications
- Fieldcraft vs. classroom learning
- Professional associations and why they matter
- Skill decay and how to reverse it
- Building a personal training pipeline
- Scenario-based training and simulations
- Developing judgment and decision-making frameworks
- Reducing cognitive bias through metacognition
- Mentorship, coaching, and knowledge transfer
- Mental and emotional resilience
- Physical readiness for operational investigators
- After-action reviews (AARs) and learning from failure
- Developing your investigative playbook
- Staying ahead of technological change
- Building a lifelong training mindset

This is the month where investigators refine not just what they do, but who they are. The job demands growth. The profession demands discipline. And excellence demands both.

December 1: Training Standards

"Learning never exhausts the mind." —Leonardo da Vinci

Training is the great separator in this profession. It reveals who is truly prepared, who is barely competent, and who is simply faking it. Investigators across the public and private sectors talk constantly about training, but what they mean by "trained" varies widely by organization, industry, or jurisdiction. That's why you can meet a police detective with two decades of experience and almost no formal interview training... and a corporate investigator with three years of experience who has more structured coursework under their belt than half a federal task force. Titles don't equal skill. Uniforms don't equal competence. And certificates don't equal capability.

Every sector—law enforcement, military, intelligence, and private investigation—defines "trained" differently. In some police departments, a new detective receives on-the-job training that looks like shadowing another detective for a few weeks before being handed a stack of cases. Meanwhile, a corporate investigator at a Fortune 100 company might complete a formal training pipeline that includes coursework, scenario-based simulations, and peer evaluations before they are trusted with a sensitive matter. A private investigator might complete the bare-minimum licensing class required by the state... or they might seek out a rigorous training academy and treat the craft as a profession rather than a hobby. As Dr. Milton Friedman once said, *"Licensure is no assurance of quality."* You can't assume anything about someone's capability based on their badge, salary, or sector.

The best investigators—public or private—don't treat training as something they completed. They treat it as something they maintain. In the private sector, where there is no academy waiting to retrain you every year, this mindset is even more critical. No one is coming to save your skills, or to mandate meaningful continuing education (many states require only a paltry eight hours per year). You must keep your skills alive yourself. I have completed thousands of hours of training and have no desire to stop taking courses. Training isn't an event; it's a lifestyle.

Takeaway: Titles don't make you qualified—competency does. Minimum standards are just that: minimums. The investigators who stand out are those who pursue training beyond the required level.

December 2: Fieldcraft vs. Classroom Training

*"Tell me, and I forget; teach me, and I may remember; involve me, and I learn." —
Benjamin Franklin*

The classroom builds your understanding. The field sharpens your edge. Every investigator eventually learns that you can ace every written exam, memorize every legal statute, and crush every scenario in a training bay—and still fall apart the first time you're alone in a parking lot at 0300 hours watching a subject who suddenly does something you have never seen before. Classroom training gives you the framework. Fieldcraft gives you the instincts.

No matter where you work, the field does not behave like a classroom. The classroom gives you the "how" —but the field gives you the "when" and "why." You learn timing, pattern recognition, people skills, improvisation, and judgment through doing. That's why some of the best investigators I have met—including those without fancy degrees or extensive credentials—excel because they have accumulated thousands of real-world reps. They have watched enough human behavior to know what a lie sounds like. They have conducted enough interviews to recognize when someone's gearing up to disclose something important. They have run enough surveillances to know when the subject is getting nervous... and when it's time to break contact.

But this doesn't mean classroom training is optional, far from it. Without a solid academic foundation—legal authorities, policy, ethics, report writing, interviewing theory—you end up with tactics but no structure. Fieldcraft without theory becomes guesswork. Theory without fieldcraft becomes fragility. You need both. The classroom fills your toolbox. The field teaches you which tool to use, how hard to swing it, and when to put it back.

The most effective investigators deliberately blend the two. They take courses, read books, attend seminars, and study best practices—then immediately go into the field to test what they learned. They ask senior investigators to shadow them. They treat every case like a rep, every mistake like a lesson, and every success like a reminder to stay humble.

Takeaway: Classrooms teach concepts. The field teaches competence. The investigator who masters both consistently delivers results.

December 3: Building a Personal Training Pipeline

"You miss 100% of the shots you don't take." —Wayne Gretzky

If you want longevity in this career, you can't afford to drift. Investigators who rely solely on agency-mandated training or the bare-minimum state requirements eventually fall behind—sometimes slowly, sometimes all at once. A personal training pipeline is how you prevent that. It's the system you build, maintain, and constantly refine to ensure you never stop growing.

The best investigators I have known—public and private—are intentional about their growth. They map out their year, identify the skills they want to develop, and pursue training just as they pursue leads: with purpose. They don't wait for a supervisor, a task force, or a company budget to approve something. They take the shot.

Many of my military colleagues were shocked when I requested to attend a private-sector course, only to have my supervisor deny it. I would then ask for permissive TDY to take it. If that was denied, I would take annual leave and pay out of pocket. When there is a will, there is a way. A personal pipeline covers three areas: baseline, advanced, and emerging skills.

- **Baseline skills** are your foundation—interviewing, report writing, surveillance, documentation, legal authorities, and ethics. No matter how long you have been doing this, these skills decay quickly when they are not practiced. They're also the skills that keep you from making career-ending mistakes. Baseline skills should be revisited at least once a year.
- **Advanced skills** elevate you beyond the average investigator: digital forensics, financial analysis, undercover work, source handling, forensic photography, or structured analytic techniques. These create differentiation. They move you from "capable" to "indispensable."
- **Emerging skills** are the horizon—AI-enabled OSINT, metadata analysis, cyber tradecraft, social engineering defenses, drone operations, and tools that barely existed a decade ago. If you ignore this category, you risk becoming obsolete in a world that changes faster than people care to admit.

Just as important is frequency. Don't cram everything into one month or one annual conference. Even 20 minutes a day of professional reading adds up to over 120 hours of self-study annually. That is more than most formal academies provide.

Takeaway: A personal training pipeline is your insurance policy against stagnation. No one will design one for you.

December 4: Skill Decay: The Silent Threat

"If you don't practice, you don't deserve to win." —Andre Agassi

Skill decay is one of the quietest, most dangerous threats in the investigative profession. It doesn't happen overnight. It creeps in slowly: a hesitation during an interview, sloppy documentation on a long surveillance day, or a forgotten legal nuance. The problem is simple: skills fade without practice. And the more complex or perishable the skill, the faster it erodes.

Anyone who has served in the military or law enforcement has seen this firsthand. A firearms qualification you once breezed through suddenly feels harder. An interview technique you could once execute in your sleep now feels rusty. The private sector sees the same phenomenon—especially when an investigator hasn't used a specialty skill in months due to fluctuations in caseload. Skill decay doesn't care what badge you carry or how many years you have been doing this. It affects everyone.

I see skill decay far too often, and many investigators are unwilling to change their attitude about it. I once conducted a CPR/AED course for embassy personnel with our health unit. Many people were grateful someone had taken the initiative to put on the course. I saw another federal agent in the hallway and asked if he was attending. He scoffed: *"CPR? I did that course 10 years ago and haven't needed it since."* I said, *"You don't think some things might have changed—or that maybe you need a rep to refresh?"* He replied, *"No, I will remember it when I need it. Besides, I am too busy."*

This is not the attitude you want to have.

Combating skill decay requires two things: awareness and reps. Awareness means being honest about which skills you haven't used recently and acknowledging that time away weakens proficiency—no matter how experienced you are. Reps mean scheduling deliberate practice. Not when you "have time." Not when things slow down. But as part of your normal rhythm. Even fifteen minutes reviewing a technique can be beneficial. Small reps compound.

If you're in a public agency, ask to attend refreshers. If you're in the private sector, build refreshers into your weekly or monthly pipeline. If you don't have access to formal training, create reps yourself—study case footage, practice note-taking, rehearse interview flows, or conduct mock surveillance drives. Repetition preserves sharpness. Skill decay is silent—until it's not.

Takeaway: Skills don't stay sharp on their own. They fade unless you fight for them. Identify your perishable skills before decay becomes a liability.

December 5: Certifications

"An investment in knowledge pays the best interest." —Benjamin Franklin

The investigative world is flooded with certifications. Some are valuable. Some are merely decorative. And some—let's be honest—are nothing more than "badge mills" selling paper to people who want shortcuts to credibility. The truth is simple: a certification only matters if it gives you skills you can actually use. If it doesn't make you a better investigator, it's just alphabet soup after your name.

Across the public and private sectors, I have seen investigators chase credentials for the wrong reasons: to pad a résumé, impress a supervisor, or appear more qualified than they are. I have also seen people skip certifications entirely out of cynicism or laziness. Both extremes miss the point. A strong credential isn't about prestige—it's about capability.

In the private sector, certifications can be essential. HR departments, general counsel, and corporate leadership often rely on them as indicators that you have met a recognized standard. Good examples include the CFE (Certified Fraud Examiner), CPP (Certified Protection Professional), PCI (Professional Certified Investigator), and CAMS (Certified Anti-Money Laundering Specialist). They don't make you an expert overnight—but they demonstrate commitment, competence, and a baseline.

In the public sector, most agencies provide internal academies and formal training pipelines so that external certifications may be less emphasized. But they can still add value, especially if they fill gaps in your agency's curriculum. Digital forensics, financial crime, OSINT, intelligence analysis, cyber tradecraft, or behavioral interviewing certifications can broaden your toolkit far beyond what a basic academy provides. The strongest investigators I have seen often pursue outside certifications on their own time—not because they need the paper, but because they need the skill (even when their agency thinks otherwise).

At Lynx, we don't just give students certificates of completion. Students may receive certificates of attendance that merely attest they showed up. A certificate of completion requires the student to demonstrate competency in the subject matter. Skill should be earned, not assumed.

Remember: A certification is a starting point, not a finish line. The course ends. The learning doesn't. The true value of a credential is how you apply what it taught you—day after day, case after case.

Takeaway: Chase certifications that give you real skill, not vanity letters.

December 6: Selecting Training Providers

"I am always doing that which I cannot do, in order that I may learn how to do it."
—Pablo Picasso

In the investigative world, not all training is created equal. The challenge is identifying what is credible versus what is a badge mill, a cash grab, or a check-the-box class that teaches you little.

I have seen investigators from every sector—law enforcement, intelligence, military, and the private sector—fall into the trap of choosing training based on convenience rather than quality. In his early years, one of my colleagues had to attend armed security guard training to obtain certification for a government contract security role. He was previously a police officer. He went to the course provider's office ready to take the course. The provider handed him a certificate after looking at a calendar and said, *"If anyone asks, you remember going to range with me last week, right?" "Look, here's your target."* He turned around and walked out. High-quality training providers share a few consistent traits:

1. **Proven instructors:** Instructor résumés matter—not the inflated version, but the real one. Look for instructors with operational experience, not just speaking experience. Someone who has actually interviewed suspects, run surveillance, worked sources, testified, conducted digital exams, or performed the skill they're teaching. Good instructors teach clearly and practically—not just recite war stories.
2. **Rigorous curriculum:** A credible course has structure, objectives, standards, and assessments. It pushes you. You leave with improved capability, not just more notes. Training should demand something from you—thinking, doing, performing.
3. **No "magic tricks.":** Avoid anyone selling secret formulas, proprietary interrogation tactics, mystical OSINT "backdoor methods," or superhuman deception-detection promises. Investigation is craft, not sorcery.
4. **Transparent standards:** Good providers tell you exactly what you will learn, how you will be evaluated, and what competency looks like. Badge mills hide behind vague promises and glossy marketing.

When evaluating a provider, ask: Who actually teaches the course? What experience do they have? What skills will I walk away with? Do they require performance, or just attendance? Do serious practitioners respect this training? Proper training accelerates your capability. The wrong training wastes time.

Takeaway: Choose training providers who build real skill, demand real effort, and deliver real value.

December 7: Scenario-Based Training

"The beautiful thing about learning is that nobody can take it away from you." — B.B. King

Classroom training gives you knowledge. Scenario-based training gives you judgment. There is a difference—an enormous one. You can memorize procedures, study legal authorities, and take notes on investigative techniques. Still, until you have been inside a realistic scenario with time pressure, uncertainty, and human behavior thrown into the mix, you haven't truly tested your skill. Scenario-based training forces you to bring everything together: observation, communication, decision-making, ethics, fieldcraft, and stress management.

Across every sector, scenarios are the closest you will get to the field without consequences. Law enforcement academies use them to test judgment under stress. The military uses them to rehearse mission profiles and inject chaos. Intelligence units rely on them to practice source meetings and elicitation. Private investigators benefit greatly from simulations that include interviews, surveillance breaks, hostile subjects, or digital evidence collection.

I have run scenario-based exercises for both public and private-sector investigators, and one pattern always emerges: people perform differently when the variables move. A trainee who is brilliant in a lecture hall suddenly struggles when a witness becomes emotional. A seasoned investigator misreads a role-player because they were not expecting a curveball. This is precisely why scenarios exist. They teach you how to think when everything is moving at once. High-quality scenario training has several key elements:

1. **Realism without recklessness:** Scenarios should mimic real investigative pressures, not Hollywood action sequences. No unnecessary theatrics—just authentic, plausible stressors.
2. **Clear objectives:** You should know what success looks like, even if the path to get there is deliberately unclear.
3. **Feedback loops:** The debrief is where the learning happens. Good instructors don't just critique—they explain, demonstrate, and correct.
4. **Role-players who stay in character:** Professionally trained role-players add depth. A poorly briefed role-player can derail an entire scenario.
5. **Injects that force adaptation:** A witness changes their story. A subject becomes evasive. A lead goes nowhere. These are real investigative frictions.

The point of scenario-based training is not to "win." It's to learn. To fail safely. To identify vulnerabilities before they cost you a case in the real world.

Takeaway: Scenario-based training builds judgment, adaptability, and confidence under pressure. Train for reality—not just theory.

December 8: Investigative Judgment

"The more you know, the more you see." —Aldous Huxley

Investigative judgment isn't something you can memorize from a book or download from a training platform. It's not a checklist, a flowchart, or a script. It's the ability to look at a situation—messy, incomplete, high-pressure—and make the right call at the right time.

The hard truth is that most investigators don't intentionally train judgment. They train procedures: how to write reports, conduct interviews, collect evidence, and run surveillance. All important. But judgment is what tells you when to press a witness, when to back off, when to break surveillance, and when a lead is worth pursuing. Judgment is the bridge between skill and wisdom. Developing investigative judgment comes from three places:

1. **Exposure to complexity:** You can't form good judgment in sterile environments. You need exposure to real people, unpredictable behavior, incomplete information, and time pressure. Ride-alongs, complex interviews, messy cases, and challenging clients build judgment faster than classroom scenarios ever will.
2. **Honest after-action reviews:** Judgment sharpens when you step back and ask: What did I see? What did I miss? What influenced my decision? What would I do differently next time? If you can't critique your own work, judgment stagnates. If you can, it grows rapidly.
3. **Pattern recognition:** Judgment grows through noticing patterns— behavioral cues, inconsistencies, timelines, correlation vs. causation, and the subtle signals people give off when they are lying, hiding, scared, or confused. The more patterns you store, the more your intuition becomes calibrated.

One technique for building judgment is running "micro-scenarios" with a partner—short, fast decision reps focused on a single variable: a shifting witness story, a sudden surveillance deviation, a contradictory record, or a last-minute change during an interview. Rapid reps build quick thinking.

I remember doing these while we were on patrol in Baghdad. One morning, my team leader—who had clearly not had his coffee yet—turned around and said, "Panico, what happens if a nuclear bomb went off right now?" I replied, "I guess we would all be dead and everything would be quiet, Sergeant." He said, "Exactly. All would be quiet. Let's practice that now." Let's just say... the moral of the story is: practice in private with someone who cares—or you will get very creative scenarios from someone who hasn't had their morning coffee.

Takeaway: Investigative judgment is trained, not gifted. Expose yourself to complexity, critique your decisions, and sharpen your pattern recognition.

December 9: Reading and Writing

"Not all readers are leaders, but all leaders are readers." —Harry S. Truman

Reading and writing shape how you think, how you communicate, how you process information, and ultimately, how effective you are in the field. It doesn't matter whether you work in law enforcement, intelligence, corporate security, or private investigations: if you cannot read critically and write clearly, your ceiling will always remain low.

Reading is fuel for the investigative mind. What you read—fiction or nonfiction—shapes how you understand people, motives, timelines, behavior, systems, and the world. Fiction sharpens imagination, empathy, and pattern recognition. Nonfiction sharpens knowledge, frameworks, and analytical thinking. Both expand your ability to see angles others miss. I read constantly. My wife sometimes gets annoyed because I always have a book open—but in this field, it's absolutely necessary. Investigators operate in a world defined by complexity, ambiguity, and hidden meaning. Reading trains you for that.

Information overload is real, especially today. There is more data, more noise, and more content than ever before. But reading—curated, consistent, intentional—cuts through that noise and makes you sharper. You don't need to read for hours a day. Even 15 minutes a day adds up to hundreds of hours per year. That alone will put you ahead of most of your peers.

On the other end of the spectrum, I once served with a Soldier who refused to read anything. Literally anything. Even a fast-food menu made him cringe. He treated reading like a personal attack. Don't be him. The world is full of investigators who don't read—and they are the ones who stagnate. In my first book, I talked about being the kid you couldn't pay to read. Now I am writing my second book. People change. But you must choose to change.

Writing is just as critical. Reading sharpens your mind; writing sharpens your clarity. Writing is how you convey ideas, request resources, articulate risk, secure equipment, justify training, communicate with clients, persuade leadership, and, most importantly, present your cases. If you can't write well in this profession, you will struggle—because your work must survive scrutiny everywhere.

Writing isn't an art reserved for the gifted. It's a skill earned through repetition. When investigators tell me they "hate writing," what they usually mean is they haven't practiced enough to be confident. To separate yourself from the pack, practice, practice, practice!

Takeaway: Read every day. Write every day. These two habits will separate you from the pack more than any certification or tool ever will.

December 10: Mentorship and Coaching

"A society grows great when old men plant trees whose shade they know they shall never sit in." —Greek Proverb

Every investigator can point to someone—an instructor, a senior detective, a team leader, a supervisor—who shaped their development. Mentorship is the reason many of us made it through our early years without crashing and burning. Coaching isn't optional in this profession; it's part of the lineage of the craft. The investigative world is built on knowledge passed from practitioner to practitioner.

I have had mentors in every sector I have worked—military, intelligence, law enforcement, and private investigations. Some taught me tactical skills. Some taught me judgment. Some taught me what not to do. And some gave me opportunities I didn't even realize I needed. Those mentors gave me a craft, a community, and a profession I have spent my life trying to honor. Giving back—coaching younger investigators, sharing lessons learned, or quietly guiding someone through their first big case—is one way to repay the system that gave so much to me. Mentorship isn't about hierarchy. It's about stewardship. To get the most out of mentorship—and to provide it—you need three things:

1. **Humility:** As a mentee, admit what you don't know. As a mentor, realize you don't have all the answers. Humility keeps the relationship healthy and the learning honest.
2. **Intentionality:** Don't wait passively for mentorship to appear. Seek out people who do the job well. Ask questions. Request feedback. Offer to help. As a mentor, be deliberate about carving out time to develop the next generation. It doesn't have to be formal. Sometimes the best coaching happens in the parking lot after shift.
3. **Transferable habits, not just stories:** War stories are entertaining. Habits are transformational. Teach the systems, checklists, mental models, and standards that actually make someone better. Pass on the process—not just the memories.

The best mentorship relationships evolve. The mentee becomes a peer. The peer becomes a collaborator. And eventually, the mentee becomes a mentor themselves. That cycle is how the profession gets stronger. It's how knowledge survives long after people move on, retire, or pass away. If you have benefitted from the guidance of a mentor—and almost all of us have—you owe it to the craft to give back. Carry the torch forward. Develop others. Share what you have learned. Plant trees whose shade you will never sit under.

Takeaway: Seek out mentors. Become one. Give back to the system that built you and help shape the investigators who will come after you.

December 11: Networks (Part One)

"No one succeeds alone." —John C. Maxwell

Investigation is not a solo profession. You may work independently, but you cannot grow independently. Every serious investigator eventually realizes the same truth: your network—your professional associations, your peers, your mentors, your contacts—is one of your most powerful tools. Still, without access to a broader professional ecosystem, you risk becoming isolated, outdated, or unnecessarily limited in what you can accomplish.

Professional associations exist to prevent that. Organizations like OSAC, ASIS, ATAP, IAFCI, IAI, ACFE, NALI, NCISS, WAD, and many others are not just alphabet soup—they are gateways to community, training, standards, and opportunities you cannot replicate on your own. They bring together practitioners from federal agencies, local law enforcement, intelligence units, corporate investigations, and private-sector firms. That diversity of perspective is invaluable.

I have benefited enormously from these networks. Some gave me training I couldn't find anywhere else. Others connected me with subject-matter experts who helped solve complex cases. Some introduced me to mentors who shaped the trajectory of my career. Below are some of the benefits of associations:

1. **Training & Continuing Education:** Most associations offer courses, webinars, conferences, certifications, and workshops that far surpass what you can find on the open market. They often maintain the highest standards in their respective specialties—financial crime, threat assessment, forensic analysis, corporate security, executive protection, or private investigations.
2. **Access to Expertise:** You can pick up the phone or send a message and reach investigators, analysts, examiners, or specialists with decades of experience. Need a forensic accountant? A digital analyst? A threat assessment professional? A seasoned PI in another state? Associations make that effortless.
3. **Credibility & Professional Identity:** Belonging to respected associations signals seriousness. It shows that you are invested in the craft, committed to standards, and connected to the broader investigative community. Clients, supervisors, and partners notice that.

You must be proactive in seeking out associations. Aside from marketing or a friend telling you about it, you will rarely have an opportunity to join one without some action on your end.

Takeaway: Associations are key for providing training, access to expertise, and nurturing your professional identity. Do your research and join up. It may even be tax-deductible. Talk to your accountant.

December 12: Networks (Part Two)

"Every person adds or takes—guard your circle, choose wisely." —Emmanuel Apetsi

Continuing from yesterday's lesson, I wanted to expand on some additional benefits of networks and associations.

1. **Advocacy & Policy Influence:** Groups like NCISS and state PI associations advocate for investigative licensing, legal protections, and operational freedoms. Without them, private investigators would lose ground quickly in legislative arenas.
2. **Career Mobility & Opportunity:** Your next partnership, referral, job, subcontracting opportunity, or training invitation often comes from someone who met you at a conference or through an association event. Doors open for those who show up.

Just as important, you need to know how to leverage these networks effectively. Some examples:

- **Join the organizations aligned with your mission,** not just the biggest names. Relevance matters more than prestige.
- **Be active.** Attend conferences. Volunteer. Join committees. Network intentionally.
- **Share your knowledge,** even if you think it's minor. What is basic to you might be transformative to someone else.
- **Connect across sectors**—public, private, corporate, military, intelligence. Cross-sector insight is an investigator's superpower.
- **Maintain relationships.** A network is something you nurture, not something you switch on when you need a favor.

The investigative profession thrives because its members share standards, methods, and knowledge across boundaries. Professional associations ensure that every generation receives more than the last—and contributes more than they took.

Takeaway: Join associations. Build your network. Invest in the community that invests in you. Professional relationships are not a luxury—they are a force multiplier for your entire investigative career.

December 13: Hubris

"Pride makes us artificial; humility makes us real." —Thomas Merton

In aviation, there is a well-known danger zone around the 200-hour mark of training. Pilots are no longer beginners—they have logged real flight time, gained confidence, and started to feel like they have a handle on the aircraft. But they are not yet experienced enough to appreciate the full spectrum of risk. It is the moment when overconfidence quietly replaces caution, and hubris begins whispering in the cockpit. Many accidents happen here—not because of a lack of skill, but because of the illusion of mastery.

Investigators hit their own version of the "200-hour mark." It doesn't matter whether you work fraud cases, internal investigations, threat assessments, criminal cases, cyber incidents, or surveillance. There comes a point when the job begins to feel familiar. You have had some wins with tough cases. You have built a little reputation. You have stopped second-guessing yourself. You start thinking, *I have got this*. That is the moment you need to slow down.

Hubris creeps in the same way skill decay does—quietly and almost invisibly. It shows up in shortcuts: skipping documentation because "I already know what happened." Cutting corners on interviews because "I can read this guy." Trusting your gut more than the facts. Assuming a pattern you have seen before must be true again and believing that your experience exempts you from mistakes.

Humility keeps you curious when the job tries to convince you that you have seen it all. It forces you to check your assumptions, revisit the basics, and verify facts even when you are confident. Humility slows you down just enough to prevent catastrophic mistakes.

When you feel yourself hitting your "200-hour moment," take it as a warning light. Re-check your fundamentals. Seek feedback. Ask questions you think you already know the answers to. Treat each case like it has something new to teach you. Every real master I have known—public or private—has the same trait: they remained teachable long after they became skilled. Experience makes you good. Humility keeps you alive.

Takeaway: When your confidence starts rising, slow down. Hubris is the silent threat that appears just as you begin to excel.

December 14: Cross-Disciplinary Learning

"The mind, once stretched by a new idea, never returns to its original dimensions."
—Ralph Waldo Emerson

One of the most significant advantages an investigator can have is the ability to pull knowledge from multiple disciplines. Modern investigations are ecosystems. A fraud case may involve psychological manipulation. A workplace threat case may require financial pattern analysis. A counterintelligence case may hinge on digital forensics and behavioral indicators. A private-sector investigation may require intelligence collection, OSINT, or advanced interviewing skills typically found in government roles.

All investigative work is interconnected. The techniques used in one discipline often carry over seamlessly into another. The more cross-disciplinary your knowledge is, the more angles you see—and the fewer blind spots you have.

Investigators sometimes fall into the trap of staying in their lane. Fraud people stick with fraud. Cyber people stick with cyber. A private investigator only wants to do surveillance. Detectives stick with criminal cases. Intelligence professionals stick with analysis. That is fine... until a case requires skill in a different domain— and you suddenly realize you are out of your depth. To develop cross-disciplinary strength:

- **Expose yourself to fields adjacent to yours.** Even an introductory class can change how you operate.
- **Study disciplines that intimidate you.** Cyber, financial crime, and forensics scare a lot of investigators, those are the very areas worth exploring.
- **Read broadly.** Books outside your field teach you patterns you didn't know existed.
- **Work cases outside your comfort zone under supervision.** Growth requires risk. I once learned about a woman in the Senior Foreign Service who takes leave of absence to study for free under chefs. It is her hobby that she enjoys developing with no connection to the government.
- **Talk to experts.** A short conversation can teach you what would take weeks to learn on your own.

Cross-disciplinary investigators become problem-solvers instead of specialists with blinders on. They adapt faster. They innovate more. And they bring a level of depth that clients, agencies, and courts immediately recognize.

Takeaway: Investigations don't live in silos—and neither should you. Expand your knowledge across disciplines and stretch your thinking through cross-disciplinary learning.

December 15: Foreign Language Proficiency

"To have another language is to possess a second soul." —Charlemagne

Foreign language proficiency is often an overlooked skill that an investigator can possess. You don't need to be fluent. You don't need to read Tolstoy in the original Russian. Even basic proficiency—greetings, simple questions, tone, cultural familiarity—can be a force multiplier during interviews, surveillance, rapport-building, and safety-related encounters. Language is access, and access is an advantage. I have seen language skills change the entire trajectory of an investigation. A simple greeting in someone's native language can soften their posture, open them up, and lower their guard during an interview. It signals respect. It signals cultural awareness. And it signals that you're willing to meet them where they are. Human beings respond to that—across every culture.

Even outside interviews, language proficiency has operational value. A friend of mine—who did not look like he spoke Spanish—was once walking alone when he overheard two men speaking quietly in Spanish about how they planned to jump him and take his money. Because he understood what they were saying, he casually broke off, changed direction, and vanished before anything unfolded.

That is the kind of situational awareness a second language can provide. Safety isn't always about weapons or tactics. Sometimes it's about understanding what others think you can't understand. In both the public and private sectors, language proficiency can also put you in a different professional tier. Many agencies, corporations, and investigative firms offer:

- **Pay incentives** for bilingual or multilingual employees
- **Foreign language** skill pay or bonuses
- **Priority selections** for overseas assignments, international cases, and sensitive interviews
- **Specialized roles** requiring cultural and linguistic capability
- **Career advancement** driven by unique skills others lack

When you speak another language, you instantly become more versatile, more deployable, and more valuable. Operationally, foreign language ability helps you do everything from understanding cultural cues that don't translate well into English to serving clients or communities that others cannot. You become the person who bridges gaps—between cultures, between subjects and investigators, between agencies and communities. That makes you a force multiplier in a profession where communication and trust are everything.

Takeaway: Learn another language—even a little. It builds rapport, enhances safety, expands your opportunities, and makes you a more effective investigator.

December 16: After-Action Reviews

"The only real mistake is the one from which we learn nothing." —Henry Ford

If there is one habit that will improve your investigative performance more than almost anything else, it's conducting regular After-Action Reviews (AAR). I learned AARs in the military, where they are non-negotiable. Every mission, every patrol, every training event—good or bad—ends with an honest review. Over time, I adapted the AAR process not only to investigations but to every part of my professional life. It works everywhere. The AAR is simple in structure but powerful in effect. It asks four questions:

1. **What was supposed to happen?** The plan, the objective, the method, the desired outcome. Without clarity here, everything else is guesswork.
2. **What actually happened?** Not the sugarcoated version. Not the "what we wish happened." The truth—unfiltered, unemotional, and accurate.
3. **What did we do well?** Strengths matter. Patterns of good performance deserve recognition so they can be repeated.
4. **What can we improve?** This is where the growth is. Concrete improvements, not vague clichés. The more specific, the more effective.

In investigations, AARs can be applied to anything, including interviews, surveillance operations, case strategy decisions, courtroom testimony, communications with clients or counsel, and even routine tasks you want to improve continuously.

The value multiplies when you codify the lessons. Write them down. Store them somewhere accessible. Review them before the next similar operation. Use them as baselines for your next iteration. Over time, your personal library of lessons becomes a customized playbook of best practices, warnings, and hard-earned wisdom.

In the private sector, AARs are often skipped because of time pressure or because people assume they are only for the military or first responders. That is a mistake. A five-minute AAR can prevent a five-hour problem later. A 10-minute AAR can prevent a repeat failure that costs money, credibility, or safety: a small investment with a massive return. AARs are not about blame—they are about improvement. They are not about ego—they are about accuracy. And they are not about looking backward—they are about preparing for the next step forward.

Takeaway: Turn every experience into a lesson. Conduct AARs, codify the results, and use them to build a stronger baseline for your next case.

December 17: Tradeshows & Conferences

"Opportunity is missed by most people because it is dressed in overalls and looks like work." —*Thomas Edison*

Tradeshows and conferences are excellent professional development opportunities in the investigative field. They combine the best elements of training, networking, and exposure to new ideas in one place. Whether you work in the public sector, corporate security, or private investigations, attending conferences accelerates your growth in ways that online courses or internal training alone simply can't.

When you attend a tradeshow, you gain access to a concentrated environment of expertise. You meet investigators from around the world, each bringing lessons, techniques, and experiences your own organization may never expose you to. You learn the latest developments in cyber investigations, forensics, OSINT, analytics, behavioral interviewing, financial crime, surveillance tools, and more. Vendors showcase technology you didn't even know existed—tools that might change how you work tomorrow.

And then there's networking—one of the most powerful benefits of all. The people you meet at conferences can become mentors, collaborators, referral partners, subcontractors, or lifelong professional allies. In law enforcement and intelligence, conferences connect you with peers who understand your operational environment. In the private sector, conferences double as business development. I have seen private investigators walk into a conference seeking training and walk out with new clients, new contracts, or new partnerships that changed the trajectory of their careers.

There is also a human element we don't talk about enough: travel. Experiencing new cities, cultures, and communities broadens you. It sharpens your people skills. It enhances your perspective. It makes you a better observer and learner.

Travel is a fundamental part of being a well-rounded investigator, and conferences provide a professional excuse to see more of the world. Less than a third of Americans have a passport. If that is you, I hope you consider changing that.

Tradeshows and conferences represent everything training should be: immersive, social, dynamic, and energizing. They remind you that this profession is alive—constantly evolving, constantly innovating, and full of people pushing investigative standards forward. If you only train inside your organization or through online modules, you miss the bigger picture.

Takeaway: Go to conferences. Meet people. Travel. Learn. Build your network and your business. You can thank me later.

December 18: International Training Opportunities

"The world is a book, and those who do not travel read only one page." —Saint Augustine

One of the fastest ways to elevate your investigative skills is to step outside your own country's training pipeline. Every nation approaches investigations differently. Their police academies differ. Their private-sector standards differ. Their intelligence practices differ. Their cultural assumptions differ. And their investigative frameworks—legal, procedural, and operational—are often shaped by history rather than convenience. When you train internationally, you are not just learning new techniques; you are expanding your worldview.

In the military and government sectors, international courses are common—UN programs, NATO academies, joint counterterrorism schools, forensic institutes, regional intelligence centers, and multinational task forces. Each brings a new lens. You sit in classrooms with investigators from Europe, Africa, Asia, the Middle East, Latin America, and beyond. You hear what has worked for them. What they failed on. What they prioritize. What constraints they operate under. It challenges your assumptions and strengthens your adaptability.

In the private sector, international training is equally valuable—sometimes even more so. Many global associations host conferences, regional summits, or specialized academies abroad. Techniques used by European financial crime units can transform how you approach a case. OSINT practices standard in Asia can expand your toolkit. Forensic processes used in the UK or Australia can refine your standards. Threat management insights from South Africa or Brazil can reshape how you evaluate risk. I have had the privilege of attending training courses with international students and of teaching them. The world is full of investigators solving problems in ways you have not seen yet.

Finally, international training expands your network in ways domestic training can't. When you meet investigators from other countries, you build relationships that last for decades. You gain contacts you can call when you are stuck, especially when your case takes you internationally. You gain insight into emerging global trends before they reach your region. And, for private investigators, you gain referral networks that bring real business. Global training isn't just a bonus—it's a professional multiplier.

Takeaway: Seek training abroad. Learn from investigators around the world. Learn how to solve problems in ways you have not envisioned yet.

December 19: Cross-Sector Opportunities

"None of us is as smart as all of us." —Ken Blanchard

Some of the most valuable training an investigator can receive doesn't come from their own agency, company, or sector—it comes from stepping into someone else's world. Multi-agency and cross-sector training exposes you to different methods, cultures, and problem-solving approaches. Whether you are in law enforcement, the military, intelligence, corporate security, or private investigations, cross-sector training multiplies your capability.

Task forces are one of the clearest examples. When federal, state, local, and sometimes private-sector partners come together on a single mission set, knowledge flows in every direction. A federal agent might learn surveillance tricks from a local detective who has spent twenty years working the same streets. A state-level fraud investigator might learn digital forensics techniques from federal specialists. Every participant leaves better than they arrived.

Joint exercises—whether homeland security drills, crisis simulations, emergency operations rehearsals, or red-team scenarios—build the same kind of collective strength. They expose gaps that no single organization could detect on its own. They teach you how other agencies communicate, plan, and respond. Most importantly, they show how your role fits into the bigger picture.

Cross-sector training also strengthens public–private collaboration. Private investigators also stand to gain enormously from these collaborations. Participating in trainings hosted by local agencies, state associations, federal outreach programs, corporate partners, or fusion centers provides many benefits. Some ways you can do this include:

- Join the Overseas Security Advisory Council (OSAC). A public-private partnership between DSS and the U.S. private sector operating overseas
- Join InfraGard. A public-private sector intelligence sharing partnership between the FBI and the U.S. Private Sector)
- Join an Information Sharing and Analysis Center (ISAC) relevant to your sector
- Assist law enforcement through referrals or contract work

Cross-sector training is not just about skills—it is about relationships. When you train with people from other organizations, you build trust that can't be replicated through e-mail or policy memos.

Takeaway: Task forces, joint exercises, and cross-sector partnerships sharpen your skills, expand your network, and sharpen your investigative techniques.

December 20: Physical Readiness

"Take care of your body. It's the only place you have to live." —Jim Rohn

Physical readiness is not a luxury in this profession—it's a responsibility. Whether you are a government agent, a corporate investigator, or a private-sector professional working cases alone, fitness is one of the few variables fully within your control. In every operational environment I have worked—military, federal, state, corporate—the same truth applies: skill, will, fitness, and gear make up the investigator's "big four," and fitness is the foundation that supports the other three.

Physical readiness isn't about being a bodybuilder or a marathoner. It's about ensuring you can meet the demands of the job without hesitation, injury, or fear. Investigators often sit for long hours, carry heavy equipment, stand in court, conduct surveillance, move quickly during field operations, and sometimes deal with unpredictable subjects or threatening situations. If your body can't handle basic occupational stress, your mind won't perform either.

Fitness improves more than strength or endurance—it enhances alertness, resilience, decision-making, and composure. A healthy cardiovascular system supports better cognitive performance. Good mobility reduces injuries during long surveillance days or sudden physical demands. Proper conditioning allows you to remain calm under pressure, even when adrenaline spikes. And a fitter investigator is a safer investigator, both for themselves and the people around them.

Officer safety fundamentals also come into play. Whether you're conducting a knock-and-talk, interviewing a hostile employee, doing surveillance on an unpredictable subject, or working a case in an unfamiliar part of town, your body is part of your safety plan. Reaction time, movement, balance, and situational awareness all degrade when fitness degrades. A weaker, slower, or exhausted investigator is automatically at greater risk. You don't need Olympic training. You need consistency. Walk. Stretch. Lift. Breathe. Sleep. Hydrate. Eat. Like someone who must think clearly for a living (because you do).

If you do physically demanding work, train appropriately. If your cases are mostly desk-bound, train intentionally to counteract the damage that sitting does. Don't be the investigator who retires at 41 and promptly has a heart attack (I have met three). The discipline you build in the gym carries over into the discipline you bring to investigations.

Takeaway: Fitness is one of the few variables you fully control. Treat it as a core part of being a professional investigator, because it is.

December 21: Mental Fitness

"The mind is its own place, and in itself can make a heaven of hell, a hell of heaven."
—John Milton

Mental fitness is as critical to the investigative profession as any technical skill you possess. It does not matter how competent you are, how much training you have accumulated, or how impressive your resume looks—if your mind is exhausted, foggy, stressed, or overloaded, your performance degrades instantly. Mental readiness is not optional. It is a professional requirement.

Just like physical readiness, mental fitness forms part of the investigator's "big four": skill, will, fitness, and gear. And here is the truth most people avoid—your mind is the node that controls all three of the others. When your mental state slips, everything else follows. Mental fatigue leads to sloppy interviews, missed contradictions, tunnel vision, hasty decisions, emotional reactivity, and critical oversights. Know this:

- You cannot muscle your way through exhaustion.
- You cannot out-train chronic stress.
- You cannot caffeinate your way out of decision fatigue.
- If your brain is operating at 60%, your investigative performance will be at 60%—no matter how hard you try.

You cannot separate mental readiness from physical readiness. They are a single system. A well-trained body supports a strong mind, and a disciplined mind supports a strong body. Together, they help you remain composed under pressure, communicate effectively, and handle uncertainty like a professional. To strengthen mental fitness:

- Protect your sleep like it is part of your job—because it is.
- Eat in a way that supports cognitive performance.
- Hydrate consistently throughout the day.
- Build stress management rituals you can rely on.
- Take breaks before you mentally hit the wall.
- Develop a recovery plan, not just a training plan.

The investigators who last the longest are not the toughest—they are the ones who treat mental readiness as seriously as firearms proficiency, interview skills, or digital forensics.

Takeaway: Your mind is your primary investigative tool and, in my view, the most powerful weapon in the world. Protect it. Strengthen it. Maintain it.

December 22: Teaching

"To teach is to learn twice." —Joseph Joubert

Every investigator eventually reaches a point where the role shifts—where you are not just doing the work, you are teaching it. Becoming an instructor isn't about rank, title, or time served. It is about stewardship. The profession only survives if experienced investigators pass on the craft to the next generation. When you become a teacher, you carry the responsibility of transmitting not just knowledge but standards, habits, and judgment. Teaching investigations is fundamentally different from conducting investigations. Great instructors share these traits:

1. **They remember what it was like to be new:** Humility is essential. Good instructors avoid gatekeeping or ego-driven teaching. They create an environment where students feel safe making mistakes—because mistakes are where the learning happens.
2. **They teach principles, not just procedures:** Tactics change. Laws change. Tools change. Principles endure. Good instructors teach why something works, not just how to do it.
3. **They use real-world examples responsibly:** Stories are not entertainment—they are vehicles for lessons. Effective instructors choose examples that illuminate the craft without violating confidentiality, exaggerating heroics, or glorifying poor decisions.
4. **They demonstrate before they evaluate:** If you cannot perform the skill under scrutiny, you cannot expect a student to. In investigations, credibility matters. An instructor who teaches interviewing should be able to interview. Someone teaching surveillance should be able to run a tail. Students can sense authenticity.
5. **They know how to correct without humiliating:** Feedback is essential, but delivery is everything. The best instructors fix errors quickly, clearly, and respectfully. They focus on growth, not embarrassment.
6. **They train with structure:** Good instruction has objectives, standards, and measurable outcomes. It isn't random. It isn't "war stories for two days." It's a progression—crawl, walk, run.

When you first begin instructing, you quickly realize how much you don't know. Teaching exposes gaps in your own understanding, and that is a gift. As Joubert said, *"To teach is to learn twice."* If the opportunity exists for you to be an academy instructor or teach a class, seize it. You will be better for it.

Takeaway: When you become an instructor, your mission shifts: pass on the craft clearly, humbly, and responsibly to the next generation.

December 23: Operational Creativity

"You can't use up creativity. The more you use, the more you have." —Maya Angelou

Investigators are often taught procedures, checklists, and standardized models, but very few are taught how to think creatively within those boundaries. Operational creativity in investigations isn't about breaking rules or inventing shortcuts—it's about seeing angles others miss, asking questions others overlook, and approaching problems with a mindset of imagination.

Operational creativity matters because cases rarely move in straight lines. Subjects behave unpredictably, witnesses change their stories, digital evidence surfaces in unexpected ways, and timelines never fit neatly into the boxes you want them to. Fraud, cyber incidents, missing persons, insider threats, surveillance challenges—all require flexibility, insight, and the ability to reframe problems. You can train creativity deliberately by:

1. **Change your lens:** View the same facts from different disciplines. What would a detective see? A forensic examiner? An intelligence analyst? Each lens exposes new patterns.
2. **Ask better questions:** Instead of "What happened?" ask:

   - "What else could be true?"
   - "What would have to be true for my theory to be wrong?"
   - "Am I missing the obvious because I am fixated on the interesting?"

3. **Borrow from other fields:** Cyber, psychology, intelligence, finance, forensics—each brings mental models that help you attack problems from new angles.
4. **Red-team your own work:** Challenge your assumptions. Build counter-theories. Pressure-test your logic. Creativity thrives when you are forced to defend your thinking.
5. **Use constraints as fuel:** Limited time, limited tools, limited access—these push you to innovate. Creativity grows when resources shrink.

One of the biggest misconceptions is that creativity means bending rules. It does not. True operational creativity thrives within legal and ethical boundaries. Anyone can be reckless under the banner of "thinking outside the box." A professional learns to innovate inside the box—within policy, law, and integrity.

Takeaway: Creativity is a renewable resource. Train your mind to look beyond the obvious.

December 24: Personal Knowledge Management

"We do not learn from experience... we learn from reflecting on experience." —*John Dewey*

Investigators deal with an overwhelming amount of information—case details, lessons learned, legal updates, interview insights, surveillance adjustments, OSINT tricks, and thousands of tiny observations collected across a career. If you don't capture and organize what you learn, it disappears. Personal Knowledge Management (PKM) is the system that keeps your hard-earned experience alive. It allows you to store, retrieve, and apply what you learn from the job, rather than relearning the same lessons repeatedly.

PKM isn't about keeping endless notes—it's about building a functional knowledge library you can actually use. Great investigators rely on systems, not memory. A strong PKM approach rests on three pillars: capture, organize, and synthesize.

Capture: means recording insights when they occur: an interview question that worked, a mistake you don't want to repeat, a tactic learned from a mentor, a legal nuance you didn't know, or a technique that made an operation smoother. It can be a notebook, a secure digital app, or a simple document—the key is capturing consistently. Lessons not written down are lessons forgotten.

Organize: means grouping information so you can find it quickly. Topic folders, tagged notes, checklists, case logs, and running "what worked/what didn't" lists all function well. The goal isn't complexity; it's retrieval. Your PKM system should help you pull a lesson forward exactly when a case demands it.

Synthesize: is where PKM becomes a force multiplier. Synthesis means turning information into insight by asking: What does this connect to? How does it change my approach? Should I update a checklist or create a new template? Does this pattern match something I have seen before? Synthesis builds judgment, intuition, and repeatable success.

A well-built PKM system gives you faster learning, stronger reports, better decisions, clearer thinking under pressure, higher-quality investigations, and a documented history of your professional growth. It also makes training others easier because you have a ready source of examples, lessons, and best practices.

Takeaway: PKM turns daily experience into long-term investigative mastery. Don't let your experience evaporate. Capture what you have learned.

December 25: Building a Yearly Training Plan

"The future depends on what you do today." —Mahatma Gandhi

The best investigators don't improve by accident—they improve by design. A yearly training plan is your roadmap for staying sharp, relevant, and adaptable in a profession that evolves constantly. Without a deliberate plan, you default to whatever your agency, company, or state requires. And minimum standards will never produce maximum performance.

Start by defining your developmental goals for the year. What do you want to improve? Interviewing? Surveillance? Report writing? OSINT? Digital forensics? Courtroom testimony? Threat assessment? Select three to five priorities. Focusing your effort increases your return. Next, build a training calendar. Break the year into manageable pieces:

- **Quarterly:** One major course, conference, or certification module.
- **Monthly:** Webinars, professional reading, scenario drills, or skill modules.
- **Weekly:** Short reps—an article, an interview technique review, or a 20-minute practice session.

Consistency beats intensity. Small, regular training investments add up faster than one large course at the end of the year.

Then address the budget. Training costs money, but planning makes it manageable. Register early to save on tuition, spread out expenses across the year, and use employer reimbursement or government training funds whenever possible. Private investigators should remember that legitimate training is often tax-deductible—something worth confirming with an accountant. Even if you pay out of pocket, never forget: training is an investment, not an expense.

Build your plan to include emerging skills—areas you may not need today but will absolutely need tomorrow. AI literacy, advanced OSINT, financial crime patterns, forensics exposure, threat management, and even foreign language development should sit somewhere in your long-term roadmap.

Finally, track your progress. Use a simple system—such as a spreadsheet, notebook, or digital log. Record what you completed, what you learned, gaps discovered, and goals adjusted. A yearly training plan gives you direction, discipline, and momentum. It prepares you for opportunities and ensures you grow in the right areas.

Takeaway: Identify your goals, build a structured plan, budget for growth, and track your progress. What you do today shapes your capabilities tomorrow.

December 26: Your Investigative Playbook

"To be prepared is half the victory." —Miguel de Cervantes

Every investigator needs a playbook—a personal system that turns lessons, skills, and experience into repeatable processes. Without one, you rely on memory, improvisation, or instinct. Your investigative playbook is a living document that captures how you conduct the craft. It forms over years of cases, mistakes, after-action reviews, and training. It organizes the workflows, checklists, templates, and habits that prevent you from reinventing the wheel every time a case begins. Think of it as the operational blueprint of your investigative brain—a structure that guides you even on your worst day. A strong playbook focuses on three core areas:

1. **Core Processes:** These are the tasks you repeat constantly: case intake, initial research, interview preparation, surveillance planning, evidence preservation, report writing, and case closure. Writing down and refining these workflows saves time and prevents inconsistency. Your playbook should tell you exactly how you handle the 80% of tasks that never change.
2. **Tools, Templates, and Checklists:** Memory is unreliable. Systems are not. Templates help standardize statements, timelines, summaries, affidavits, and interview outlines. Checklists keep you from missing steps during interviews, scenes, or digital evidence collection. Tool lists ensure you don't hit the field without critical equipment.
3. **Lessons Learned and "Never Again" Notes:** Every investigator has had moments they never want to repeat—a missed question, a lost detail, a rushed assumption, a poorly structured report. Capture these lessons. Write them down. Make them part of your playbook so you never fall into the same trap twice.

Your playbook should evolve continuously. Update it after major cases. Add new techniques learned in training. Modify workflows when better methods emerge. Use it to mentor newer investigators. Eventually, your playbook becomes one of your greatest professional assets—a roadmap for consistent performance and a foundation for leadership responsibilities.

Most investigators have experience. The strongest investigators have systems. Systems create reliability. Reliability builds reputation. And reputation opens doors—into leadership, specialized assignments, and opportunities given only to people who can perform at a high level every single time.

Takeaway: Build and refine your investigative playbook. Preparation and repeatable processes set the stage for long-term professional growth.

December 27: Thinking Routines

"Thinking is the hardest work there is, which is probably the reason why so few engage in it" —Henry Ford

Good investigators don't just have skills—they have thinking routines. These are the mental habits, daily practices, and internal processes that guide how they approach information, evaluate evidence, question assumptions, and make decisions. A thinking routine is the invisible backbone of investigative excellence. It is what keeps you sharp when cases get messy, timelines get complicated, or details start to blur together.

Most people drift through their day reacting to whatever shows up. Investigators can't afford that. The profession demands intentional thinking: structured, disciplined, and repeatable. A strong investigative thinking routine includes several key habits:

1. **Daily Information Calibration:** Before diving into tasks, orient your mind. Review your active cases, your priorities, and the key questions still unanswered. Ask yourself: What do I know? What do I need to know? What assumptions am I carrying?
2. **Evidence-First Thinking:** Your routine should force you to separate fact from interpretation. Start with what you can prove. Then consider what the evidence implies. This protects you from bias, tunnel vision, and premature conclusions—the silent killers of investigations.
3. **Pattern Recognition & Anomaly Hunting:** Train your brain to look for both the patterns that repeat and the details that don't fit. Patterns show you the truth. Anomalies show you the lie.
4. **End-of-Day Reflection:** Take a few minutes at the end of each shift to review what you learned, what you missed, and what needs follow-up tomorrow. This isn't journaling—it's cognitive maintenance.

These routines don't require special equipment or extended hours. They require consistency. Like physical training, mental training compounds—small daily reps turn into long-term capability. When you talk to seasoned investigators and ask how they think, you hear the same patterns: clarity, skepticism, curiosity, structure, and discipline. None of that happens by accident.

Takeaway: Your most important investigative tool is your thinking. Build a routine that keeps your mind sharp, structured, and curious.

December 28: Stepping into Responsibility

"The reward for work well done is the opportunity to do more." —Dr. Jonas Salk

At some point in every investigator's career, the opportunity to lead will appear. Sometimes it is a formal promotion. Sometimes it is simply being the one who steps forward when everyone else hesitates. Leadership is not about rank—it is about responsibility. And the people who consistently produce good work will be asked to carry more of it. Salk was right: the reward for being competent is being trusted with greater responsibility. That is not punishment—it is confirmation that you matter.

Yet throughout my career, I have known countless people who avoid leadership at all costs. They choose comfort over growth. They shy away from supervising others, taking charge of complex cases, making decisions, or being accountable when things go sideways. They stay "worker bees" even though they are capable of much more. They fear the pressure, the expectations, or the loss of personal freedom. But avoiding responsibility does not protect your career—it limits it.

Competent investigators should step up. The profession needs leaders who are ethical, thoughtful, and steady—not ones chasing titles or avoiding effort. When strong people refuse leadership, weaker people fill the vacuum. And everyone suffers—teams, clients, agencies, the profession itself. If you have the skills, the temperament, and the willingness to grow, leadership is not optional. It is part of your duty.

Leadership also makes you a better investigator. Supervising cases forces you to see the big picture: timelines, evidence flow, team dynamics, resource allocation, investigative strategy, and the human factors that make-or-break operations. If formal leadership roles are not available, create informal ones like:

- Mentor a junior investigator.
- Volunteer to brief the team.
- Offer to run the timeline or manage evidence.
- Take point during a chaotic scene.
- Provide structure when the group is disorganized.

Stepping up may mean sacrificing comfort. It may mean more work, more accountability, more stress, and fewer easy days. But it also means more influence, more trust, more growth, and more opportunity. You do not rise in this profession by hiding from responsibility—you rise by carrying weight well, and then carrying a little more.

Takeaway: If you are competent, ethical, and capable, seize leadership opportunities—even when they are inconvenient.

December 29: Recognition & Awards

"Appreciation is a wonderful thing: it makes what is excellent in others belong to us as well." —Voltaire

Many organizations are quick to counsel, reprimand, or document failure, but painfully slow to document excellence. They produce negative paperwork with urgency and positive paperwork as an afterthought. That imbalance creates resentment, burns out good investigators, and sends the message that exceptional performance is expected—but not worth acknowledging.

I have never believed in that approach. In the military, I counseled my Soldiers positively just as deliberately as leaders elsewhere document negative behavior. A positive counseling statement recognizes effort, reinforces standards, and gives people something to anchor their confidence in. It shows them you see their work. And when someone goes above and beyond, I write award nominations—even the long, narrative-heavy ones most people avoid.

I once wrote my own supervisor up for a competitive award after she led a major operational test for the U.S. military. The project was enormous, complex, and undeniably successful. She carried a weight that most people didn't even recognize and certainly not commensurate with her rank (far above it). Yet no one else bothered to nominate her. They assumed someone else would or didn't care. They assumed leadership would notice on their own. They assumed she didn't need recognition. She won the competition and was awarded—but only because someone took the time to tell her story.

In most organizations, you can write awards for subordinates, peers, and supervisors. You don't need special authority—just the initiative to document excellence when you see it. The only people who hesitate are those who don't realize how powerful recognition can be.

But recognition must be done correctly. When everything is special, nothing is. But the opposite problem—**never** awarding, failing to recognize effort, or tying awards to rank rather than performance—is just as damaging. I have seen units violate U.S. Army regulations by assuming certain grades "don't need awards," or tying them to rank. That is not leadership. That is laziness wrapped in tradition. You create a record that follows the person for years.

Take the time to document excellence. Take the time to write the nomination. Take the time to articulate why someone's contribution mattered. Your words might be the only acknowledgment they ever receive for that achievement.

Takeaway: Recognition is a leadership responsibility. Do not hoard praise, do not tie awards to rank, and do not overlook excellence.

December 30: Career Longevity

"It is not the strongest of the species that survive, nor the most intelligent, but the one most responsive to change." —Leon C. Megginson (summarizing Darwin)

A long career in investigations is not guaranteed. It must be earned, preserved, and actively protected. Some investigators burn bright and burn out. Others plateau early and spend decades repeating their first three years of experience. A smaller group—those who build true longevity—remain sharp, adaptable, relevant, and professionally engaged well into the later stages of their career.

They don't get stuck. They don't get cynical. They don't drift. They evolve.

Longevity comes from adaptability, not raw talent. The investigative world you enter is not the investigative world you will retire from. Laws change. Technology changes. Threats change. Investigative tools, court expectations, digital evidence, surveillance methods, and public–private collaboration all shift constantly. Investigators who cling to old methods because "that's how we've always done it" slowly fall behind—sometimes without realizing it.

The next key to longevity is continuous training. Investigators who stay relevant treat training like nutrition, not medicine. They do not wait for agencies or firms to mandate it. They seek it. They invest in it. They maintain their edge through year-round development—not a couple of courses every few years. The investigators who remain dangerous—in the best professional sense—are usually the ones who never stopped being curious.

After training is reputation. Over a long career, your name becomes your currency. Reliability, integrity, professionalism, and consistency will outlast any job title or badge. Careers collapse quickly when those elements erode. They flourish when your reputation becomes the reason people trust you with complex cases, high-stakes work, promotions, or leadership roles.

Finally, longevity requires purpose. People burn out when they forget why the work matters. The best investigators sustain their careers by staying connected to the mission—protecting people, uncovering the truth, preventing harm, solving problems, or giving clients clarity. Purpose fuels persistence. Persistence fuels longevity.

Takeaway: Longevity is built, not inherited. Adapt to change, train continuously, guard your reputation, and know your purpose.

December 31: Who You Intended to Be

"There is nothing noble in being superior to your fellow man; true nobility is being superior to your former self." —Ernest Hemingway

If you have made it this far, you are not just reading a book—you are building a life around a craft. Over the last several hundred pages, we have walked through casework, fieldcraft, interviews, surveillance, writing, training, judgment, fitness, leadership, networks, and the dozens of pieces that make this profession work. None of it was about perfection. All of it was about direction. The real question this last entry asks is simple: Who are you becoming as an investigator—and is it who you intended to be?

Somewhere along the way, you chose this field: law enforcement, intelligence, corporate security, private investigations, or another corner of the investigative world. Maybe it was curiosity. Perhaps it was service. Maybe it was a rare circumstance. Either way, the job has a way of reshaping you. It hardens some people. It humbles others. It can sharpen your mind and dull your empathy, or sharpen both if you are deliberate. Mastery in this line of work isn't just about building skills. It is about building a character that can carry those skills forward.

Mastery, as you have seen across these entries, lives in the small things: showing up prepared, training when no one is watching, writing clearly, treating people with respect, protecting your integrity, doing AARs after the hard days, building your playbook, refining your thinking routine, investing in your body and mind, and staying a student long after the title says "senior." The investigator you intend to be is built one decision at a time.

The future of this profession will demand even more from investigators than the past did. More technical skill, more cross-disciplinary knowledge, more ethical clarity, more resilience, more adaptability. AI will evolve. Threats will evolve. Laws will evolve. People will remain people. Complicated, inconsistent, and surprising. Your edge won't come from trying to predict every change. It will come from becoming the kind of investigator who can adapt to any change.

If there is a single thread running through this entire book, it's this: You are not stuck with the investigator you were yesterday. You can sharpen your skills, strengthen your systems, broaden your perspective, and address your weak spots. You can be the investigator your younger self wished they had to learn from. You can be the one who leaves the profession better than you found it.

Takeaway: Becoming the investigator you intended to be is a lifelong project. A daily choice to pursue mastery, stay humble, and keep growing.

What's Next?

You have just completed one year of *The Daily Investigator: 366 Lessons to Make You a Better Investigator.* What do you do now? You get ready for January 1st to reread this book all over again. As the U.S. Navy SEALs say, *"The only easy day was yesterday."*

Thank You

Thank you for picking up a copy of *The Daily Investigator: 366 Lessons to Make You a Better Investigator.* You are what makes this profession special. If you learned something, please consider leaving a review on the platform where you purchased this book.

Acknowledgements

I want to thank the following people in no particular order:

All of my mentors and the people who have shaped my experiences over my lifetime.

All of my friends and colleagues whose own experiences helped round out this book.

My wife and children's patience for the countless hours I spent working on and refining this book.

My cousin, Armando Palmieri, for reviewing early drafts of this book and providing his insight and experience from a career with the FBI and as a private investigator.

My brother, Dominic Panico, for providing additional private investigator insight, ensuring I met the mark in this important sector.

My editor, who wishes to remain anonymous given his former profession, for making sure this book was readable and made sense.

My graphic designer, Rekha Sahni, for making a great cover for the different versions of this book.

My typesetter, Penny Brucker, for making sure this book flowed.

My Spanish translator, Angélica Alfonso, for editing and proofreading the Spanish version of this book.

About the Author

Edward Panico is the founder of Lynx Security Group, a private investigation, security consulting, and training company. For over 21 years, Mr. Panico has worked both domestically and abroad in intelligence, investigations, and security matters with the U.S. Military and with the U.S. Department of State. Mr. Panico has trained hundreds of domestic and foreign military, intelligence, and private-sector personnel worldwide in law enforcement, security, and intelligence.

While employed with the U.S. Military and U.S. Department of State, he received extensive training and experience in risk mitigation, anti-terrorism/force protection, crime prevention, criminal investigation, counterintelligence, dignitary protection, physical security, access control, security operations, intelligence collection, investigations, interview/interrogations, and physical surveillance.

He maintains an active security clearance as part of his commitment to the U.S. Government, which also provides him with ongoing access to specialized training not available to those fully entrenched in the private sector. Mr. Panico is a recipient of the Military Intelligence Corps Association Knowlton Award and over 30 U.S. Military and U.S. Department of State service awards.

Mr. Panico holds an M.S. in Criminal Justice with a concentration in Law Enforcement and Crime Prevention from the University of Cincinnati. He also holds a B.A. in Intelligence Studies from American Military University and an A.A.S. in Intelligence Operations Studies from Cochise College.

If I Can Help You Further

If you or your organization needs consulting or training, please e-mail me at edward@lynxsecuritygroup.com so we can connect and execute.